LENIN

LENIN

Hélène Carrère d'Encausse

translated by George Holoch

HM
HOLMES & MEIER
New York / London

Published in the United States of America 2001
by Holmes & Meier Publishers, Inc.
160 Broadway • New York, NY 10038

Originally published as *Lénine,* copyright © Libraire Arthème Fayard, 1998.

This book was published with the assistance of the French Ministry of Culture.

This book has been printed on acid-free paper.

designed by Brigid McCarthy
typesetting by JoAnne Todtfeld

Library of Congress Cataloging-in-Publication Data

Carrère d'Encausse, Hélène.
    [Lénine. English]
    Lenin / Hélène Carrère d'Encausse ; translated by George Holoch.
        p. cm.
    Includes bibliographical references and index.
    ISBN 0-8419-1412-5 (cloth : alk. paper)
    1. Lenin, Vladimir Ilyich, 1870-1924. 2. Heads of state–Soviet Union–Biography.
3. Revolutionaries–Soviet Union–Biography. 4. Communists–Soviet Union–
Biography. 5. Soviet Union–History–1917–1936. I. Title.

DK254.L4 C2813 2001
947.084'1'092–dc21
[B]
                                                          2001024537

Manufactured in the United States of America

In Lenin we have the person
who was created for this age
of blood and iron.

—Trotsky, *O Lenine*
(Moscow, 1924)

CONTENTS

Part Four
The End of the Dream
(1917–1924)

FOREWORD

"Lenin's tomb is the cradle of the Revolution" proudly proclaimed the thousands of banners streaming above an immense crowd on the day the founder of the USSR was buried. That was in January 1924. Sixty-eight years later, in January 1992, the USSR had ceased to exist; communism and revolution were discredited; and the statues of communist leaders, knocked from their pedestals, were lying in parks, pitiful testimony to a vanished glory. However, facing the Kremlin on Red Square, the mausoleum—the "cradle of the Revolution"—still held the embalmed body of Lenin which had been offered for the worship of crowds for three-quarters of a century; it was what Stalin called a "revolutionary relic." Eager crowds no longer come to contemplate the "beloved leader" (*Vojd'*), but the memory of Lenin has not entirely faded from consciousness.

Lenin's fate after his death was indeed strange. He exercised power for only a short time—from late 1917 to the first days of 1923—was then removed from it by illness, and died a year later. The Bolsheviks, in a panic at the void created by Lenin's death, decided, against Russian tradition, the wishes of his widow, and probably the wishes Lenin would have expressed had he been able, to preserve the dead man's appearance of life and thus to keep him among them. Embalmed, exposed to the view of pilgrims in his glass coffin, Lenin became the object of a quasi-religious veneration. The Bolshevik Party claimed that it was responding to the requests of the working class: "When we doubt the Revolution or are on the point of making a mistake, it will be enough for us to contemplate Lenin, and he will set us on the right road."[1] The objective was simple: to save Lenin's legacy—and the Leninism[2] that Stalin invented as soon as the "guide" was dead. Lenin had to escape from the ordinary human fate, and his death must only be an appearance. "Lenin lives" was the slogan of the post-Lenin years, and the mausoleum confirmed its accuracy.

As years and decades passed, the fate of Lenin turned out to be more surprising still. The twentieth century has abounded in great charismatic heads of state who put themselves forward as saviors of their people in the name of communism (Stalin, Mao, Ho Chi Minh) or against it (Hitler, Franco, Salazar). All fell from their pedestals as soon as death reduced them to silence. Even those, like Mao, still protected from the "hell" of political figures by a mausoleum, have not escaped from the implacable challenges to their merits and their work.

Stalin, who briefly shared Lenin's mausoleum from 1953 to 1961, was brutally removed when he slipped from the status of "greatest man of all time" to that of a "criminal." Only Lenin was spared the decay of great men that had been carried out by death and time. He avoided it when Stalin was put on trial beginning in 1956 and when the publication of *The Gulag Archipelago* in the early 1970s showed the true totalitarian face of the USSR, opening the floodgates of accusations against it. He even escaped after 1985, when in the USSR and the rest of the communist world, the idea of closing the time of revolutions and the political systems they had established gradually took root. And still Lenin in his mausoleum was preserved from this revisionism until 1992. Even today, the fascination he holds for some of his compatriots is expressed sometimes by continuing loyalty to the party that he founded and sometimes by strange demonstrations of faith. For example, in 1992, a Christian-Leninist Party was created, calling on Russians to come together around Lenin in order to hear the word of Christ.[3] Its slogan–"We are Leninists, we bear the ideas of Christ"–expresses a curious syncretism which manifests the intellectual confusion following the death of communism, along with a certain survival of the myth of Lenin.

This posthumous fate, so specific to Lenin, can be explained in various ways. First, unlike other dictators he was not an isolated figure whose glory depended on his charisma and momentary power. Lenin was situated in the persistent tradition of utopias and in the mythical trinity of Marx-Engels-Lenin (in which Stalin for a time became a fourth member, later to be denounced as an impostor). The founding fathers of Marxism, who did not live long enough to see how their followers put their ideas into practice, have escaped from the accusations made against the communists. And Lenin long benefited from their protection. Also, for three-quarters of a century, the worldwide influence of communism protected the figure who had been the first to transform utopia into a system of power. Challenging Lenin would have implied that the communist states were depriving themselves of the legitimacy conferred on them by a man idealized by his successors and the Leninism with which they had clothed themselves, that is, supreme reference and inherent truth. The survival of communist systems required this kind of legitimation. On that basis they were at liberty to criticize Stalin and to reject large parts of his policies in the name of the "return to Lenin."

With communism rejected and the struggle abandoned, the idol has no more reason for being. The USSR has entered into history; Lenin now belongs to those who reflectively weigh the merits of men and events without worrying about political exigencies or imperatives. It is now possible to ask the necessary questions about Lenin: Who was he, a criminal responsible for one of the most terrible tragedies of the century, or a victim of the sudden reversals of history, to whom another, perhaps final reversal will one day do justice? What role can be attributed to his personality in the political actions and the political evolution from which it is difficult to dissociate the man from his country? What role was played by the political environment in his choices and their consequences, the backwardness of Russia, and the delay of the revolution outside Russia? Was

Lenin the embodiment of a terrible century in which contempt for humanity was constant or a visionary who outlined (perhaps too soon) the road to a peaceful future that would be beneficent to mankind?

The ambition of this book is to help remove Lenin from ideological passions in order to situate him in the history of a century that has come to its end and which, whether we like it, has been dominated more than anything by Lenin's ideas and will.

PART ONE

FROM ULYANOV TO LENIN
(1870–1900)

Chapter One

APPRENTICESHIP TO LIFE

HOW DOES ONE BECOME THE "HERO OF THE REVOLUTION," especially of the "proletarian revolution," that is, the "rebellion of the down-trodden"? Does one have to have been one of them to personally experience misfortune and poverty? Once power had been conquered and held, this was how the statue of the hero of the Revolution began to be built. The formative years were described with a proliferation of details that all suggested that they could have led only to the creation of the hero. The fate of Vladimir Ulyanov, so ran the legend, was to become Lenin and to establish a new world.

> Vladimir Ilyich Lenin (Ulyanov) was born in Simbirsk on April 10, 1870. He grew up in a harmonious family that loved ideas and hard work. In addition to the influence of his mother and father, that of his brother Alexander Ilyich was very helpful to him. This beloved brother was a model for him. His great idealism, his determination, his self-mastery, his sense of justice, and the generally high level of his moral qualities characterized Alexander Ilyich from childhood, along with a great capacity for work, a very useful example for Vladimir Ilyich. Living together in adjoining rooms until Alexander left for Petersburg, and afterward during summer vacations, Vladimir Ilyich could see what interested his brother and what he read. In the two last years, Alexander Ilyich brought with him for the summer books on economics, history, and sociology, and in addition *Das Kapital* by Karl Marx. The execution of this beloved brother had a powerful effect on Vladimir Ilyich and in itself impelled him onto the path of revolution.

Thus begins the biography of Lenin composed after his death by his sister and close collaborator, Anna Ulyanova-Elizarova, for the celebrated Granat encyclopedia prepared for the tenth anniversary of the October Revolution and containing the lives of nearly two hundred of its leaders.[1] This biography fostered the legend of Lenin as it was taught to all Soviet children for three-quarters of a century. In its most popular version, it insists on the modesty of his origins and way of life. Lenin was born, says the legend, in a tragic empire, in

3

which a people deprived of rights was at the mercy of the arbitrary rule of tyrants. The future Lenin, like so many of his compatriots, was said to be of very humble, or even of serf, origin, living in a family that was certainly affectionate but whose difficulties from the outset impelled the children to understand the world in which they were growing up and to reject it.

A PRIVILEGED CHILDHOOD

Legend and reality did not match. Lenin was born in Simbirsk in April 1870, the third child in a family that would have eight children, two of whom died at an early age. The time of Vladimir Ilyich Ulyanov's birth was, for Russia, a relatively happy period. The czar-liberator Alexander II had abolished serfdom in 1861. Significant reforms were coming one after the other; the hope of political modernization occupied people's minds. But extremist movements did not see things in this way, preferring a radical break to reform. Terrorists were stalking the czar-liberator, and, after a long series of failed attempts, they finally managed to kill him in 1881.

Terrorism, however, was unknown to the childhood of Vladimir Ulyanov. His native town, where he went to school and spent his adolescence, was favorable to family life and the education of children. It was a typical Russian provincial town. To be sure, it had grown constantly, increasing in population from ten thousand in 1800 to forty-three thousand in 1870. This was the period of the rapid urbanization of Russia. By the turn of the century, its nineteen largest urban areas would each have more than one hundred thousand inhabitants. Set on the banks of the Volga, Simbirsk was a quiet town whose many churches and monasteries were hidden in superb parks. It was a town in which Russians, Tatars who still felt at home along the whole length of the river, and Chuvash lived side by side. No doubt Orthodox missionaries had carried Christianity into conquered territory after the fall of the khanate of Kazan in 1552, but the Tatars remained fiercely attached to Islam. The schools provided for these "foreigners" showed the intention of the Russian government to maintain peace among the various communities of a heterogeneous empire of which Simbirsk was a representative sample. Nor were strictly Russian educational establishments lacking: two secondary schools, one of which was for girls; religious schools; an Orthodox seminary; an institute for commercial studies; and an institute for training midwives. Finally, two large libraries were accessible to everyone, Russians and "foreigners," and contributed to the studious atmosphere of the town.

Contrary to the legend, young Ulyanov's family was neither poor nor proletarian. The house in which he grew up was pleasant, spacious, and had two stories, a sign of relative prosperity; it also had several servants. This was the usual way of life for the head of the family who, after being a mathematics teacher, had been appointed to the coveted position of inspector of public schools in the province of Simbirsk. The ancestry of the father of the future Lenin, Ilya Nikolaevich Ulyanov, was long referred to in order to attribute serf origins to the hero of the October Revolution. Lenin did have a serf great-grandfather, Vassili Ulyanov, but he was freed early, well before the reforms of 1861. Haunted by the desire to give Russia the trappings of a civilized country, Alexander I (1801–1825) and Nicholas I (1825–1855) were indeed aware of the difficulty of reconciling that ambition with continuing serfdom. Even though they did not dare to abolish serfdom, they encouraged the individual emancipation of serfs. This explains why the proportion of serfs in the population of the empire, which had hovered around 50 percent in the late eighteenth century, had fallen to 37 percent in 1858. This decline demonstrated that serfdom was already condemned in the nation's mind before it was abolished by law. As a serf Vassili Ulyanov had been one of the beneficiaries of this disfavor. He had settled in a town where his descendants had continued the social rise thus begun. His son, Nikolai Vassilievich, was a tailor in Astrakhan. His grandson, Ilya Nikolaievich, Lenin's father, studied mathematics at the University of Kazan, and then, as we have seen was a teacher, a school inspector, and was finally promoted to the rank of state counselor, which meant that he had acceded to the status of hereditary noble. From the status of serf to that of a noble covered with medals, the change in three generations had been great.

Ilya Nikolaievich Ulyanov was a quintessential representative of the Russian Empire in its most notable quality: the capacity to be a melting pot for extraordinarily diverse civilizations and peoples. Ilya Ulyanov was of course Russian, but his mother was Kalmuk. After Catherine II reduced their autonomy, the majority of Kalmuks who remained in Russia gave up Buddhism and lived in Astrakhan. That was where Lenin's grandmother was married; it is to her Mongol origin that the rather pronounced Asiatic face of Lenin can be traced, and of his father before him, notably the slanted eyes. This Kalmuk ancestry in no way prevented the ennoblement of the father.

Ilya further complicated family genealogy by his marriage to Marya Alexandrovna Blank. Lenin's future maternal grandfather, Alexander mitrievich Blank, was a Jew from Zhitomir; his father was a Jewish merchant, and his mother was Swedish. His conversion to Orthodoxy opened many doors: to the faculty of medicine, to the upper administration (he was appointed police doctor and then a hospital doctor), and especially to the hereditary nobility to which he acceded in 1847. He also purchased the estate of Kokushkino, which was later to be a source of income and a refuge for Lenin's mother and her children. If we consider the fact that Jews in the Russian Empire were in principle prohibited from occupying official positions and from owning land, this remarkable social advancement confirms the forceful assertion of the great Russion historian, Leonard Schapiro, that the Russian authorities were hostile to Jews who identified themselves as such, but that conversion removed all prohibitions that had been imposed.

When Alexander Blank married, the Swedish background of his mother was joined by the German background of his wife, Anna Groschopf, the daughter of rich landowners and a devout Lutheran. Ilya Ulyanov married their daughter, Lenin's mother.

Certain characteristics stand out from this apparently complicated genealogy, most notably the national and religious diversity so similar to that of the empire. In Lenin Russian, Kalmuk, German, and Swedish ancestry mingled. He was the heir of varied religious and cultural traditions: Orthodoxy, Judaism, Protestantism, and, in the background, the Buddhism of his Kalmuk ancestors. This rich and varied heritage was supported by the cultural values of a remarkable family. His mother spoke three languages—Russian, French, and German—and was a good pianist. His father was very cultivated. He and both of Lenin's grandfathers had a higher education, in medicine or mathematics. Material comfort came from both sides of the family, and both held important positions. In addition, the Blank family owned an estate worked by peasants (serfs until 1861), from which they derived income. Both branches of the family had acceded to the hereditary nobility, and Vladimir Ulyanov himself later lay claim to it. In April 1891, it was he who made sure that his mother was listed on the register of the nobility of Simbirsk; later, his signature was sometimes "Vladimir Ulyanov, hereditary noble."

Settled into a world that seemed immutable, in which social and material status determined the place of the individual in society, the Ulyanov children could rightly consider themselves privileged. In the Simbirsk secondary school, they benefited from their father's prestige. Their home was harmonious, with an attentive mother and an indulgent father. A convert to liberal ideas on education, Ilya thereby helped his children to flourish. Among his brothers and sisters, Vladimir was closest in his childhood to his sister Olga, one year younger than he, who died at the age of twenty. Perhaps the most troubling, the one who disturbed the family peace, was Alexander, four years older than Vladimir and already interested in political problems, the black sheep of a family that had until then been settled in a comfortable conservatism. Ilya Nikolaievich, a high official respected by everyone and those who were close to him could hardly think otherwise in light of the reforms which in those years were bringing real modernization to the empire.

In this peaceful family atmosphere, young Volodya was a brilliant student. The principal of his secondary school, Fedor Kerensky, was a man with a career resembling that of his father. He was later inspector general of schools in Turkestan, as Ilya Ulyanov had been in Simbirsk. It is an irony of history that the parallel careers of the fathers were, for a time, matched by the parallel fates of the sons. Vladimir Ulyanov was fleetingly a lawyer and the leader of the October Revolution; Alexander Fedorovich Kerensky, also a lawyer, but a celebrated one and a remarkable orator, was one of the leading figures of the February Revolution.

THE END OF HAPPY DAYS

Before these two adolescents were carried by history to the front of the stage, two events transformed the life of Volodya Ulyanov and gradually removed him from the path that seemed prepared for him.

The first was the sudden death of his father from a cerebral hemorrhage at the age of fifty-five in early 1886, when he had just turned sixteen. The effects of this death were immediate. Marya Alexandrovna probably reacted quickly by asking the government for a pension that would allow her to provide for the education of her children. She also had the estate inherited from her father and its associated income. But the family no longer benefited from the prestige of the father.

More tragic in its consequences was the execution of Alexander Ulyanov, the turbulent older brother. He was twenty, his father had just died, and he was doing brilliantly as a science student in the University of Saint Petersburg. Russia was in a strange period in 1886. Alexander III, who had succeeded Alexander II in 1881, was haunted by the regicide that cost his father's life. He was deeply troubled by the conclusion that reforms had not at all placated the terrorists and convinced that the country required unwavering authority in order to bring an end to terrorism. The chief procurator of the Holy Synod, Constantine Pobedonostsev, had written to him immediately after the murder: "The time is terrible, but there is not a moment to lose. It is now that Russia must be saved. If they sing you the old siren songs claiming that you should stay calm, continue in the same liberal spirit, and make concessions to what they call public opinion, do not believe it, it would mean Russia's downfall and yours."[2] Thus encouraged in repression, Alexander III pursued revolutionary organizations with zeal, determined to dismantle them and to execute all the captured terrorists. This policy of rigorous repression did nothing to stop the movement. Assassination attempts, now directed against him, proliferated, as did revolutionary organizations. One of them was the source of the tragedy that forever plunged the Ulyanovs into mourning. In Saint Petersburg, Alexander had befriended a young noble, Piotr Shevyrev, the founder of a terrorist section of the *narodnia volia* (People's Freedom), which was very active among the students of the capital. In 1887, the group plotted an attempt against the emperor; the date was set for March 1 in order, in the minds of the conspirators, to create an impression by an explosive commemoration of the murder of Alexander II.

Alexander Ulyanov, who was in the process of writing his thesis on spider crabs, was one of the authors of violent proclamations calling for an uprising. But the police were on the alert, discovered the plot, and arrested the principal conspirators. The program drawn up by Ulyanov, the science student, demanded nationalization of the land and of businesses and the establishment of democracy. The czar commented, "This is the same as the Paris Commune."[3]

Fifteen of the indicted were tried by the special tribunal of the Senate; all were sentenced to death, but ten of them were reprieved in the end. If Alexander Ulyanov was not, this was because in the course of the trial, he proudly proclaimed his responsibility, thereby lessening that of his fellow conspirators. Thereafter, he rejected any clemency and any demonstration of repentance. It did no good for his mother to plead his cause in Petersburg and to call for clemency from the monarch in the name of her husband's services to the empire; her son's intransigence led the czar to reject any gesture of generosity.

Alexander Ulyanov and those sentenced with him, including Shevyrev, the linchpin of the movement, were hanged on May 11, 1887.

What influence did this tragedy have on the future Lenin? The question is difficult to answer. Soviet legend closely linked the martyrdom of Alexander and the revolutionary vocation of his brother. If we closely examine his activities during these terrible months for his family, we see that Vladimir Ulyanov quietly continued his studies and successfully passed the examinations that admitted him to the University of Kazan, where he was to study law. At the university, he benefited from the necessary protection of his former secondary-school principal in Simbirsk. Fedor Kerensky indeed feared that Alexander's name would weigh on Vladimir and prompt the authorities to suspect him as well.

Vladimir Ulyanov's attitude was rather indecisive. He did not yet show a very strong interest in political life, but he was gradually affected by the agitated atmosphere of the university. Demonstrations continued even though they were prohibited. Students were prompted to present themselves as spokesmen for the young, a considerable portion of whom had lost all hope of going to the university, either because the entry fees had been harshly raised, blocking candidates of modest means, or because of discriminatory measures limiting the access of Jews to higher education.

The University of Kazan was in as much turmoil as that of Saint Petersburg, and, although he did not show excessive zeal, it is unquestionable that Vladimir Ulyanov, impelled by curiosity and the general movement, was present at student meetings of which the authorities disapproved. But the brutal sanction to which he was subject was out of proportion to his rather episodic and passive participation in these meetings and debates. It was rather determined by the name that he bore. Once the authorities wished to make an example, it was a Ulyanov that had to be chosen. Was he not suspect from the outset? In December 1887, despite the ardent pleas of Kerensky, who was still concerned for the fate of his protégé, he was excluded from the university, required to leave Kazan, and placed under house arrest on the family estate. His mother, who had gone to Petersburg a few months earlier to try to save the life of her eldest son, made the same journey to save Volodya's education. It was no longer the emperor whom she had to persuade, but the minister of police, Durnovo, who turned a deaf ear. He openly stated that the brother of a terrorist could only be dangerous. It didn't matter that Volodya had not yet shown any revolutionary intentions. His name was enough to condemn him.

THE "BROTHER OF THE HANGED MAN"

Dismissed from the university, forced for a time to live in the country, deprived of all contact with his former fellow students, Vladimir Ulyanov found only two ways to fill the time period of his exile and prepare for the future: studying so that he could present himself as soon as possible as an external candidate for the bar examination, and, above all reading. But what should you read when you are the brother of a martyr of the political struggle, when you are suspected of holding advanced ideas, and when, at the university, you have noted the prestige of socialist and anarchist thought? It goes without saying that this is the kind of reading to which Vladimir now turned. Because he was suspected of revolutionary sympathies, he might as well discover what the accusation meant. Marx, Russian social literature, and, above all, Chernyshevsky, whom he later called his intellectual mentor, all served for him to see clearly into himself and also to understand what was happening in his country. It was probably then that the memory of Alexander took on importance for him, and he inwardly became the "brother of the hanged man."

Diligent reading of writers who were nefarious in the eyes of the authorities did not prevent Vladimir from pursuing his original plan of securing the diploma that would make it possible for him to be a lawyer. By 1892, it was done; he had a degree from the University of Saint Petersburg, even though this was not an easy matter for an external candidate. He settled in as a trainee lawyer in Samara, for which he received authorization.

His career as a lawyer deserves little attention. It was brief, and Vladimir Ulyanov never handled an important case. A few boundary disputes between landowners and a few financial matters in which he was directly involved were the extent of his activity, the only one in his life that gave him a hope of earning a living. But earning a living was never one of his real concerns.

And then, police rigor against him was relaxed. After the harsh years of repression, after the great catastrophes–famine in 1891, cholera in 1892, followed by inevitable social disturbances–a certain peace had returned to Russia. The grip of the authorities was loosened. In the atmosphere of the end of a reign–Alexander III died in 1894–relatively disorganized protests developed in the major cities and among the national minorities. Vladimir Ulyanov seized the opportunity to leave Samara in September 1893 and settled in Saint Petersburg, where he worked for a short time in the office of a lawyer named Volkenstein.

THE DISCOVERY OF THE WORKING CLASS

The two years in Saint Petersburg, from September 1893 to December 1895, were the only years in which young Ulyanov had any contact–very limited, in any event–with the working class. According to his sister, in the biography published under her name that has already been mentioned, they were also years in which his profession as a lawyer was a means of earning a living, which is more doubtful.

The most important thing was his meeting with a young woman already very involved in political, if not revolutionary, activity, that is, Nadezhda Krupskaya, who became his faithful collaborator and his wife. This young woman, who was infatuated with advanced ideas, was an austere and not very charming figure. Nadezhda Krupskaya was a few months older than Ulyanov. Like him, she claimed noble ancestry through both parents. It is notable that she pointed this out in the autobiography she submitted to the *Granat* encyclopedia, which was written after Lenin's death. She wrote that she was of noble but poor origin because her parents, who were both orphans, had been raised "at the expense of the State" and had thus been able to pursue advanced studies. Her father, a career officer, was accused of subversive activities, tried, stripped of his rank, and dismissed from the army. He died soon thereafter, in 1883, when his daughter was only fourteen. It was then left to his widow, a woman of strong character, to see to the education of her daughter and to their material existence. Both of them lived from the mother's private tutoring and from renting rooms to students. Nadezhda completed her secondary education brilliantly, "with a gold medal," she wrote. She was briefly interested in the ideas of Tolstoy, very fashionable at the time, and then she turned toward the working class to which, over the course of the next four years, from 1891 to 1895, she devoted an important part of her time. She gave evening and Sunday classes, not only to adults, but also to the children of needy families. Her centers of political interest helped to orient her activity, and in this she was not at all exceptional. Toward the end of the century, there were many young people, especially young women, from the nobility who considered it a duty to help raise the level of popular education. Twenty years earlier, populism had already expressed this desire to go to the people, but in that case the people were the peasants.

The growth of the working class in the course of the years of rapid industrialization fostered the enthusiasm of idealistic youth about workers. Already involved in this activity for two years when Vladimir Ulyanov entered her life, Nadezhda Krupskaya helped him make contact with the working-class world of which he knew nothing. "It was at that time," she asserts, "that I became a Marxist."[4] This is a sketchy assertion that is difficult to verify. What is certain is that, in a capital in which political debate was very vigorous in the small circles frequented by both students and already renowned intellectuals (such as Petr Struve), Ulyanov and Krupskaya encountered many participants and thereby acquired the reputation of sympathizing with advanced ideas. In Krupskaya's house as well, with her mother at the center and partly because of the participation of the boarders, there were frequent meetings, which Vladimir Ulyanov attended assiduously.

Was he also an assiduous suitor? He probably often went with Nadezhda to her classes for workers. They went together to many evening gatherings, political, not social, it goes without saying. But it seems that they did not yet express feelings going beyond the limits of a solid friendship and a common interest in political discussion.

It cannot be forgotten that, from childhood, Vladimir Ulyanov had been surrounded and freed from all material difficulties by women. His mother and sisters had always guarded his tranquillity. In Saint Petersburg, it is likely that he properly appreciated the welcome he received in a house where he found something resembling what he had always known, that is, a mother providing a protected life for her child. The two women would be separated only by death.

Krupskaya's mother always followed her daughter and shared her life. He also found in the personality of Nadezhda, whose interests and activities were similar to his own, something of his sisters: Olga, his favorite, who was already dead; and Anna, who would join the circle of women that made up his permanent entourage. But despite his frequent visits to Nadezhda's apartment, Vladimir did not clearly present himself as a suitor, and no one could yet foresee that their fates would be forever joined.

For the moment, the attention of both was increasingly focused on left-wing ideas. The situation in Russia was propitious for such developments. Emperor Alexander III had been succeeded in 1894 by a young monarch with a not very assertive character but who was full of goodwill. He intended to continue the work of his father, to maintain autocracy, which he thought the only system suitable for Russia; at the same time, he wished to secure the love of the people. From that came policies alternating between rigor and flexibility, from which the greatest benefit was derived by dissident groups who multiplied and extended their activities.

MEETING THE "FOUNDING FATHERS"

Early in 1895, Vladimir Ulyanov left Russia for the first time. He went to Switzerland to meet the major historical figures of Russian marxism, Plekhanov, Axelrod, and Vera Zasulich. He received a lukewarm welcome. For these prestigious figures, the young man visiting them offered few attractions. Physically, he provoked surprise by his premature aging. At twenty-five, witnesses asserted, he could be easily taken for nearly forty. His small size and slight build, precocious baldness revealing a huge forehead, thin hair, and a beard whose reddishness was already dulled, all had the effect of emphasizing his Asian appearance (inherited from his Kalmuk grandmother) and his remarkable and disconcerting eyes. He had a gaze that was too sharp, too insistent, eyes of an indefinable color, the "gaze of a wolf," said some. His physical appearance very early prompted everyone to give him two nicknames that caused his age to be forgotten: "the Old Man" or "the Bald One."

The reticence of his elders was not simply a reaction to his physical appearance; on an intellectual level, the meeting led to a certain lack of understanding. Shortly before, under the pseudonym "Tulin," Vladimir Ulyanov had published a virulent critique of Struve's book on populism. The "founding fathers" of Russian marxism found that the young Ulyanov demonstrated great narrow-mindedness and that he was driven more by a polemical spirit than by a veritable grasp of Russian problems at the end of the century. If the meeting was nevertheless a success (his hosts encouraged him to publish a political newspaper in Russia), it was because they appreciated their young visitor's desire to act. But beyond encouragement and promises to work together, it is legitimate to think that the gap that was constantly to widen between Plekhanov and the future Lenin first appeared at that moment. Plekhanov had probably seen behind Ulyanov's will the cynicism that would later manifest itself. As for Vladimir, he glimpsed and rejected Plekhanov's principles as a refined intellectual.

This very brief trip marked the final phase of the Saint Petersburg period. Ulyanov now wanted to be active in the revolutionary movement. He wrote a good deal (essentially, as we shall see, to criticize populist ideas), composed occasional manifestos, notably for May Day, and tried to bring out the paper that Plekhanov and Axelrod had suggested he create. It was to be a clandestine paper, *Raboche Delo* (The Workers' Cause), and he would write all its articles. He was ready to publish on December 9, 1895, but the police intervened. The future Lenin and most of his associates were arrested, and the equipment seized. For a year and two months, while trial preparation went on, he was in a prison that was not too harsh, engaged in tireless activity, receiving books to continue his education, and using his reading to help with his own writing. He was able to communicate (probably clandestinely, but effectively) with his friends, especially Nadezhda, who was not arrested until 1896 for participation in the major strikes in May and June that mobilized large numbers of workers. Through his various correspondents, Vladimir Ulyanov sent out short pamphlets and instructions to various groups, strengthening the authorities' conviction that they were dealing with a dangerous revolutionary. That justified his sentence to "exile" (banishment) in February 1897. He was then compelled to spend three years in Siberia.

A COMFORTABLE EXILE

Here we should pause to take note of the methods used by the czsarist regime that its successors accused of being so bloodthirsty. After a prison stay that bore no resemblance to the imprisonment in the Lubyanka of later victims of Soviet terror (who had no access to books and could not draft and send out pamphlets), Lenin was released for three days to "settle his affairs," wrote his sister, and to organize his own travel to Siberia. This man, who was considered dangerous, spent the three days meeting with friends in the revolutionary movement. He then left under rather special conditions.

His mother, whose concern for him was constant, again approached the authorities with two rather surprising requests to the minister of police. First she asked that her son be allowed to go into exile on his own, as a free man, "without escort," as Anna Ulyanova-Elizarova explained, apparently unaware of the enormity of the request. On the pretext of her son's fragile health, Marya Alexandrovna asked that he be allowed to stay in a place with a mild climate, such as the town of Krasnoyarsk or the southern Yeniseysk region. He seconded the requests, which were accepted for the most part, and he was thus able to travel comfortably on the Trans-Siberian at his expense, or more accurately at the expense of his mother. He was sent to Shushenskoe village near the small town of Minusinsk, where he spent three years. The clemency of the authorities did not stop there. After six months in prison, Nadezhda Krupskaya was exiled to Ufa in the Bashkir region. She then asked the authorities to allow her to go to Shushenskoe to join her fiancé Vladimir, so that they could marry and live together.

The authorities agreed, and in early 1898 she arrived with her mother, who was to share their life. Not only did the wedding take place but, at the insistence of Krupskaya's mother, it was a religious wedding, following the Orthodox rite into which bride and groom had both been baptized a quarter-century earlier. The contempt in which Marxists held religion seemed not to trouble the couple, who conformed to tradition without protest.

All in all, the exile of Vladimir Ilyich and his new family was very tolerable. In her narrative, which is noteworthy for its attempts to erase any trace of indulgence on the part of the authorities, to describe the period of exile as one of work and reflection, Anna Ulyanova-Elizarova cannot avoid mentioning some of the conveniences in the life of "deportees" under the czars: "Only two Polish workers were living in Vladimir Ilyich's village, but in other nearby villages there were comrades whom he met for holidays and weddings." Lenin's example reveals that exile prevented neither weddings nor gatherings among residents of various places. During this period, Lenin often engaged in physical activities that he was fond of: hunting, fishing, and long walks encouraged by wild and splendid nature. There were also of course the intellectual activities complacently emphasized by his sister: the translation of the then famous book by the Webbs, *The History of Trade Unionism,* and the composition of short personal works for which he had gathered material in prison, and of pamphlets that he sent abroad. Although they were published, the authorities were not impelled to restrict the activities of this exile who was so zealous in his struggle against the regime. His wife played a considerable role in these polemical works; she helped with translations and put together material for future works. More than a young bride, Nadezhda was a collaborator, indispensable to a Lenin who was intent on dividing his time between the pleasures of nature and intellectual work. As for the material life of the household, this was left to Nadezhda's mother, freeing her daughter and son-in-law from any practical worries.

Several other aspects of this life deserve mention, most notably that like the other exiles whom they met for pleasant evenings where they sometimes enjoyed the results of the hunt, the Ulyanovs suffered no restrictions beyond the requirement of living in their assigned location. But they had great freedom of movement over a relatively large area and could visit other exiles in the region and organize hunting or fishing expeditions. Even though these revolutionaries had been deemed dangerous, they also enjoyed broad opportunities to meet others. Not only were they not deprived of the right to meet, but they were also not kept apart from the local population among whom they frequently engaged in active propaganda. Exile, for those sentenced to it, was an opportunity to broaden their social contacts and to carry revolutionary ideas to the outposts of the empire. The local authorities observed this agitation without reacting, because the condition of "exile" involved no restrictions. The enemies of the regime were treated with surprising leniency and even with deference, as numerous accounts attest. Nor were they compelled or even asked to perform the slightest work organized by the authorities. In short, beyond the obligation to reside in Siberia, they were free to live as they liked, to see whoever they liked, and to engage in all the leisure or subversive activities they pleased. From the comfortable journey on the Trans-Siberian to this calm existence, it is impossible not to notice the distance between the fate of the enemies of czarism and that later inflicted on the "enemies of the people." The cruelty and unrestrained violence of the Bolsheviks in power were not taught to them by the weak and civilized czarism of the late nineteenth century.

No doubt, in the early part of the century, the situation of exiles had been enormously harsher. But even then it cannot be forgotten that the wives of the Decembrists, who had traveled to Siberia in frightful conditions, had managed to join their husbands and to share their life in exile. Under the Soviet regime, individuals hunted down by the authorities—generally with no reason, haphazardly because of "deportation quotas," or for the sole crime of belonging to a suspect social or ethnic category (Crimean Tatars, Chechens, Ingush, and so on)—were torn from their homes and families and generally lost all contact with them.

Moreover, this "exile" of entirely relative harshness did not last very long. In 1900, Lenin was allowed to leave Siberia, free to go where he wished, except for major university and industrial centers where the authorities feared that former exiles, armed with the prestige of their time in Siberia, would immediately become influential agitators. After a brief stay with his family in Moscow, Vladimir Ulyanov decided to settle in Pskov. As for Nadezhda, who still had a year of exile in front of her when her husband was released, she chose to return to Ufa where she had maintained close contact with revolutionary circles. Hardly troublesome, the authorities that had allowed her to move to Shushenskoe three years earlier, similarly authorized her return to the Bashkir region. They hardly cared about the reason for the request. It may even be said that they seemed unconcerned that Krupskaya was again engaged in revolutionary activity that was difficult to ignore. She stayed in Ufa until 1901, when she expressed the wish to settle abroad, which was of course granted. At each move, Krupskaya was followed by her household, that is, her mother from whom she was inseparable, her books, and all the necessities of daily life. If the exile was not gilded, it was certainly not lacking in comfort.

With the end of exile came the end of the Ulyanov couple's apprenticeship for the life of revolutionaries. As though to further emphasize this break, which occurred when both were approaching thirty, Ulyanov became "Lenin," the only signature he would ever use. Before that, he had in turn been "V. U.," "Tulin" (referring to the town of Tula), "Petrov," or "V. Ilin." It was under the name of Lenin, which he adopted in 1901, that the "hereditary noble Ulyanov" entered history, transformed the destiny of his country, and to some degree shook the foundations of the entire world.

Chapter Two

RUSSIA IN THE CRUCIBLE OF CHANGE

THE EMPIRE OF "ALL THE RUSSIAS"

BY 1900, RUSSIA WAS NO LONGER THE COUNTRY DESCRIBED A mere few decades earlier as a place of barbarism and backwardness. What was constant, no doubt, was its immense size and the diversity of its population. It had continued to grow in size, even though, in 1867, a few years before Lenin's birth, the Russian Empire had removed itself from the American continent by selling Alaska to the United States. But it remained an immense Eurasian entity, whose borders were not definitively established until 1895. The empire was made up of two worlds: Russia itself and its western possessions–the Baltic provinces, Finland, Poland–turned entirely toward Europe, and the second Russia stretching to the east and south, the quasi-colonial territory of Siberia, the Far East, and the steppes. These two Russias encompassed large populations that were disparate in civilizations, levels of development, and ways of life.

The total population of the empire was very large, 123 million according to the 1897 census, whereas that of the United States was only 95 million, and of Germany, 68 million. But the population was scattered over an immense territory and badly distributed, with an average population density of seven inhabitants per square kilometer. The birthrate was very high, but mortality, particularly infant mortality, was high as well. Russia had experienced numerous demographic catastrophes, famines, and epidemics. But at the turn of the century, the progress of agriculture and medicine seemed to suggest that such misfortunes were a thing of the past. The great famine of 1891 and the cholera epidemic of 1892 were, or at least the Russians hoped, the final tragic episodes of their collective life.

Cultural and ethnic diversity were the other dominant characteristics of the population. The 1897 census showed that 55.7 percent of the inhabitants of the empire did not speak Russian and thus were not deemed to be Russians. These populations with various languages were also distinguished by their beliefs, which often determined their way of life. The Christian majority–Orthodox, Catholic (persecuted by the empire), and Lutheran–was concentrated in the western part of the country. The south and east contained Muslims, usually but not always Turkish-speaking, and Buddhists, especially in Siberia. Finally, in the

Caucasus, which was partly Christian, nearly one hundred minor peoples and languages rubbed shoulders. Geography, as well as cultural variation, helped to foster different patterns of behavior. Russian peasants had fought against the forest to conquer living space; the sedentary populations of Central Asia had struggled to obtain the water necessary for survival; and nomads had fought to preserve migration zones.

The empire that had conquered all these peoples in four centuries, from the fall of the khanate of Kazan in 1552 to 1900, had not had the time to deal with the question of their future unity. Russia juxtaposed Russians and outsiders (*inorodtsi*), and was in the end, as an English traveler wrote, the "land of all the Russias."[1]

Because of his exile to distant Siberia, Lenin was able to get a sense of the immensity and human variety of his country. After a childhood in European Russia that itself was diverse, the stay in Siberia made him aware of the enormous size of Russian territory and of the richness of its landscapes and its civilizations. The Russia of towns, the peasant colonists of Siberia, the Chuvash that he met in exile but also in Simbirsk, and the Tatars he encountered in childhood and again in Kazan, all helped from the outset to give him a precise view of the empire. He had benefited from this experience to raise the colonial problem at an early stage, something that only slightly concerned most of his friends.

A CHANGING SOCIETY

The diverse empire was also an empire in movement in which progress and problems ran in tandem. The emancipation of the serfs was an act of considerable political significance in 1861, because it transformed them into citizens. But the agrarian problem was still far from being resolved. Although peasants had the right to purchase land from then on, they generally lacked the means to do so. Many of those who were too poor to exercise the right had given it up; others had gone into long-term debt. The countryside of the last decades of the century juxtaposed large landowners, rich peasants, owners of tiny parcels, and landless peasants. Communal farms (*mir*), which had been preserved by the reform, grouped peasants together and redistributed land every five or six years. In a country in which 80 percent of the inhabitants were peasants, "land hunger" and hostilities between rich and poor occupied a considerable place. Rural agitation was endemic, and no one could be unaware that the countryside was dominated by rampant subversive tendencies that any organized political movement could exploit. The regime was far from unaware of the fact and, in order to pacify the peasantry whose agitations were troubling, tried to encourage rural migration to Siberia, an American-style solution more attractive to the authorities than to the peasants. By 1900, barely one million peasants had embarked on the adventure of colonizing the available land.

In the space of two decades, the choice of economic development based primarily on industry that had been made by Alexander III on the death of his father had borne fruit. Russia was experiencing very rapid urbanization, and peasants discouraged by rural poverty were tempted to move to cities. Although Russian cities had for very long been primarily markets whose inhabitants were drawn by the lure of trading, by the late nineteenth century industrialization had accelerated urban development and stabilized the urban population. Moscow and Saint Petersburg, each of which had a population of between one million and one million two hundred thousand in the early twentieth century, were large centers in which all kinds of industries were present. Remarkably, industrial development extended to the colonial part of Russia, and non-Russians widely participated in it, which was not without consequences for the growth of major social movements. Finally, the expansion of the railroad, vital for such a large country, helped to change the life of the empire by further fostering urbanization and human exchanges.

This rapid economic transformation resulted in the birth of a working class that was still small in size—fewer than three million—but was concentrated in the major industrial cities. This nascent working class was far from passive. Its material conditions were very harsh, a fact of which it was acutely aware, perhaps because the break with rural life had been brutal, and cities in a constant state of flux were not very welcoming. The scenes of this galloping industrialization were large factories where the living conditions and human relations differed hugely from those of the village. Finally, in a period of nascent capitalism, businessmen were generally implacable toward their employees, denying them any rights. But workers were not defenseless. Two-thirds of them had learned to read, often thanks to classes given by young people attached to their cause, as Nadezhda Krupskaya had done before her arrest. They were also able to decipher or to have read to them Marxist tracts, to think about their problems, and to come together around shared demands.

This growing awareness on the part of a poor and mobilizable working class was the source of the strikes and protest movements of the last decade of the nineteenth century, but also of some improvement in working-class conditions. Confronted with the rise of the workers' movement, the government was forced into a few concessions. At the conclusion of the major strikes that paralyzed the Saint Petersburg textile industry in 1896 and 1897, Sergei Witte, then overseeing economic policy for Nicholas II, undertook a reform of working time. The law adopted limited the work day to eleven and one-half hours, night work to ten hours, and made Sunday a day of rest. In light of the social legislation in force in the industrialized world at the end of the twentieth century, these provisions seem to be outrageous, and no one would dare to imagine that they might be an improvement. But for the Russia of the time, in which legal unions and the right to strike did not exist and in which there was nothing to limit arbitrary management, this was a success for the workers.

Indeed, temporal comparison makes a good deal less sense than spatial comparison of labor legislation. Although by 1878 the law in England limited the workday to ten hours and required time off for Saturday afternoon and Sunday, the famous "English week" was seldom imitated elsewhere. In France, a country that the Russian revolutionaries considered advanced, social legislation in the late nineteenth century was far from exemplary and would have been quite satisfactory to Russian managers. Unlimited before 1848, the working day had then been reduced to twelve hours. From then until 1914, despite temporary and local measures, many businesses followed the 1848 law, and a ten-hour day was more exceptional than not.[2] It was imposed for women in 1900. Only underground miners and children were less harshly treated by the end of the nineteenth century. As for the weekly day of rest, although it had been respected in France for religious reasons until 1881, it was abolished at that date and not restored until 1906, though it had been obligatory in Germany since 1891. In this area then, the status of the Russian worker was rather close to that of his French counterpart. It was with respect to legal unions and the right to strike that Russia was an exceptional case. Everywhere else, in England, always at the forefront, but also in Germany, Belgium, France, and Italy, legal unions and the right to strike were part of the workers' status once they were achieved between the 1870s and the 1890s.

Whether despite or because of the existence of these rights, from 1895 on mobilization of workers became a common factor throughout western Europe. Although strong movements were staggered in time from one country to the next, developments were analogous, and governments everywhere had to find responses to popular demands. How could Russia escape from this agitation when Russian workers were informed through an active revolutionary movement of the struggles taking place elsewhere and were aware of their own backwardness when it came to rights and freedoms? This explains why they attempted to seize them by force.

A STAGNANT GOVERNMENT

Russian society was then in the midst of transformation. Of course, it still had a majority peasant population. But the dynamic elements, those that gave evidence of the necessary adaptation to a modernized economy lived in the cities: workers, students, and the intelligentsia as a whole, to which we return. What was still missing from this social landscape was a bourgeoisie which, had it existed, might have contributed both to progress and to stability.[3]

In the face of this changing society, the regime lacked resources. At the summit of the state, the young monarch who had ascended the throne in 1894 was subject to many influences, which all encouraged him to ignore the need for change stirring his country: the weight of the legacy of his father, to begin with, and the political conservatism of Alexander III; the influence of the chief procurator of the Holy Synod, Constantine Pobedonostsev, tutor of the late czar, who intended to keep the son totally loyal to the autocracy he had inculcated in the father; but also the young Empress Alexandra, passionately attached to her new country and to the Orthodox faith she had embraced at the time of her marriage, but who had a rather troubling understanding of the religion to which she had converted, drawing from it the certainty of a sacred mission blending mysticism and political conservatism, which once again produced an obsession with autocracy. Naturally irresolute, with little awareness of the state of a society with which he was hardly deeply familiar, the monarch was susceptible to these pressures. Moreover, he had a vision of his people closer to what it had been in the eighteenth than to what it was in the late nineteenth century. The "people"–the real Russian people–were for Nicholas II an idealized *muzhik*. As for striking workers and demonstrating students, he considered them minorities manipulated by agitators and thought that the "true" people paid no attention. Although, under the influence of Sergei Witte, the great modernizer of Russia, he continued the work of economic development begun by Alexander III, he did not grasp its profound consequences: the parallel modernization of thought and the need to adjust, at least in part, the political system to the economic and social changes underway. For Nicholas II, economic progress and political status were two separate realms and should remain so. And the more Russia progressed in material terms, the more, thought the emperor, respect for moral and political tradition should be imposed. The Orthodox Church helped to fix him in this conservative attitude.

Was the Russian state in a position to deal with the growing agitation at the turn of the century? Indeed not. One of the most surprising aspects of this powerful empire, whose bureaucratic inefficiency and corruption had been copiously described by writers from Gogol on, was that in a time of modernization, it did not have enough of an administration to ensure its normal operation. In the late nineteenth century, the administrative structure of the Russian state was enormously less developed than those of such states of western Europe as France and Germany in the same period.[4] To the lack of sufficient personnel, linked to Russia's budgetary problems, were added a poor territorial distribution of offices and civil servants and widespread corruption. The administration was for the most part concentrated in the capital and in central Russia. But the provinces, much less colonial outposts, were barely served. This situation produced the excessive power of officials who were as scarce as they were unscrupulous. Indeed, although some figures in the upper levels of the Russian administration possessed outstanding intellectual and moral qualities, petty local officials had for the most part inherited the depraved moral behavior that had long characterized these *chinovniki*. They were inclined to take advantage of power that they exercised with no administrative supervision.

The Russian state compensated for the lack of sufficient numbers of officials by emphasizing the system of social surveillance, that is, the police. The assassination attempts that had punctuated the life of Alexander II and then that of his son had led to the attribution of substantial powers to the minister of the interior, who was chiefly responsible, from 1883 on, for state security and the police. Security was the responsibility of the police authorities, acting through local police forces, the principal tool of social control. Between 1883 and 1898, the regime was concerned with directing and monitoring police activities by establishing supervisory bodies charged with ensuring the legality of police actions, but the situation changed after 1898. Social agitation had resumed, and the government accordingly decided to strengthen police institutions. The number of police officials and local officers increased, and use of emergency powers grew more frequent; seen from the outside, Russia tended to resemble a police state. This judgment must be balanced by certain characteristics specific to the functioning of Russia.

Three elements permanently weakened a policy based on the hope of neutralizing subversive forces by means of police surveillance.[5] First came respect for private property, the possessions, and economic freedom of individuals, even if they were considered dangerous political criminals. Neither prison nor exile authorized the state to deprive someone of his or her possessions. Revolutionary movements and sometimes their members received donations and subsidies which the state, even when it was aware of them, never touched. Transfers of funds abroad to finance publications that were then sent into Russia to foment insurrection were carried out with complete legality. The second weakness of the system was the ability of Russians, particularly the intelligentsia, to go abroad to study, to take refuge, or to carry on subversive activities. Getting a passport was all the easier at the end of the century because the authorities preferred to see individuals considered dangerous leave the country. London, Zurich, Paris, and Berlin were all very valued centers of Russian revolutionary life. This explains why the Ulyanov couple had little trouble going abroad after their Siberian exile. The third cause for the weakness of the regime had to do with the "scruples" of the governing elite. It believed in the need for a firm, repressive system. On the other hand, it wished to be seen, especially outside Russia, as a modern elite respecting criteria of authority accepted everywhere. From this divided conception of authority, which was sometimes found at the lowest levels of the system, flowed contradictory ways of acting that contributed little to effectiveness.

Thus, although relying on a significant police apparatus and arbitrary rule in order to maintain civic peace, the Russian state was principally characterized by its weakness and ineffectiveness. In principle it was a police state, but in reality it was not very repressive, as a few figures suggest. In the decade preceding Nicholas II's ascent to the throne, there were seventeen executions for political crimes, and we know that most of the condemned had really committed assassinations. Through the entire reign of Alexander III, a grand total of four thousand people were arrested and incarcerated for political reasons[6] (it is important to point out that at the time, political opponents of the regime were not transformed into common criminals, as was the practice in the USSR); Nicholas II's record was even smaller. For a population of 123 million, and for troubled times in which assassinations of high officials did occur, it is a record that makes it inaccurate to call the Russia of the decades preceding the Revolution a "police state." The most that might be said is that some of those governing the nation had the ambition to make it so.

The major victims, not of surveillance, but of a certain tolerance by the police for the outrages that they suffered, were the Jews. There were 6 million of them living in the empire at the end of the century, most of them in "residence zones" to which they had been assigned.[7] The last two decades of the century were particularly tragic for them, marked by discrimination (notably the university's *numerus clausus*), repeated pogroms, and finally, after the publication of a vicious forgery, *The Protocols of the Sages of Zion,* in 1895, by the growth of an atmosphere of universal suspicion. The regime thus closed its eyes to a tragedy experienced by an entire community of the empire. It also closed its eyes to a foreseeable consequence of the situation that was costly to Russia, the exodus of a population: the Jews who were able to decided to flee to neighboring European countries or even to America. Several choices were open to those who remained: to turn toward organizations favoring a return to the promised land, to join the revolutionary struggle within specifically Jewish organizations, or finally to become a part of the struggle being led against the system by the entire revolutionary movement.

THE INVISIBLE CRISIS OF THE CHURCH

Late nineteenth-century Russia had another dominant institution that combined hierarchy and moral authority, the Orthodox Church. Orthodoxy was the leading religion of the empire, and the Autocephalic Church was the state church, one of the components of national life and the political system.

The church had been under state control since the time of Peter the Great, who had abolished the patriarchate in 1721 in order to block the church's desire for independence, replacing it with an administration, the Holy Synod. The chief procurator of the Holy Synod was in fact a high official chosen by the monarch. Subject to political authority since the eighteenth century, the Orthodox Church had become stagnant, with its sumptuous rituals inherited from Byzantium and complete intellectual conformity. The regime expected the church to confirm its legitimacy and to support the society's certainty that all the government's decisions and actions were in harmony with the divine plan. In exchange for this submission to the interests of the political system and this stabilizing role, the Orthodox Church enjoyed immense authority because of its status as the national church. Catholics and Lutherans were reduced to a semilegal existence; Judaism was synonymous with social exclusion, and Jews had to be baptized to become full citizens of the empire. Only Islam, the religion of the conquered peoples of the southern part of the empire, was implicitly accepted by the regime. Non-Russians enjoyed a special status in the empire; they were exempt from military service, authorized to open schools, and allowed many places of worship. General Kaufman, the governor general of Turkestan, prohibited the Orthodox Church from establishing a diocese and engaging in missionary activities in Tashkent.[8] The Russian government expected that this peaceful coexistence with the Muslims would induce them to discover for themselves the virtues of Russian Orthodox civilization and to embrace them willingly.

Despite the limits imposed on it in the southern part of the empire, the Orthodox Church was in favor of territorial expansion; it supported the empire's attempts to conquer more territory in Asia, from which it expected an expansion of its sphere of influence. But conformity and adhesion to the imperial regime and its plans did not command unanimous support in the church. Although the upper clergy, the dignitaries, were fully integrated into the system, and the badly educated and isolated rural clergy followed the hierarchy and asked few questions about the future, a certain number of clerics, especially in the large cities, were aware of the agitation prevalent in Russia. They thought that it was not the church's only calling to support a regime deaf to the cries of the people, that it should not necessarily be on the side of the rich and powerful. The disquiet that began to take root in a small segment of the clergy, unquestionably an elite, would finally lead to the separation of church and state in 1918.[9] After two centuries of subjection, the church emancipated itself in less than two decades. This reawakening of authentic religious consciousness was a still hidden but real component of the underground movements that were shaking the political order of the empire. As for the rest, the regime at the end of the nineteenth century had little awareness of these developments as well.

THE INTELLECTUAL REVOLUTION

With a society in movement and a stagnant government, it is not surprising that the Russian intelligentsia made this contradiction the kernel of its thought. In this context, it is necessary to evaluate two closely connected phenomena that transformed the course of Russian history in the early years of the twentieth century: the growth of the intelligentsia and the development of political and social thought that gradually became a basis for action.

In order to understand these phenomena, it is worth returning briefly to the first figure who attempted, in his brutal and rapid manner, to transform Russia, Peter the Great. This remarkable monarch conceived the project of extracting his country from its backwardness and its oriental heritage—Tatar and Byzantine—in order to modernize it and root it in Europe. All of his reforms were inspired by this project: the creation of a powerful state, the abolition of the independence of the church, and the reliance on foreign elites and techniques. In her own way, Catherine the Great continued the plan. Determined to transform their country, and willing to use the harshest methods to do so, these two monarchs were without doubt enlightened heads of state; they were despots, but their despotism was at the service of a desperate search for progress. After them, the situation of Russia was no longer as it had been. Their successors, heirs to a powerful state and conquerors of a vast empire, acted primarily to strengthen that power. With the exception of Alexander II, whose reforms changed the social organization of the country, the czars thought primarily in terms of power. Probably none of them can be accused of complete blindness. But starting in the late eighteenth century, when the Enlightenment and the spirit of the French

Revolution spread throughout Europe, Russia did not participate in the movement, took refuge in its Asiatic traditions, and cut itself off from the rest of Europe. Although this break was barely felt in Russia itself, precisely because of its isolation, until the first decades of the nineteenth century, everything thereafter became a source of conflict.

In this context, the "intelligentsia," peculiarly Russian in its makeup, its development, and the role that it played, takes on some importance. What gave it its uniqueness was the fact that it did not form a well-defined sociological group. Limited in numbers and coming from varied backgrounds, from the nobility to the most deprived lower classes, it took shape by becoming aware of Russian problems and looking for appropriate solutions that were as diverse and changing as the intelligentsia itself. It defined itself primarily by its rejection of a "stagnant" order, and by the "revolutionary" spirit with which it opposed that order. The Russian intelligentsia was an amalgamation of moods and ideas, an ideological community that was constantly expanding to include men from ever more varied backgrounds, and that changed by adapting itself to a shifting intellectual history. Its members very soon moved away from their origins and settled into a precarious existence in a closed circle. In a period in which the proletariat was not yet widespread in Russia, the intelligentsia, through the calling it proclaimed for itself, sought to be the representative of the silent people. And because of its material conditions, it proclaimed itself to be the first Russian proletariat.

Its history can be divided into two periods. Before 1870, it saw itself as the true instrument of history. After 1870, it placed itself in the service of a "historic" class, first the peasantry, then the working class, which, it believed, were the real actors in the change that had to be accomplished.

HOW COULD RUSSIA BE CHANGED?

Russian history in the nineteenth century is largely a history of intellectual movements animated by the intelligentsia and following one another with increasing speed. The time of the revolutionary movement did not arrive until the beginning of the following century. What is worth noting at the outset is the richness and diversity in the thinking of the intelligentsia, in contrast to the rigidity and relative intellectual poverty of the ruling class. Even outside the intelligentsia, the major figures of the century from the nobility or relatively comfortable classes, such as Pushkin, Gogol, and Tolstoy, also represented subversive thought in the eyes of the authorities. Without rehearsing this history in detail, it should be recalled that its point of departure was 1825, when young officers from the nobility, having discovered the ideas of the Enlightenment and the French Revolution through the Napoleonic wars (and also through Freemasonry which was then making inroads in Russia), rose up against the political stagnation of their country, in what was known as the "Decembrist" movement. In the feverish days of December 1825, these young idealists thought they could bring down the entire system by removing the monarch. They called upon the French ides of liberty, equality, and fraternity, and they found themselves in absolute solitude. Russian society as a whole had not heard their call.

There were several reasons for its indifference. Challenging the legitimacy of the monarch was not yet acceptable, as the church confirmed. But also the call for "liberty" was still premature. "Liberty" remained an abstract term for the Russians of the early nineteenth century. Aware of their problems—serfdom, poverty, the arbitrariness of those in power—and troubled by them, the Russian people aspired to social justice above all. Because they had not understood this, the conspirators of 1825 stood alone against the regime, and their martyrdom did not shake people's minds. But the lesson was not lost. After 1825, the theme of social justice, the hope of the whole society that was rooted in the hearts of the destitute, replaced that of liberty and dominated all movements of thought. The Decembrist plot was nevertheless a warning shot for the regime, which was not unaware of the need for reforms, but was hesitant to undertake them. For its part, convinced that the regime would always be incapable of reforms, the intelligentsia thought that they could be accomplished without and against the authorities. From then on, the link between the desire for reform and the struggle against the regime was established, and for a long time. It was the source of the tragedy of Alexander II and, up to a certain point, of that of Nicholas II.

After the failure of the Decembrists, the intelligentsia began to consider the nature of the changes needed in Russia and the steps that would make it possible to modernize. This was the time of the great debate between those who wanted to resume the path pointed to and followed by Peter the Great, who believed in a Russia developing like Europe, through the growth of capitalism and the rejection of the specificities of Russian history, and those who defended a "Russian road." Before anyone else, a friend of Pushkin's, Pyotr Chaadayev, in his first *Lettre philosophique*, written in French and published in 1836, raised the question of the historic development of Russia and suggested the necessity of adopting the European road. Declared insane and prohibited from further publishing, Chaadayev had nevertheless brilliantly opened the way for "Westernizing" thought, notably for Belinsky.[10]

The response to this plea in favor of Westernizing Russia came from the group known as "Slavophiles," led by the theologian Alexey Khomyakov, the brothers Ivan and Constantine Aksakov, and Ivan Kireyevsky. Contrary to received ideas, this movement was far from being original in Europe, even though it was animated by the affirmation of virtues specific to Russia: spirituality, generosity of the people, and solidarity, as opposed to the harshness and corruption of Western capitalism.[11] The Russian tradition was certainly at the center of this way of thinking, but the Slavophiles were in fact connected to European and especially German romanticism; like Schelling, Schlegel, and Franz von Baader, they nostalgically defended their vision of a lost paradise.

The Westernizers were no less romantic in their own way. From noble families (except for Belinsky), as were most of the Slavophiles, they opposed serfdom for moral reasons, in the name of a certain sense of guilt specific to their class; and they advocated a constitutional political system. Both camps were rather ignorant of the realities of Russia and thought about its future primarily in moral terms. Gradually the dividing lines between them began to blur. In time, Chaadayev was less severe in his criticism of Russian specificity, and Khomyakov declared his admiration for England. Herzen, who had begun as an intransigent Westernizer, was disappointed by the "bourgeois" French revolutionaries of 1848 and gradually came to agree with certain Slavophile ideas. The West had been corrupted, he thought, by its mercantilism and its bourgeois spirit; Russia was not yet corrupt because it had not adopted the capitalism that had engendered those two monsters. Hence, shouldn't capitalism be avoided and Russia be encouraged in the future to develop the communal organizations that were original to it and could lead it to make progress?

This suggests two important aspects of Russian thought. First is the horror of the bourgeoisie, considered the embodiment of decadence and corruption. In this way, Russian thought is very distant from Marx, who on the contrary emphasized the natural virtues of the bourgeoisie, its entrepreneurial spirit, and the mission that devolved on it in social history. The other idea, whose essence Herzen suggested and that Marx would accept only very late and with many qualifications, is that historic processes are plural, adapted to the diversity of situations and historic conditions. The possibility of avoiding capitalism, a hypothesis that was in vogue in the second half of the twentieth century, was totally novel in the middle of the nineteenth. Even though Marx was not yet widely recognized as an intellectual leader, the necessity for the capitalist stage or its inevitability was a certainty already well established in most minds.

Whereas political debate in Russia was for the most part linked to the legacy of the Decembrists and to the argument between Slavophiles and Westernizers until the great reforms of the czar-liberator in 1861, afterward everything changed: the nature of ideas, their influence, and the intelligentsia itself.

"THESE MAGNIFICENT YOUNG FANATICS"

Then came the time of the nihilists: Pisarev, Dobrolyubov, and especially Chernyshevsky whose influence on Lenin was large. This movement, with no equivalent elsewhere, was very characteristic of the spirit of the Russian intelligentsia, which was radical, intolerant, and not inclined to debate but to the denial of any idea opposed to its own. For the nihilists, the only thing that counted in the life of the mind was what would serve social progress. They turned their backs on literature, philosophy, and art, and asserted that only the exact sciences were useful. There also emerges from their writings an extraordinary human type, the "new man," ascetic, austere, solitary, whose fate is identified with that of the community. *What Is to Be Done?* by Chernyshevsky and the *Revolutionary Catechism* by Nechaev clearly illustrate this conception of the future. The greatest Russian writers of the time gave a prominent place to the nihilist movement and its ideas. In *Fathers and Sons*, Turgenev popularized the term "nihilist" (it is true that he had a polemical intention) and sketched a psychological portrait of these men. In *The Devils*, Dostoevsky was inspired by the murder of the student Ivanov, decided and organized by Nechaev. Bakunin, who was very close to Nechaev[12] and helped to spread his influence, wrote of him: "I have here with me one of those young fanatics who know no law, fear nothing, and have absolutely decided that many of them should perish under the blows of the government as long as the Russian people have not rebelled. They are magnificent, these young fanatics, godless believers and plain-spoken heroes."[13]

The reforms undertaken by Alexander II, especially the abolition of serfdom, forced the intelligentsia to adopt a way of thinking that was not entirely negative. The reforms also suggested to them that they should address the people directly and gain their support in order to avoid having the people turn toward the czar. It was a time in which populism, anarchism, and an early revolutionary movement organized and embodied by Tkachev all flourished.

Like nihilism, "populism" was a specifically Russian movement in part connected to the disappointment Herzen had shown in his view of the West. Following him, the populists had thought about the social reality of a Russia dominated by the peasantry, and had concluded that it was that reality that should be the basis for their action. They had also considered the failures experienced by the intellectual movements that had preceded them and, recognizing the isolation of their predecessors and the lack of understanding that had greeted them, they concluded that it was necessary to find a popular base. Another problem concerned them: the place of the intellectual in the struggle. Until then, intellectuals had seen themselves as privileged historical actors; for the populists, intellectuals should step aside in favor of the "historic" social class, the peasantry. Their function was to serve the peasants, not to guide them. If the populists were intent on granting the peasantry a central role, this was because, like Herzen, they thought that it was a social class foreign to and unassimilable by capitalism and thereby capable of giving birth to a new society that capitalist corruption would not succeed in degrading. Thus, for the first time, political struggle in Russia made a place for the popular masses. The ideas of the populists were also marked by the distance from the thinking of their immediate predecessors. In his *Historical Letters*, Lavrov used as a basis the positivist thought of Auguste Comte and Herbert Spencer. The exact sciences that enjoyed so much prestige were displaced by the attention given to the individual person, to the demand for social justice imposed by love of one's fellow man. Whoever fate had favored should pay for their good fortune by placing themselves at the service of others. The desire to expiate a privileged birth thus led enthusiastic young people, won over by populist preaching, to "go to the people," to go to the countryside to educate the people and call on them to become aware of their historical role and of their suffering.

This generosity was disappointed and misunderstood. The peasantry remained attached to the monarch and to the faith that legitimated the existing order, whereas the populists proclaimed their contempt for religion and that very order. The peasants greeted these naïve young people with pitchforks, or worse, called the police. The populists were right in attempting to base their action on social reality. However, they failed to inform themselves about the peasants' state of mind. Certain that the peasantry agreed or was ready to agree with all of their ideas, they came up against two contradictory phenomena: a poverty stricken social reality, as they had imagined it; and a social conscious-ness that had not grasped that poverty and the forms of struggle that would make it possible to get out of it. In addition (a lesson that would not be lost on others, including Lenin), the populists had not imagined that the good will they demonstrated would turn out to be ineffective if it were not supported by an organization. When the leaders were arrested, the movement collapsed. But their lack of success does not in any way diminish the importance of the pop-ulists in the political history of Russia. Their great merit was to have understood the changes that had occurred in Russia after 1861, and to have demonstrated–by failing, no doubt, but the lesson would be learned–that no political move-ment could succeed without organization. The door was thereafter open to rev-olutionary organizations.

"Anarchism" also holds an honorable place in the genealogy of the Russian revolutionary movement, and it also makes up a part of Russian tradition. Its leader in Russia was Bakunin, an aristocrat who, like most populists and Slavophiles, thought that the Russian people were endowed with special virtues. First was a tradition of rebellion whose model was Pugachev.[14] Bakunin intend-ed to give new life to this tradition by calling the people to insurrection. In his view, the people had another quality that was decisive for the future, the absence of state consciousness, of an inclination for organization, and he contrasted this particularity to the "innate statism" of the Germans. This is why Bakunin was convinced that Russia would be the privileged site for the abolition of all organ-ized social life.

MODELS FOR ACTION

Opposed to Bakunin's thought, engaged in constant polemics against him and against the populists, Piotr Tkachev played a significant role in the development of Russian revolutionary thought and in the genealogy of Leninism. Like many revolutionary thinkers, he had come from the provincial petty nobility, but he had been a student in the capital, where he had been quick to discover subver-sive ideas and activities. So much so that, having entered the university in 1861, he was almost immediately arrested for taking part in various demonstrations. He was imprisoned for two months in the Peter and Paul fortress. From the out-set, he had thus acquired a twofold experience of agitation among students and of repression.

Developed over the course of very many articles published under various pseudonyms in Russian journals, Tkachev's thinking was in a sense a summing-up of the thinking of the populists and the anarchists, as well as of their experiences and failures. Like the populists, he thought that the historic opportunity of his country was the lack of a bourgeoisie. But against them, he had little belief in the specific virtues of the people. Of course a revolution could not be made without them, he thought, but the people had to be organized, directed, guided, and not entrusted to a supposedly innate historical wisdom that did not exist. Rejecting the populists' reliance on the peasants, Tkachev just as vigorously condemned Bakunin's rejection of the state. The state should not be destroyed, he said, but replaced by rigorously organized revolutionary institutions. Society is not changed by dislocating the order of its life and turning it over to the initiative of the masses. It is changed by taking power, organizing it, and holding on to it. Tkachev thus opened a new road that broke with the past thinking of Russian intellectuals, but also moved some distance from the ideas of Marx. He recognized the revolutionary capacities of Russia, but pointed out that the conditions for it were specific. In addition, he thought that revolution meant seizing and holding on to power not by the masses, but by a minority of perfectly organized revolutionaries. Tkachev was the first to say that the conquest of power is at the heart of the process of social transformation. He was also the first to propose a method for that conquest of power, to describe its "techniques," and to specify its purpose: the preservation and indeed the strengthening of the power that had been conquered. Organized, rigorous, precise, Tkachev was in fact the first theoretician of the Russian Revolution. He adapted Marx's thinking to the Russia of the last decades of the nineteenth century. His journal *Nabat* (The Tocsin) and his correspondence broke with purely speculative revolutionary thought and showed Lenin the path to follow. The pre-Marxist period was coming to an end in Russia; the time for thought calling upon the important Western marxist movement had come.

First the Russian intelligentsia made a final attempt to reach its goal by an organized attack on the political system. Propaganda, demonstrations, strikes by workers, and terrorism were all combined in two successive revolutionary terrorist organizations, *Zemlya i Volya* (Land and Freedom) and *Narodnaya Volya* (People's Freedom). *Zemlya i Volya,* which dominated the 1870s, set up a real organization in the middle of the decade to coordinate the activities of its members scattered throughout the immense territory of Russia. Vigorous propaganda and spectacular demonstrations (the red flag was hoisted to the top of the cathedral of Kazan) were met with implacable repression. To avenge her imprisoned comrades, a young aristocrat, Vera Zasulich, shot the governor of the capital in 1878, inaugurating the "year of assassinations" and the evolution of *Zemlya i Volya* toward systematic terrorism. There were attempts against government representatives and against the czar. The period concluded with the proclamation of a state of siege in the most troubled regions and by the transformation of *Zemlya i Volya* into *Narodnaya Volya,* the final variant of the movement dominated by two remarkable revolutionary figures, Nikolai Kibalchich and Andrei Zhelyabov. This time, it was a genuine secret society whose sole purpose was terrorism. The objective was to bring down the tyrant by the armed struggle of a strong combat organization. The goal was reached on March 1, 1881, when the conspirators finally succeeded in killing the czar-liberator.

The consequences, however, were ambiguous, because the death of the czar resulted in the cancellation of the constitutional proposals that he had been about to sign. Instead of constitutional reform, the conservative policy recommended to Alexander III by Pobedonostsev prevailed and delayed the political progress of Russia for a quarter century. The assassins were hanged on April 3, 1881; the successful attack against the movement's principal target had simultaneously demonstrated its impotence.

With the arrival of Marxism in Russia, a different intellectual elite moved to the front of the political stage. Lenin gradually became one of its most prominent figures. A page of Russian history had thus been turned on March 1, 1881; the prehistory of the revolution was over. From then on, the debate on Russian specificity moved to the background of the concerns of those who wanted to change Russia.

Chapter Three

THE ORIGINS OF BOLSHEVISM

WHEN VLADIMIR ULYANOV LEFT SIBERIA IN 1900, NOW UNDER the identity of Lenin, the conditions in Russia were already very favorable for the development of an organized revolutionary movement claiming to be Marxist. The last decades of the century had seen a concurrent evolution of Russian society and the Russian intelligentsia, along with a change in Marx's relations with Russia, all of which contributed to the rapid spread of Marxism in the country.

MARX AND RUSSIA

Marx's Russophobia is sufficiently well known to require little comment. What is less well known is that he was always haunted by Russia and that in the course of his work he had become a real specialist on the "Russian question." He had at first been obsessed by his vision of a "plan for universal aggression" that he believed Russia was harboring, and by the barbarism of the methods that would be used to carry it out. As evidence, he relied on the apocryphal "Testament of Peter the Great," which he always believed to be authentic. Marx's hostility was strengthened by Russian violence against Poland, particularly by the terrible repression of the 1863 uprising. At the time he wrote that support for Poland was the "test of a truly socialist consciousness." The constant reiteration of this virulent antipathy to Russia was hardly likely to bring him the support of Russian intellectuals. It is easy to understand that, until the 1880s, they had adopted positions and joined movements that were rather distant from Marxism.

At the very moment that he was lamenting the fate of Poland, Marx was beginning to take a new look at Russia. The emancipation of the serfs and the agitation of the intelligentsia gave him a sense of rapid change. Volume I of *Capital*, published in 1867, was translated into Russian in 1872, and Marx made the acquaintance of one of the translators, the populist Nikolai Danielson (who used the pseudonym Nikolai On). In an 1871 letter, Danielson assured Marx that his book had provoked great interest in Russia.[1] Thereafter, Marx grew increasingly curious about Russia. He learned the language, read Chernyshevsky and Flerovsky,[2] and entered into sustained correspondence with several intellectuals, including Pyotr Lavrov and Vera Zasulich. As early as 1870, he noted that "a terrible social revolution is inevitable" in Russia.[3]

As a result he developed an interest in the Russian "commune." Vera Zasulich questioned him about the possibility of using this particularly Russian social organization for revolutionary purposes. Although surrounding his answer with reservations, Marx concluded: "If the Russian revolution gives the signal for a proletarian revolution in the West, and if they support one another, the current system of collective property in Russia could serve as a point of departure for communist development."[4] This was probably for Marx more a theoretical hypothesis than a concrete prospect, and many of his other writings confirm his doubts. In the end, what was at issue was considering Russian specificity as a historic opportunity and imagining a development different from that of the rest of Europe, making it possible for Russia to avoid the stage of capitalism, that is, to advance at an accelerated rate toward socialist forms of production. In a certain sense, Marx thus seemed to agree with the populists and with Chernyshevsky, who were desperately seeking a means of doing away with czarism without having to travel over the long path of European history or give up Russia's special social and economic structures. Although his answer remained ambiguous in the end, designed neither to encourage nor to discourage his Russian friends in their support for populist approaches, once Marx died, Engels was much more intransigent on the subject. Writing to Danielson in 1890, he reduced Marx's rather restrained remarks to the expression of a judgment based on the immediate circumstances. At the time, he explained, terrorism seemed to announce the end of czarism, and it seemed entirely appropriate not to encourage Russia to develop capitalism. But by 1890, Engels noted that the industrialization of Russia had led to the growth of the working class and the birth of capitalism. The discussion between Marx and Zasulich was therefore no longer timely.

On the links between revolution in the West and in Russia, whether on the basis of the preservation of the peasant "commune," Engels wrote a good deal designed to dissipate any ambiguity that might have been created by Marx's positions. He stressed that the European revolution had priority, not an autonomous revolution in Russia. Everything would become possible for Russia once the socialist revolution had won out in Europe.

Although these debates might have seemed rather theoretical in the last decade of the nineteenth century, it took only a few years for their practical implications to be noticed. In any event, they had the virtue of setting Russia, until then not very respected by European socialists, at the center of their concerns. They also had the advantage of making Marxism a decisive reference for the development of Russian thought at the end of the century.

RUSSIAN MARXISM: ORTHODOXY AND REVISIONISM

Brilliant minds soon came surging through the door opened by Marx. Philosophers and economists, who raised the question of the transformation of

Russia in their own way, sharply emphasized the disagreements between their analyses and those of Marx's orthodox Russian disciples.

That orthodoxy was embodied by the man who was considered the father of Russian Marxism, Georgy Plekhanov (1856–1918). After a period as a militant in Land and Freedom under the influence of Chernyshevsky, and then in various Bakuninist organizations, he converted to Marxism at the time that he was forced to flee the country in 1880. He then began the difficult life of an exile that did not end until his return to Russia in 1917. In the interval Plekhanov lived in Geneva, was banished from Switzerland from 1889 to 1894, and settled in France, from which he was expelled five years later. His wanderings took him to London before he could finally return to Switzerland. His life as a perpetual outcast, his very broad culture, and his rigorous attachment to Marxism explain the enormous prestige he enjoyed among the Russian intelligentsia.

The little group gathered around him in Geneva, which called itself the Emancipation of Labor Group, was made up of Pavel Axelrod, Lev Deych, and Vera Zasulich. This was the first Russian Marxist Party, and they were its only members. They devoted themselves to: the propagation of Marx's doctrines in Russia and the establishment on their basis of a revolutionary movement that would take its place in the international socialist movement; and to the destruction of the prestige and influence of the populists.

Plekhanov's intellectual authority over the intelligentsia explains the swift propagation of Marxism in Russia, demonstrated by the success encountered by the publication of *Capital.* But the "founding fathers of Russian Marxism" were politically weak, because of their distance from Russia and their lack of real contact with the Russian working class on which they had founded all their revolutionary hopes.

Nevertheless they managed to propagate in their country a Marxism unblemished by the desire to "co-opt" Russian specificity. Through them a rationalistic Western form of thought penetrated into Russia and struck strong blows against populism and an entire "Russian" vision of the future.

Plekhanov fought tirelessly against those whom he saw as the evil geniuses of Russian thought, who rooted it in an isolation from which only Marxism, he thought, could rescue it: Tkachev, Bakunin, and all the populists without exception. In *Our Disagreements,* published in 1885, he vigorously attacked the populists' conception of history in the name of the unity of the historical process: "Russia," he wrote, "will necessarily follow the same path as Western societies, even if its great backwardness might bring about a swifter transition toward and decline of capitalism. The mistakes of the Western proletariat might also instruct the nascent Russian proletariat and help it to speed up the course of events." In Plekhanov's view, counting on the specificity of Russian rural organization was dangerously utopian. He often wrote that capitalism and the class struggle could not be avoided. And he lucidly foresaw the perils of a revolution laying claim to socialism that had not fulfilled the necessary preconditions: "It would be a political monster . . . a tsarist despotism disguised in communist colors." This warning from 1885 is evidence of exceptional prescience.

Plekhanov particularly attacked Tkachev's voluntarism, accusing him of fostering a terrible reaction by attempting to force the course of history. Beyond this attack against Tkachev, it was with Lenin–a Lenin still unknown to the world, who was still really an adolescent–that he was already crossing swords. Arguing against obscurantism and in favor of a rational approach to history, from that time forward Plekhanov always represented the rigorous Marxist, the Westernizer determined to make the European path of development prevail in Russia. But at century's end, Russian Marxism was a movement of thought of great diversity to which a remarkable contribution was made by another current, the "Legal Marxists." Of course the success of Bolshevism was soon to throw its representatives into obscurity for a long period. They nonetheless introduced into Russia ideas very close to those being developed at the time by German "revisionism." They were contemptuously called Legal Marxists by their opponents, who denounced what contributed to their notoriety, their ability to propagate their ideas legally. Indeed, they lived legally in Russia and published their writings there, often successfully passing through the censor. And their works sometimes reached a wide public by the standards of the time. The best known was Petr Struve, a contemporary of Vladimir Ulyanov's who outlived him by twenty years.[5] Along with him, Nikolai Berdyaev, Mikhail Tugan-Baranovsky, Semyon Frank, and the future theologian Sergei Bulgakov made up a brilliant constellation. All these thinkers born around the same time as Lenin were more intellectuals reflecting about the fate of their country than men of action. Their opponents accused them of dreaming of reforms and not, as consistent Marxists, working to make revolution the goal of Russian development. They also accused them of advocating legal means to reach their goal, synonymous with ineffectiveness in the eyes of these critics.

All of them later rallied to liberalism. If they had first chosen Marxism, this was because at the turn of the century, liberalism did not yet exist in Russia, and the entire debate was organized around Marx's ideas. They also turned toward Christianity, and Sergei Bulgakov became the greatest and most original Orthodox theologian of the twentieth century. These men shared a commonality of thought about Marxism without blindly accepting any of its axioms. They separated Marxism as a scientific explanation of historical processes, to which they subscribed, from a certain number of moral principles, which in their view belonged to an independent sphere. For example, they attributed absolute value to democracy and civil liberties and in the end considered Marxism a useful theory of society, but did not wish to make it into a political weapon. In 1894, Struve published in Saint Petersburg *Critical Remarks on the Economic Development of Russia*, a book that provoked much interest and many debates. But it was a disturbing book for Marxists, because Struve rejected the idea that the state oppressed society. On the contrary, he wrote lucidly, society needs the state and will still need it in the system that replaces capitalism. His positive view of capitalism, of its capacity to evolve and to prepare its own disappearance to make way for a better order, contradicted the strongly held Marxist idea of the pauperization of the working class. However, this very rich thought did not seem at first to trouble the Russian Marxists with whom Struve and his friends maintained close ties.

In the background of the great debates stirring the Russian Marxists, at home or in exile, Marxism also took on another form: action. Its privileged stage was Saint Petersburg, the political capital of the empire, but even more important, the intellectual and economic center where ideas and social forces confronted one another.

THE BEGINNINGS OF MARXIST REVOLUTIONARY ACTION

After a few relatively calm years due to the repression following the assassination of Alexander II, the capital began the last decade of the century in a state of great agitation.

A social movement that was at first pre-Marxist and then won over to Marxism took shape in the capital at the time. Marxist and populist political circles were organized, all the more disturbing to the authorities because strikes and demonstrations were shaking the country: demonstrations took place in the capital to celebrate labor day (the first attempt of this kind in Russia took place in Saint Petersburg in May 1891). The government was particularly alarmed by the major strikes in Lódz in May 1892, to which it reacted sharply. The numerous arrests among small and dispersed groups of intellectuals, particularly those who called themselves Social Democrats and who were the principal targets of the repression, made it necessary for them to organize.

Early in 1893, a revolutionary movement was set up by a student at the Technological Institute in the capital. Stepan Radchenko was endowed with a genuine conspirator's temperament. For him and his comrades, it was unthinkable to leave the responsibility for action to the workers. Russian conditions, they thought, required clandestine political activity that had to be secret, organized, and hierarchical, in which intellectuals would play the role of guides. The ideas of *Narodnaya Volya* had found a significant opponent. Radchenko had faithful followers. For example, German Krasin, who became the theoretician of the movement, but especially a small group of four women who taught in the Sunday schools for workers, which was established by a philanthropic manufacturer named Vargunin. Among them was Nadezhda Krupskaya.

The moment has come to situate Vladimir Ulyanov in this movement. We have already seen, from the perspective of his private life, how he participated in some revolutionary activity during this period. We must now consider his place in the Marxist movement. When he arrived from Samara after a brief stay in Nizhni-Novgorod (towns where a number of exiles lived), armed with a recommendation to the Radchenko group, Ulyanov also had in his favor the fact that he was the brother of a hero of the revolutionary movement, and the name of Alexander was his best passport. He met the principal leaders of the group, but did not make a particularly favorable impression on them: "His unattractive and common physical appearance did not impress us very much," noted one of the participants in the meeting, Mikhail Alexandrovich Slivin.[6]

It took almost a year for him to be fully accepted and become involved in the group's activities. This idle time bothered him little; he took advantage of it for a summer vacation with his family in 1894. He might have thought he deserved it, because it coincided with the completion of an essay, "Who Are 'the Friends of the People' and How Do They Fight against the Social Democrats?"[7] In this work, he criticized the populists and defended Struve. More important than this first attempt at a book was his meeting with Yuli Martov and the necessity of making a choice between agitation as a revolutionary means (advocated by Martov), and action and propaganda.

With Martov, Ulyanov found himself facing the great debate among Marxists seeking directions for action in Russia. At the source of the debate, and of the meeting, was a book that Martov had published, *Ob agitatsii* (On Agitation), whose author, Arkady Kremer, was one of the founders of the Jewish socialist party, the Bund. Martov was to become close to Lenin, and it is worth pausing for a brief description of him and an outline of his career. From a family of Jewish intellectuals, Yuli Tsederbaum, as he was named, had a deeply influential childhood. His mother was Viennese, and he learned German and also French, the language his parents used at home. His grandfather, a renowned Jewish intellectual, had established one of the first newspapers addressed to the Jewish community of Russia. His father, who was living in Constantinople when Yuli was born in 1873, had followed this example and was a correspondent for several Russian newspapers. Raised in a well-educated and well-traveled family, which after Constantinople had settled in Odessa, a city with a large Jewish community, the young Tsederbaum was not particularly conscious of being a Jew or of belonging to a community different from the Russian people. But the pogrom in Odessa following the murder of Czar Alexander II in 1881, which miraculously stopped at the Tsederbaums' door, left the eight-year old child with a memory of frightful scenes and helped him to discover his origins.

Another moment in this developing consciousness came in 1889. Shortly after the 1881 pogrom, the Tsederbaums had moved to the capital. Yuli had been admitted to a gymnasium when, in 1889, the police called their Saint Petersburg residence permit into question, a permit that was available only to privileged Jews. After some uncertainty the authorization was confirmed, probably because of the high level of education and resulting social status of the head of the family. The incident came close to depriving Yuli Tsederbaum of the possibility of studying in the capital, affected him deeply, and soon turned him toward illegal activities in student groups. Arrested in 1892, released, and arrested again in 1894, he was expelled from Saint Petersburg and prohibited from living in any university town for two years. He moved to Wilno (now Vilnius, capital of Lithuania), met Kremer, and began to consider along with the local Social Democrats the problems of the workers' movement. It was then that he became "Martov."

From that time on he made a strong impression on everyone despite his unattractive physical appearance. Rather ugly, stooped, and disheveled, he gave the impression of being slightly deformed. However, as soon as you met his eyes, glittering with intelligence behind thick glasses, his unattractiveness was forgotten, and you saw only the brilliant, extraordinarily cultivated man and the remarkable dialectician. In Martov, Lenin found an exceptional collaborator and interlocutor whose attachment, until a dramatic break, indicated that he had been able to discern in Lenin the future hero of the Revolution.

Ob agitatsii, the pamphlet by Kremer that Martov had published, posed problems for Social Democrats that were to cause serious divisions. Relying on the experience of the Polish working class, Arkady Kremer drew the conclusion that workers had to struggle to resolve their own difficulties, to begin with their economic difficulties, and that by doing so they would come into conflict with the authorities, thereby giving their struggle a political character. Two themes came out of his analysis: workers had to "act" rather than study; they would learn in struggle, and the duty of Social Democrats was to urge them to action through "agitation." It was the "awareness of their economic interests" that prevailed among the workers. The activity of Social Democrats therefore had to shift from propaganda and education to agitation of the working class.

The Social Democrats debated and divided over this choice between agitation and continuation of the work of education. Lenin devoted himself for the most part to intellectual work, always favored throughout his life. He studied the living conditions of the working class and labor law; in short, he became an "expert in the working class," but with no real experience in the field. In his view, the principal concern was to go beyond the little group to which he belonged to join the circle of "major" marxist theorists, and through them to reach the prestigious founding fathers exiled in Switzerland. The publication of Struve's book, *Critical Remarks on the Question of the Economic Development of Russia*,[8] would, he thought, provide the opportunity. The work, which was oddly authorized by the censor, had great success, the immediate effect of which was the spread of marxist ideas—and hence the discrediting of the populist notion that Russia had to follow a specific historical course—to a wider public than the one that had been reading Social Democratic pamphlets. It opened a wide-ranging debate in Russia. Ulyanov wrote a cautious review. In January 1895 he caught a chill and decided to go abroad for treatment, and it was then that he received a passport with no difficulty. It was the ideal occasion to finally meet the founding fathers.

We have already noted his meeting in Switzerland with Plekhanov and Axelrod. For the young revolutionary of twenty-five, these elders were impressive in every respect. Axelrod, then forty-five, the son of a poor Jewish innkeeper from Ukraine, had very early discovered the revolutionary cause while working to help educate Jewish children in order to ensure their emancipation. Contrasted to this typical representative of the Jewish intelligentsia of the empire, who sought in revolution a response to the oppressed status of his people, was the aristocratic figure of Plekhanov. Like many young aristocrats of his generation, Plekhanov had joined socialism through populism, because he thought he had contracted a debt to the people. In 1895, this forty-year-old was physically imposing; he was handsome, distinguished, extremely cultivated, and courteous but distant.

When Ulyanov met with Plekhanov, Struve was with him. The two men were comparably brilliant and knew it. They respected one another. To introduce himself to Plekhanov, Ulyanov had a good visiting card, related to the positions he had taken. At the same time as Struve's book, the Russian censorship had authorized the publication of Plekhanov's *On the Question of Developing a Monistic View of History*. Ulyanov had given an enthusiastic commentary on it at a meeting of Social Democrats, and Plekhanov had been informed of it. However, as we have seen, he was only half-charmed by this young man intent on pleasing him. The effect Ulyanov produced on almost all his interlocutors, on Struve as well, though not negative, was marked by a certain distrust. Struve wrote: "The impression Lenin made on me, which will remain with me always, was unpleasant. . . . I immediately sensed him as an enemy, even when we were still close. . . . The brutality and cruelty of Lenin—that I noticed at our first meeting—were inseparably linked with an irrepressible passion for power. . . . What was terrible in Lenin was the mixture of personal asceticism, the ability to flagellate himself, and the ability to flagellate others, which expressed itself in an abstract social hatred and a cold political cruelty."[9] Struve's retrospective view of the young Ulyanov coincides to a certain extent with Lunacharsky's habit of mentioning the "Asiatic" characteristics of Lenin.

After passing through Paris to met Marx's son-in-law, Paul Lafargue, Ulyanov returned to Saint Petersburg in September 1895. It was then that he met Martov, just as impatient as he to go into action. Of the two friends—relations between them were very close before their break—Martov was the more enterprising. He argued for concrete decisions, whereas Ulyanov was still hesitant and more inclined toward intellectual activity. The result of their alliance was the formation of the Union of Struggle for the Emancipation of the Working Class, bringing together the disciples of Radchenko and those close to Martov. It consisted of seventeen members, including the four women who taught in the Sunday schools, and five "alternates." It was already a small hierarchical organization, closed to workers, elitist. Ulyanov was the editor in chief of all publications. But, as we know, on December 16, 1895, the authorities, aware of all this commotion, intervened and arrested most of the members of the group.

In prison but not inactive, Ulyanov drafted a program intended to make possible the survival of the group. This document, which was easily sent out of prison and widely distributed, is a curious one. Its author still seems uncertain about the line that should be followed. Insofar as it asserts the primacy of the economic struggle and decrees that the party should "assist" and not guide the working class, the program could have come from the pen of Kremer. These are arguments that Ulyanov, when he had become Lenin a few years later, was to denounce with virulence.

The Russian situation at the moment was very contradictory. The strikers of 1896 had had no imitators. But the economic crisis that was to develop at the end of the century was already affecting some sectors of the economy, particularly the metalworking industry. Threatened with layoffs, the workers were reduced to silence. The number of strikers fell from sixty thousand in 1897 to forty-three thousand in 1898. After a slight increase in 1899, the first year of the twentieth century recorded only twenty-nine thousand.

Revolutionary hope was thus retreating, and exile did not seem to be a tragic break with the workers' movement. The exiles met for discussion before their departure: Should their movement open itself to the working class? The clearly negative answer of Martov and Lenin was supported from a distance by Plekhanov. Social Democracy at the time was able to establish unity on the basis of such views.

Lenin's years in Saint Petersburg, his only time in Russia before the Revolution, are difficult to sum up if we wish to define his intellectual development. When he left for Siberia in 1897, he condemned the opening of the party to the working class. But less than two years earlier, he had adopted as his own the ideas of agitation and assistance to the working class. He had not yet completely abandoned the populism of his youth, which was mixed with the ideas of Marx. It was not until the end of the century that he resolutely turned his back on the temptation of "economics first." In the end, what emerges most clearly from his activity is his capacity to fight in the realm of ideas, to engage in polemics, and to write. He would always be more at ease with the intelligentsia than with workers, whom he hardly knew, and who, he was afraid, although he did not say so, if they were better educated, would form an elite able to compete with the intelligentsia to which he belonged.

THE FIRST ORGANIZATIONS

Kremer, the importer of "economism" into Russia, was also the founder of the Bund, that is, one of the first working-class organizations in the empire. Until then, everything had played out in the heartland of Russia, but it was the Poles and the Jews that gave a jump-start to the organized political movement. To begin with, there was the Polish Socialist Party, founded by Roman Dmowski in 1893, which tended to favor purely Polish interests. Against this "nationalist" tendency, the internationalist elements of the party, led by Rosa Luxemburg and Leo Jogiches, soon split off and founded the Social Democratic Party of the Kingdom of Poland. Rosa Luxemburg already understood, as Marx had a few years earlier, that the time had passed when Polish interests had to be taken into account because, insofar as it was more advanced than Russia, support for Poland was a way of weakening the empire of the czars. In 1890, Russia's rapid economic growth and political development required organization of the workers' struggle throughout the empire in order to bring the proletariat together and avoid dissipating its energies in sterile national dissensions. The revolution had to take place in the heart of Russia.

The trajectory of the Bund was more complex. This Jewish socialist movement was created in 1897 at the particular instigation of Martov and Kremer. It was called the General Union of Lithuanian, Polish, and Russian Jewish Workers. It is easy to understand what led Martov, Kremer, and their friends to set up this union. In the troubled Russia of the late nineteenth century, the situation of Jews was particularly difficult. Confronted with persecution and residency restrictions, their community at the time was divided. Some dreamed of a return to Palestine, and Zionism attracted many followers. But against the Zionists, the advocates of integration argued passionately that socialism, based on the solidarity of the working class, was the most effective response to the ostracism they suffered. To defend this cause, they relied on the social particularities of the Jewish community. It was primarily urban, concentrated in the western part of the empire, where industrialization was progressing most rapidly. The Jewish working class that was growing so quickly was generally dispersed in small businesses, less subject to police control than large industrial firms. Because of these characteristics, the Jewish working class had been able to construct bonds of solidarity and forms of organization that made it an advanced element of the proletariat of the empire. If it is further noted that it was characterized by a high degree of intellectual development, which differentiated it from workers from rural areas who had been hastily urbanized and were still ill-adapted to cities and factories (which was characteristic of the majority of the Russian working class), the propensity of the Jewish proletariat to unite and to give evidence of a genuine class consciousness is easy to understand.

The advocates of integration invoked these characteristics. The leaders of the workers' movement were then working to bring Jewish and non-Jewish workers together, asserting that they shared the same condition, and that what separated them, Judaism, was of little weight. To be sure, the most common language in Jewish workers' groups was Yiddish, but that was for the simple reason that it was the best means of communication. Nevertheless, the first Jewish intellectual to recognize the difficulties of the assimilationist program was Martov, who was himself completely assimilated. Addressing the Jews of Vilna on May 1, 1894, he declared that the interests of Jewish and Russian workers were not always identical; that of course they had to struggle together, but that the Jews could not completely trust the Russians. Martov therefore concluded that they needed their own organizations.[10] The opinion was all the more adopted because Russian anti-Semitism at the time had taken on terrifying proportions and had become a daily reality.

It was against this specific vision of a Jewish workers' movement that the Bund was established. To be sure, at the moment of its formation, it was an organization of the Jewish working class.[11] But in Martov's view, that was only a temporary concession to the specific conditions of Russia. The aim was the internationalization of the working class, and this was a way of preparing it.

This political activity of Poles and Jews functioned to some degree as an example for the marxists of Saint Petersburg, opening the way to the creation of a real organization of Russian Social Democrats, which came into being in 1898.

THE MINSK CONGRESS

Nine people met in Minsk in March 1898 and founded the Russian Social Democratic Labor Party, or RSDLP. The meeting in Minsk had its source in the rivalries among various regional workers' organizations, particularly Vilna, base for the Bund, and Kiev. Its intent was to accomplish the unity of workers' organizations. But it was the Bund that played the decisive role in the organization of the Minsk congress. The nine participants represented the Marxist organizations of Saint Petersburg, Moscow, Kiev, Yekaterinoslav, and, it goes without saying, the Bund with three delegates. The congress lasted for three days, from March 1 to 3; elected a central committee of three members; and adopted a program drafted by Struve, which claimed allegiance to the ideas of People's Freedom, but without recourse to terrorism. On adjournment, the congress decided to hold another plenary session six months later, but the delegates were soon arrested and deported, and the RSDLP went into hibernation.

In this first attempt at an organization bringing together all the Marxist groups scattered throughout the territory of Russia, two aspects are noteworthy.

First was the aspiration to go beyond the national problems that were then beginning to trouble the multiethnic empire and to make the organization of the working class an instrument for the integration of national minorities. The vocabulary used indicates this, because the party was called a party "of Russia" *(Rossiiskaia)* and not "Russian" *(Russkii)*; it thus clearly addressed all workers of whatever origin living within the borders of the empire, not only the Russian working class.

In the second place, the program elaborated by Struve, following the example of the *Communist Manifesto,* described a revolutionary process in two stages. The first, dominated by the bourgeoisie, would lead to democratic progress; in the next one, the proletariat would assume its historic task and establish socialism. Struve pointed out that in this process the weakness of the Russian bourgeoisie made it incapable of fully playing its role in the stage of democratic progress; as a consequence, the Russian proletariat was given a decisive role from the outset. In other words, Struve managed to reconcile in this document Marx's conception of the revolution and the particular political conditions of Russia.

Even though it did not have the hoped for results, the role of the Minsk congress in the turbulent history of the Russian revolutionary movement should not be underestimated. Up to that point, the political stage had been dominated by the populists, and then by the fight conducted against them, in the name of a different historical vision, by the "founding fathers" of Marxism, Plekhanov and Vera Zasulich. But, for nearly a quarter century, intellectual debate and terrorism had prevailed over attempts to organize a nascent working class. With the Minsk congress, and despite the rapid disappearance of its participants, a new period opened, one in which the necessity of a revolutionary organization, a program, and precise rules of operation was to be recognized by everyone and mobilize the energy of the Marxists, Lenin above all.

Finally, it is surprising to see how quickly the names of the men who ventured to create this first party in Minsk disappeared from memory, and how quickly the revolutionary stage was taken over by those who had until then played minor roles. The nine delegates in Minsk sank into oblivion, perhaps because of repression, but especially because none of them later played a significant role in the party that was in the process of formation. On the other hand, Vladimir Ulyanov, absent from Minsk because of his exile in Siberia, where he was engaged in thinking and writing, was soon to come forward as the real organizer of the Bolshevik Party, a party that was to formulate aims and impose a direction on the Russian revolutionary struggle that no one at Minsk could have imagined.

In the spring of 1898, the real history of Lenin was about to begin.

PART TWO

PROFESSIONAL REVOLUTIONARY
(1900–1914)

Chapter Four

UNITY: ONE PARTY, ONE PROGRAM, ONE LEADER

ON FEBRUARY 11, 1900, THE EXILE OF VLADIMIR ILYICH ULYANOV came to an end, and he left Siberia. But the man hurrying from Shushenskoe to Russia and the outside world was no longer Ulyanov. Toward the end of 1897, he had written a pamphlet titled *The Tasks of the Russian Social-Democrats,*[1] which was published in Switzerland in the following year and was the first to be signed with the name he had permanently adopted, Lenin. At first, the name was merely a pseudonym, chosen in reference to the Lena River flowed lazily through the region of his exile. It might have been only one of his many masks. But the accidents of history assured that the name Lenin survived as the designation of a man who had done more to transform the history of the world in the twentieth century than any of his contemporaries. The permanence of the name chosen by chance during his exile is probably connected to the fact that Lenin lived outside Russia beginning in 1900, and that he therefore had no need to hide behind changing identities. Quite the contrary, his activities from 1900 on imposed a stable identity on him to which both his audience and his opponents could refer with no risk of error. From then on, the requirements of clandestine existence were replaced by those of political combat carried out from abroad, and hence in fairly stable conditions of safety.

PSKOV: FINAL MONTHS IN RUSSIA

At the conclusion of his exile, Lenin looked for a place of residence that would be only temporary, because he already intended to settle outside Russia. He chose Pskov, where Radchenko and other of his former associates were living. The exile of Alexander Potresov and Martov ended at the same time, and they joined him there, making Pskov a center of marxist activities. During this brief period, the former exiles were provided with material to refine their theoretical views, because the turn of the century was marked by furious debates among marxists, in which Lenin had already played an appreciable role during his exile.

In *The Tasks of the Russian Social-Democrats*, Lenin had already sketched his views on the role of the workers' party and the nature of the alliances that it could form with other social forces. For Lenin, only the Social Democrats were fighting against absolutism in a coherent way, and they should therefore use other social forces for their purposes with no spirit of compromise. Lenin's ideas, from the outset, came into conflict with those of the "Economists," young Social Democrats gathered around Ekaterina Kuskova and Sergei Prokopovich, whose ideas were set out in Kruskova's *Credo*. For the "Economists," the specific situation of Russia had to be taken into account by Marxists; the "economic" demands of the working class ought to mobilize the social-democratic movement which, by forming an alliance with the liberal opposition, would be performing a much more useful task than if it were to establish an autonomous party. When Lenin read this program while still in exile, he mobilized his friends and secured sixteen signatures for the text that he drafted to vigorously condemn the arguments of the *Credo*. This anti-Economist manifesto was published in Geneva by the Social Democrats living on the shores of Lake Léman.

The Economists were not the only ones troubling Lenin. He was disturbed above all by the progress of Eduard Bernstein's reformist arguments in Russia, and by the philosophical evolution of Struve and Bulgakov. The fear of seeing Russian Marxism turn toward heterodox positions haunted him from that point on and impelled him to consider with more precision the response that should be made in terms of program and organization. He devoted his time in Pskov to this question. The discussions with the faithful Potresov and Martov led Lenin to the conclusion that it was urgent for Russian Social Democrats to have a battle organ, a newspaper published abroad that would express the positions of orthodox Marxism.

He called a working meeting of his friends in Pskov in May 1900 at which Struve and Tugan-Baranovsky were also present. In Lenin's view, the alliance with these Legal Marxists was intended to lend more weight to his proposal. The paper that came out of the meeting was called *Iskra* (The Spark), to which both the Pskov group and the Legal Marxists were to contribute. But for the idea really to get off the ground, they had to secure the agreement and participation of Plekhanov, a task undertaken by Lenin, Martov, and Potresov. This required leaving the country, and thus the end (with the exception of the 1905 interlude) of Lenin's life in Russia until 1917.

Before leaving on this lengthy exile–this time an exile in freedom–Lenin had to settle family affairs, above all to reunite with Krupskaya.

In 1900, she was still facing another year of exile. When Lenin left Siberia, he went with her to Ufa before going to Pskov. In May, about to leave Russia for a long time, he went to bid her farewell in one of those family expeditions that were so important to this man so deeply attached to his family. He went to the Bashkir region with his mother and his sister Anna; the two women were in Podolsk and Lenin in Pskov, and the three Ulyanovs met in Sizran. From there they traveled by boat on the Volga as far as Kazan where they changed ships and, sailing from one river to the next, reached Ufa by way of the Kama. It was a pleasure trip, neither the shortest nor the least expensive way from Kazan to Ufa, that Lenin would always remember fondly. "How pleasant it was sailing with you and Aniuta in the spring of 1900," he recalled in a letter to his mother.[2]

Before this trip, he had decided to go to Saint Petersburg for a meeting with some Social Democrats and to take care of various matters. Because he was barred from the city, he stayed in Tsarskoe Selo, the favorite residence of the imperial family, which was a further violation of the restrictions imposed on him. He was arrested, taken to the police station, and then jailed for three weeks in uncomfortable conditions, noteworthy for the troublesome presence of bed-bugs in his cell.

The fecklessness of the czarist system of surveillance can only provoke surprise. By 1900, Lenin had already become well known to the police, through his revolutionary activities in Saint Petersburg, which had led to his imprisonment and exile, and then through his activities in the group of exiles in Pskov. He paid for his clandestine trip to the capital from which he was barred with a brief prison term, to be sure, but with no further penal consequences. There was no thought of a further sentence. He then asked to go to Ufa to visit his wife, who had resumed her subversive activities in the town, and although the request was at first rejected, this was only temporarily; a few days later, he was authorized to organize the family meeting already described. Then, having decided to go abroad, he was given a passport without the slightest difficulty, in exchange for the modest sum of ten rubles. The Russian police were probably comforted to know that the revolutionaries were out of the country rather than stirring up trouble in Russia, but they could just as well have sent Lenin back to Siberia; his disregard of legal restrictions gave grounds for that kind of decision. The extremely tolerant behavior of the police in May 1900 made it possible for Lenin to leave his country undisturbed in order to prepare, outside its borders, the overthrow of the system.

THE BEGINNINGS OF *ISKRA*

On leaving Russia, Lenin went to Germany to make contact with the Social Democrats, while Potresov went to Switzerland to solicit the assistance of Plekhanov and Axelrod, who had already promised to provide it. Points of detail remained to be settled in a final meeting with Plekhanov. The decision to publish *Iskra* had been made, but the place and conditions of publication had yet to be determined. Plekhanov wanted *Iskra* to be published in Switzerland, proposed himself as editor in chief, and said that he could arrange access to a printer. Lenin and Potresov had already negotiated with Clara Zetkin in Germany; she had promised them the services of a clandestine printing press, and they had decided that the paper should be published in Munich. Anna Ulyanova-Elizarova explained the preference for Germany over Switzerland by her brother's wish not to be confined to the closed and quarrelsome circle of

Geneva émigrés. It is more likely that Lenin felt from this moment that Plekhanov's moral and intellectual authority risked obscuring his own. Plekhanov's participation in the project was indispensable, but Lenin refused from the outset to have the patriarch of Russian Marxism considered the ultimate arbiter. In 1900, although there was no opposition in the ideas of the two men, they were totally distinct in temperament. Behind the apparent cordiality, their meetings in Switzerland, from 1895 to the 1900 meeting to settle the final details for publication of the paper, were always characterized by a more or less hidden mistrust on both sides. The decision to print *Iskra* in Germany caused a great commotion. The editorial offices, with Lenin, Vera Zasulich, Martov, and Potresov, were set up in Munich, although the first issue was printed in Leipzig. For security reasons, the location of printing was frequently changed, and moved from Leipzig to Munich, then to London, and finally to Geneva.

Lenin now had the organ of battle he had long dreamed of and that Plekhanov had urged him to establish five years earlier. The first issue was published on December 24, 1900. Lenin took care of writing several articles, organizing the shipment of paper to Russia, and, above all, defining its line. For him, *Iskra* was already the starting point for the party that was to assemble and lead the Russian revolutionary movement. From its very first appearance, it was very well distributed in Russia, to which it was brought clandestinely and then distributed to the most active Marxist groups in the capital and the major industrial and university centers. Following the instructions of the leadership, each issue was read and discussed by small groups; it passed from hand to hand and ended up reaching an appreciable number of readers. Copies were posted on walls at night and torn down by the police in the morning, but in the interim they had been read by hundreds of sympathizers and curious passersby. Lenin was chiefly responsible for *Iskra* and derived considerable authority from that position. From the outset, he made it an organ of struggle against ideas of which he disapproved, that is, economism and reformism, to which many articles were devoted from the establishment of the paper until 1903, the year when he became occupied by problems of organization and thus had less time to devote to polemics. In these articles and elsewhere, Lenin gradually forged a personal view of revolutionary struggle which found full expression in *What Is to Be Done?* But even before his views were clearly formulated, he contended that the function of the paper was to unify the Russian political organizations that called themselves Marxist. Indeed, the Russian Marxist movement in 1900 was still diffuse and characterized by ideological flexibility; it was still a juxtaposition of groups and forums for discussion rather than an entity tending toward unity. For Lenin, the newspaper that he controlled had to be an "agitator and collective organizer." Because he had a precise idea of the function of *Iskra*, he threw himself fully into it and thereby lay claim to its particular authority. Krupskaya later remarked that Lenin–the impassioned chess player–gave up the game from that time on, not wanting it to distract him for an instant from the work of the paper.

Krupskaya's term of exile had ended, and she joined him in Munich, still accompanied by her mother. The three remained inseparable and thenceforth led a regular, indeed bourgeois, existence. However, when the Munich printer of *Iskra* found the work too risky, they had to move to another city, and Lenin decided to choose another country.

London seemed to be the safest place for these activities, so *Iskra* was transferred there, and the household moved without hesitation. Lenin liked London a good deal, but he soon discovered a personal drawback to life in England: his meager knowledge of the language. During his Siberian exile, he and Krupskaya had translated the Webbs' *History of Trade Unionism*, but there was a great difference between a translation struggled through with the help of dictionaries and grammar books and a conversation with an ordinary Englishman. As a result he plunged into the study of English with the same doggedness he showed in writing his diary or fighting his opponents. In general he brought exceptional persistence and concentration to everything he undertook. This consistency in any task that he considered necessary gave him a great advantage over those around him who were often less consistent.

On several occasions this character trait had unfortunate consequences. Exertions that were too intense exhausted him and damaged his nervous system, which was probably fragile. This happened to him in 1902 when he was about to leave London for Geneva, where the paper and its editors were again emigrating. Lenin then fell into a semi-depressive state which obliged him on his arrival in Geneva to spend two weeks cloistered at home, seeing no one.

Before leaving England, he had met for the first time a young revolutionary nearly ten years his junior, Lev Davidovich Bronstein, who in 1902 had just adopted his permanent pseudonym, Trotsky, borrowed from a prison guard in Odessa, a city in which he had spent two years. After prison, exile, and flight to Samara where he had been in contact with the local *Iskra* group, Trotsky had clandestinely traveled to Austria, where he had met Victor and Friedrich Adler, and then come to London to join the staff of the newspaper. Curious about everything, brilliant, and cultivated, he might have expected a warm welcome at the outset. In fact, Lenin subjected the newcomer to a veritable inquisition before accepting him. Of course, he later trusted him, but in the discussions among the editors of *Iskra*, everything indicates that Trotsky was more taken with Martov and Vera Zasulich than with Lenin, who made decisive judgments about everything with no subtlety. If we are to believe Trotsky, Lenin noticed this on several occasions but attributed his young colleague's attitude to what he considered pernicious influences rather than to the growing awareness of divergences among the editors. When the *Iskra* group moved to Geneva, it was Plekhanov that Trotsky had difficulty in dealing with, whereas Axelrod was rather close to him. In 1903, he officially joined the editorial staff of *Iskra* when control over the newspaper slipped from Lenin's hands.

WHAT IS TO BE DONE? UNITY

Lenin had been considering since 1900 how to ensure that the revolutionary movement was cohesive and effective. Ideological battles, *Iskra*, and his articles were all harnessed to this fierce determination to forge the tool of the revolution in accordance with his central idea that only "unity"–of will, of the program, of the organization–would make it possible to realize the revolutionary project. *Iskra*, an organizing and unifying organ, was a first step in that direction, but it was far from being the real instrument of which he dreamed. Haunted by ideas taken from Tkachev, it was the party that he had to invent and impose. In 1902, he wrote *What Is to Be Done?*–a systematic exposition of his views on this instrument of the revolution.[3] His central argument, which the whole dispute with the Economists had anticipated, was that the primacy of politics could not be called into question.

Analyzing the situation of his country, the consequences of rapid industrialization, and the growth of the working class, Lenin concluded that the weakness of that class made it necessary for a structured organization to take leadership over it. But reducing Lenin's thinking to this circumstantial observation would be a dangerous distortion. For, beyond the difficulties specific to a nascent working class, he was raising the general question of class consciousness of the workers, to which he gave a negative response: "The history of all countries shows that the working class, exclusively by its own effort, is able to develop only trade union consciousness. . . . Political class consciousness can come to the worker only from outside, that is, outside the economic struggle, outside the relations between workers and employers."

This is the foundation of Lenin's argument. The lack of innate class consciousness among workers condemned their spontaneous movements to end in compromise or retreat. Spontaneous movements of the working class, of which there were numerous examples in the first years of the century, led to economism and not to genuine revolutionary consciousness. "The spontaneous development of the working-class movement leads to the subordination to bourgeois ideology. . . . Trade-unionism means the ideological enslavement of the workers by the bourgeoisie. Hence, our task, the task of Social-Democracy, is to combat spontaneity. . . . Without revolutionary theory there can be no revolutionary consciousness."

Then what is to be done? The answer for Lenin was very simple: "We have said that there could not have been Social-Democratic consciousness among the workers. It would have to be brought to them from without." To rectify the trade-unionist consciousness of the working class, it therefore had to be pushed toward an authentic revolutionary movement; it had to have the assistance of those who, outside the working class, had an awareness of the general problems of society, that is, the intelligentsia.

At this point Lenin silently departed from the views held by the Social Democratic movement and supported by the "historical" Russian Social Democrats, such as Plekhanov. In their view the intelligentsia had to form a revolutionary movement with the workers that had no specific structure, with the party understood as an organization including them all, considering all capable of participating in historical change. Lenin had a very different view of revolution; it had to be organized and led by professionals, the "vanguard" of the working class, bearers of its class consciousness and of the revolutionary theory of which the workers had no innate sense. Only the party, in Lenin's view, was the true creator of class struggle, the instrument that could instill in the working class the class character that would keep it from straying into error and falling under the ideological dominance of the bourgeoisie. The important thing for him was that the workers' movement be guided by the right "ideology," precisely the one brought to it by the party. The party was thus the "only" possessor of proletarian consciousness.

This explains the importance that Lenin gave to the organization and operation of the party. This vanguard had to be organized in accordance with its historical mission, which was particularly difficult to accomplish because what was involved was bringing down the established order. That implied that the party had to be centralized, hierarchical, authoritarian, and that it reject endless debates and verbalism. Its organization was governed by the principle of unity, "unity of will," expression of class unity and of the will of the party. This unity of will could be established only by the elimination of all individual wills, mistakes, and deviations, that is, by a purge. The epigraph to *What Is to Be Done?* is a letter from Lassalle to Marx containing the assertion that "a party becomes stronger by purging itself." Lenin was referring to two organizational models: the "factory," of course, that imposed on men discipline, collective behavior, obedience to a plan transcending them; and even more the "army," with rigid structures, organized in preparation for combat, the purpose governing its rules and ensuring their efficacy. As an organization of professionals whose tasks were defined according to the principles of the division of labor, the party had to establish a rigid hierarchy of authority emanating from the top, spreading through all levels, and in the final analysis imposing its decisions on everyone.

For a Russian intellectual, these ideas did not sound entirely new. In 1874, Tkachev, who had so impressed his avid reader Lenin, had already written: "The people by themselves are making a social revolution and organizing their life on a better foundation. Obviously, the people are indispensable for the revolution. But only a revolutionary minority can lead it."

What Is to Be Done? was an exposition of Lenin's theoretical vision, but it remained to establish the theory in the real world. He needed the agreement of the Social Democrats, and this was the purpose of the Second Congress of the RSDLP held in July 1903, beginning in Brussels and then moving on to London.

On its publication, *What Is to Be Done?* provoked little hostile comment. Plekhanov did assert that Lenin had exaggerated the dangers of spontaneity, and many of his colleagues found his emphasis on centralism a bit excessive. But, in general, they were all aware of the difficulties of the struggle against autocracy under the political conditions in Russia and hence of the requirements of clandestine action. With some qualifications, but with no deep disagreements, Lenin's companions tended to share his analysis.

THE SECOND CONGRESS: THE SOCIALISTS DIVIDED

Nevertheless, a break did take place in Brussels and London during the stifling days of the summer of 1903. The congress held in the two cities was grandiloquently called the Second Congress of the RSDLP, which was a formal claim to continuity with the Minsk meeting. In reality, what was at issue this time was an attempt to give life to a party that did not yet exist.

In 1903, establishing a real party was an imperative that all the Social Democrats understood. Two immediate threats made the effort necessary, both of which were changing the relations in Russia between Social Democrats and the working class.

In the first place, the use of "police unionism" or "yellow unionism," put in place by the minister of the interior in 1901 and 1902, was already producing disturbing effects. Union "entryism," called *Zubatovshchina*, after its inventor Serge Zubatov, drew into unions established and protected by the police large contingents of workers attracted by the ability to demonstrate and legally to demand improvement in their working conditions. The Social Democrats could only be concerned about this development in the working class, because it reduced the ranks of their followers and seemed to support the arguments of the Economists.

A second problem was emerging at the same time, the competition of the Socialist Revolutionaries (SRs) who argued simultaneously for unity of the opposition and for the use of terrorism to speed up the struggle, and who thereby exercised strong influence over the elite, from students to the intelligentsia in the broadest sense.

In the face of these threats to their authority over the working class and the elite, the Social Democrats were almost all convinced that more than anything they needed a strong organization to react effectively to such challenges. When the congress of the RSDLP met, the mood of its most eminent members was already very gloomy and even aggressive, particularly in the case of relations between Plekhanov and Lenin. However, the Second Congress was to be marked less by these disagreements than by the dramatic and definitive break between Lenin and the man who had supported and followed him for nearly eight years, the unconditional Martov.

Plekhanov had considered *What Is to Be Done?* an intellectual exercise marred by its author's excessive temperament, but no one had thought that it might contain the sketch of a real program for the party. For Lenin's colleagues, it was at best an entirely personal description of a desirable party, which still needed a serious program and rules of operation.

Plekhanov had set to work on the program in the course of the year 1902. He produced a document that provoked a sharp reaction from Lenin as well as from Martov, and from Potresov, who always supported Martov. The dispute focused principally on two questions: the role of Social Democracy in the revolutionary struggle, and the definition of certain elements specific to Russian economic and social life that the Social Democrats could tolerate. For Plekhanov, Social

Democracy was the guide of the workers because their interests were the same. Lenin, on the contrary, was determined to demonstrate what separated them, and was therefore inclined to accuse Plekhanov of surrendering to the ideas of the Economists on this point. He also criticized Plekhanov for his indulgence toward small-scale production and the petite bourgeoisie, both doomed to disappear according to Lenin, whereas Plekhanov assigned them a positive role in the Russian revolutionary process. Plekhanov was therefore asked to revise his text and to submit to the editors of *Iskra* a version taking into account the objections of Lenin, whose vehement intransigence made a strong impression on his colleagues. The second version satisfied Plekhanov's critical readers no more than the first, and even less because he had replaced the expression "dictatorship of the proletariat" with "power of the proletariat." Lenin then called on the authority of Marx, who had stated as far back as the early 1850s that "class struggle necessarily leads to the dictatorship of the proletariat."[4] After a vigorous debate, he succeeded in having the expression restored to Plekhanov's draft, which was finally adopted.

The divisions among the editors of *Iskra* shown on this occasion grew even sharper over the following months. Plekhanov was supported by Vera Zasulich and Axelrod. Against them, Martov and Potresov, rather disrespectfully calling them the "old ones," took Lenin's side, even though they were troubled by his violence and lack of consideration for anyone who dared to disagree with him. Potresov later noted that this early on Lenin's brutal character and his certainty that he was always right made his supporters wonder whether they were doing the right thing. Martov said the same, and even before he got to Brussels, he already had a sense of what might separate him from Lenin, although he had not yet clearly expressed his fears. But the debates, Lenin's extraordinary will to power, and his manipulations as well finally made Martov realize the conflict between them and the fact that it was irremediable.[5]

On the eve of the Second Congress, the antagonisms within the editorial staff of *Iskra* were obvious. For that reason, all decisions concerning the content of the paper had to be submitted to a formal vote which usually had the same result: two groups of three confronted and neutralized one another. In this charged atmosphere, the editors headed for Brussels, where the congress was to open on July 30.

The Russian Social Democrats hoped for a degree of security in Brussels; it had been promised by the Belgian socialists, particularly by Emile Vandervelde, who had obtained the premises where they were able to hold their first sessions. The Belgian police, alerted by Russian agents, monitored the debates despite frequent changes of location designed to escape surveillance, and after a few days told the delegates to leave Belgium immediately. They adjourned to London, where some trade unionists gave them refuge in a church.

The congress brought together delegates from the twenty-five principal organizations in Russia, as well as those of the Bund. In theory, each organization had two votes. In fact, some organizations had sent only a single delegate, so that the forty-three present had fifty-one votes. In addition, fourteen delegates had only an advisory role. The arrangement was in accordance with the views of Lenin, for whom it was important that the supporters of *Iskra* have a majority. Nor was he unhappy to note that only four workers were attending the congress.

The first item on the agenda was the adoption of the program presented by *Iskra*, a careful blend of Plekhanov's contribution with Lenin's amendments, followed by the adoption of the party rules. The program was very seriously and lengthily debated, and adopted with a few amendments that had little effect on the fundamentals. The overthrow of the autocracy and the calling of a Constituent Assembly elected by the people were presented as the first stages of the revolutionary program, securing easy agreement. In the course of the debate, the question of a possible contradiction between democratic freedoms which, for some, were an absolute value, and the "interests of the [p]arty" stirred the delegates. On this point, Lenin, a supporter of the subordination of all democratic principles to the interests of the party, received Plekhanov's support. This suggests how influential, despite Plekhanov's hesitations about them, the ideas of *What Is to Be Done?* had become. By 1903 the party was considered the supreme point of reference, the holder of the truth, and the only body capable of exercising authority correctly. As a consequence, the "interests of the [p]arty" as defined by itself became in turn a supreme value, leaving little room for the principle of freedom or for democratic demands.

The congress did not split on this issue. On this point, Lenin succeeded in imposing his views, and the program remained in force until 1919. The irreparable split came over the issue of the party rules. When they heard Plekhanov support Lenin in the earlier debate, Axelrod and Martov had been devastated. Their anxiety prefigured the split which soon occurred, in the course of the second major debate, having to do with the definition of "party member," where both conducted an implacable fight against Lenin.

The first paragraph of the rules established the conditions for joining the party. On this point there were two irreconcilable views, Lenin's and Martov's. For Lenin, membership presupposed personal involvement in a party organization, which meant not only agreement with the entire program, but also active participation in the life of the party. Martov, who had prepared an alternate draft before the congress and vigorously insisted that his version also be presented to the delegates, offered an enormously more flexible definition of "party member." For him, anyone was a member "who gives cooperation to the Party under the direction of one of its organizations." In other words, for Lenin, in order to be a member of the party, one would have to occupy a precise place and play an active role in a hierarchical and centralized organization, whereas for Martov, anyone who felt close to the ideas of the party could call himself a member. This apparently abstract dispute in fact involves two eminently concrete debates.

First, the view defended by Lenin in his preparatory draft underlay his entire conception of an organization of professional revolutionaries, rigorous, disciplined, and subject to permanent internal control. For him, only such a conception, separating the party from the working class and placing rank and file organizations under organized authorities, would make it possible to translate a revolutionary program into action.

The second concrete problem was the problem of authority. The mass organization favored by Martov would leave the initiative to the rank and file and in fact prohibit the leadership of the party from imposing its directives. For Lenin, this conception inevitably involved a dilution of party authority and a challenge to the personal authority of its leader, that is, his own.

Martov was certainly not alone in holding this view, which was close to that of an appreciable fraction of German Social Democracy, but among the Russians he was in a minority. The debate, however, evolved in an unexpected direction. Lenin's harshness and Martov's oratorical skills had an effect. At the outset Lenin seemed to have the majority, and Plekhanov had given him his support. "I have listened carefully to the arguments on both sides," said Plekhanov, "and the more I listen the more certain I am that Lenin is right. . . . The opponents of opportunism must vote for Lenin's proposal because it closes the Party's doors to opportunists." But Axelrod openly supported Martov, while Vera Zasulich and Potresov silently expressed their sympathy. At the very last moment, Trotsky too, although he was not yet part of the *Iskra* editorial staff because of Plekhanov's very strong opposition to his candidacy, leaned in favor of Martov. He violently attacked Plekhanov's support for Lenin's position and tore apart the argument he had made defending the efficacy of Lenin's method of combating opportunism. Trotsky's speech was brilliant, remarkable for the oratorical skills that always served him, and it was therefore effective.

Despite a final speech by Lenin aimed at weakening Martov and Trotsky, the vote that followed, in which he had expected to win a majority, finally went against him. The roll call vote was twenty-eight for Martov and twenty-three for Lenin. The remainder of the text was adopted without changes, but the blow was hard for Lenin. It was his first major defeat since he had begun to play a significant role in Russian Social Democracy.

At this point, despite an attempt to preserve appearances, the break between the two men was complete. Since the beginning of the congress, Martov had grown increasingly troubled by Lenin's authoritarian behavior and his conviction that his ideas were the only ones with any foundation. Lenin's tone in arguing against Martov had humiliated him on several occasions. This sensitive and cultivated man, passionately loyal to Lenin for years, had been unable to bear the harshness and arrogance of a man he had so long supported. He suddenly saw in his former friend nothing but the passion for power. Lenin's feelings were no less violent. Martov had opposed him, inflicted a cruel defeat on him, and was attempting, he thought, to remove him from the leadership of the party which he claimed without wishing to admit it. The difference in temperament between the two men, who were aware that what was at stake beneath their theoretical debate was indeed the exercise of power, explains the succeeding events. Although he was remarkably intelligent, Martov was impulsive and uncalculating; emotions often overcame his powers of reasoning. In contrast, Lenin—the passionate chess player—had all the qualities the game requires.

Everything for him was coldly calculated. He moved instantly from friendship for Martov to hatred and the desire to eliminate him politically. From then on his intelligence was fully devoted to that purpose; what was really at stake, it should again be stressed, was power in the party.

The debates that followed were to have considerable and unexpected consequences on the life of the party for they brought about another reversal in the balance of forces and suddenly put Martov and his supporters in the minority. The discussion had to do with the status of the Bund, which was calling for the right to form a separate organization that would alone, in its view, have the ability to represent the Jewish proletariat. Beyond the problems of organization, the Bund's demand led to a broader debate on the national question, about which the party soon had to make a determination. But for the moment, the delegates were required to decide on the organization of the party. In recognition of the importance of the national question, should it be given a federal structure, and indeed should it be given the task of defending calls for national emancipation?

The demands presented to the Party Congress by the Bund were along the lines of debates that had been stirring the Socialist International since the late nineteenth century. Austrian Social Democrats had already produced many analyses and proposals that had strongly disturbed the workers' movement. Despite the famous radical phrase from the *Communist Manifesto,* "the workers have no country," the Austrian Socialists Renner and Bauer had concluded on the basis of the example of the Austro-Hungarian Empire that workers felt the greatest solidarity with the national group to which they belonged, and only secondarily to their social class. They feared that if the workers' movement did not take this into account, national loyalties would in the end obliterate class solidarity. In their works, as well as at the Berlin Congress of 1899, they therefore asked that Social Democrats integrate national demands into their program, while at the same time rejecting the idea of a federalization of the workers' movement.

Aware of the Austrian debate, Lenin and the majority of Russian Social Democrats understood from the outset that it could soon penetrate into the Russian Empire, whose ethnic complexity was far greater than that of the Austro-Hungarian Empire. In the demands of the Bund, which had been given the special status of "autonomous organization" in the party by the 1898 Minsk Congress, they glimpsed the seeds of future demands from social democratic organizations on the periphery of the empire. The presence at the London Congress of Georgian delegates under the leadership of Noi Zhordania, who had secured passage with Bund support of an article concerning use of the national language, indicated that national demands were very close to being expressed in Russian Social Democracy and that the Bund was not totally isolated in that respect. This explains why, in the debate provoked by the Bund's demands, the delegates were so intransigent, particularly the editors of *Iskra,* suddenly reconciled in shared opposition to the Jewish workers' organization. The vote went against the Bund. Seven indignant delegates immediately left the hall, five Bundists and two Economists who had sided with the Bund while seeking special status for themselves. As a result Martov's majority for the preceding vote no longer existed, and Lenin took the opportunity to return to a position of force with a one-vote majority. Having seen the situation turn in his favor, he asserted that the group he headed had become the majority and gave it the name "Bolshevik." His opponents, now in the minority, were called "Mensheviks."

This entirely unilateral decision is interesting in that it expressed a balance of forces, personality clashes, and a great diversity in the perception of events, while also suggesting the broad outlines of the future. The majority that Lenin boasted of was fortuitous, by only one vote, and due to the Bund's departure before the end of the congress. The determination of Lenin (who had been in the minority and might have remained there had Martov been more skillful in debate) to fix this "moment" in the majority permanently by enshrining it in a vocabulary and drawing from it an inviolable definition of the balance of forces in the party, is revealing about his voluntarism and lack of scruples. These were the characteristics that would lead him to seize power and to monopolize it. On the other side, the docility of Martov and his friends, who allowed themselves to be named Mensheviks, thereby permanently identified as the minority, prefigured their future weaknesses. Respectful of the vote even though it expressed only a momentary truth, they had agreed to a name that set them in a position of inferiority. In all their struggles against the Bolsheviks, the Mensheviks would be similarly paralyzed by their excessive scruples and their serial surrenders.

The congress ended with another victory for Lenin, giving him control over *Iskra*. Arguing from the stalemates among the editors, he had suggested that the board be reduced to three members, and he similarly proposed that the authority of the Central Committee of the party be reduced in practice. Lenin was reassured by the victory that he had won over Martov and the certainty that his majority would remain solid because the Bundists and Economists had walked out. With the decisions he was to impose concerning the organization of the ruling organs of the party, he thought he had secured his revenge. With a vote of twenty-five in favor, two against, and seventeen abstentions (only forty-four voting delegates were left), the congress appointed Lenin, Plekhanov, and Martov to run *Iskra*. But, outraged by the dismissal of Vera Zasulich, Axelrod, and Potresov, and convinced that the small editorial staff would turn *Iskra* over to the control of Lenin alone, whom Plekhanov was not strong enough to oppose, Martov refused to participate. The very high number of abstentions suggests the doubts that had taken hold of the delegates.

With respect to the Central Committee, Lenin had also devised a strategy likely to reduce its weight. As it was organized at the conclusion of the congress, the party had two centers of authority: one, the "Central Committee," located in Russia, with overall responsibility for the various local organizations; the other, the "organization committee," that is *Iskra*, located outside Russia and protected from the Russian police. It went without saying that the two centers did not have the same weight. The Central Committee was of course weaker, exposed to arrest and thereby to instability of membership which would frequently have to be changed. The editorial committee of *Iskra* or the organization committee was on the contrary protected from changes in personnel, and its stability gave it greater authority. Lenin had moreover indicated this difference by attributing to the former "practical leadership" and to the latter "ideological leadership." In addition there was a semantic distinction: the organization committee had a function of "command," whereas for the Central Committee the term was *rukovodstvo* or "leadership."[6]

At the close of the congress, the split within the party was obvious. Lenin had become the master of *Iskra*; the organization of the party which was inseparable from that of its newspaper, was largely dominated by his supporters. Those who had lost were very bitter. Even though Plekhanov had a position of honor in the new leadership, it was blindingly clear (as he himself must have seen) that he was only a fig leaf. Contact between Zasulich, Axelrod, Potresov, and Martov and Lenin was practically broken off, and Plekhanov was close to thinking of joining them. But the convulsions of the divided party were far from over, and Lenin's triumph this time was of short duration.

A PYRRHIC VICTORY

In late 1903, the situation that had been so favorable to Lenin at the conclusion of the congress was reversed. The Bolsheviks and Mensheviks met again in October in Geneva, where Lenin seemed at first to have complete control over *Iskra*. But the Mensheviks soon became aware of the hostility that his authoritarianism and intolerance were provoking. With the support of Trotsky, Martov began a virulent attack on the Bolshevik stranglehold on *Iskra*, pointing out that only exceptional circumstances had made the takeover possible. After briefly backing Lenin, Plekhanov argued for a compromise with the Mensheviks, and his approach attracted a number of Bolsheviks. Encouraged by this support, he asked that the editorial staff of *Iskra* be restored to six and that the editors who had been excluded be recalled. Intransigent as usual, Lenin rejected this "conciliatory" approach and, confronted with a hostile coalition, walked out of *Iskra*, unwilling to accept the loss of his dominant position. As a result "his" newspaper fell into the hands of the Mensheviks, as Plekhanov restored the former editorial staff, without Lenin. Former supporters such as Martov had become his most implacable opponents.

For Lenin, the loss of *Iskra* was a real tragedy. First, he was obliged to recognize that his authority among émigré Social Democrats was much less than he had thought after his London triumph. He was also cut off from the Russian movement, to which *Iskra* was a link. At the beginning of this period of separation, his isolation was total.

As had happened in the past, Lenin also had to deal with the weakness of his nervous system which often betrayed him in times of political crisis. He fell into a state of depression, from which Krupskaya managed to rescue him by organizing a vacation in the Swiss Alps, where tourism, walking, and many hours of restorative sleep succeeded in bringing him back to health. By late summer 1904, he had recovered his balance, but, more importantly, he had new plans and had found new collaborators.

In reading Iskra during his period of solitude and depression, Lenin had been able to recognize the degree of Menshevik hostility toward him. There was no issue of the paper that did not contain articles challenging his views. Through them, his former friends, Axelrod, Martov, and Plekhanov were also attempting to provide a solid theoretical basis for Menshevism, designed to undermine the Leninist conception of the relations between intelligentsia and proletariat. Plekhanov had launched a veritable crusade against him, in which he denounced the man, his intolerance, and his brutality, but also constantly criticized his conception of the party, whose totalitarian character Plekhanov grasped with lucidity. Trotsky joined the chorus of critics to call Lenin a "potential Robespierre," and imagined that Lenin would one day decimate the members of the party of the Revolution. This no doubt premonitory vision was based on the call for "purging" used as an epigraph for *What Is to Be Done?*

However, as the months went by, Lenin's isolation was eased, and new sympathizers came forward. First there was a doctor of his own age, Alexander Malinovsky. An early supporter of the revolutionary movement, he was known by his pseudonym Bogdanov. His theoretical (he had debated with Berdyaev) and philosophical works had already given him great notoriety and sustained relations with the most celebrated Russian writers. Having joined the Bolsheviks in 1903, the following spring he went to see Lenin, who was delighted with this visit from a choice recruit. Bogdanov was to bring Lenin friends such as his brother-in-law Lunacharsky. He provided financial support and access to intellectuals living in Russia, with whom he had close ties. He also went along on the couple's vacation, during which Lenin gradually recovered his nervous equilibrium and his taste for battle.

Another newcomer in his life in this period of solitude, whom he met through Bogdanov, was Anatoly Vasiliyevich Lunacharsky, a brilliant mind, the perfect embodiment of the Russian intellectual elite. Trained as a philosopher, a polyglot, remarkably learned in may areas, he had entered into contact with the Marxist movement very early. He had met Lenin's sister, Anna Ulyanova-Elizarova in Moscow in 1899. Inseparable from Bogdanov, he came to see Lenin in Geneva to propose that he collaborate on the newspaper that was to be launched to replace *Iskra*. More than a politician, Lunacharsky was an intellectual of high quality, often undone by weakness of character and instability.

A third choice recruit was Leonid Borisovich Krasin, born in 1870 like Lenin, in a small town in Siberia. Before meeting Lenin, Krasin was already better known than the others for his militant activities. After university he had begun work as an engineer in Baku, where he played a significant role in the Social Democratic movement then developing in the oil capital and throughout the Caucasus. He later set up a clandestine printing press that printed *Pravda* and revolutionary tracts and organized their distribution throughout the empire. In 1903, he was elected to the Central Committee as a Bolshevik sympathizer. To

Lenin's great disappointment, on the committee he argued against Lenin's rigid position and in favor of a necessary reconciliation with the Mensheviks. Aware of the role that a man with such a talent for organization could play in the party over which he dreamed of regaining control, Lenin attempted, with eventual success, to win him over.

Finally, in the first rank of the people who helped him to escape from solitude was of course Krupskaya. At the same time that she was taking pains to entertain her husband, she put her former connections in the movement at his service and worked effectively to make it possible for him to reestablish contact with Social Democratic organizations in Russia.

When they returned from vacation, everything was ready for Lenin to undertake a new project and to become able gradually to recover his ascendancy, or at least some of his authority, over his former companions

VPERYOD OR THE NEW *ISKRA*

With Bogdanov's financial assistance and the help of his contacts, Lenin re-created what he missed most, what he could not do without, a newspaper. It was urgent for him to take action because his personal situation had been declining throughout 1904. Not only had his former Russian colleagues turned their backs on him, but also European Social Democracy as well, whose most prestigious German members condemned his excesses of thought and language. Karl Kautsky, probably the greatest moral authority in the movement, denied him the pages of *Die Neue Zeit* where Lenin had asked to present his point of view on his dispute with the Mensheviks. Lenin, who often bore grudges, never forgot the insult, to which he responded many years later by calling the old master the "renegade Kautsky." Rosa Luxemburg, another leading Social Democrat, joined the chorus of critics and pointed out that Lenin was above all "Russian" in his behavior, imbued with the still barely civilized attitudes of his country. Lenin did not forget that insult either. For years Lenin and Rosa Luxemburg engaged in polemics on many subjects,[7] even though they did not really disagree on the essentials of such serious problems as the question of national minorities. But the dispute with Junius (Luxemburg's pseudonym) in 1916,[8] would recall in its violence the hostility that arose between them during this early period of internal conflict among Russian Social Democrats. Finally, although August Bebel, another authority, suggested a compromise, Lenin refused to listen to him, persuaded that German Social Democrats were in favor of his enemies. He was not entirely wrong. This early, leaders of the European workers' movement were troubled by the excesses of the bolsheviks which seemed not at all compatible with their own polite manners and reformist tendencies.

The end of 1904 marked the end of Lenin's torment. In the course of the year, he had written a new work, *One Step Forward, Two Steps Back: The Crisis in Our Party*,[9] in which he settled accounts with the Second Congress.[10] The work, published in Geneva, consists of a defense of the positions he had taken at the

Congress. When he returned to Geneva from the vacation to restore his health in August 1904, he called together twenty-two Bolsheviks who were close to him and set up a "committee of the majority," in which Bogdanov, elected to a leadership position, was to play a very active role. That fall Bogdanov returned to Russia and worked to organize groups under the authority of the new committee. Before leaving he worked with Lenin on preparing for the publication of the new newspaper that was intended to demonstrate his recovered authority and strengthen the position of the bloc or committee that had been christened "of the majority." The first issue of *Vperyod* (*Forward*) was published in December; it was an organ over which Lenin exercised complete control. The paper signaled, if that were still necessary, the break between the two tendencies of Russian Social Democracy. It was the anti-*Iskra*, and in issue after issue Lenin attacked the rival publication with relentless virulence. For his part, the patriarch Plekhanov denounced in every piece by Lenin "the oil thrown on the fire to heighten the conflict."

From that moment on, with his vigor fully restored, Lenin began to prepare for the Third Congress of the RSDLP, which was to be held again in London in the spring of 1905. He had passionately wished for this congress in order for it to sanction his patient reconquest of the party. But his determination came up simultaneously against opposition from the Mensheviks and from organizations in Russia concerned with the sterility of the schism that weakened the movement as a whole. Five of the six members of the Central Committee working in Russia expressed their opposition to the idea of this congress and argued that "Social Democracy in Russia needs serious directives and propaganda material and not disputes. Stop arguing and get to work!"

For Lenin the first and only urgent task was to restore his authority over the party and to reconquer the power he had lost. This is why he dismissed a suggestion from Gleb Krzhizhanovsky, an old acquaintance from the movement in Saint Petersburg in 1895 who had been elected to the Central Committee at the Second Congress, to come to Russia to sound out the local organizations. As an advocate of reconciliation, Krzhizhanovsky had come to Geneva precisely in order to express the feelings of militants inside Russia. He had urged Lenin to come to see for himself, to talk with them instead of continuing to imagine their views from his comfortable Swiss refuge. Lenin had bluntly refused, offended at such naïveté.

But luck smiled on Lenin unexpectedly. In Russia the police interfered with party activities and managed to arrest nine of the eleven members of its ruling body. Krasin escaped from the roundup. The arrests were providential for Lenin because they suddenly got rid of the internal opponents of his position. He immediately grasped the windfall represented by the police action that sent his comrades to prison, and he made this cynical comment: "This will weaken the Mensheviks for a long time."

Hence it was a Central Committee reduced by circumstances to a mere fragment that gave its agreement to the holding of what was called the "Third Congress of the RSDLP." The name was no doubt extravagant, because it was in fact a meeting of Bolsheviks, and hence a break with the preceding one. The thirty-eight delegates, most of them from Russia, full-time militants, "professionals" as *What Is to Be Done?* had prescribed, sided in advance with Lenin, ready to condemn Menshevik positions without reservation.

The Mensheviks were not passive. They had called on August Bebel as a mediator, and he had proposed establishing a tribunal of five independent personalities to attempt to settle the dispute. The idea, accepted by the Mensheviks, was violently rejected by Lenin, who answered that the forthcoming congress would have to settle a disagreement that was not about persons but ideas. Bebel withdrew, horrified by Lenin's behavior, but at the same time not very confident in the political seriousness of his opponents. Put on the spot by Lenin's decision to hold the congress, the Mensheviks decided to call their supporters to Geneva, but they called the meeting they organized a "conference" instead of a congress. As they had done two years earlier, out of legalism or weakness, they adopted a modest stance that gave up to Lenin the benefit of being a true representative of Social Democracy.

The debates in London, like those in Geneva, were dominated by the events that had been convulsing Russia since January and by the possibility of a transformation and development of the events into a revolution. As a result, the problems of party organization, its relations with the proletariat, and the definition of future prospects seemed more timely than ever, and the confrontation was all the sharper.

The Mensheviks, who controlled *Iskra*, had in their ranks the most prestigious personalities of Russian Social Democracy: Plekhanov (undermined, however, by the support he had recently given Lenin), Axelrod, Martov, and the former supporters of Lenin, Potresov, and Trotsky. Observing the development of a revolutionary climate in Russia, they all argued that the party should embody a revolutionary opposition and not undertake attempts at the seizure of power or the sharing of power, considered premature. Their hostility to the program of centralizing the party advocated by Lenin, understated until then, was now out in the open.

THE THIRD CONGRESS:
THE BOLSHEVIZATION OF THE ORGANIZATIONS

In London, Lenin had to rely on new allies: Krasin, who defended the position that had now been adopted by Lenin that the party should participate in the provisional revolutionary government; Bogdanov, who had been very active in Russia in preparing the congress; and Lunacharsky, who presented to the congress at Lenin's request a resolution on armed insurrection. Despite all this the seeds of the break between Lunacharsky and the founder of the Bolshevik Party were already perceptible. Indeed, their relations would always be difficult, oscillating between Lunacharsky's militant intention to be useful to Lenin and his doubts as an intellectual which would often separate him from the father of Bolshevism. In any event the Third Congress represented a phase of support by

Lunacharsky for the Bolshevik leader, even though Lenin was already unable to accept Lunacharsky's adhesion to Bogdanov's ideas. Although he said nothing out of the need to maintain the short-term agreement, the silence was soon broken.

Newcomers had also joined Lenin, including Lev Borisovich Kamenev, a very young man who had joined *Iskra* in 1902 and conducted polemics in its pages with Berdyaev and Struve, and then returned to Russia to organize militants, first in Tblisi and then on the Party Committee in Moscow. In 1904, he had broken with the now Menshevik *Iskra,* adopted Lenin's positions, corresponded with the newly created *Vperyod,* and prepared for the Third Congress by traveling to the local committees supporting the Bolsheviks in the Caucasus, Central Russia, and the Urals. The Committee of the Caucasus elected him as its representative to the Third Congress.

Another recent recruit was Alexei Ivanovich Rykov, the child of peasants from Saratov, who had joined *Iskra* early on and played a decisive role in setting up Social Democratic groups in Moscow.

These newcomers were not allies that Lenin could easily manipulate, and the Congress of London demonstrated that although the founder of Bolshevism had been able to bring together his supporters, he was not facing a monolithic organization. A number of delegates who had come from Russia stood up to him. Those he contemptuously dubbed *komitechiki* (leaders of local committees) were led by Alexei Rykov who, with all the enthusiasm of his twenty-three years, opposed him without the slightest difficulty. Because he came from the country, Rykov would always doubt the possibility of carrying out a socialist revolution in an agrarian society without a long period of transition. In the course of the congress, a "reformist" tendency could clearly be seen taking shape, the aim of which was to limit Lenin's powers. Even the loyal Krasin launched a vehement critique of the "emigration," the excessive weight of which in the party, according to him, was a brake on its growth. Lenin was Krasin's target, as everyone clearly understood, but this did not prevent the majority of delegates from vigorously applauding his speech.

Another difficulty that Lenin had to confront had to do with relations with the mensheviks, whom he dreamed of excluding from the party, something to which the majority of delegates was hostile. Despite their opposition they finally adopted the proposals that Lenin, as a good tactician, had put forth cautiously. The Mensheviks were thus condemned on the ideological level, but they might individually remain party members if they accepted all the conditions and party discipline and if they recognized the legitimacy of the Third Congress. In sum Menshevism was excommunicated, but its members could survive in the party if they accepted total submission. The congress also voted in favor of the immediate organization of armed insurrection, a decision to which Lenin attached vital importance.

The Bolshevik Central Committee elected at the conclusion of the Third Congress included Lenin, Krasin, and Bogdanov, a triumvirate that was to rule the party until 1908. It also contained in its ranks Rykov, giving a place to the turbulent *komitechiki.*

Л Л Л

Lenin's authority over the party at this point is difficult to evaluate. On the one hand, he had imposed the greater part of his views; the holding of the congress made the Bolshevik faction the equivalent of the RSDLP, and he himself was now identified with the party, whereas the exclusion of the Mensheviks seemed to have cast them out of Social Democracy. Finally the call for armed insurrection and the recognition of the centralization of the party sanctioned the revolutionary views favored by Lenin, who was looked on as the true representative of Russian Social Democracy.

However, the reality was more complex. First, he had had to fight hard to impose his views. The apparent unanimity on the break with the Mensheviks was contradicted by a secret resolution which gave the Central Committee the mission of looking for ways of reaching an understanding. Thus on the one hand, the congress condemned the Mensheviks and called on the organizations in Russia that were connected with them to accept the majority's positions and submit to it; at the same time, the wish to restore unity persisted, and the Central Committee was entrusted with implementing it. The attitude of the Mensheviks helped to maintain the hope of a return to unity. Although their meeting in Geneva was full of attacks on the Bolsheviks, the very fact that its organizers had used "conference" and not "congress" to identify it revealed their reservations. We should probably see the refusal to dub a factional meeting a "congress" as a manifestation of their legalism, a scruple totally foreign to Lenin. But also, by doing so, they avoided the acceptance of a definitive break and thereby provided encouragement to the associates of Lenin who accepted his intolerant behavior only with reluctance.

Nor was the Socialist International very indulgent toward Bolshevik extremism. Lenin's radical positions were at odds with the views of the majority of the Social Democratic movement, and in particular with the orientation of the German party. Between Plekhanov, a refined intellectual with a Western air, and the brutal figure of Lenin, there is no doubt that the International preferred the former; in its view the latter illustrated a Russian peculiarity that Social Democracy would have difficulty integrating into its strategy.

If Lenin had won over the fence sitters at the London Congress, this is perhaps because no major figure had been able to stand up to him for any length of time, except for Krasin, whom he also won over, if only for an alliance of a few years. He also won out over the Mensheviks, a victory like the preceding one in 1903 that was short-lived and had little substance. When the London Congress ended in April 1905, Russian Social Democracy was obliged to turn its attention from formal debate to the revolutionary combat that had begun a few months earlier in Russia.

The revolution of 1905 was to obliterate all the discussions and pose a severe challenge to Lenin's authority.

Chapter Five

1905: ORDEAL BY FIRE

WHILE THE BOLSHEVIKS AND MENSHEVIKS WERE DEBATING, Russia was on fire, gradually entering into a revolution neither the outbreak nor the disorderly course of which had Lenin foreseen.[1] There had, however, been enough to alert him. The disastrous war against Japan provoked the indignation of the Russian people who recognized the futility of the military defeats and the incompetence of its leaders.[2] It also produced a string of disorders. Demoralized troops were exposed to the agitation of revolutionary militants who operated along the routes taken by reinforcements headed for the Far East. Major railway junctions lent themselves particularly well to the movement. They were meeting places for railway workers, who already supported the revolutionary cause, and students, who had been dismissed from universities during the troubles of 1899–1901 and drafted into disciplinary battalions assigned to guard rail lines, and who carried on agitation in the places where they were forced to live. Some political organizations were involved in the movement. This troubled period witnessed in particular the strengthening of Socialist Revolutionary (SR) Party, heir of the populists, whose increasing power enabled it to replace the declining terrorist organizations, Land and Freedom and People's Freedom.

The growing agitation in Russia took legal political forms—the *zemstvos* organized and met in a congress to advocate reforms—but also involved illegal actions. Everyone sensed that, in one way or another, not only did the Russian political system have to change, but it also had to change very quickly. Unfortunately, at the head of the state, an anxious and indecisive monarch did not understand social impatience and responded with a measure that would have seemed revolutionary a half-century earlier but was laughable in 1905. This was the decree of December 12, 1904, which, rather than announcing even limited reforms, spoke vaguely of necessary reforms that would be carried out, according to the document, to satisfy zemstvos, peasants, workers, and people charged with crimes. Nicholas II was convinced that he had responded to the growing agitation in the country. As a consequence, forty-eight hours later, the government gave a solemn warning to the society: agitation should immediately come to an end; the decree is a response to social demands; and the debate is therefore over. This misreading of the social mood opened the way to the great tragedy of

January. No one paid attention to calls for calm. Students were agitating, and the working class, silent until then, was about to make a dramatic entry on stage.

BLOODY SUNDAY

On December 20, 1904, a strike broke out in the Putilov factory, on the minor grounds of the dismissal of four workers. It was enough to inflame the suburbs of the capital and then the entire capital itself.

In order to understand these events, we have to consider for a moment a peculiar characteristic of Russian trade unionism early in the century, the manipulation of unions by the authorities put in place by the head of the Saint Petersburg political police, Sergei Zubatov.[3] Because of this very special kind of unionism, the regime thought it was protected from large-scale workers' movements, or at least hoped to be able to control them. That explains why the activities of Father Gyorgy Gapon, who would lead the demonstration on Bloody Sunday, did not trouble the authorities; they saw him as being in their service. But Gapon was not Zubatov. He was not corrupt, and he was convinced that he had the sacred mission of reconciling the czar and the people.[4] Inspired by deep faith, and gifted with genuine charisma, by 1904 he had enlisted nearly twenty thousand workers in his union (a much larger figure than the members that Social Democratic organizations could claim). Thus his intervention in the Putilov factory dispute was received favorably by both workers and authorities. But Gapon failed to achieve a negotiated settlement and decided to call a general strike and a mobilization of the people to demonstrate to the government the solidarity and determination of the workers.

In January 1905, the situation was still fluid on both sides. It was to the monarch that the strikers turned; they addressed a petition to him, and it was he, they thought, who had the power to resolve the crisis. The petition was drafted by Gapon with the help of a few liberals and was to be presented to the czar on Sunday, January 9. By this point the Putilov strike was nothing but a pretext. What the people were asking from the monarch was a total reform of the political system, a reform in which they wanted to be involved. Gapon's supporters intended the petition to express general popular feeling, and for this purpose they gathered many signatures in factories, public places, and streets.

The authorities knew about all these developments because Gapon kept them informed of the preparations for the demonstration. A peaceful procession was to present the request of the people to the monarch on Sunday, a day of peace, the day of the Lord, a term that also meant "resurrection" in Russia. The people were indeed preparing for a new birth or a new life. Because the authorities, fully informed, did not react openly, Gapon was persuaded that they accepted the procedure. He did not know that at the time Nicholas II noted in his diary: "All the factories in Petersburg have been on strike since yesterday. Troops have been brought in from nearby to reinforce the garrison. Until now, the workers have been calm. Their number is estimated at one hundred twenty thousand. At the head of their union is a kind of socialist priest named Gapon. Mirsky came during the evening to present his report on the measures taken."

The misunderstanding was obviously complete. On one side the petitioning and confident people, and, on the other, a monarch who would shut himself up in his country residence, Tsarskoe Selo, to avoid all contact with the people coming to meet him, leaving it up to his subordinates to react on their instincts to the unfolding of the demonstration.

Because the crowd was peaceful and unarmed, and because it believed its proposal had been heard and accepted, it paid no attention to warnings or to the order to disperse. Because the regime had neither understood nor listened to the crowd, the troops facing it opened fire and, panicked by equally panicked demonstrators, carried out an atrocious massacre. The Sunday of the people's peaceful march to their monarch became in a few hours *Bloody Sunday*, the Sunday of the break between the people and the czar. Gapon summed it up in the tragic cry: "There is no God any longer. There is no czar."

The toll for Bloody Sunday was very heavy. Conservatively, losses amounted to several hundred dead and wounded. But beyond the tragedy affecting the victims, the political consequences were disastrous. Autocracy was forever condemned in the eyes of a population that had borne it for so long. And the deaths of Bloody Sunday were added in popular consciousness to the futile deaths of the Far Eastern disaster, further proof, if proof were necessary, of the contempt in which the system held the life of its subjects. What kind of regime could kill its children or allow them to be killed? How could it claim any legitimacy?

The misunderstanding between people and monarch, already great, was to grow even deeper. For Nicholas II, the bloodbath of January 9 had demonstrated that the government was too weak, and he decided that harsh measures were necessary to restore order. For the people, the only response to the bloodbath, the only way to demonstrate their solidarity with the dead, lay in continuing the struggle. Workers' agitation spread to the provinces—Moscow, Saratov, Riga, Lódz, Warsaw, Vilna—and there were violent peasant uprisings in the countryside. Terrorism, which had subsided for a time, also reappeared. On February 4, 1905, Grand Duke Serge, the emperor's uncle and governor of Moscow, was shot by a student named Ivan Laliaev, a follower of the Socialist Revolutionaries. Students had indeed joined the movement, abandoning classes, ignoring prohibitions, and organizing demonstrations in universities themselves, and linking up with workers everywhere.

BIRTH OF THE SOVIETS

While Bolsheviks and Mensheviks were disputing at a distance in their London and Geneva meetings, in Russia the at-first spontaneous revolution was beginning to get organized and finding channels for the formulation of precise demands. The Congress of zemstvos in Moscow in April called for the establishment of universal suffrage and the calling of an assembly that would prepare the needed reforms. A month later the Congress of zemstvos formulated more precise political demands, opposing the "rights of the nation" (a new and as yet poorly defined concept) to those of the monarch. Associations and groups were formed everywhere, held countless meetings, and passed resolutions. The peasants themselves drew up lists of grievances. In May 1905 a Peasant Congress was convened, and traditional patterns of jacquerie resurfaced.

In the course of this agitated month of May, an event occurred that was to attract the attention of Social Democrats of all tendencies. In Ivanovo-Voznesentsk, a center of the textile industry, striking workers elected a soviet that would last for two months. This was a significant political innovation. Soon thereafter the mutiny on the battleship *Potemkin* in the port of Odessa revealed that the flame of rebellion was spreading from one end of the country to the other, in all circles and in every imaginable form.

For political movements, preeminently for the Social Democrats, the question of what was to be done had been posed. In the first place, what was to be done about the soviet, the spontaneous organization of the working class?[5] Should they support it, or try to co-opt it? What should be done in general with the social forces that had been unleashed? Should they be organized? In what direction should they be pointed? The Socialist Revolutionaries had their eyes fixed on the countryside. The liberals were attempting to "co-opt" the unions. Before the Social Democrats had decided what path to follow, the answer came from society itself. In the autumn local strikes and sporadic demonstrations had suddenly spread throughout the country, and the strongest union, the railway workers, called a general strike. In the capital a soviet was created in mid-October that assimilated the experience gained since May in Ivanovo-Voznesentsk and by all the other soviets that had sprung up on its model.

The Saint Petersburg Soviet, which was established on October 14, 1905, lasted for fifty days. It was made up of 562 members elected by factory workers, and almost all its deputies were from the working class, most of them metalworkers. An Executive Committee (*Ispolkom*) of thirty-one members included nineteen representatives of the parties of the left who observed the work of the Soviet but had only an advisory role. The Mensheviks had quickly understood the importance of the organization, for whose creation they had been practically responsible. A young lawyer named G. S. Khrustalev-Nosar was elected head of the executive, and the two vice presidents were the Menshevik Trotsky and the Socialist Revolutionary Nikolai Avksentiev.

The Soviet organized itself and began publishing a weekly paper, *Izvestia Sovieta Rabochikh Deputatov* (News of the Soviet of Workers' Deputies), which in 1917 would be claimed as an ancestor by *Izvestia*, the newspaper of the Soviet State (after major changes, it has even survived the collapse of the USSR).

As the soviet was coming into existence, the emperor was hesitating, frightened at the sight of a country paralyzed by strikes and engaged in the establishment of autonomous government institutions. By temperament, and out of loyalty to his father's policies, Nicholas II was tempted to rely on force. But a fraction of his entourage argued for flexibility, particularly the former prime minister Witte, who had just managed to limit the extent of the military catastrophe in the Far East at the Portsmouth conference. Given the prestige gained from the remarkable treaty he had succeeded in negotiating, he was in a position to influence the monarch, to demonstrate to him that the resources for repression no longer existed in Russia and that he had to come to terms with society. On October 17, 1905, the imperial Manifesto announced to Russia that some of its demands would be satisfied: universal suffrage and the calling of an elected assembly. The country was about to enter a new political era.

Although the liberals considered the Manifesto insufficient, it impelled them to prepare an effective strategy for the elections that it promised. They established the Constitutional Democratic Party (known as the Kadets) and prepared for the electoral battle. But the socialists were hardly inclined to follow the same path. Although the Manifesto had stirred interest in large sectors of society, it had not put a stop to agitation. The Petersburg Soviet did not disarm, but on the contrary multiplied calls to continue strikes and demonstrations. "The proletariat should not lay down its arms," said *Izvestia*. And *Novoe vremya,* a paper hostile to the revolutionary movement and aware of the importance of Khrustalev-Nosar as the president of the Soviet, wrote: "Today there are two governments in Russia, Witte's and Khrustalev's."

The regime was not indifferent to this point of view, and it played simultaneously the card of concessions (coming elections, measures favoring the peasantry) and the card of repression. There were many arrests, including Khrustalev. Trotsky succeeded him as president of the Soviet, conferring great prestige on the post, although his tenure coincided with the last days of the mass organization. It was soon abolished, and Trotsky was arrested and put on trial. But its example had spread to the provinces, particularly to the other capital, Moscow, which succeeded Petersburg as a revolutionary center.

From a distance Plekhanov had been concerned about this kind of repression and had warned against any premature movement that, according to him, would have the effect of diverting the course of change undertaken by the regime and giving new impetus to autocracy. Ignoring his warnings the Soviet had called on the people to refuse to pay taxes and to rise up in order to force the calling of a Constituent Assembly. Although this summons, set out in a *Manifesto to the Russian People,* had little effect among the people, it certainly provoked a brutal reaction from the authorities, that is, the arrest of members of the Executive and the banning of newspapers.

The regime reacted all the more quickly and violently because this call from the Soviet was merely the visible form of the insurrection that was being prepared at the same time. Indeed, barely present in the Soviet, the Bolsheviks were involved in organizing for armed struggle in the cities, and for this purpose they bought weapons and supplied them to small groups prepared for battle. Saint Petersburg, dominated by the Soviet and the Mensheviks, was not very favorably disposed toward these plans, but in Moscow tracts calling for insurrection covered the walls and barricades were set up throughout the city.

In December 1905, when repression struck and all the leaders of the Soviet were arrested, the army, made up of peasants, helped to turn the page on the revolution. A few months later, Trotsky was sentenced to exile, but he escaped before reaching his destination. In Moscow the workers kept up a fierce battle for a while before being defeated in turn. With the revolution over, the time had come for political solutions and for analysis as well.

LENIN IN THE FACE OF THE REVOLUTION

From January to December 1905, the Bolsheviks, and Lenin above all, had anxiously observed events that contradicted their predictions and analyses. Although the party was well organized, it had played a minor, practically negligible role in the rising agitation. The momentary success of the soviets showed that the working class was capable on its own of inventing its own forms of organization. Workers' spontaneity leading to political awareness did not fit with Lenin's deeply held views.

At the beginning of the movement, Lenin had no intention of returning to Russia, unlike Trotsky, who crossed the border shortly after Bloody Sunday to participate in the movement, first in Kiev and then in the capital.

Following up on the October 17 Manifesto, on October 21, Nicholas II had proclaimed the political amnesty that had been called for since January and that he had been unable to bring himself to grant. Considered insufficient inside the country, the amnesty nevertheless had the consequence of making the return of exiled revolutionaries possible, thereby breathing new life into nascent political organizations. In her memoirs about Lenin, Nadezhda Krupskaya presents him as very impatient, after January 1905, to return to Russia. However, he showed himself perfectly capable of overcoming that impatience, returning only after the amnesty had been proclaimed. Having taken his time, he returned to Saint Petersburg on November 8, and his first activity in Russia was journalism.

Krupskaya presents an entirely personal version of this period: "In late summer 1905, Vladimir Ilyich showed his foresight by saying that we would soon start a newspaper and that its offices would be on Nevsky Prospect. I laughed at that as something that was hardly likely, but three months later, the sign for the offices of *Novaya zhizn'* [New Life] was indeed glittering on Nevsky Prospect."[6]

The reality was somewhat different.[7] In the fall of 1905, before the Manifesto had been issued, a group of intellectuals, on the left but independent of any party, had come together in the capital in the hope of publishing a newspaper that would express the social aspirations that had come to the fore in those troubled months. This initial group made up of the philosopher Minsky and the poets Zinayda Hippius and Constantine Balmont, was joined by Maxim Gorky and writers close to him, such as Leonid Andreev, and finally some Bolsheviks, including two members of the Central Committee, Bogdanov and P. P. Rumyantsev. Minsky managed to secure authorization to publish his newspaper even before the Manifesto had given the signal for the liberalization of the regime. Although he was in charge, editorial responsibilities were given to Gorky's second wife, the actress Marya Andreeva, who had given up the stage for political activities tied to her Bolshevik sympathies.[8] The strange alliance thus formed between writers more concerned with esthetic problems than partisan commitment and Bolsheviks can be explained primarily by the exalted, not to say euphoric, atmosphere that prevailed in Russia throughout 1905. The "political springtime" gradually gave way to revolutionary action, but for months the expectation of change and the hope of living through a great moment survived. Speaking of those months when nothing had been finally decided, Nikolai Valentinov, an incomparable witness, evokes the atmosphere of France in 1848 and the description given of it by Flaubert in *L'Éducation sentimentale*.

Everything changed with Lenin's return to Russia; without losing a moment, he rushed to the offices of *Novaya zhizn'*, seized control as though he had created the paper, and made it into his tool. From the outset, he published article after article imposing in an authoritarian way his views on "the reorganization of the [p]arty" and the "proletariat and the peasantry." Four days after he joined the paper that did not belong to him, his article of November 13, "The Party Organization and Party Literature," led to a veritable Bolshevik takeover of the publication that had originally been created as a bridge between left-wing writers and militants. Those who rejected this insidious takeover had only to leave; others who were less decisive kept silent, and *Novaya zhizn'*, as Lenin had told Krupskaya some weeks earlier in Geneva, became his newspaper.

He wrote: "Literature must become *part* of the common cause of the proletariat, a cog and a screw of one great Social Democratic mechanism. . . . Newspapers must become the organs of the various Party organizations, and their writers must by all means become members of these organizations. . . . [W]e are discussing Party literature and its subordination to Party control."[9]

This article, although written in the heat of action, that is, with Lenin belatedly obliged to take a position on a revolution that was coming to an end, is nonetheless troubling. His authoritarianism had already shown up in debates among the Social Democrats, but he had never so frankly presented his conception of intellectual life, involving its mobilization and complete subordination to the party. The seeds of the totalitarian practices of the bolshevik state are already present in this article.

Having printed, along with eight other papers, Trotsky's call for a boycott of taxes, *Novaya zizhn'* was banned in early December. And yet the press was not muzzled. Prohibited papers were immediately replaced with new publications or, more accurately, by new titles with the same editors. The imperial Manifesto had proclaimed freedom of the press; although it repressed the revolutionary movement, the government held to its promise to maintain freedom of expression. Among the flood of papers that were constantly being created, reflecting the positions of the Bolsheviks, the Mensheviks, the Socialist Revolutionaries, and the liberals, Lenin always had his own platform. Thus he successively edited *Volna* (The Wave) *Vperyod* (Forward), *Ekho* (Echo), and *Proletary* (The Proletarian), published in Vyborg.

To finance the press, all parties found sponsors who might have been expected to support more conservative positions, that is, large industrialists and sometimes aristocrats, showing how true it was that 1905 was a revolution greeted with enthusiasm by the greater part of society. For his publications, Lenin benefited from the enterprising spirit of Krasin, who had been his most zealous supporter since the Third Congress. He was also helped by Gorky, who was extremely successful in collecting funds. In 1906 Gorky and Marya Andreeva went to the United States to secure funds needed to finance their press, but also for arms purchases and for subsidies provided to full-time party workers. These collections of funds were not by far the only resources for the Bolsheviks who found, as we shall see, in "expropriations" an additional means of resolving their financial problems.

During this period in Russia, Lenin's life was stamped by his position as unchallenged leader of the Bolsheviks. The role of the Mensheviks in the soviets and the personal prestige of Trotsky together had helped focus attention on them and bring out the absence of the Bolsheviks during the months of agitation, as well as the fact that they had no leaders of stature, except for Lenin. It is therefore not surprising, as Valentinov pointed out, that the Bolshevik faction mobilized around its leader and took pains to make his life free of material constraints. After two brief stays in Moscow in December 1905 and March 1906, principally devoted to spending time with his family, Lenin decided to settle more permanently in a protected place. Discreet about their material conditions, whose difficulties she constantly described with complacency, Krupskaya frequently explained that Lenin had to lead a wandering life in Russia, relying on the goodwill of others for a place to spend the night and on occasion meeting his wife in modest restaurants in the capital. In fact, by February 1906, Lenin, who was attached to a stable and comfortable life, which he had managed to create even in his Siberian exile, decided to settle far from police surveillance, in Finland.

In Russia in 1906, in the political climate created by the revolution, the Manifesto, and the ambiguous attitude of the regime made up of concessions and repression, Finland was in a strange situation of distance from the empire. This is why Lenin settled in Kuokkala, sixty kilometers from the capital, where he had the impression of being practically outside Russia. The time of constant moves and separations from Krupskaya was over. The couple rented the ground floor of a large dacha, and the second floor was occupied by Bogdanov and a few other Bolsheviks. Within a few weeks, the "family life" to which Lenin was always attached was reconstituted. Krupskaya's mother joined them to take care of the housework with the help of a servant. Krupskaya had always admitted that she was a bad housekeeper and indeed was uninterested in domestic chores. Her mother took care of that as long as she lived. Thereafter Lenin's sister Marya completed the family circle. Activities were divided up in a perfectly organized manner.

Lenin spent most of his time in Kuokkala, from which he led the party and its papers, and where he wrote articles and saw Bolsheviks who had come for his instructions. Krupskaya went to the capital almost daily to maintain contact. In May 1906 Lenin and his family made a brief attempt to settle in Petersburg, but, anxious to avoid any surveillance, he soon cut the experiment short and returned to Kuokkala, where he stayed for almost a year. From time to time, he participated in gatherings of Bolsheviks, although he very infrequently spoke at public meetings.

Perhaps it was because of the extreme tension of those months, when no one could predict the future of the revolution, that Lenin again fell into a spectacular nervous depression. In May 1907, he had gone to the Party Congress in London, where the Bolsheviks were in the majority and his theses on "democratic centralism" were adopted as party rules. We return to this congress that was a triumph for him, but was also the scene of a very hard battle against the Mensheviks. When he returned to Kuokkala, Lenin so strongly impressed Krupskaya and his friends with his state of nervous and physical exhaustion that his wife decided to renew the treatment already used in the past, to take him away from all his activities and abolish his cares through isolation. He left for a two-month rest in an isolated spot in the Finnish forest, and no Bolsheviks knew where to reach him. In the fall, restored by these two months of solitude and physical activity, he returned first to Kuokkala and then, fearing the effects of increasing reaction, to refuge in a village near Helsinki. Here too he was worried by anticipated insecurity. The couple then decided to leave Russia and went through Åbo to Stockholm.

In the course of this winter expedition, crossing the ice to reach a small island where a fishing boat was waiting for him, the ice gave way under his weight, and he came close to drowning. Valentinov asked the relevant question: Was Lenin's good luck not what was going to cause the misfortune of Russia?[10] What would have happened if, in December 1907, the man of the October Revolution had disappeared in the frigid waters of the gulf where he had imprudently ventured? The question is unanswerable.

The journey from Stockholm to Geneva was easy, and the life of exile resumed; it would last another ten years. For Lenin this decade was made up of dark years in which his revolutionary will would find few outlets. And his retrospective view of the two years during which the empire had come close to collapse gave him little comfort. Could he really be satisfied with the small role that his party had played in the tumultuous events? Could he be satisfied with the way he himself had led the party in the course of those two years of revolutionary hope?

A REVOLUTION WITHOUT THE BOLSHEVIKS

On his return to Russia, Lenin had been caught short by events and by the success of the Soviet, as he had earlier been caught short in January 1905. He had foreseen none of this. He had been able to see the spontaneous revolutionary activity of the working class develop for months without the help of directives from any party. Then he had witnessed the working class's efforts to create representative organizations for itself, first in Ivanovo-Voznesentsk and especially in Petersburg. The movement that had become more politicized with each passing day was a cruel disavowal of his own postulates and confirmed a twofold failure in his thinking, intellectual (he had not foreseen these developments), but also political, because the Mensheviks, naturally confident in the working class, had been able, if only belatedly, to participate in the revolution, thereby demonstrating the mistakes in analysis made by their sworn enemy.

It was therefore advisable to think about the way of restoring the Bolsheviks to their position, and Lenin did this in two areas. First he tried to define an immediate strategy for revolutionary struggle. Second he attempted to resolve the problem of elections to the Duma and the attitude to be adopted toward it.

What strategy should be adopted for the revolution? Lenin was confronted with two questions: How was the Menshevik-dominated Soviet to be judged? What direction should be urged on a working class that did not give up its arms? After observing the Soviet, a spontaneous manifestation, with great suspicion, Lenin recognized his mistake. The Soviet existed, it was imitated in other Russian cities, and an attempt should be made to bring it into the Bolshevik orbit, although it was already quite late for that. Never hesitant to abandon from one moment to the next a tactical position that he had defended up to that point, Lenin proclaimed, in the name of a pragmatic vision of reality (evidenced in many articles) that the Soviet was the privileged instrument of the proletariat, that it should be developed, and that it should later become the principal institution of the provisional government that would be formed as soon as the revolution had been won.

In order for the revolution to win out, it remained to decide on and to lead a decisive action, a general insurrection. In late 1905, the situation was becoming increasingly tense. Workers were multiplying strikes and demonstrations; mutinies were breaking out here and there, indicating that the army, shaken by the fiasco of the Russo-Japanese War, had doubts about the indecisive regime; finally postal and rail communications were practically paralyzed. The conditions for insurrectional action had indeed come together.

For its part, the regime, considering that the October Manifesto had granted the maximum possible concessions, expected society to respond by a return to calm. When that did not happen, it thought repression was necessary.

Between continuing agitation and the threat of brutal repression intended to bring it to an end, Lenin saw only one possible strategy: armed insurrection, able to transform agitation into revolution and to change Russia for good. Even before leaving Geneva for Petersburg, to everyone who asked him how to act, he feverishly repeated that only insurrection was a response to the situation that had been created in Russia since January 1905. And it was up to the Bolsheviks, organized in small groups of "professional" revolutionaries, to lead that insurrection.

Moreover, competition on the scene with the Mensheviks could only favor the Bolsheviks if an insurrection did break out. The Soviets had been an opportunity for the Mensheviks, who had very quickly adapted to them and from the outset found their place in the popular movement that was stirring Russia. In addition, they had powerful orators in their ranks, able to address the workers and their representative organizations while not claiming, as Lenin did, to exercise authority over them.

FROM THE STRATEGY OF VIOLENCE TO ELECTIONS

Confronting these leaders, talented orators such as Trotsky and, to a lesser degree, Khrustalev-Nosar, the Bolsheviks had the greatest difficulty in swaying the crowds. As for Lenin, during his entire time in Russia, he scarcely ever stood up in public meetings. Because insurrection was the terrain in which Bolsheviks felt the most comfortable, he worked for it by issuing many precise directives: armed insurrection, formation of an Army of the Revolution, a provisional government, and so on. To prepare for the uprising, the Bolsheviks acquired arms, formed assault groups, printed tracts calling for an uprising and covered the walls of Petersburg and Moscow with them, and participated everywhere in the building of barricades.

The Mensheviks, for their part, were rather persuaded by the appeals for calm from Plekhanov, who was in fact addressing the Bolsheviks more than his own supporters, but Lenin's supporters paid no attention. Attentive to everything coming from the party, the workers were more inclined to listen to Bolshevik calls for violence and immediate insurrection. The direct consequence was the Moscow workers' uprising of December 1905 and its defeat, which cost the working class a good deal of blood that Lenin was later criticized for having shed in vain.[11] But Lenin did not give up his calls for insurrection. For example, after the Duma was dissolved in July 1906, arguing from the failure of the parliamentary experiment, he advocated a return to violent action. Moreover, he suggested that the deputies of the second Duma take advantage of their immunity to incite the people to revolt. The regime could not fail to react to this kind of insurrectional speech, and even more to the exhortations by some deputies to the working class and the army inciting them to join the struggle. In July 1907, the government denounced a plot against the state; many deputies were accused of complicity and were arrested, and the Duma was dissolved, depriving them of the fragile protection of their immunity. Failed attempts at insurrection and repression put an end to the workers' movement, which gradually sank into discouragement and demobilization. In 1905, 2,750,000 strikers had participated in revolutionary action; in 1906, there were a million fewer; their number fell to 750,000 in 1907 and continued to decline until it sank to 50,000 in 1910. The militants of the movement grew equally scarce, and revolutionary organizations collapsed.

A propagandist for insurrection, Lenin had unquestionably lost the battle. It remained to find out what benefit could be derived from the reforms and particularly from elections. The division of the Socialists on this question was obvious. Unlike the Kadets, who hoped that the Duma would pave the way for a constitutional monarchy, Socialists of all stripes believed nothing of the kind. But all of them, except the Bolsheviks, thought that, even so, they should try to use the Duma for their own purposes. Divided on electoral strategy, the SRs and the Mensheviks in any event decided to participate in the elections and to fight to elect deputies who, with the protection of their immunity, would be able to defend their arguments publicly without risk.

Lenin alone opted for a position radically hostile to the elections.[12] The Duma, he said, was a complete trick; this fools' bargain deserved a simple response, a boycott of the elections. Despite this slogan, and despite Bolshevik attempts to block the voting by violence, the election took place in April 1906. The Kadets won 179 of the 486 seats. Despite the boycott decided by the SRs, their preferred party, the peasants had ninety-four deputies, who formed a group with the title *trudoviki* (Labor). The Mensheviks, shaken by Lenin's attacks on what he called "parliamentary cretinism," but nevertheless tempted by electoral participation, had chosen a semiboycott that was badly understood by the voters. As a consequence of this excessively ambiguous attitude, only eighteen deputies were elected under their aegis.

The first Duma had a short life, and was replaced in 1907 by a second that was elected in the same way. This time the socialists had changed their strategy. Recognizing the popularity of the Duma in the society at large, indicated by a high level of participation in the first vote, they had replaced a boycott with a very active electoral campaign. But there was no lack of difficulties. Although the government had refrained from interfering in the campaign in 1906, it gave its support, in the form of material assistance, in 1907 to parties that were close to it, generally grouped together under the name of Octobrists (supporters of the policies set out in the Manifesto of October 1905). Other parties had to enter the battle with few resources and with a semilegal status, which did not prevent their success. The assembly that came out of the elections was a triumph for the Socialists, with 133 deputies claiming the label, including 66 Social Democrats (mostly Mensheviks) and 37 SRs; to this should be added 98 Labor deputies. On the other side, the right had only 52 deputies (19 Octobrists and 33 representatives of extreme right-wing parties), and the Kadets fell from 169 in the first assembly to 98 in the second. The second Duma thus leaned clearly to the left, and the Mensheviks found themselves, as they had in the soviets in 1905, in a much better position than the Bolsheviks.

The success was short lived, because the government, convinced that it was confronted with an ungovernable assembly, persuaded the czar to dissolve it. In addition, he decided to change the election law so that the results would be more in accordance with his wishes. The third Duma, elected in the fall of 1907, witnessed a collapse of the left, with only thirty-two deputies, half of whom were Social Democrats. The Socialist Revolutionaries had decided to boycott the vote and were therefore absent from the third Duma. This time, however, Lenin had been more in favor of participation.[13] Taking note of the decline of the workers' movement and the widespread feeling of discouragement, he had concluded that the elections at least represented a final opportunity to articulate revolutionary arguments in public. No doubt he understood that the election law made it impossible for the candidates of the left to win, but he thought it was better to assert the presence of the left during the campaign than to turn the working class over to progovernment parties alone. In his view participation in the elections was a last chance to avoid a break with the working class. He was thus alone with the Mensheviks in defending the position that participation was necessary, an argument he made at the Kotka Party Conference in July 1907, held to fix the Social Democrats' attitude toward the elections.[14]

Lenin's argument in favor of participation in the elections had been far from winning unanimous support in the party. After the elections the Bolsheviks who had argued against him, chiefly his two lieutenants, Krasin and Bogdanov, fierce supporters of a boycott, demanded that the Social Democratic deputies immediately leave the Duma. The violent conflict between Lenin and the "left-wing Bolsheviks" led by Bogdanov (who had been the leader of the few Bolshevik deputies in the second Duma) foreshadowed the coming break, which would go beyond tactical considerations to a profound ideological disagreement. The *otzovisti*, as he called the advocates of the recall of the deputies, won the support of the Bolshevik organization of Saint Petersburg and condemned any form of legal activity, which they considered impossible in a period of reaction. Despite his desire not to cut the party off from the masses by a radical refusal to exist in the open, Lenin could not resist the movement, and finally accepted its positions. He nonetheless did not recapture the support of the extremists who were hostile to him. They formed a separate faction and even established their own newspaper, adopting an ephemeral title, *Vperyod.* In this, they were following the example Lenin himself had given a few years earlier when he set up a newspaper in opposition to *Iskra* and the Mensheviks. In the dark year of 1907, he was the victim of breaks and rejections that he was so used to imposing on others. "Unity," the basis of the party that he had advocated with such forcefulness, was undermined.

ATTEMPTS AT RECONCILIATION WITH THE MENSHEVIKS

The divisions among Bolsheviks ought not to conceal the essential point that in the period from 1905 to 1907 a deep desire for unity inspired all the Social Democrats. The desire was strengthened by the ebbing of the revolutionary movement and the need to define a strategy, taking into account both the failure of the revolution and the opening of parliamentary prospects in Russia. The split was still recent, and no one thought of perpetuating it. Lenin accepted the idea of a reconciliation with the Mensheviks in part because his supporters were strongly in favor of the step and they put pressure on him to engage in a dialogue. But Lenin was also, as always, convinced that his analysis of events was correct, and he therefore expected the Mensheviks to join and support him. He no doubt wished for reconciliation, but it would have to take place around Bolshevik positions.

In December 1905 an all-Russian Bolshevik Conference was held in Tampere, Finland, at which the need for unity was discussed, a position that the Mensheviks also supported. We might note that Lenin met there for the first time a young Georgian revolutionary sent to the conference by the Caucasus organization, who had at first joined the Mensheviks who were powerful in the region. This was Josef Vissarionovich Dzhugashvily, better known at the time as Koba, and after 1910 as Stalin. There would be little to say about this meeting between the two men were it not for Koba's memoirs noting the impression, or rather the lack of any impression, made on him by this first meeting with the leader of the Bolsheviks:

> I had hoped to see the mountain eagle of our Party, the great man, great physically as well as politically. . . . How great was my disappointment to see a most ordinary-looking man, below average height, in no way, literally in no way, distinguishable from ordinary mortals. . . . How great was my disappointment to see that Lenin had arrived at the conference before the other delegates were there and had settled himself somewhere in a corner and was unassumingly carrying on a conversation, a most ordinary conversation.[15]

In April 1906, Bolsheviks and Mensheviks met secretly in Stockholm. The Mensheviks were in the majority, with 72 delegates representing 34,000 militants, whereas the Bolsheviks had only 46 representing 14,000 militants. The status of the meeting was rather difficult to determine. Dubbed the *Reunification Congress,* the Stockholm meeting was for the Bolsheviks the Fourth Congress of Social Democrats, whereas the Mensheviks, who did not recognize the validity of the Bolshevik Third Congress in London in 1905, considered the Stockholm meeting as the only legitimate Third Congress. Because of this disagreement, the meeting for unity was not incorporated at the time into the sequence of Social Democratic congresses. It was only later that it found a place in the chronology of Communist congresses developed by the Bolsheviks.

In 1906, however, the success of the Stockholm meeting was genuine. With unity restored the party also welcomed into its ranks the Bund and the Social Democratic Parties of Poland and Latvia. The Central Committee elected at the conclusion of the meeting reflected the restored unity and the uncomfortable position of Lenin, who was generally considered responsible for the split. The three Bolsheviks elected to the governing body were Krasin, Rykov, and V. S. Desnitsky, whereas Lenin was not, and the Mensheviks had seven seats.

Lenin in the minority was a situation that was difficult for him to accept, and which, as usual, he set to work to change. By late 1906, on the occasion of the debate over the attitude to adopt for elections to the second Duma, while strongly declaring his attachment to unity, he fought against the Mensheviks' position by proposing an electoral alliance with the liberals in order to block the path to a "hard" right that the electoral law was intended to favor.[16] The opposition between Lenin and the Mensheviks was such that a meeting had to be organized in January 1907 to attempt to reconcile their viewpoints. Persuasive, and strengthened by the presence of forty-two Bolsheviks (ten more delegates than the Mensheviks), Lenin secured a favorable vote, but agreed in exchange, as a gesture to unity, to explore possible alliances.[17] This did not prevent him from asserting in a pamphlet that the Mensheviks had been "sold to the bourgeoisie."[18] They responded by appealing to a party tribunal, before which Lenin argued that he had indeed insulted the Mensheviks, but that political combat, even against associates, legitimated the use of any means. Lenin's brutality was an expression of his certainty that after the difficulties encountered in Stockholm, the balance among the Social Democrats was again tilting in his favor. This was to be confirmed by the London Congress.

The Fifth Party Congress convened in the British capital in April 1907 and at first seemed to reflect the reconciliation negotiated at Tamberle and Stockholm, which had been called for primarily by the rank and file. All the principal Social Democratic leaders were in London: Plekhanov, Axelrod, Martov, Potresov, Rosa Luxemburg, Trotsky, Bogdanov, Krasin, Gorky, and Irakli Tsereteli, but also newcomers who were beginning to become known in Russia and would gradually come to play important roles, such as Zinoviev, Kamenev, Tomsky, Kliment Voroshilov, Hanetsky, and Stalin. The 165 delegates of the Russian Party had been joined by 44 delegates from the Bund, 26 from Latvia, and 45 from Poland. The Russians were divided into 90 Bolsheviks and 85 Mensheviks. Despite this apparent balance and speeches with a unitary flavor, the congress reflected the fierce struggles that had been taking place in Russia since the Stockholm Congress. In the minority at Stockholm, the Bolsheviks on the scene, especially in the two principal Russian cities, controlled or at least held important positions in local organizations. In Saint Petersburg, the Party Committee was split between them and the Mensheviks, but a troika was in overall charge. Its strongest figure was Grigorii Evseevich Radomilsky, already known in the party as Zinoviev. As Trotsky later noted, he was a "born agitator, endowed with remarkable political flair and always likely to get carried away."[19] Lenin had already shown his confidence in him by sending him to organize the failed insurrection in Kronstadt in 1906. The troika gradually moved the Petersburg Committee to the side of the Bolsheviks. Kamenev was especially active in Moscow, whose Central Committee was dominated by historical Mensheviks such as Fedor Dan, Martov, and Noi Zhordania. But Lenin thought that it was the Petersburg Committee that could ensure the victory of his supporters. Zinoviev in the capital and Kamenev in Moscow had prepared the congress and had spared no effort to ensure the preeminence of Lenin's supporters.

The debates in London brought him support from the Polish and Latvian delegates, whereas the Mensheviks could count only on the Bund, exasperated by Lenin's authoritarian centralism. The presence in London of the major Social Democratic figures had little influence on the course of events. The Bolsheviks, a little more numerous, strengthened by the larger number of allies, had the wind in their sails. The debates, which took place in a church, were often brutal and expressed a hardening on the part of Lenin's supporters. Confronting them, the Mensheviks were on the defensive. Axelrod argued for bringing together all the workers' parties and groups in Russia. Tsereteli, one of the most brilliant orators in the Duma,[20] called on the Social Democrats to adopt a realistic attitude, to recognize the necessity of the stage of bourgeois democracy in order to foster political progress in Russia. Trotsky was almost alone in defending a conciliatory position, attempting to persuade his colleagues that the most important thing for the future of their movement was to avoid any new split.

Lenin showed himself to be inexorable, calling some hypocrites and others reformists. He was convinced that success was in his hands, first of all with the election of a Central Committee dominated by his supporters, including Zinoviev, along with Lenin himself, and with Krasin and Bogdanov as candidate members. He could also boast of another victory: the congress had agreed to establish in the party rules his cherished principles of democratic centralism and submission of the minority to the majority. Finally he had secured the adoption of rules for periodic meetings—an annual congress and quarterly conferences. The Social Democratic Party had thus acceded to Lenin's wishes, and its organization had become more constraining. Lenin's principal concern was probably to arrange for the coexistence of rival groups within a single party in a way that would not weaken it. In the majority in 1907, he was not unaware of the fact that that position was precarious. Indeed, shortly after the London Congress, his close supporters Bogdanov and Krasin moved away from him. What was important to him was to maintain the means of fighting against the Mensheviks, of weakening them in a period during which he was obliged to coexist with them. In the course of this stage, he particularly needed "democratic centralism" with the emphasis on "democratic," in that it authorized an appeal to the rank and file for the election of the leadership, as well as "freedom of discussion." It was not an accident that into the Central Committee elected at the conclusion of the Congress, Lenin had introduced young professional revolutionaries, such as Zinoviev, who were to return to Russia to work on the scene to "Bolshevize" the organizations.

This approach was easy to understand in light of developments in Russia. The failure of the revolution and of attempts at insurrection and the development of a parliamentary process prompted the Mensheviks to condemn clandestine action in favor of integration into the system that was taking shape. The Mensheviks thought that the liberal bourgeoisie could be an effective ally in developing the Russian workers' movement along the lines followed by Western Social Democracy. Axelrod, and he was not alone, always held to this position, which Lenin attacked all the more violently because he was aware of the discouragement of the working class and the breakup of the entire movement.

In 1907 the Social Democrats as a whole thought that the urgent task was to learn from the failure of 1905 in order to determine the path that they should take to survive.

THE LESSONS OF A FAILED REVOLUTION

Divided from the outset by their differing views of the course of Russian history, Mensheviks and Bolsheviks drew from 1905 lessons that supported their respective convictions and hence their division. The Mensheviks saw the course of events as a confirmation of the correctness of their attachment to rigorously orthodox Marxism. Socialist revolution–Marx, whom they claimed to follow, had said it explicitly–cannot occur in the absence of a strong proletariat, which in turn could not develop outside a capitalist system and a bourgeois revolution. The Mensheviks thought that 1905 had been an unfortunate attempt to accelerate the process. Its failure had confirmed the impossibility of skipping historical stages, and that the insurrectional activities encouraged by Lenin would not lead, as events had shown, to the achievement of revolutionary aims. "It was a mistake to take up arms," Plekhanov hammered out. Nor was it correct, the Mensheviks asserted, invoking Marx, Engels, and the experience of the 1848 revolution, to count on an alliance between the working class and the peasantry, a class that was reactionary by nature. This was the basis after 1906 for their alliance with the liberal parties, inside and outside the Duma, and their wish to set up in Russia a large association of workers, a nonpartisan alliance, with a view to instituting and extending the system of Soviets to the entire country.[21]

For Lenin this analysis was unacceptable as a whole and in each one of its elements. He held that 1905 had shown that the proletariat existed as a national force and that it was ready to bring down the autocracy. Although in the aftermath of 1905 he agreed with the Mensheviks that the stage of bourgeois political democracy was inevitable, he supplemented this proposition with the observation that the Russian bourgeoisie would not go beyond that stage, because it was "inconsistent, egotistical, and cowardly," frightened by the proletariat to such an extent that it was always ready to change sides. Only the proletariat was consistent, and aware of the need to go beyond the bourgeois revolution in order to win. How was this to be accomplished?

Lenin answered in the summer of 1905 in *Two Tactics of Social Democracy in the Democratic Revolution.*[22] The first condition articulated was alliance with the peasantry.[23] By 1905 he was convinced of the importance of the Russian peasant question and of the revolutionary potential of peasant demands, to which the political system was not providing sufficient responses. It was up to the party, he believed, to channel this potential and use it for its own benefit. "The peasant proprietor in Russia is on the eve of a democratic movement of the whole people with which he must sympathize."[24] According to Lenin the result of this common struggle will have to be "a democratic revolutionary dictatorship of workers and peasants."[25]

The second element of this definition of revolutionary success was one about which Lenin was in agreement with the Mensheviks: the democratic revolution "would inflame the countries" of the West (a formulation also used by Trotsky), and the consequence would be an acceleration of the Russian revolutionary process and an end to its isolation.

Trotsky also contributed to the debate with various writings drawing the lessons from 1905. The assessment he made of events was based on two experiences. First during the 1905 revolution he had been a major actor in the Petersburg Soviet, and even its president at the end. The Soviet was not a matter of abstract reflection for him, because it had for a time been the center of his revolutionary activity. In addition he had spent the following year in prison, during which time he had had ample opportunity to think about the events he had just lived through. He had then formulated his ideas in works that would in the end be considered most fully to represent his thinking.

Having presided over the Soviet, Trotsky was in a position to define its role in the revolutionary process:

> The Soviet organized the toiling masses, led strikes and political demonstrations, armed the workers, and protected the population against pogroms. Similar tasks were carried out by other revolutionary organizations, before, during, and after the Soviet. But they did not have the same influence. The secret of that influence lies in the fact that the Soviet was not organically isolated from the proletariat in the course of its struggle for power.[26]

In Trotsky's analysis this evaluation of the role of the Soviet, which aroused a good deal of suspicion in Lenin, posed the problem of the Social Democratic Party. Should the Soviet take its place? Trotsky's answer was unambiguous. In a time of revolution, he thought, the revolutionary front should be as broad as possible, and the Soviet had been able to accomplish this by integrating the whole working class into the movement. This was something that the party, accustomed to the requirements of its underground existence and therefore turned in on itself, was unable to do. However, Trotsky did not deny that the party remained the indispensable source of the revolutionary ideology that inspired the Soviet. The Soviet was not the "pure product" of Social Democracy, but it was the bearer of the party's ideas of proletarian socialism.

Trotsky thus set up a division of labor between party and Soviet. In the prerevolutionary phase, the party's role was to educate and influence the workers. But when the revolution got under way, it was the workers themselves who created the institutions for their struggle, the Soviets. Although before the revolution, the party was the vanguard of the working class, thereafter it became one of the components of the workers' movement and its own institution, the Soviet. This view was to enter into the theory of permanent revolution that Trotsky developed in thinking about the lessons of 1905. In the end what he took and kept from the events in which he had participated was the deep impression produced on him by the entry of the masses into the revolutionary movement. From this he maintained the certainty that the Russian proletariat could act only "massively" as a political force, and that no party should dominate it when that happened.

This shows what separated him from Lenin, whose convictions about the role of the party and its place in the workers' movement even in revolutionary circumstances had in no way been affected by the events of 1905.

The disagreement between the two is clear, and even though Trotsky made numerous efforts to preserve the unity of Social Democracy, Lenin could not tolerate his approach, both because of the virulence of his criticisms of Bolshevism and the authoritarianism of its leader and because, in order to satisfy his adversary, Lenin would in fact have had to renounce the very essence of his thinking. Until 1917 nothing would reconcile the two men.

Л Л Л

The first Russian revolution was in many respects an unexpected time for Lenin. To be sure, he had returned to Russia as soon as the revolution had spread through the country. But he had not done so at the outset. As a man of study, when he heard of the convulsions of his country, he had consulted all the writings dealing with insurrection; for example, the analyses of Marx and Engels of the 1848 revolution. Then he had attempted to persuade his Russian correspondents that their task was to organize an armed uprising.[27] But he was also a party man, and it was important for him to take control out of the hands of the Mensheviks. While strikes and demonstrations were growing, he devoted himself to organizing the London Congress, which convened at the very time that Ivanovo-Voznesentsk was becoming a center of the workers' movement that would give birth to the first Soviet in Russia.

During the first months of the revolution, Lenin led the activities of the Bolsheviks from abroad; he did not return to Russia until November. The October strikes, which he had not foreseen and which conformed neither to his analyses nor to the program presented at the Third Congress, led to the formation of the Petersburg Soviet. He considered the institution with uneasiness, but was obliged to take it into account. His stay in Russia, from late 1905 to 1907, was not marked by intense revolutionary activity. He saw himself as head of the party, but also as a thinker and a journalist. He wrote and advocated insurrection, but was hardly involved in events. He spent the bulk of his time at a distance from the agitation, in Finland, or in a semiclandestine existence. Further, he went to Social Democratic Congresses in Stockholm and London. There were not many workers' meetings at which he spoke. It is true that he was not unusual in this respect, and that Trotsky was practically the only well-known Social Democrat to play a visible role in events. Although his lieutenants, Bogdanov, Zinoviev, and Kamenev, were active on the ground, in the Soviet or the Bolshevik organizations of the capital, Lenin seems to have thought that his status as head of the Bolshevik faction made it necessary to consider his safety as a priority.

This revolutionary period was also revealing about the extraordinary weakness of his nervous system. On two occasions, in 1905 and after the 1907

London Congress, he sank into such impressive states of depression that he had to be removed from all political activity, either by the organization of long vacations or by isolation from all contact with his colleagues in some hidden spot deep in the Finnish forest. No one has determined the causes of these collapses. There was extreme nervous tension, of course, but was it caused by the revolution, by the desperate attempt to bring about an insurrection and his distress at its failure? Or else, do the persistent conflict with the Mensheviks and the struggle to impose his authority on the party explain the fact that Lenin, at moments, turned out to be unable to carry on any political efforts? In reference to one of these crises, his sister called his illness the "sacred fire."

In 1907, with the revolution over and his stay in Russia at an end, there was nothing for Lenin to do but to go abroad and resume his work. A new exile of ten years awaited him. From the disappointments of 1905, he was to draw many writings, in search of a new point of departure for a revolutionary movement that was to appear quiescent for several years. However, perhaps the most important of Lenin's observations—as yet unformulated, but beginning to take shape—was that 1905 had not taken place in just any circumstances. What had ignited the spark and provoked the popular revolt was the lost war in the Far East. From that intuition, years later he would draw fruitful conclusions and a plan of action which on that occasion, he thought, might not fail.

Chapter Six

TIME IN THE WILDERNESS (1905–1914)

THE END OF THE REVOLUTIONARY ADVENTURE BROUGHT
Lenin and Krupskaya back to Geneva. This new exile made Lenin gloomy.
"Accursed city! Coming back here, I feel as though I'm crawling into my grave."

His feelings in early 1908 are easy to understand. Not only had the revolution
been a failure but also, even worse, the Russian workers' movement was in a
state of complete collapse. Strikes that had mobilized workers were declining in
number, and the militants who had been so dedicated to the party for two years
were drifting away. By 1910 they would be reduced to less than ten thousand,
one-tenth of their number in 1905. Social Democratic organizations were disappearing for lack of participants, or because the remaining members were wearing themselves out in futile quarrels and splitting into rival sectarian groups.
Indeed, Russian society as a whole was weary with the unrest that seemed to
have produced few positive results. The regime was aware of this weariness, and
it also recognized that, despite its apprehensions and the military reverses it had
suffered, it had been able to count on the support of the army to resume control
over the country. Most important, like Lenin on his side, it had seen how the
revolution had come up against two obstacles: geographically, it had never succeeded in going beyond the cities; and politically, leaving aside Lenin's planned
insurrection that had not been carried out, its goals had been too vague and
were now incomprehensible to the society at large.

REFORMS AGAINST THE REVOLUTION

As a result, the regime was able to recover control over the situation by combining repression and concessions. Arrests swept up all identified leaders, beginning with the radical deputies in the Duma. In December 1905 the regime had
arrested the members of the executive of the Soviet after they called for a boycott of taxes; similarly, in June 1907 the announcement of the discovery of a plot

against state security allowed it to arrest most Social Democratic deputies, dissolve the Duma, and dismantle a number of organizations.[1] The Social Democrats who had escaped arrest immediately left Russia.

It is fair to note here that the third Duma, often casually referred to as a "rump parliament," in reality represented progress in Russian political life. Improperly elected, subject to pressure from the regime, it was nevertheless a manifestation of an irresistible institutional shift. The Duma was no longer the momentary expression of the imperial will. It lasted for its full term of five years and had its own life, governed by legal documents. In 1907 Lenin had clearly sensed the direction of events, and this had been the reason for his reversal of position on the assembly. An inflexible supporter of a boycott of the elections to the first two Dumas, he completely reversed positions on the third. For him the first two had been "police traps"; in 1907 he placed his hopes in the Social Democratic representatives to the new Duma and fought against the *otzovisti*, led by his old friend Bogdanov.

The government for its part intended to control the Duma through a restrictive electoral system, but this was only one of the elements of a policy designed to recover control over society. Its essential points were contained in the programs of Stolypin, who had been leading the government since the summer of 1906.

Nicholas II had selected Piotr Stolypin because he was a man of the soil, and he made agrarian reform the centerpiece of his policy. He had sensed, and his intuition corresponded to Lenin's analysis, that the 1905 revolution had suffered from the distance between working class and peasantry.[2] Peasant agitation had been strong early in the century, but it was independent of the workers' movement which had neither gained support from the peasants nor been able to spread to the countryside. As we have seen, Lenin had clearly recognized and commented on this weakness of the working class; he sought remedies for it in the "democratic revolution of workers and peasants" that he advocated at the conclusion of the analysis of 1905 that constituted the bulk of his work on his return to Switzerland.

Stolypin's plan was to outstrip the revolution by attaching the peasantry to the regime; he did this beginning in 1906 through a series of laws freeing the peasants from the commune, distributing communal lands, and encouraging peasants to settle in Siberia, where future prospects for adventurous colonizers were considerable. To agrarian reform was added an enormous effort to educate rural society, through schooling, technological training, and sanitary improvement. Everything was put in place so that the rural world would change rapidly and so that the growth of private property among an educated peasantry would convince it to turn its back on calls for revolution.

Political concessions and plans for social reform also won over the liberal intelligentsia who were discouraged by the failure of 1905 and by the turbulent disputes of the socialists. This intelligentsia was tempted to play the hand it was dealt in order to carry the regime as far as possible down the path of progress.

Lenin found little comfort in his enforced exile. From a distance, he was able to observe the ruins of the workers' movement, Russian economic progress, and most of all a political life that seemed to be in the process of settling down. The repression, very harsh in 1906 and 1907, was easing. Lenin was acutely aware of the race underway between the regime and the revolution, and the latter did not seem to have the stronger cards during those years.

YEARS OF WANDERING

Exiled and discouraged, in 1908 Lenin began to live the life of a wanderer. Feeling oppressed by Geneva, in late 1908 he left for Paris, where he was to spend nearly four years. This was followed by a stay in Cracow, closer to the Russia in which he glimpsed new grounds for hope. At the beginning of the war, he returned to Switzerland, but not to Geneva, which he had come to hate; he stayed first in Berne and then in Zurich.

This wandering exile later became the basis for the Soviet legend of Lenin confronting the worst material difficulties. Valentinov has researched the origins of this legend of poverty, set out in the memoirs of Anna Ulyanova-Elizarova, but he absolves her of responsibility because, according to him, when she began to write her memoirs, the party had already created the beautiful story of the revolutionary living in poverty. The first writer responsible for the "invention" was, it seems, an obscure Bolshevik who owes his place in the history of the period to this contribution. This man, named Vladimirov, visited Lenin in Paris and recounted that he was living there in "a small room with an alcove and a minuscule kitchen." In fact, and Lenin himself confirmed this, his two Paris residences, on rue Bonnier and then on rue Marie-Rose, were neither minuscule, nor sordid, nor lacking in comfort. They were adequate for the reconstitution of the family group. On rue Bonnier the couple was joined by the inevitable and indispensable mother of Nadezhda Krupskaya, and sometimes by Lenin's mother or one of his sisters, each of whom obviously had a room; and Krupskaya notes that there was, in addition to their own bedroom, a salon. The following year the Lenins moved to rue Marie-Rose, where their new apartment was smaller by one room, but Lenin's mother and sister had by then returned to Russia, and only Elizaveta Vasilievna was living with them. This apartment had something that was luxurious for the time, central heating, of which Lenin made a good deal.[3] He often referred to it in letters to his mother.

This family atmosphere, fully managed by Krupskaya's mother with the help of a servant, was necessary for him to work, and he recovered a balance that had been shaken in the course of the preceding years. Moreover, Krupskaya was able to serve as an intermediary, take care of his contacts with the outside world and protect him from the importunate, because he was not fond of visitors and frequently complained of the interminable and sterile chattering of émigrés. The Bibliothèque Nationale, to which he frequently went by bicycle (he praised this means of travel for its health benefits, something he could discuss endlessly), provided him with inexhaustible resources for his writing, primarily for his political and philosophical polemics with his former friend and faithful collaborator, Bogdanov.

But before coming to these works, another subject deserves attention, because it had serious consequences on Lenin's relations with the international socialist movement and with the Mensheviks. This is what in contemporary terms would have to be called the "affairs," that is, affairs of money.

THE "EXPROPRIATIONS" – A CONTINUING SCANDAL

Although Lenin had received financial aid from various sources for his own living expenses and his publications, a continuing problem preoccupied the party: finding the money to finance its activities. Krasin, who had given himself the title of "finance minister of the party," was the real director of the "expropriations," which at a certain point were an almost inexhaustible source of enrichment for the party. Before him, Gorky had already undertaken to fill the party coffers with private funds that he collected in America, but this paled in comparison to the "expropriations" that were to create a scandal in the workers' movement.

Long before the Bolsheviks used this method to build up a war chest, expropriation had been advocated by Kropotkin, who had fled to Geneva to escape the Russian police thirty years before Lenin. In his *Memoirs of a Revolutionist,* published by Élisée Reclus in 1855, the great anarchist linked revolution and expropriation, which he called indispensable for revolutionary success.[4] But, he went on, "It [expropriation] must be carried out on a grand scale. On a small scale, it would be seen as nothing but common pillage."[5] It was precisely "common pillage" that characterized the Bolshevik practice of expropriation and provoked the indignation of the international socialist movement.

It had begun before 1905, but became spectacular in the succeeding period, which saw a few particularly striking episodes. The most celebrated was the expropriation of Tblisi in 1907, Stalin's masterstroke.[6]

These armed attacks (which the use of the term popularized by Kropotkin was intended to cover with respectability) had proliferated throughout the empire in 1906. But the Social Democratic Congress of Stockholm had condemned expropriation of either public or private property. Indeed, the Social Democrats had learned that armed groups were indulging in unbridled criminality in the name of the party, establishing an association between combat organizations and uncontrollable bandits. From that time on, the reputation of Russian Social Democracy suffered from the confusion between what Lenin considered necessary to secure financial resources and pure and simple criminality. The method was no doubt effective, because with those funds the Bolsheviks were able to buy weapons and to finance the publication of tracts, that is, to assert and strengthen their power. In 1907 the hope of an insurrection, which Lenin used to justify the violence, no longer existed. Hence the decisions taken at Stockholm merely made the illegality of the method more obvious. However, terrorism and expropriation continued.

At the heart of the system was the man who was still a faithful lieutenant to Lenin, Leonid Borisovich Krasin. In the postrevolutionary period, when any political effort seemed futile, he put his exceptional talents at the service of terrorist action. He played this role as an engineer and economist whose skills were recognized by the entire party. After the failure of 1905, he was the real leader of the armed militants, the *boyeviki*, who continued the struggle when the revolution was over by engaging in systematic terrorist action against the forces of order, institutions, and, especially, "expropriatable" property.[7] To continue the battle along these lines, weapons, explosives, and money were needed. All this was obtained through Krasin, who negotiated arms purchases everywhere (his favorite suppliers were soldiers returning from the Far East and foreign traffickers), organized the manufacture of explosives, and provided courses of instruction for terrorists, who made ample use of them. It was also Krasin who organized the attack against the house in which Stolypin and his family were staying on Aptekarsky Island.

Krasin's most loyal and most famous lieutenant, Semyon Ter-Petrossian, better known as Kamo, was born three years after Stalin in the same village near Tblisi, Gori. He was a companion of Stalin's, a specialist in assassination and arms trafficking (the party had him buy weapons abroad in 1906), and, according to Krupskaya, "passionately attached to Ilich, Krasin, and Bogdanov." Working with Krasin, with Stalin in the background, Kamo was the one who planned the expropriation of Tblisi in 1907, that is, robbery of the state bank using bombs and guns. This spectacular operation, carried out in broad daylight in front of a large crowd, demonstrated how common the practice of expropriation had become in Russia in 1906 and 1907.

The condemnation by the Stockholm Congress carried little weight against the habitual practice, and Lenin openly applauded these often substantial seizures of money. His unreserved acceptance of this "financial policy" comes through in the affectionate and admiring tone used by Krupskaya in talking about the perpetrators of these exploits. It is also demonstrated in the fact that, after a series of nerve-wracking misadventures (arrest in Germany, feigned madness, deportation to Russia, and condemnation), as soon as he was free, Kamo immediately joined Lenin in Paris, where he was, according to Krupskaya, warmly received.

In any event the Bolsheviks could not pretend to be unaware of these expropriations. When Kamo was arrested in Germany, it was established that he was in the process of preparing a bank robbery. At the same time, another of Lenin's associates, Maxim Maximovich Litvinov, was arrested in Paris carrying five hundred ruble notes which turned out to be part of the haul from Tblisi. This was not an accident, because Litvinov had been charged since 1906 with "managing" the funds coming from expropriations. For several years he had also been in very close contact with Lenin, who relied on him to take care of the financial link with the secretariat of the International Socialist Bureau. Litvinov deposited with the Bureau the funds derived from expropriations, obviously without revealing their origin, and then used them for weapons purchases, thus providing a respectable cover for the proceeds of armed robbery which European Socialists did not at first question. However, the arrest of Litvinov and of other Bolsheviks changing stolen notes abroad suddenly enlightened the Social Democrats.

To the affair of the five hundred ruble notes was added the discovery in Berlin of paper and prototypes intended for the printing of counterfeit rubles. In this case as well, the police captured those Bolsheviks who were responsible for the plan. The scandal was all the greater because the counterfeiters had hidden their material in the offices of *Vorwärts*, the organ of the German Social Democratic Party. The Mensheviks immediately expressed their indignation: Axelrod proclaimed that they could not continue to coexist in the same party with outlaws who, in addition, disregarded shared commitments; Plekhanov was just as violent. But protests and moral condemnations made little impression on Lenin.

However, he was not at the time in a position of strength, and, at the request of the Mensheviks and of some Bolsheviks more scrupulous than he, he was obliged to agree to have an investigating commission examine the affair. The choice of Gyorgy Vasilievich Chicherin to head the inquest was not very favorable to Lenin. The offspring of an aristocratic family, after university Chicherin had been a diplomat before breaking with his milieu to engage in revolutionary activity. By temperament, he felt rather close to the Mensheviks, and even though, in 1907, the Russian Social Democrats had been reunified, he was enrolled among the opponents of Lenin and the Bolsheviks. He was designated to conduct the investigation of the "affairs" precisely because, in the émigré circles in which he was charged with important responsibilities (he was secretary of the Social Democratic organization abroad), he commanded genuine respect from all his colleagues. They were happy to recognize that this "red aristocrat" had a perfect education allied with strong administrative skills. Chicherin also enjoyed the esteem of European Social Democrats with whom his duties placed him in frequent contact. The investigation he was charged with troubled Lenin, even though at the beginning he was convinced that Chicherin would be unable to assemble proof of collusion between him and the counterfeiters. Chicherin did succeed in identifying Krasin as the man behind the operation and tried to trace the responsibility back to Lenin.

Lenin's reaction to this kind of threat was always the same: He sidestepped the difficulty by securing a change in the composition of the body posing the threat. Thus he suggested that the investigation be turned over to a real commission, not Chicherin alone, and managed to pack it with Bolsheviks. As a result Krasin was exonerated from any responsibility, the affair of the counterfeit notes was buried, and the commission recommended the reintegration of the entire Caucasian group (including Stalin), which had been expelled because of the party's indignation at its exploits in Tblisi. Through this clever maneuver, Lenin was thus able to straighten out a situation that was apparently very compromising for him. But in doing so, he further exasperated the Mensheviks whom he had already accused of bearing false witness against his supporters.

Nor did his cleverness disarm Chicherin. And Krasin, along with Bogdanov, began in turn to move away from him to join the supporters of a boycott of the Duma. The break with these two loyal followers would not be long in coming.

STEALING AN INHERITANCE

Rid of the counterfeiting and expropriation affairs–but not of the considerable funds acquired that made it possible for him to manipulate the party–Lenin was involved in another affair that was just as harmful to his reputation, that is, the affair of the Shmit inheritance, or, rather, to give the affair its proper name, the "seizure" of a legacy organized by the Bolsheviks.

In her memoirs Krupskaya recounted the Shmit episode in a very novelistic and moving fashion:

> A young student of twenty-three, Nikolai Pavlovich Shmit, nephew of the industrialist [Savva] Morozov, became a Bolshevik in 1905. He provided money for *Novaya zhizn'* and for buying arms. He was arrested in 1905, tortured, and killed in prison in 1907. Before his death, he managed to express his wish to leave his fortune to the Bolsheviks. His young sister Elizaveta Pavlovna Shmit decided to give her portion of her brother's legacy to the Bolsheviks.[8]

At this point the story Krupskaya tells becomes barely comprehensible, unless we introduce an ingredient that is already well known, the financial and human manipulations so cherished by the Bolsheviks. In reality Shmit had two sisters and a brother, only one of whom, Catherine, was of age and could legally dispose of her fortune. The two others, Elizaveta and the brother, were minors and could therefore give nothing to the Bolsheviks. Wishing to get its hands as quickly as possible on a fortune that no legal testamentary bequest had attributed to it, the party set out to get around the two sisters by means of a matrimonial plot over which Krupskaya casts a very deceptive veil. According to her, because Elizaveta was still a minor, she had contracted a fictitious marriage with a Bolshevik named Ignatiev, in order to accomplish her brother's will by means of this subterfuge. In reality Elizaveta married another Bolshevik, Viktor Taratuta. And here the true story becomes immensely more interesting: Taratuta went to join Lenin in Geneva and turned over the coveted legacy to him.

The truth is even more complicated than it appears, and the order of the narrative needs to be changed in order to account for everything. In 1905, Taratuta, who was close to Lenin, was secretary of the Moscow Committee, which was Bolshevik, and was in charge of its treasury. At the London Congress, Taratuta had been promoted to candidate member of the Central Committee because of Lenin's authority over the composition of the governing body, and had later joined the founder of Bolshevism in Kuokkala. It was at that point that he entered on the stage of the Shmit inheritance affair. He fell in love with the minor sister, Elizaveta, and married her, but the marriage could not be legally entered into because Taratuta was living underground, with a variety of fictitious identities. In order for the young woman to be able to dispose of her legacy, the Bolsheviks then thought of marrying her to Ignatiev who was living legally under his own name.

At the end of this rather convoluted and hardly moral story, Ignatiev disappeared from the scene, leaving Taratuta master of the situation and of the part of the fortune that was supposed to come to Elizaveta Shmit. He transferred (at least he wrote that he did) considerable sums to the Bolsheviks through Lenin and Bogdanov, whose friendship had not yet been broken off.[9] In fact Taratuta turned over to the Bolsheviks only the part of his wife's fortune that came from Nikolai Shmit's legacy, keeping for himself what came from what her father had left her. This explains why Bogdanov, who was suspicious of Taratuta because of his past activities as a provocateur or even an informer, suddenly called him a "pimp."

The story didn't end there. Because the party could not put its hands on the fortune of the young brother, who was only fifteen and for whom marriage was thus unthinkable, it went after the elder sister, Catherine. The party's emissary on this occasion was another Bolshevik named A. M. Andrikanis, who, unlike Taratuta, was living legally under his own name and could therefore marry the Shmit heiress without difficulty. Andrikanis had no peace, because the party considered him as a simple intermediary who was required to turn over without hesitation the part of the Shmit inheritance he had obtained through the marriage.[10]

At this point there began a twofold farce, first between the husbands and the Bolsheviks, and then between the two factions of the Russian Social Democrats. Although Taratuta managed without too much trouble, incurring only insulting judgments, in reconciling his interests and those of the party by keeping some of his wife's property, the same thing was not true for Andrikanis. When he arrived in Paris in 1908, Catherine Shmit's husband decided not to turn over the coveted fortune to the Bolsheviks. Taratuta was deputed by the party to straighten out this recalcitrant brother-in-law, who was suddenly prey to scepticism about the revolutionary cause. Admonitions, threats, everything was tried. Taratuta went so far as to suggest physical liquidation of the rebel, who appealed to the Bolshevik Center and received this reply, signed by Lenin, Zinoviev, and Kamenev: "We confirm that in the Z (designating the complainant) affair, comrade Viktor [Taratuta] acted according to our directives and under our control. We accept no accusation against comrade Viktor."[11]

To escape from pursuit by the Bolsheviks, Andrikanis ended up giving them some of the Shmit legacy but kept the bulk of it for himself and decided to break all ties to the party. Taratuta was tempted to do the same, but the party had a stronger hold on him. He had to give in to the combined pressure of Lenin, Bogdanov, and Lunacharsky and surrender a much larger portion of the family fortune. The contempt in which he was held by a number of Lenin's associates seemed to suggest that he was done for, but he never lost Lenin's favor and after 1917, following a hiatus of some years, the "pimp" reappeared in his entourage.

The conjugal farce was coupled with a much more serious dispute involving European Social Democracy, the perennial conflict between Bolsheviks and Mensheviks on the question of money. Contrary to Krupskaya's assertions, Shmit had shown interest in Russian Social Democrats in general, not the Bolsheviks alone. The seizure of the inheritance was thus coupled with an attempt to seize the dead man himself, whom Krupskaya tried to turn into a Bolshevik martyr with her imaginative stories. In reality, like a number of Russian industrialists early in the century (including his uncle, Savva Morozov, an enthusiast for contemporary art), Shmit was convinced that Russia needed a revolution, and he sided with the revolutionaries, particularly the Social Democrats, and not with any individual faction. When the Bolsheviks, through their rather unusual maneuverings, appropriated the inheritance (they finally obtained only a part of it, but they claimed all of it), the Mensheviks found this unacceptable. They were aware of Shmit's attachment to all components of the Social Democrats; they also knew that Lenin intended to use the money to impose Bolshevik domination over the movement as a whole. Finally this dispute over an inheritance coincided with the time at which Russian Social Democracy had in principle been reunified, so that what belonged to the Bolsheviks was also the property of the Mensheviks. Lenin saw things differently and attempted to conceal the existence of the inheritance from the party, intending to keep the money from the Mensheviks and their allies in the Bund; they discovered the matter almost by chance.

Indeed the Shmit affair surfaced at a moment when the Social Democrats, theoretically reconciled but in fact riven by the dispute over recalling the deputies from the Duma, were once again attempting to find the grounds for a compromise advocated by the "conciliators."

Another conflict then broke out over the party press. With the help of Shmit's money, Lenin had been publishing the paper *Proletary* since early 1908, and had used it for fierce attacks on the Mensheviks and the "conciliators." He now proposed a truce. His offer certainly contained elements attractive to his counterparts: He would stop publication of *Proletary*, and the Mensheviks would do the same for *The Voice of the Social Democrat* (*Golos social demokrata*). All would then come together in the party's central organ, *Sotsial Demokrat*, whose editorial staff would take on Lenin and Zinoviev; two Mensheviks, Dan and Martov; and a representative of the Polish Social Democrats, Warski. But the sharing of editorship and intellectual resources implied the sharing of financial means. No more separate "coffers," proclaimed the Mensheviks, who demanded explanations about the Shmit inheritance and that the money from the bequest be placed in neutral hands in whom both parties had confidence. The intimate Russian enemies once again turned to the respectable and respected German Social Democrats. Clara Zetkin, Karl Kautsky, and Franz Mehring were chosen to receive the fortune and to distribute funds to both parties as and when they were needed.[12]

The agreement did not last long. First, Lenin had decided that the funds would be transferred to the trustees in stages and that it was appropriate for him to keep a small portion as compensation for stopping publication of *Proletary*. The Mensheviks, who had refused to stop their own publication, immediately complained about Bolshevik malfeasance in the transfer of money. Barely reconciled, Bolsheviks and Mensheviks entered into a battle of interests of unprecedented violence, with torrents of invectives and insults that ended up in the courts. In the meantime they exasperated the German Socialists. Claiming that the agreement had been broken by the Mensheviks, Lenin demanded that the Germans return the money that had been deposited to him and him alone. One by one the trustees grew discouraged. Kautsky withdrew, and then Mehring. Clara Zetkin made a final attempt to reconcile the adversaries by proposing restitution of the funds to the party as belonging to all. Nothing worked. Lenin accused her in turn of lying, the courts got involved, and until the war Mensheviks and Bolsheviks continued to insult one another and to fight for possession of the Shmit inheritance.

The principal winner in financial terms was Lenin. He had kept (and the Mensheviks were not wrong on this point) a significant portion of the funds that had earlier been deposited with him.

As early as 1910, the Bolsheviks were not lacking in resources. Expropriations, legacies, and gifts from wealthy financiers had amply filled their coffers. Of course they had lost the respect of the German Social Democrats, exasperated by the disputes among Russians and by the coarseness of the Bolsheviks, particularly of their leader. But they would never want for money in the future. Trotsky once called this kind of financial operation "expropriation within the Party."

In this troubled period of the history of the Bolshevik movement, money "affairs" were joined in 1909 and 1910 by the "Malinovsky affair."[13] Roman Malinovsky was a protégé of Lenin's but, more importantly, he was one of the recruits of the czarist political police, the Okhrana, who proliferated in the ranks of left-wing parties. A metalworker, he had been secretary of the Saint Petersburg union. After a brief period under arrest which persuaded him to move to Moscow, he was again arrested and then released, at a time when the Bolsheviks were being arrested in droves. Among his fellow prisoners, Nikolai Bukharin had from the outset suspected he was playing a double game and accused him of having joined the Bolsheviks on orders of the Okhrana. The Mensheviks, with whom he had been involved until his widely noticed move to the Bolsheviks in 1909, were equally suspicious. It thus came about that after the wave of arrests that devastated the workers' movement in 1909 and 1910, they publicly accused Malinovsky of having provoked those arrests. A Social Democratic commission was set up, which was presided over by Hanetsky, an associate of Lenin, who vouched for Malinovsky through him. Suspicion nevertheless remained, and the Mensheviks, angered by Lenin's conduct (he accused them of slandering an honest "militant"), added another grievance to their anti-Bolshevik file: Lenin's entourage, they said, was corrupt and dangerous because it was manipulated by the Okhrana.

Although Lenin had been able to secure the financial resources to keep his faction alive in the years between 1907 and 1910, his cynicism and brutality had isolated him. His close associates, Bogdanov and Krasin, as well as Gorky and Lunacharsky, broke with him. Two men replaced them, Zinoviev and Kamenev, who would not leave him until the war, although in January 1910 they opposed him over the attitude to be adopted toward the Mensheviks, whose support Kamenev wished to recover. This rebellion was of short duration. Under Lenin's guidance, Kamenev published a pamphlet two years later, *Two Parties*, which confirmed the split in the ranks of the Social Democrats.

BOLSHEVIKS AND MENSHEVIKS: THE DIVORCE

Lenin's conduct toward the Mensheviks and the German Social Democrats created a good deal of hostility against him. In late 1908, under his influence, a party conference adopted positions hostile to those he called the "left-wing liquidators." The following year he had a Bolshevik meeting condemn "expropriations" (to which he had closed his eyes while simultaneously using them as the basis for his faction's prosperity and capacity for action) and demanded the dissolution of the last groups of *boyeviki* (another fighting method that he had used unscrupulously until then). This sudden attack against the left drove away his previous supporters and left him almost alone but convinced that he was right to act in this way.

In January 1910 the Central Committee met in Paris. It had never really accepted the division of the party and attempted, without much success, to reconcile the various tendencies. Lenin then relied on the majority he had attained at the London Congress in 1907 to demand that everyone follow him. Arguing on the basis of his failures in Russia, as well as his lack of scruples, the Mensheviks and Bundists refused to surrender leadership of the party to Lenin. Unity was an unrealizable dream.

His intolerance explains why Lenin was the object of the most vigorous attacks from all directions at the Congress of the Socialist International held in Copenhagen in August of 1910. The Russian Social Democrats thought of him as the great divider who might well become the party's gravedigger.

In 1911 Lenin was exhausted by internal struggles, loss of support, and solitude. Many of those who had left him were drawn to *Pravda*, published in Vienna by Trotsky and Adolf Yoffe,[14] or joined Bogdanov and the group around *Vperyod*. As usual his nervous system gave way, and he needed rest. He settled into the Zinoviev household in Longjumeau, near Paris. During these difficult years, the Bolsheviks had established in this suburb a school for cadres directed by Zinoviev. Militants were trained there so that they could be sent back to Russia to reorganize the movement, which was in the process of falling apart. The school in Longjumeau was in competition with the one that Gorky, also separated from Lenin, had created in Capri for the same purpose. Although he was resting, Lenin engaged in some vigorous Bolshevik propaganda at the school.

It was already clear that the Social Democrats could not remain indifferent to the reawakening of the workers in Russia and merely continue to pick at its wounds. Demonstrations had started up again, first in the universities, and they were followed by strikes by the workers. Although there had been only fifty thousand strikers in Russia in 1910, their number doubled in 1911; and on May 1, four hundred thousand workers stopped work. In April 1912 strikes in the gold mines on the banks of the Lena in Siberia were so widespread that the government intervened, arresting the strikers' delegates, and when the crowd of miners came to demand their liberation troops were set on them. Volleys of shots without warning produced a large number of casualties: nearly 150 dead and hundreds wounded. The massacre, which is what it was, transfixed Russia and provoked waves of strikes and demonstrations throughout the country.

Before the rebirth of working-class agitation had reached all the industrial cities, the Social Democrats had convened a conference in Prague in January 1912. Lenin had carefully prepared for the event, counting on recapturing the majority at the conference. Many of the "graduates" from the school in Longjumeau had been given the mission on their return to Russia to engage in agitation to bring together Lenin's supporters and ensure that they send his most ardent advocates as delegates to Prague. The preparations turned out to be effective, because most participants in the conference represented underground Russian organizations, and rather few delegates, Bolshevik or Menshevik, came from émigré circles. The conference was to confirm the division of the party into two irreconcilable factions.

Lenin succeeded in imposing his authority in Prague. Along with him, the Central Committee elected at the end of the conference included Zinoviev, Sergo Ordzhonikidze, Yakov Sverdlov, and Malinovsky (still suspect in the eyes of the Mensheviks). Lenin then gave Malinovsky responsibilities on the daily paper that the conference had decided to create, *Pravda*. The first issue appeared in April 1912; following successive seizures, it was obliged to change its title but always maintained the word *Pravda* in various combinations. Aware of the moral authority commanded by Plekhanov, Lenin again attempted to associate him with the publication, but he soon gave up in the face of the old master's refusal.

In the meanwhile Trotsky reacted to the appropriation of his title. In August 1912 he convened a conference in Vienna to attempt to restore some unity to the party, but it failed; Bolsheviks and Mensheviks rejected any dialogue. The result of the conference was the creation of the August Bloc, a heterogeneous alliance that set up an organizing committee that had little activity.

At the same time, there was a furious polemic between Lenin, against whom the Bloc was directed, and Trotsky. Lenin accused his opponent of shifting from one tendency to another and of political inconsistency. Trotsky repeated over and over that Lenin was making hay out of the backwardness of Russia and its working class.

The Duma was another privileged site for the confrontation between Bolsheviks and Mensheviks. In 1912, the mandate of the third Duma, which had completed its full term, came to an end. The coming elections for the fourth Duma required that an electoral strategy be defined. Of course the 1907 election law was still in force and still as unfavorable to the Social Democrats. However, this time Lenin was excited by the vote, and, as in 1907, advocated participation.[15]

He was so involved in the 1912 voting that when he was called on in November to attend a meeting of the International Socialist Bureau of which he was a member, he said that he could not come because of the elections to the Duma.[16] Around the same time, he replied to a reminder of dues owed addressed to him by the liaison office of the Socialist International that the Duma elections were taking up all the resources of the party.[17] After the vote, while complaining about the high rate of abstention and about voting irregularities, he enthusiastically greeted the election of thirteen Social Democrats, including six Bolsheviks. Among those elected to the fourth Duma, the Socialist Revolutionaries could pride themselves on the entry into the parliament of a man who was to play a great role in it and who was coincidentally an old acquaintance of Lenin's: Alexander Kerensky, the son of his protector in Simbirsk.

In the early stages of the new assembly, Bolsheviks and Mensheviks managed to preserve the appearance of a unity that the Prague conference had in fact destroyed. This surface unity lasted only until the summer of 1913. The conflict then reached the Duma, and the Social Democratic group in the assembly ceased to exist. The Bolshevik faction was from then on presided over by Malinovsky, who acted as Lenin's agent there, too.

This split in the parliamentary group had two consequences. First, the Duma in turn became a stage for confrontations between Bolsheviks and Mensheviks. Malinovsky constantly engaged in invective against Menshevik deputies, and he was seconded by *Pravda*. In addition, the more than suspect personality of Malinovsky, of whom the Bolsheviks as well as their opponents grew increasingly wary, unquestionably cast a shadow on all the Social Democrats.

In 1912 and 1913, Malinovsky created a major scandal in the Bolshevik Party. The suspicions that had long weighed on him, which Bukharin had in vain brought up with Lenin, were revived by a series of arrests for which he alone could have been responsible. First, in late 1912, the secretary to the Bolshevik faction in the Duma, who was married to Alexander Troyanovsky, was apprehended while she was carrying a message from Lenin. Then it was the turn of Sverdlov, a Bolshevik militant from his early youth, who had been co-opted onto the Central Committee in 1912 at the age of twenty-seven. He had escaped from Siberia and taken refuge in Saint Petersburg, where his arrest took place after a meeting with Malinovsky. Stalin himself was arrested in similar circumstances. In all these cases, Malinovsky had been near the underground hiding places or informed of the movements of those questioned by the police. From all sides—Bukharin again, Troyanovsky, but also Martov and his brother-in-law Fedor Dan—people warned Lenin, urging him to withdraw his confidence from a man who was openly accused of being an Okhrana agent.[18] It was a waste of effort. Far from paying attention to these pleas, Lenin, who was then living in Cracow, made Malinovsky one of his preferred table companions and threatened to take those who accused him to court. He signed vengeful communiqués that were published in *Pravda*, saying that "after investigation, we are completely convinced of the innocence of Malinovsky," and refused to have a party tribunal get involved.

The Malinovsky affair thus helped poison still further, if that were possible, the atmosphere inside Russian Social Democracy. Some of Lenin's associates could not deal with his blindness. For example, Troyanovsky, exasperated, broke with him; the two men did not become reconciled until late in 1920. As for Malinovsky, a veritable spokesman for Lenin in the Duma, in 1914 he tried to lead the deputies into a collective resignation. His failure, but even more an increasingly precarious personal situation (the president of the Duma, Mikhail Rodzianko, had been informed of his police activities), suddenly led him to make an unexpected gesture: He handed Rodzianko his resignation in a spectacular way and declared that he was withdrawing from political life. He immediately disappeared from Russia and resurfaced only during the war when, captured by the Germans, he still benefited from the help of his protector. Unfortunately, his resignation added to the confusion prevailing among the Social Democratic deputies.

The press, as always, was an echo chamber for this unending dispute. Lenin controlled *Pravda* with an iron hand. Although Malinovsky was in charge of financial matters, the editor in chief, Miron Chernomazov, was also an Okhrana agent. With the help of these two provocateurs, Lenin made the paper a tool for his furious attacks against his principal opponents, the Mensheviks. They responded with the same virulence in the press organ they had created in Russia, *Luch* (The Ray). The Menshevik paper, however, could not withstand competition from its Bolshevik rival, because the material resources needed to keep a paper alive and to ensure its circulation were in Lenin's hands. Money questions thus continued to weigh heavily on relations among Social Democrats, and the Mensheviks constantly complained of having been financially dispossessed by unscrupulous adversaries.

CRACOW, CLOSER TO RUSSIA

In the summer of 1912, Lenin and his family had left the French capital to move to Cracow. It was not that Paris was hard for the exile, but he wanted to be closer to Russia now that social agitation was again gaining ground and the workers' movement appeared to be reborn. Cracow was also a more convenient place for directing and controlling *Pravda.*

Settling in Cracow was, however, not a simple matter. For the Austrian authorities, Lenin was not a particularly desirable guest. However, a loyal follower who had joined him in the hard years, Yakov Hanetsky, intervened successfully. He was a strange figure, who also used the name Fürstenberg; he had been a member of the Polish revolutionary movement, had been a delegate to RSDLP Congresses since 1903, and had been elected to the Central Committee at the Fifth Congress. Having gradually become involved in all of Lenin's financial affairs, he managed to negotiate the authorization for him to settle in Cracow, where he was joined by two other loyal followers, Zinoviev and Kamenev.

The two years that Lenin spent in Cracow were peaceful and relatively happy. He wrote articles, went for long walks, and met many emissaries from Russia. In 1913, he was for a time joined by Stalin, a Bolshevik whose merits he had recognized since the time when "expropriations" had helped fill the party coffers. Lenin's favorable opinion of "Koba" had been obvious since 1912. At the Prague conference where he had "his" Central Committee elected, he insisted that Stalin be co-opted and appointed as a member of the "Russian Bureau," although his candidacy had been coolly received by those participants who remembered his role in the "expropriations." If Lenin pushed Caucasians in general, and not only Stalin, to the forefront, this was because their region made up a veritable Bolshevik citadel. Ordzhonikidze was promoted at the same time as Stalin. And Stalin also played a role in setting up *Pravda* the same year, when he and Molotov were appointed to the editorial staff. The contribution of Stalin and Molotov would not be worth mentioning had it not been that they defended in the paper, against Lenin, a conciliatory line. They were then called "spineless" and replaced by Sverdlov who undertook to impose once again on the paper the line defined by Lenin. Even so, Stalin did not lose Lenin's favor; on his arrival in Cracow in 1913, Lenin greeted Stalin warmly and gave him a task that he considered very important, the composition of an article on the national question for a journal controlled by the Bolsheviks, *Prosveshchenie* (Enlightenment).

This is not the place to examine Lenin's ideas on the national question. What should be noted is that he called on Stalin in 1913 because he needed to clarify his own views in this area, not in order to derive a theory from them, but purely for reasons of political strategy. The national question was indeed a subject of vigorous debate among the Russian Social Democrats in 1912 and 1913. And at the Vienna conference organized by the Mensheviks in August 1912 (which Lenin called the conference of "liquidators"),[19] the leaders of the national Social Democratic organizations—the Bund, the Latvian and Caucasian Social Democratic Parties, and representatives of the Polish and Lithuanian Socialist Parties—called for the adoption of a program for the nations. Lenin considered these demands dangerous. He thought that they threatened to weaken the unity of the workers' movement, perhaps even to cause the party to dissolve, a threat that Lenin had earlier seen the Bund representing for the Social Democrats.[20] In addition party discipline, requiring complete adherence to principles developed as early as 1903, was challenged by these particularist demands. Lenin was all the more troubled by them because it was precisely the strongholds of the Socialist movement (including the Caucasus) that were affected by these ideas, which were derived from the arguments of Otto Bauer and his disciples, very respected figures among European Social Democrats. To combat everyone who was attracted by a national conception of Socialism, Lenin felt the need to use a Bolshevik who was involved in national problems. He had at first thought of the Armenian Stepan Shaumyan, who had already considered the problem and put together arguments and documentation, but Shaumyan was in the Caucasus. It was then that the Georgian Stalin providentially arrived in Cracow. Lenin gave him the task without hesitation and wrote to Gorky: "We have here a marvelous Georgian who is writing a long article '*enlightening*' the proletarian solution to the national question."[21]

The purpose of the article that he asked Stalin to write was clear. It was a polemical work designed to call Russian Social Democrats to order and to accelerate the process of breaking with the Mensheviks and their supporters by giving a theoretical explanation of their conflict. Excluding the Bundists, the Caucasian Mensheviks, and beyond that, all the other Mensheviks, would have been difficult without a solid reason, because the International would have taken offense. Sticking to his usual method, Lenin therefore intended to demonstrate that the opponent was wrong. But there is no basis for thinking that he gave the "marvelous Georgian" the task of preparing a theoretical article. Deep thinking, theory, was always the responsibility of Lenin himself. It was up to his collaborators to cross swords in the genre of polemics.

Further, to lend a hand to Stalin, whose command of German was very rudimentary if not nonexistent, Lenin recruited Bukharin and Troyanovsky (he had not yet quarreled with the latter) to help him research and translate the documentation on the subject. The result of this work was, as we know, the pamphlet *Marxism and the National Question*, which he always claimed as proof of his gifts as a theorist. And he would also drape himself in the term the "marvelous Georgian" to show how deep his ties to Lenin had been. But that is another story. The essential point in this context is the importance that Lenin attributed to the work of his collaborator at a time when the conflicts with the Mensheviks were a source of problems for him with the Socialist International.

THE INTERNATIONAL CAUGHT
BETWEEN THE INTIMATE ENEMIES

The International was founded in Paris in 1889; after a period of complete flexibility it was given a more institutionalized organization in the early years of the century. The International Socialist Bureau (ISB) was thus set up in Brussels in 1900 as a permanent organ. At the Amsterdam Socialist Congress of 1904, the International listed as one of its tasks safeguarding socialist unity in all countries. The split of the Russian Social Democrats consequently became a constant concern for the leaders of the International and the Bureau. The situation was all the more difficult because, at the outset, Plekhanov was one of the two Russian representatives, and the better known, to the ISB.[22] In addition major Social Democratic figures, such as Kautsky and Bebel, were inclined to prefer the Mensheviks to the Bolsheviks. Finally, after the Third Congress of the RSDLP, which the Mensheviks refused to consider legal, Lenin challenged Plekhanov's right to continue to represent the Russian Social Democrats and tried to force the International to replace him with a Bolshevik who would be designated by the Central Committee elected at the Congress–in other words, someone chosen by Lenin. In the end it was Lenin who became the representative of the

Bolshevik faction to the ISB in 1905, although he did not appear there during the entire time of the first Russian revolution.

On the other hand, between 1907 and 1912, the International occupied a major place in Lenin's activities and helped to soften the time in the wilderness that those years of exile and often discouragement meant for him. Moreover, relations with the International were improved to some degree by the proliferation of steps in favor of unity in 1909 and 1910, which strengthened the conviction of European Social Democrats that the division was the result of "classic émigré disputes" rather than of basic conflicts. This notion seemed to be corroborated by two events in 1910. Lenin proposed to the ISB that Plekhanov, who had been ousted in 1905, rejoin the body; Plekhanov, on his side, agreed to cooperate with the Bolsheviks against the "liquidators," and wrote: "We belong to the same Party."[23]

Lenin attended a Congress of the International for the first time in 1907, in Stuttgart, and he was even a member of the bureau presiding over the work of the Congress.[24] *Le Peuple* described his presence in these terms: "Seated to the left of Rosa Luxemburg was Lenin, socialist leader of the defunct Duma. With his small blonde mustache, his large forehead made even larger by premature baldness, his piercing gaze, and his energetic and clever face, he is a truly impressive figure."[25] This first participation in an international forum made him very happy. He was convinced that he had found a platform from which he could combat reformism, and he was allied with Rosa Luxemburg on many points. This encouraged him to continue his cooperation with the International, and for four years he attended all its meetings. In a certain sense, his difficulties inside Russian Social Democracy were made easier to bear by his feeling of participation in the leadership of international Socialism. But this happy optimism came to an end in 1912. The International, which had believed that it was helping to reduce dissension among Russian Social Democrats, and Lenin, who believed that he was accepted and understood by the International, were both obliged to surrender their illusions.

The Russian Social Democratic Party was not the only one that was publicly divided. But, for the International, it was probably the most serious case. In January 1912, after the Prague conference, Mensheviks and Bolsheviks were permanently split. The International considered this situation to be as scandalous as it was unacceptable. Offers of mediation proliferated, but both sides rejected them with equal vehemence. For the Mensheviks the rejection was based on the feeling of having right on their side and that they were confronted with a form of violence that could not be overcome by any rational means. No doubt Plekhanov was much more flexible than his colleagues and asserted that any mediation was acceptable, because it was division that was not. Lenin's deafness to offers of mediation came in part from his intransigence, but also from his awareness that in the eyes of the International, he was the "bad guy," the one interfering with harmony. On this point he was not wrong.

The International had always thought, and continued to do so, that disputes among the Russians had to do primarily with personalities, and that emigration was a condition that was likely to foster and embitter such squabbles. No one in the ranks of the International really believed that there was a major basic dispute between Mensheviks and Bolsheviks about the nature of the Russian revolution. This mistake in assessment helped to give the exchanges between Russians and European Socialists the character of a dialogue of the deaf, which was to continue up to the Russian Revolution and the death of the Second International. In these conditions it was Lenin who spoke with the greatest violence, on whom all the grievances of the Mensheviks were focused, and who was considered a man capable of everything. It was impossible not to think in this context of the "affairs"—expropriations and stolen legacies—which he instigated and from which he profited. The leaders of the International were horrified by them, as they were by his coarseness when efforts at mediation did not suit him as, for example, in the way he treated Clara Zetkin. They contrasted this coarseness with the measured and courteous tone of Plekhanov and Martov, more in keeping with their European habits.

Rosa Luxemburg hardly helped improve Lenin's reputation. She was considered the principal specialist on Russia in the International. As a Russian speaker, and because of her experience with the Polish workers' movement, she was the oracle on the "Russian question." Luxemburg shared Lenin's views on many questions, but, like Kautsky, she believed that the time was not ripe for a debate on revolution in Russia and that all that counted were Lenin's maneuvers which had the effect of undermining Social Democratic unity in Russia. In 1912 the gulf between the two figures quickly became unbridgeable, because they also came into conflict over a particular problem, the split that took place in the Polish Social Democratic organization. Close associates of Lenin came out in opposition to the governing committee of the Social Democratic Party of Poland and Lithuania, led by Tyszka (Leo Jogiches) and Rosa Luxemburg, and called on Bolshevik support. The principal figures were Yakov Hanetsky and Karl Radek. The latter was both remarkably intelligent and remarkably muddled and unstable. He was disliked by German Social Democrats for his opportunism, his lack of scruples, and the scandals around him. In 1908 he had even been accused of theft. Lenin's support for his positions in 1912 was not calculated to improve Luxemburg's feelings toward the leader of the Bolsheviks.

The Prague conference, the Polish conflicts, and the pressure of Rosa Luxemburg on the International all explain why that body decided to take up the Russian question in 1913. Aware that he was looked on with increasing disapproval, Lenin had moved away from the International in that year. He no longer attended ISB meetings and turned his mandate over to Kamenev, who was then living in Paris. The official reason was that Cracow was too far from Brussels. In fact Lenin would have felt himself in a difficult position. Nor did he attend the meeting that took place in London in December 1913; he left it to Litvinov, who replaced Kamenev for the occasion, to reply to Luxemburg, who was supported by Kautsky. The meeting justified neither the efforts of Luxemburg and her supporters nor Lenin's worries.[26] After a few calm preliminaries, the affair was referred to a special conference which was supposed to be convened a few months later in Brussels and which would bring together all the organizations, factions, and groups associated with Social Democracy in Russia. The program that the ISB had given itself was clear: either this confrontation would make it possible to move forward on the path of mutual understanding, or else it would fail, and there would then remain the final recourse, the International Socialist Congress scheduled for August 1914 in Vienna.

Consequently Lenin carefully prepared for the coming conference, drafting a report on Social Democratic unity in Russia, gathering the documents with which he intended to supply his delegation, and attempting to ensure that a maximum of organizations favorable to his positions would be represented. He meticulously selected the three-member Bolshevik delegation, the most eminent member of which and the one closest to him was Inessa Armand, and entirely drafted their various speeches. Everything seemed to be fully prepared, except that Lenin's plan had a weak point, his own absence. He was wrong not to go to Brussels and to entrust the reading of his report to Armand. His absence made a bad impression; it was considered an evasion inspired by the fear of being disavowed, while his representatives, disconcerted by the debates, sometimes lacked presence of mind. At the conclusion of very animated discussions, Kautsky's resolution, which was hostile to the Bolsheviks, was adopted. Lenin was only half disappointed, because he had harbored few illusions about his chances of winning out. Because unity had not been achieved, the Vienna Congress would have to deal with the question again, and Lenin was determined to attend that one in person to fight against the Mensheviks, against reformism, against the entire International if necessary.

The plan, like the Congress, came to nothing. On the date for which it was scheduled, war had broken out, dragging Europe into the cataclysm and confirming the bankruptcy of the International, which had been able neither to reconcile the Russian rivals nor to prevent the war. Lenin had stopped believing in its value since 1912 and saw in its collapse a confirmation of the correctness of his views.

TIME IN THE WILDERNESS, BUT FRIENDS TO SWEETEN IT

The years from 1907 to 1914 were certainly difficult ones for Lenin in the political realm: Revolutionary hope had flown, he suffered many attacks, and experienced moments of great isolation. What helped him through this time in the wilderness, when he found it hard to imagine the slightest revolutionary renewal, much less the possibility of the Bolsheviks assuming a dominant position, was his entourage. In the camp of his supporters, those years were marked by serious breaks but also by the arrival of new disciples.

Men who were close to him and whom he admired suddenly distanced themselves from him. This was true first for Bogdanov, who broke with him in 1907 on the question of the attitude to adopt toward the elections to the third Duma, and briefly seized leadership of the Bolshevik faction from him. Beyond the dispute about power, there was a philosophical opposition between them, even though Lenin always attempted to minimize their differences. Bogdanov invited opponents of Lenin such as Trotsky and Lunacharsky to teach in the party school in Capri. Lenin's establishment of a school in Longjumeau to counter the Capri school and the ideas that it spread was not enough to appease him.

Krasin, who had been loyal to him for so long, left him in turn in 1910. Trotsky, who had for a time been his protégé, had already done the same.

In contrast to successive desertions were new disciples: Zinoviev, Kamenev, and Hanetsky, who all became his intimates in the years before the revolution and did not leave him until the return to Russia.

But it was the family group that really comforted Lenin. It was a group made up of women; those from his early life, his mother and sisters, who came for fairly long visits in his various places of exile, were joined by the two women who would leave him only when death decreed.

Nadezhda Krupskaya, whom he married in Siberia in 1898, was simultaneously his wife, his chief of staff, his public relations officer, and his secretary. Devoted and indefatigable, despite delicate health, she was also the object of constant attention from her husband. On countless occasions he sought out the best doctor for her. On countless other occasions, he carried on conversations with Inessa Armand about Nadezhda's temperature when she had a cold. They were a surprising couple of comrades, but they were inseparable, no doubt bound by ties of affection and esteem, and by the revolutionary program. Only death put an end to this quarter century of companionship. During their long life together, they had only minor difficulties. Despite their revolutionary activities, they rarely experienced real insecurity. Their exile was rather peaceful. Their successive residences abroad almost always kept them safe from the imperial police. Except for a very few moments, they did not feel hunted like so many of their comrades.

Material life was also quite comfortable, for many years thanks to financial aid from Lenin's mother, and thereafter through assistance from the party. Always adequately housed, able to secure the help of a servant, they were spared the poverty that so many revolutionaries had to confront. The ordeals that they had to deal with were matters of feeling. They were both unhappy because Krupskaya could not have children, so much so that when they were in Poland, they offered to adopt the Zinovievs' little boy, an offer which was of course refused. Finally there was the unhappiness tied to the dilemma created when Armand burst into their life.

Elizaveta Vasilievna, Krupskaya's mother, was really the faithful keeper of the hearth for them. She took care of everything, until her declining health and her age made it necessary for a full-time servant to take her place. She remained in Lenin's household until her death in 1915. Her relations with her son-in-law were courteous, calm, no doubt tinged with esteem and even sympathy. But Elizaveta Vasilievna always remained reserved toward Lenin, believing, as she frequently said, that it was not normal for a man not to work.

And then in Lenin's life, beginning in 1910, there was a female figure whom Bolshevik prudery strove to reduce to the customary comradeship, but who in fact occupied a place in his heart. Considering the place reserved for Inessa Armand in Lenin's life does not mean giving in to unhealthy curiosity or the temptation to gossip. Once that place is recognized, the portrait of the man receives a different light than that the carefully crafted legend has always tried to conceal. That place can be obscured all the less because it played a role in his political development.

Inessa Stephan-Wild, Armand by marriage, was born in Paris in 1874 from a French father and a half-English mother. Raised in London after the death of her father, Inessa left for Russia at the age of fifteen to stay with her grandmother and an aunt. Like many of their compatriots, these two women had settled in Russia where, in the late nineteenth century, French women were sought out by the most distinguished families as tutors and governesses; and they sometimes made rich marriages that could not be hoped for in France. In addition to being beautiful and able to speak perfect English and Russian, Inessa was an excellent musician. As in certain sentimental novels of the time, she was governess in a rich family and, at eighteen, married the son of a prominent Russian merchant. With a handsome, rich, and amiable husband and five children, her fate seemed settled until the revolutionary temptation turned her away from that comfortable road. She was active in Social Democratic groups, left her husband for her young brother-in-law (a sacrifice to the myth of free love), was arrested and exiled, but was still protected by an abandoned but indulgent husband who saw to the children. As Marxism required, she took courses in economics; finally, when she arrived in Paris in 1910, she met Lenin, who held for her the prestige of the revolutionary leader.

This relationship, on which fragments of letters shed light, posed for Lenin the serious problem of Nadezhda Krupskaya. Research by serious historians suggests that she soon became aware of the situation—she had never left Lenin and sensed his slightest change of mood. She suffered, rebelled, and then with dignity proposed to give up her place.[27] But Lenin thought differently. The affair with Inessa Armand was discreet; Krupskaya remained the respected wife and gradually developed a friendship for Inessa, which was mutual. This was certainly not a ménage à trois. The Lenins and Inessa met frequently and sometimes traveled together, but all of them demonstrated remarkable dignity and deep mutual respect. In 1913, Inessa, who could not bear Cracow, a city that she found boring, and perhaps also troubled by a difficult romantic situation, left for a while and settled in Paris. It was Lenin who decided to break things off, while maintaining close ties to Inessa. In December 1913, she wrote to him that she "could get by without the kisses" if she could only be near him. In a letter of May 1914, Lenin begged her: "Do not be angry against me. I have caused you a great pain, I know it."[28] A month later he asked Inessa: "When you come, bring all our letters here." What has been preserved of their correspondence is both confident and unhappy, and revealing of the sacrifice that Lenin imposed on himself and on Inessa. We can understand the reasons if we consider his character. He had never had the free notions of many Bolsheviks on the subject of love. He would vigorously criticize the argument by Alexandra Kollontai in favor of free love and more generally of sexual freedom. A man of order, a prude, he would always remain faithful to the education he had received in a united family whose behavior was dictated by the moral code of Russian society in the late nineteenth century.

The late General Volkogonov, who had access to the Russian presidential archives, claimed that Lenin had also had an illegitimate child.[29] If that turns out to be true (but the secret in this matter seems well preserved), it would simply show how careful Lenin was to prevent his reputation for morality from being undermined, and also how important it was to him not to wound those close to him.

Starting with the outbreak of the war, Inessa Armand became primarily, along with Krupskaya, the collaborator whom Lenin needed the most. Indeed, he had written to her: "[My] fullest friendship, absolute admiration and confiance of mine are confined to only 2–3 women."[30] Representing Lenin, speaking in his name at various Socialist congresses, or participating in them with him, she was also part of the group that returned with him to Russia in April 1917. When she died, a broken Lenin, overcome with a sadness that struck everyone present, accompanied Inessa to her final resting place. Despite the distances imposed on the heart, everything indicates that the love he bore for her had remained intact.

His family life and the role played by matters of the heart attest that although Lenin was incomparably harsh with his opponents and abstract in his sympathy for humanity in general (Gorky said that he "loved men as they would be when the revolution had changed them"),[31] there was another Lenin, the man who was warm and loving to those in his closest circle. It would be unfair not to add this Lenin, whose company was reserved for a few privileged people, to the one who entered the history of his country and of the world beginning in the late nineteenth century. This observation suggests a question: Was there a moment, when he held enormous power, when the Lenin who was so attentive to those who were close to him extended his capacity to love others to those who did not belong to the narrow circle of his affections? With his time in the wilderness coming to an end and the pace of events picking up speed, who was the Lenin about to confront the period of action? Was he the brutal man thinking only of subjecting everything to his will? Or was he a Lenin full of human feeling for those who were dear to him and had helped him keep up the flame of hope when everything seemed to be lost?

PART THREE

REVOLUTION AT ANY COST (1914–1917)

Chapter Seven

THE DEFEAT OF RUSSIA:
FOR THE GOOD OF THE REVOLUTION

ALTHOUGH IN 1905 HE HAD NOT ANTICIPATED THAT REVOLU-
tion would come out of Russian setbacks in the Pacific, by 1914, Lenin had long
ago drawn the lessons from the past and criticized his own blindness. He would
have no further doubt that war was the opportunity for revolution, but the question was whether he might hope that war would come, particularly in Russia,
where it had been the spark setting off an abortive revolution. Lenin did not
dare to think that a similar opportunity would arise again, and he wrote to
Maxim Gorky in 1913: "A war between Russia and Austria would be of great
value to the revolution. But there is little likelihood that Francis Joseph and
Nikki will give us that pleasure."[1]

Further, was the International not prepared to mobilize all its forces in order
to avert the threat of war? Because international tension had grown, beginning
with the Moroccan crisis in 1911 and continuing with the Balkan Wars, the
International had constantly been debating how to prevent a confrontation
among peoples for whom class solidarity made warfare unthinkable. Peace and
peace alone was the only conceivable prospect for the majority of European
Socialists. Very few, and almost all of them were Russians, thought about a revolution that might come out of a possible conflict. As early as 1907, at the
Stuttgart conference where the antiwar struggle had mobilized all the participants, Rosa Luxemburg, Lenin, and Martov had managed to slip through an
amendment going far beyond the views of the majority: "In case war breaks out,
socialists have the duty . . . to use with all their strength the economic and political crisis created by war to stir up the lowest levels of the people and to speed
up the fall of capitalist domination."[2]

The Russians' position is easy to understand, because they were obsessed
by the memory of 1905. Lenin was to hold to this linkage between war and
revolution, and to develop it constantly in the succeeding years.[3]

RETURN TO SWITZERLAND

In early July 1914, no one really believed that war was coming. Heads of state and party leaders, including those in the International, and private citizens who could afford it were all getting ready to go on vacation. In his excellent book, *La Grande Guerre des Français*, Jean-Baptiste Duroselle notes that despite the assassination of the archduke of Austria on June 28, 1914, complete calm reigned through almost the entire month of July in Europe, so much so that President Poincaré and Prime Minister Vivendi set out for Russia on July 16, and Vivendi wrote at the time: "We went toward peace with our heads held high and our spirits calm."[4]

Lenin was one of the few political leaders who saw the rising storm behind this apparent calm. Austria did send an ultimatum to Serbia on July 23, but for a few more days, the diplomats persisted in believing in the chances for peace. Lenin reacted immediately, and wrote a letter to Inessa Armand on July 25 that begins: "My dear & dearest friend! Best greetings for the commencing revolution in Russia."[5]

The meaning of the message was clear. Lenin no longer doubted that war was coming, nor did he doubt its result: revolution in his own country. Holding this belief in the last week of July 1914 required visionary abilities, because Russia had never inspired so much confidence in its allies. Poincaré's visit indicates as much, and from the military review he witnessed at Tsarskoe Selo on July 23, the French president was convinced of the great military strength of his ally. Moreover, Russia had triumphantly celebrated the tercentenary of the dynasty the year before, and the demonstrations of popular enthusiasm suggested to those in power that the time of violent crises might very well have come to an end. Economic development was continuing, and 1913 was a year of exceptional grain harvests and satisfactory industrial production; inflation remained at a modest 2 percent. Of course not all economic obstacles had been overcome. But Lenin himself, in a 1913 article, before war renewed his hope, had noted the rapid progress of Russia and had wondered about the possibilities of revolution in that context.[6] It was indeed possible to assume that Russia would continue to progress on the path of constitutional monarchy, as many liberals hoped, or that moderately revolutionary tendencies would develop, as the Mensheviks thought. The International gave them its support and, armed with that, they thought they could mobilize the Russian workers' movement around themselves. On the eve of war, the least plausible hypothesis was that of radical revolution and Bolshevik triumph. It was difficult to imagine at a time when Lenin's friends were internationally isolated and domestically weak, and when their program was far from coinciding with the aspirations of most of Russia's social forces, who wanted their country to evolve peacefully.

For Lenin, that no longer had the slightest importance; the war had arrived, and he just had to wait for Russian defeat and its consequences.

His defeatist vision was shared neither by the majority of the International nor by his compatriots. The International met in Brussels on July 29 and 30, and adjourned without having decided on any concerted action to preserve peace. It was counting strongly on the Vienna Congress, planned for August, to adopt measures likely to prevent the conflict. War forestalled the congress, and the most vehement Socialists turned their backs on internationalist phraseology. On August 4, the Social Democrats in the Reichstag voted in favor of war credits. Vandervelde joined the Belgian government, and in France the *union sacrée* encompassed all parties. The Socialists, who had always and everywhere been so quick to denounce their own rulers, suddenly discovered that the responsibility for war lay with the rulers of the enemy countries. As a result, the war was called "defensive" by the German Socialists, whereas French and Belgian Socialists joined in blaming "German aggression." The notion of "just war" suddenly replaced that of unacceptable war. Only the Russian Social Democrats in their own country opposed the war and refused to vote for the credits requested for defense. While Lenin attacked the betrayal of the French and German Socialists, in Russia it was the Bolsheviks who were accused of treason. Lenin had in addition sent to Kamenev, who had returned to Russia to manage *Pravda* and lead the Bolshevik group in the Duma, blunt instructions intended to define the attitude of its deputies. He ordered that they solemnly declare to the Duma their opposition to the war and their desire to see Russia defeated, because on that would depend civil war and the salvation of the working class. The intervention of the police and the arrest of all the deputies put an end to these impulses.

In fact, aside from the Bolsheviks, Russian Socialists were very divided. Like the leadership of the International, the majority of Menshevik leaders came out in support of the war effort from the day it was declared. This was the position of Plekhanov, and of Potresov, who had remained in Russia. But a minority around Martov and Axelrod inclined toward internationalist positions. There was also division among the SRs, where Viktor Chernov came close to Lenin's views. The most important thing was that Lenin's position did not go unnoticed by the leaders of the Central Powers, who soon discovered the use they could make of this unexpected ally. He wrote a short article that he thought should serve as a guide for everyone inspired by the revolutionary spirit: "The Tasks of Revolutionary Social Democracy in the European War," dated late August 1914. This article sums up his vision of war changing into revolution, and provides precise instructions for the defeatist activities that his supporters were supposed to engage in.[7] In particular, he recommended that they go into the trenches to tell ordinary soldiers: "Take your rifles and turn them against your officers and against all capitalists!"

However, once the war had begun, Lenin had to take care of his personal situation as a foreigner residing in a country at war against his own. The Austro-Hungarian authorities were at first troubled by his presence and subjected him to surveillance and then arrested him for a few days. Appalled, because he was hardly used to this kind of treatment, Lenin turned to the faithful Hanetsky, who appealed to the authorities of the Austro-Hungarian Empire and to his friends, notably the Social Democratic representative Viktor Adler, and secured his release.[8] In order to accomplish this, Hanetsky referred to Lenin's defeatist positions, indirectly favorable to the Central Powers. In addition to his release, Hanetsky secured permission for Lenin to leave without difficulties for Switzerland.

At first Lenin settled in Berne, an active center of Russian émigré life. As soon as he arrived, he brought together the Bolsheviks living in the federal capital and presented to them his view of the war and his program: "This is a war for imperialism. For pillage. We should not ask for peace. That's a slogan for priests. The slogan of the proletariat should be to transform the war into a civil war in order to destroy capitalism for good!" He explained that he was indeed talking about the defeat of Russia, because, he went on, "Tsarism is a hundred times worse than kaiserism."

During this meeting Lenin also elaborated on a theme that had first appeared in his brief article-program of late August, the separation from the empire of various regions–Ukraine, Poland, the Baltic provinces–as a foreseeable consequence of the war and the defeat of Russia. From that time on, he would constantly return to two ideas: the necessity for an international mobilization of Socialists to unleash civil wars everywhere, and the possibility that the Russians could speed up the disintegration of the Russian Empire. From Berne, and later from Zurich where he settled in 1915, he was to devote himself to fostering these ideas, with the implicit assistance of the Central Powers.

Lenin's years in Switzerland were hard years for him. In many letters he complained of having to confront a very harsh existence with very few resources. Many historians have adopted Krupskaya's assertions about these years of poverty in which Lenin is supposed to have been tormented by the hope of finding literary commissions to earn a subsistence. Letters sent to Gorky and Alexander Shlyapnikov were pleas for help.[9] However, Nikolai Valentinov, whose research on the couple's finances was very thorough, was far from accepting this position. In opposition to it, he quotes many letters from Lenin thanking his sisters for various transfers of funds, and he notes that, just before the war, Krupskaya had received an inheritance from an aunt in Novocherkassk. Dmitri Volkogonov, who carefully explored the archives dealing with Lenin's financial affairs, also maintained that the material difficulties about which he complained during the war were purely relative. No doubt, in 1915 and 1916, the death of his mother and the disorganization of the party in Russia may have caused temporary difficulties. But his lamentations at the time are better explained by discouragement than by lack of money.

He was consumed with impatience, while events were slow to take the direction that he advocated. In Russia itself, the patriotic fervor of 1914 had made him into an outcast. and the major defeats of 1915 did not lead, as he had hoped, to civil war. The very duration of the war, which went on month after month, year after year, was a surprise to him. During the war, he devoted a good deal of time to writing, and he produced major works, including, *Imperialism, the Highest Stage of Capitalism.* He wrote articles, but *Pravda* was banned, and he felt the lack of that privileged rostrum for publication. Above all, in his exile, he was solitary, practically cut off from the socialist movement in Russia. Even in Switzerland, where his revolutionary compatriots were legion, his extreme positions on the war alienated many of them. In Russia, the situation was even worse: The deputies who had been arrested, with Kamenev at their head, were tried for "high treason" and sent to Siberia, where they joined Sverdlov, Stalin, and Ordzhonikidze, who had been sentenced to exile before the war. The first consequence of these repressive measures was that the Bolshevik organization and the Russian Bureau of the Party had practically ceased to exist. It was not until 1916 that Shlyapnikov returned to Russia, undertook a reorganization of the dismantled Party, and became Lenin's liaison.

In her memoirs Krupskaya recounts how the isolation in which her husband lived in Switzerland in this period demoralized him. Furthermore, the years in Berne and Zurich were years of private sorrows. The death of Krupskaya's mother, which affected Lenin only indirectly, was followed in 1916 by that of his own mother, to whom he had always been very close and whom he had not seen for years. Soon after this very affecting event, his sister Anna Ulyanova-Elizarova was arrested in Russia. He learned of it from a coded message from his brother-in-law and reacted very strongly; not only did he feel affection for her, but she also was indispensable to him despite what he considered her lack of political training. She had been his courier under the pseudonym of "James." With his mother dead and his sister arrested (although for only a short time), all the ties to the family past to which he was so attached were unraveling.

The death of his mother-in-law also had practical consequences for the life of the couple. Nadezhda Krupskaya had never shown any interest in housekeeping. Her mother had always been the one to make sure they were comfortable. She did have the help of a servant, but with Elizaveta Vasilievna gone, there was no one to give the servant the necessary instructions. This probably explains why the Zurich apartment and Lenin's rather shabby clothing at the time produced a deplorable impression on some visitors. Inessa Armand was sometimes in Switzerland, where she went on vacation with the couple, a habit that persisted, and sometimes in Paris. Lenin's correspondence with her during those years was substantial (only Hanetsky received as many letters), but her absence also weighed on him. There remained, although it was tenuous, sporadic, and discouraging, political activity.

REBUILDING AN INTERNATIONAL

The inability of the major European Socialist figures to stand up against the war had shattered those who continued to lay claim to genuine internationalism. They were haunted by the idea of lifting the International from its failure and rebuilding an organization that would take up the torch that had fallen in July 1914.[10] The initiative came from Swiss and Italian socialists who began to consider ways of reassembling the fragments of the International as early as September and had a secret discussion of the subject in Lugano. Their plan had the support of Clara Zetkin who, although despairing at the near-disappearance of the movement to which she had devoted her life, had the idea of beginning by organizing a meeting of Socialist women. The result was the Berne meeting in the spring of 1915, with the participation of Krupskaya, Zinoviev's wife Lilina, and a few less well-known Bolsheviks.

Concealed behind them, Lenin undertook to change this pacifist meeting into a movement in the service of his ideas. The conference had prepared a manifesto with a moderate tone, addressed to women and saying in substance: "Women workers of all countries at war, join together!" Lenin's collaborators or spokeswomen attempted to replace it by or add to it a radical resolution weakening the impact of the manifesto that had already been drafted. The resolution of the Bolshevik women (clearly Lenin's handiwork) called for a break with "all" the "treacherous" Socialist and workers' parties and the immediate establishment of a new International, and it concluded with a call for the transformation of the war into a civil war.

The delegates to the Berne meeting who were not Bolsheviks could not accept a resolution of this kind. They did not want to alienate the existing parties but rather intended to pressure them to adopt a pacifist position. They were convinced that all was not yet lost, even though the war was already in full swing, if they were to address the masses. The slogan that Lenin wanted to impose on them—"Long live the Third International!"—was foreign to their way of thinking. Under his urging, the Bolshevik delegates adopted for themselves the intransigent attitude that was habitual to him. Clara Zetkin implored them to withdraw a resolution that would weaken the common position. In the face of their refusal of any discussion, she appealed to Lenin, and, after prolonged negotiations that almost killed her (she had a heart condition), she finally extracted a compromise from him. The Bolsheviks would sign the common resolution, but their own resolution would be included in the final report.

If Lenin in the end decided not to cut off all ties, this was because he had already sensed a strategy likely to lead to the triumph of his ideas. A few weeks later, a new opportunity presented itself. Also in Berne, Socialist youth organizations were meeting in the wake of the women's congress. Lenin hastened to provide the young Bolsheviks with the resolution that had just been presented by Krupskaya and Lilina, and a similar battle took place, this time leading to a deadlock.

Lenin soon renewed his efforts, this time without calling on intermediaries. On September 5, 1915, the Italian Socialists finally carried out the plan they had been nurturing for a year, that of summoning an international antiwar Socialist conference. To the Swiss village of Zimmerwald came delegates from Russia, Germany, Poland, France, Italy, Hungary, Holland, and more. The delegates to the conference demonstrated great courage by attending, because contacts with representatives of an enemy country in wartime were obviously considered acts of treason. Many of them had come to Switzerland clandestinely, and they took it out on Lenin because, as a resident of the country, he ran no risks. For that reason they thought his virulence entirely out of place.

Two groups were the focus of attention at Zimmerwald, because the future of the International would depend on their conduct. On the one hand, the French and German delegates whose countries were at war declared at the outset: "This war is not ours." And they confirmed their intention to work for a "peace without annexation," the only way, they thought, to soothe future national hatreds. These delegates–the Germans Hofman and Georg Lebedour, and the French Alfred Merrheim and Borderon–were wildly applauded, because the delegates listening to them found hope for the rebirth of the International. The second group, the Russians, had a very different effect. The Russian delegation was not homogeneous; it contained Bolsheviks, Mensheviks, and SRs. But Lenin had a number of supporters among them that was not negligible. In the course of the debates, it became clear that he had the support of eight of the thirty-eight delegates, including Fritz Platten, the secretary of the Swiss Social Democratic Party. Then aged thirty-two, Platten had been a locksmith and a draftsman and during the war, fascinated by Lenin's speeches, had become one of his followers. After 1917 he was one of the founders of the Comintern and of the Swiss Communist Party.

During these difficult years for Lenin, the arrival of new disciples was of great comfort. At Zimmerwald he dismissed the ideas that had been accepted at the Berne conferences; against the resolutions in favor of peace supported by the majority of the delegates, he attempted to set out his own program: a break with the Second International, the immediate creation of a new body for the working class, and the promotion of radical slogans, in particular a call for universal civil war. In the minority, he was not included in the executive setup in Berne at the conclusion of the conference, under the name of the International Socialist Commission; its members were two Italians, Odino Morgari and Angelica Balabanov, and two Swiss, Robert Grimm and Charles Naine. But even though he had had no influence on the manifesto that had been passed unanimously (he himself voted for it reluctantly), Lenin drew some satisfaction from the conference, because he had been able to count the number of his supporters, who were identified as the "Zimmerwald Left." This group produced a more radical declaration than the general manifesto although it did not go so far as to call for general insurrection, as Lenin had asked.

The opportunity to go further with his group was provided in April 1916 at the Kienthal conference, a continuation of the Zimmerwald meeting. The political climate inside the Socialist delegations was already different from that of 1915, which explains the progress of his position. Indeed, there had been no response to the appeals for peace and the continuation of the war cruelly emphasized the isolation of the Socialists. Moreover, in certain countries, particularly in France and Germany, the "Zimmerwaldists" were a minority among the Socialists carried away by patriotism. For example, in Germany, the Social Democrats were divided over the question of war credits, and Liebknecht, spokesman for the Zimmerwaldists, was expelled from his parliamentary group. With the gulf growing inside the movement, those who were agitating for peace were inclined to go on the offensive.

Forty-three delegates attended the Kienthal conference; this time Lenin was at the head of a larger group of supporters than at Zimmerwald, able to secure twelve votes for his resolution. Throughout the conference, he was seconded by his two lieutenants, Zinoviev and Radek, who had already been very active at Zimmerwald. In 1915 he and Zinoviev had published some of their articles in a volume entitled *Socialism and the War*. Then he had devoted himself to organizing the Zimmerwald Left and providing it with propaganda. At Kienthal, Zinoviev presented himself as a delegate from Latvia, which was admissible because Latvia was part of the empire. As for Radek, who was still a militant in the ranks of German Social Democracy, he was at the same time beginning to become a part of the Bolshevik faction and, along with Paul Levi, was even attempting to create a pro-Bolshevik faction in the German workers' movement.

As at Zimmerwald, Lenin presented a radical resolution which called on the working class then in uniform to "lay down their arms and turn them against the common enemy, the capitalist governments." The majority resolution, though rejecting such a radical appeal, went further than it had the year before. Drawing the conclusions from a seemingly endless war, it agreed that pacifism was indeed not enough and that it had to be supplemented with "the struggle for socialism."

The resolution thus went in the direction advocated by Lenin. He was of course defeated on the point for which he had constantly argued, a break with the Second International. But on this issue as well, the delegates moved closer to him by expressing severe condemnation and denouncing the inability of the International to defend the cause of peace, that is, the cause of the proletariat. Although Lenin's radical resolution received only twelve votes, the majority of participants were no longer very far from sharing his views. They all recognized that his contribution to the development of the international Socialist movement was very important, if not decisive. The idea of a Third International was already taking shape in the minds of the delegates.

REFLECTIONS ON IMPERIALISM

Although the Zimmerwald and Kienthal conferences had for a time mobilized Lenin and given him the opportunity to exercise his authority over the Socialist movement, they had not been enough to overcome his sense of isolation. His real refuge in these hard years lay in intellectual work. The 1914 war forced him to deepen his thinking in an area in which he had glimpsed his disagreement with a majority of the Second International as early as 1907, that is, the problem of colonial exploitation. In commenting on the work of the Stuttgart congress in that year, Lenin had begun to investigate the link between colonization and the revolutionary weakness of the European proletariat.

Many Socialists in the early twentieth century were aware of the beneficial effects of colonial policy on the material conditions of European workers, who might thereby feel less inclined to think of revolution as a means of escaping from their fate. Kautsky, Luxemburg, and Rudolf Hilferding had clearly seen and articulated the problem, and raised the question of how to bring it to an end.[11] It had been the subject of much debate at Stuttgart, and Lenin had written at the time: "Thus in certain countries the material and economic basis is created for the contamination of the proletariat by colonial chauvinism."[12]

For several years he hesitated about the tactics to be adopted in order to isolate the proletariat from colonialist contagion, but like his socialist colleagues, he remained convinced that the solution would come from the Western proletariat. The 1914 war opened a new phase in his thinking, because the differences among Socialist reactions to the war, he said, raised a question which was impossible to avoid: Were these opposing attitudes not linked to the status of the Socialists' respective states? Lenin recalled that at Stuttgart there had been divisions on the colonial problem between Socialist parties from the powers possessing an empire, not very inclined to challenge the colonial phenomenon, and those from states without colonies, who were much more critical of colonization. In 1914 Lenin witnessed the collapse of Social Democracy in countries where it was strong, enjoying a quasi-official status, all of which held vast possessions (Germany, France, Belgium); and he contrasted that with the strength of Russian Socialism, even though it was quasi-clandestine, and its determination to preserve the peace. Of course Russia also had colonies, but the nature of the Russian Empire was very different from that of the other European empires. It was characterized by territorial "continuity," the intermingling of populations, and, above all, from 1905 on, the growth of the revolutionary movement on its colonial peripheries. Lenin attempted to integrate these disparate phenomena into a coherent whole and concluded that imperialism provided an explanation for the crisis through which European socialism was passing.

This effort at theoretical analysis to which Lenin devoted the bulk of his time, patiently gathering material in Swiss libraries, produced two works, both of which were published in 1916. *Imperialism, the Highest Stage of Capitalism*[13] is the result of a considerable work of documentation, the elements of which are contained in what constitutes perhaps one of the most interesting aspects of Lenin's work and his method, the *Notebooks on Imperialism.*[14] Twenty-two notebooks dated 1915 and 1916 contain a summary of his reading in preparation for the writing of his work and demonstrate a vigorous method based on the determination not to miss any available source of information. This is the work that led to *imperialism.* No doubt, it can be noted that the economic analysis, based on the work of Hilferding and J. A. Hobson, provides nothing new. But Lenin's ambition was both theoretical and tactical, or it amounted to providing a theoretical basis for the tactics that he advocated. Wishing to supply an explanation for the overall development that he had observed in the world since the beginning of the century, he systematically developed the idea that he had sketched out in 1907, that is, that the colonial phenomenon explained the corruption of the Western proletariat. Colonial profits, he wrote, had allowed the bourgeoisie to foster the "opportunist," that is, moderate and reformist, tendencies of the working class. By arguing in this way, Lenin was in agreement with his vision of a proletariat about which he had been asserting since *What Is to Be Done?:* that it had no innate class consciousness, but that it favored trade unionism to the extent that it had an innate sense of its immediate interests. In those circumstances how could it not be corrupted by colonialism, which had the capacity to improve its condition?

But, while Lenin unmasked and denounced the corrupting action of colonialism on the Western working class, when he looked at the colonized masses, he detected reverse consequences. Revolted by a domination from which they could expect no benefit, these masses sought salvation in national action. The development of national feelings in the colonial context was for Lenin the positive effect of imperialism. In 1916 he asserted that the national struggle against imperialism was a fundamental component of the general struggle of the proletariat for its emancipation. The struggle for national liberation in the colonies weakened the colonial governments and gave new strength to the proletariat. *Imperialism, the Highest Stage of Capitalism* was not published in Petrograd until 1917, but the positions it took were the basis for a dispute with Rosa Luxemburg in 1916.

In that year, angered by Lenin's ideas on the national question, she published under the pseudonym of Junius, *The Crisis of German Social Democracy*, in which she forcefully attacked the Bolshevik leader and defended against him a Eurocentric vision of the revolution. "It is only from Europe," she wrote, "only from the oldest capitalist countries that can come, when the time is ripe, the signal for the social revolution that will free mankind. Only English, French, Belgian, German, Russian, and Italian workers, all together, can lead the army of the exploited and enslaved of the five continents." To be sure, herself from the empire of the czars, Rosa Luxemburg did not leave the Russian workers out of her list. Lenin could not accept this underestimate of the dominated countries, or of those who were late in industrializing. His answer to Luxemburg was stinging: "National wars against the imperialist powers," he wrote, "are inevitable, progressive, and revolutionary."

These words come from "The Junius Pamphlet," dated July 1916.[15] In it he reasserted his belief in the usefulness for the European revolution of movements agitating the colonial world. The ideas he then developed about the links between European revolution and national agitation in the colonies in essence came from his analysis of a question that was decisive for Russia, the national movements and the place that the workers' movement should give them in its strategy. On this question Lenin's thinking was evolving very quickly, and the years of solitude made it possible for him to produce an original work that broke with the tradition of the workers' movement.

NATION AND REVOLUTION

The national question was not an unprecedented concern for Socialists. Although Marx and Engels had only been moderately interested in it, carefully analyzing the concrete problems posed by nations, but not developing a theory of nations as such, their successors confronted the problem very early on. This was especially true of those who lived in or came from multinational empires. At the turn of the century, Kautsky (born Czech, an Austrian citizen living in Germany), Karl Renner, and Otto Bauer devoted a good deal of their time to attempting to understand the national phenomenon and to define its relationship to revolutionary dynamics. Austro-Marxism, the name given to this current of thought, involved both recognition of the national phenomenon, of the "nation" as a permanent category of history, and the desire to make it coexist with proletarian internationalism.

The success of Austro-Marxism in Russia explains the fact that Russian Social Democrats very early came to grips with the problem, less in theoretical terms than for the purpose of working out a strategic response. Like the Mensheviks, Lenin accepted from the outset the principle of national self-determination, but explained that the expression in fact referred to "self-determination of the proletariat."

In his writings on this question up to 1912, he limited himself to these strategic concerns. But even before the war, it seemed to him necessary to pursue the analysis further. In August 1912, at the Menshevik conference in Vienna, known as the "liquidators'" conference, a committee made up of Trotsky, Martov, and Berg (representing the Bund) was charged with developing a program on the future of the national minorities. Because the majority of the Caucasians and Bundists were close to the Mensheviks, the latter were obliged to pay attention to their demands. This was all the more the case because the Socialist Revolutionary Party was a dangerous rival to all Social Democrats in this area. Since 1905 it had been gradually developing a national theory that recognized the importance of the problem and made the right to self-determination an integral part of its program. The Mensheviks understood that if they did less than the SRs, they risked desertion to them of the Jewish and Caucasian Socialist battalions.

In the Duma in December 1912, Georgian Deputy Akaki Chenkeli called for the creation of "institutions necessary for the development of each nation." In doing so he deliberately violated party discipline. This was more than Lenin could tolerate, and he demanded that the RSDLP reprimand Chenkeli and; more important, silence supporters of such ideas.

However, Lenin never stopped at simple administrative measures. Polemics, in his view, were the best weapons for fighting against ideas that he rejected. For this reason, in 1913, with Stalin at hand in Cracow, he mobilized for a crusade against the Caucasians, the Bundists, and anyone who might be tempted to follow their example.

Lenin did not resign himself to having others respond in his place to what he considered a dangerous heresy, and, what is more, a threat to the unity and discipline of the workers' movement. He thought about the most appropriate response until 1914,[16] and then, between February and May, drafted *The Right of Nations to Self-Determination.*[17] In this work, and in all the shorter ones that he devoted to the problem during the same period, he rejected the idea that the struggle for self-determination turned the masses away from the struggle for revolution. Far from accepting the postulate that the national struggle was a matter for the bourgeoisie, he asserted that it was on the contrary the duty of the proletariat. It was indeed a matter of struggling against a form of oppression, and the proletariat was by nature the opponent of all forms of oppression. In this context Lenin stressed the necessity of recognizing the principle of self-determination in the revolution and the effect that this legitimation of national struggles would have on the development of internationalist consciousness. Against his opponents on the left, such as Rosa Luxemburg, he linked internationalism with recognition of national aspirations by relying on three arguments.

First, accepting the necessity for self-determination meant resolving the difficulties of a multinational state by pacifying the relationships among the various communities, particularly among their proletarian elements, and hence within the party. This recognition freed the party from national resentments and placed it in a better position to claim to represent the interests of "all" workers.

Second, in the prerevolutionary period, this program would ensure to the working class and its party the cooperation of nonproletarian national movements, which would strengthen the party and speed up the course of the revolution.

Finally, it was a way of combating nationalism and educating the proletariat in an internationalist spirit. The corollary of self-determination was national equality, of which neither the proletarians of the oppressing power nor those of the oppressed power had a natural awareness. For Lenin this principle therefore had a pedagogical virtue. His determination in defending it was both strategic and based on an internationalist concern. Since the Stuttgart congress, he had been haunted by the awareness of the chauvinism animating the proletariat of the dominant nations and had been dreading its effects on the future.

At first sight Lenin's positions seem close to those held by Otto Bauer.[18] In reality he refused to ratify the national phenomenon in the manner of Bauer. In particular he rejected recognition of the "national culture" at the heart of Bauer's argument. For Lenin the concept was created by the bourgeoisie, because national culture was always the culture of the ruling class. The only culture that he found acceptable was the "international culture of the worldwide workers' movement."[19] But Lenin was not very precise in defining the culture of the workers' movement. Unlike Stalin, who had emphasized these cultural aspects in his 1913 article, he gave little room to such questions in his thinking, although he recognized in passing that a culture could not exist independently of national forms, first of all a language. Relations among nations were of interest to him primarily in economic and ideological contexts. Although he discussed the problem of national culture, he did so in order to condemn the idea of the cultural autonomy of national groups that was cherished by the Caucasians. Lenin's silences in this area indicate the difficulty he had in considering the nation as a real historical category; while making certain allowances for it, he tried to keep it within a restricted and temporary compass and to neutralize its political content by contrasting it with the international culture of the proletariat.

Then what might be the outcome of a struggle for self-determination? Lenin could see only two possibilities: full and total adhesion to a unitary proletarian state as soon as the proletariat had won out or else separation. He considered the second possibility rather as a solution to the national problem in the pre-revolutionary stage. In that case it would have the effect of weakening the existing state and opening the way to revolution. Once the revolution had taken place, Lenin could not imagine that the union of all the proletarians of the various national groups would not take place. The pedagogical slogan of self-determination, adopted by the workers' movement in the period of revolutionary struggle, would necessarily have sufficiently changed consciousness for national differences subsequently to dissolve, so that all that would remain would be the unity of proletarian consciousness. Under any circumstances Lenin rejected the intermediate solutions of autonomy or federalism.

This internationalist pedagogy led him from the very beginning of the war to assert the necessity of dismantling the Russian Empire.[20] On November 29, 1914, he returned to the question in an article on the national pride of the Great Russians.[21] Lenin's desire to support national struggles in the Russian Empire then came up against the convictions of many socialists who thought that, by his appeal to national sentiments, he was weakening the workers' movement as a whole. After Rosa Luxemburg and the Polish left, Nikolai Bukharin, Georgy Pyatakov, Yevgenya Bosh, and finally Radek[22] came out against this position, whose first effect, they said, was to divide the proletariat and divert it from the only goal it should pursue, the revolution. Lenin replied in a series of polemical articles which, for two years, merely repeated his views. In 1916 he published a radically innovative work, "Socialist Revolution and the Right of Nations to Self-Determination."[23] For the first time, a global vision of the national phenomenon could be seen in Lenin's thinking. He distinguished among three situations:

- First, in the advanced capitalist countries (Western Europe and the United States), progressive bourgeois national movements had completed their task, and integration had been accomplished.
- Second, in the two multinational European empires, the national struggle was in progress. The proletariat could only play its role in that struggle and win if it defended the right of nations to self-determination.
- Finally, in the colonial and semicolonial world, with a population of one billion, bourgeois democratic movements barely existed. Socialists had to take the lead in struggle, demand the immediate end of colonization, and support all rebellions, if necessary with revolutionary war.

With this work Lenin finally found himself in a comfortable position with respect to his colleagues. He was defending a coherent point of view which linked the national problem to imperialism and in which the revolutionary struggle quite naturally integrated the stage of the struggle for self-determination. Moreover, at a time when national agitation was growing in importance everywhere, and not only inside the Russian Empire, this global vision had the virtue of concealing the historically backward and specific character of Russia and conferring on it a central place in the revolutionary movement.

In appearance Lenin granted a substantial place to the national phenomenon in his vision of history in the period of revolutionary struggles. But the appearance concealed an entirely different reality. In fact he was intent on describing the "practical" conditions in which the right to self-determination would be exercised, and that description pointed principally to the limits on that right. To be sure he wrote that the right extended as far as separation and that it was to be exercised by means of popular vote, but the right was not unlimited. It came up against geographic constraints. For example, he wrote, in Russia it could apply only to national minorities located on the periphery, not to those enclosed within Russian territory.

The second limit concerned the body that would make the decision. It was up to the party to decide whether and when the right could be exercised. It was the supreme decision-making body because it was the consciousness of the masses. It had to decide each case "by adopting the point of view of the interests of the general development of society and of the interests of the proletariat's class struggle for socialism."[24] Moreover, Lenin refrained from specifying which party organs would in the end make these decisions, according to what criteria of judgment, and taking into account which national aspirations. Finally, he clearly stated that union was permanent after the revolution but that separation was always subject to revocation. This fragility of the "right to divorce" was all the more evident because, for him, the context for the life of a postrevolutionary society was by definition a large centralized state. Even before the revolution, a state of that kind might appear to be the most propitious setting for the development of class struggle; but it was definitely necessary after the revolution.

Thus, although Lenin's analysis of the respective struggles of the proletariat and the national minorities was very thorough in 1916, his principal purpose, in the light of the war and the collapse of the International when faced with the rise of nationalist feeling, was to abolish the opposition between the two categories of aspiration, to reconcile them, and thereby to propose in advance solutions that would be applied after the revolution.

Л Л Л

For Lenin the war years as a whole were certainly difficult, solitary, and, in appearance, full of despair. Between 1916 and 1917, he had come into conflict with the majority of the International, which had already considered him an unscrupulous agitator before the war. Also, despite the relative success of the Kienthal conference, he had been rejected by the Socialist left, extremely irritated by his insistence on analyzing and integrating the national phenomenon.

For those who had been close to him in exile during the period of building the party—Martov, Trotsky, Bogdanov, Krasin, among many others—he had become a dangerous man, hungry for power, and yet, in their view, one who had already failed irreversibly. For many of his compatriots, he was purely and simply a traitor who favored a position that was unacceptable until 1917, the defeat of his country. For the major figures of European Socialism, his leftism was in contradiction with the general development of the workers' movement. Finally, for those on the left, such as Rosa Luxemburg, who might have rallied to him, his arguments on nationalism made him a reformist.

No one could see, during these years when he was subject to general opprobrium, that Lenin was in the process of finding answers to all the questions that had long troubled him: How could he reconcile his revolutionary will with the particular situation of a multiethnic and backward Russia? How could the revolutionary spark be ignited in Russia? How could his party, which was so much in the minority, be made into an instrument for the seizure of power? It was by developing a national strategy for the revolution, by setting the nation at the heart of the revolutionary process, that he thought he could succeed. Early in the century, he had forged the tool of his revolutionary will. In the war years that were so discouraging and at first sight so sterile, he began to glimpse a national strategy capable of speeding up the course of the revolution. Because this strategy seemed to be reformist rather than revolutionary, he was thought to have been converted to the ideas of Otto Bauer. In fact, on the heart of the problem, he was on the side of Rosa Luxemburg, convinced that only the proletarian revolution counted. But his analyses and his instincts both told him that, with Russia's national minorities, he held a formidable lever with which to carry out the revolution. To the inventor of the party was then joined the strategist who, within a few months, would have the opportunity to put his intuition to work. He had grasped the possibility that Russia's weakness, its backwardness, which was principally a backwardness in integrating its national minorities, might very well in the end transform it into the vanguard of the revolution.

In 1905 Lenin had had a remarkable intuition: he had understood that an unsuccessful war could unleash a revolution. The interminable First World War was another source of inspiration for him, entirely unrelated to Marxism; he then sensed that the use of national impulses might very well become the privileged instrument for the global victory of the proletariat.

Chapter Eight

ALL POWER TO THE SOVIETS (FEBRUARY – OCTOBER 1917)

"NOT ONE PARTY WAS PREPARING FOR THE GREAT UPHEAVAL. Everyone was dreaming, ruminating, full of foreboding, feeling his way. . . . Revolution–highly improbable! Revolution!–everyone knew this was only a dream–a dream of generations and of long laborious decades. Without believing the girls, I repeated after them mechanically: 'Yes, the beginning of the revolution.'"[1]

This is how Nikolai Nikolaievich Himmer, better known by the name Sukhanov, a political journalist and economist with ties to the Socialist movement, described his reaction in Petrograd on February 21, 1917, when a young typist working in the next office told him that the Russian political system had collapsed. His incredulity might seem surprising in light of the fact that he was very well informed, at the center of the capital's political life, and in contact with the entire opposition. But it is easier to understand Sukhanov if we remember that no one in the late winter of 1917 had really thought of preparing for the revolution.

Russia's situation was certainly disastrous. The war was sweeping along its endless procession of dead, wounded, and prisoners, and misery was spreading throughout the country. The scorched earth policy followed by the imperial armies–full of the memory of the effective opposition to Napoleon–had had contrary effects in the world war: A swarm of deserters, civilians, and the wounded was streaming down the roads leading to the center of Russia and invading cities where nothing was ready to deal with refugees.

These masses felt abandoned by a regime that had been able neither to prevent military defeats nor to prepare measures capable of relieving their suffering. Accumulated resentment and the problems posed in the cities by the influx of newcomers provoked discontent on the point of turning into rebellion.

The economic situation was not much better. The conversion of industry to deal with military requirements had certainly made it possible to speed up the manufacture of equipment needed for defense. But it had been achieved at the expense of an almost complete cessation of the production of consumer goods, the shortage of which affected prices. The peasantry, in particular, could buy nothing in exchange for what it sold, and quite naturally tended to consume their local harvests or to work less. The mobilization that had taken peasants from the land also helped to reduce production. Like industrial prices, agricultural prices climbed, while wages remained relatively stable. Shortages and the decline in the standard of living affected not only the working-class population but also the social strata that had been relatively protected until then, the middle classes and bureaucrats. Although those classes had held back from the revolutionary movement in 1905, their growing material difficulties would impel them to take part in 1917.

The muffled but growing discontent of both cities and countryside was joined by another source of difficulty for the Russian regime, the crisis of the empire, which had still been imperceptible in 1905. At the very beginning of the war, Poland, Lithuania, and Galicia had been invaded by the armies of the Central Powers, and their populations had been encouraged to rebel against Russia in the name of their national feelings. In 1915 and 1916, Germany played the card of the disintegration of the empire of the czars, establishing a Finnish army to fight Russian troops, proclaiming the independence of Poland (the Russian part alone, of course), and setting up Polish contingents in the hope of saving its own troops on the Eastern Front. Above all, it used the Union of Nationalities, created by neutrals during the war, to bring together émigrés from the national minorities of the Russian Empire and encourage them to propose programs calling for national independence.[2] This effort, whose impact was not at first recognized by the Russian authorities, helped to develop a nationalist current in Poland, the Baltic States, and Ukraine that was only waiting to show itself. Even in distant Central Asia, this kind of propaganda led to a rebellion of nomad tribes in 1916, which immediately removed part of the region from czarist control. As a Soviet specialist in Turkestan was to write later, "Here, 1917 and the end of the empire began in 1916."[3]

Finally, at the same time the regime was paying the price for what had allowed it to accomplish fantastic economic progress in the course of the preceding three decades: the structure of Russian capitalism. Foreign capital had played a decisive role in the development of Russia. But, beginning in 1915, French and English capitalists, the principal investors, were troubled by Russian military disasters and persistent rumors of a separate peace, given some credibility by the national origin of the empress, a German princess. The idea took root that a change of regime might be a better guarantee for investments in Russia than a vacillating monarchy. The Russian liberal bourgeoisie was thinking along similar lines. As for the people, it suspected the regime of paying with Russian blood for a development policy based on foreign loans. Were the military sacrifices accepted by the empire in order to contain the German army on the Eastern Front not so many concessions to implacable creditors?

Confronted with rising discontent and suspicion, the regime dissolved in short order. Military and civilian leaders blamed one another for the disaster. The emperor was cloistered at military headquarters, and the empress, ever more unpopular, chose government ministers, changing them frequently, thereby creating in the society the disturbing feeling that it was now governed by nothing but the fantasies of an unbalanced woman.

Urgent decisions that no one in government was making were dealt with by private initiatives. The Red Cross and aid organizations that sprang up spontaneously in the cities tried to resolve the problems of the refugees, the wounded, and everyone who asked for help. The same thing was true of the disorganized economy, which had left the inhabitants of the cities on their own. In this area as well, committees established by people of good will were created to deal with problems of food supply. Hence, in a near power vacuum and confronted with growing disorder, the Russian population went through an apprenticeship in self-management and self-government. This was a quasi-revolutionary situation of which no one was really aware, neither those involved, nor the regime, nor the opposition, and even less those living in exile.

Sukhanov's surprise at the proclamation of the revolution thus had no equal but the surprise of Lenin.

THE BIRTH OF REVOLUTIONARY POWER

The February Revolution began in Petrograd (the name given to Saint Petersburg at the beginning of the war to remove the Germanic flavor of its name) and took only six days to eliminate the monarchy. This quick and easy revolution contained many surprising aspects: the victory of a proletariat on its own, without leaders, in a well-defended capital; the immediate spread of the revolution through an enormous country; and the disappearance of the monarchy while the political class was still discussing its transformation. The unfolding of events makes it possible to understand how Russia had reached that point.

Petrograd could be defended against riots. The lesson of 1905 had been learned by the regime. The capital had a garrison of one hundred sixty thousand men and a plan for the repression of rebellion was stored in its governor's files. On February 23, ninety thousand people (striking textile and metal workers and women) assembled for a demonstration against material hardships and because it was International Women's Day. Work stoppages and processions were spontaneous expressions of the popular discontent that had been increased by the shortages and strikes which had proliferated throughout the winter. But no party or leader had thought it necessary to guide or control these masses. At the end of a day of relatively moderate demonstrations (calls for bread and peace), the participants returned home, convinced that repression would come down on the movement. Nothing of the kind happened. The regime, despite being well prepared for events of the kind, did not react. And the demonstrators, flabbergasted by the passivity of the authorities, took to the streets again on the next day, more sure of themselves and more aggressive.

Their numbers increased; petit bourgeois and students joined them; and revolutionary songs began to be heard, punctuated with political slogans taking over from economic demands. Gradually all of Petrograd was taken up by the movement, and the terrified government only then decided that the troops should intervene. But it was only on February 26, three days after the beginning of the demonstrations, that the crowd and the army came face to face and orders to disperse were replaced by firing. The people called on the army to join them. So powerful was the invitation that the following day one regiment after another swung into insurrection. The most prestigious among them joined the mutiny. Workers seized the weapons of the soldiers that had joined their camp and were finally in a position to defend themselves. They opened the prison gates and freed their leaders—themselves mere workers—who had been arrested two days earlier. On February 27, the regime no longer existed, and another one had to be invented. The insurrection spread throughout the country.

For lack of leaders on whom to confer power, the crowd turned to the Duma that the czar had just dissolved. Challenging that decision, the Duma immediately elected a Temporary Committee, containing representatives from all parties except the right. The Duma leaders assembled in this committee sought to save the political system by adjusting it; they called on the czar to allow them to act. But Nicholas II, unaware of the magnitude of the revolution, remained deaf to these plans, wanted to use force, and found himself isolated. After attempting to save the system by imposing a constitutional monarchy on the czar, Rodzianko, president of the Duma Committee, finally dropped the czar and accepted his abdication. Nicholas renounced the throne in favor of his sick son, and then designated as his successor his brother Grand Duke Mikhail, who dared not accept without the agreement of a Constituent Assembly that did not exist. The monarchy subsequently disappeared without a fight on March 3, 1917.

Rodzianko's negotiations and the czar's hesitations had already been overtaken by a political reality that was changing from moment to moment. The Tauride Palace, seat of the Duma, was also the meeting place for the Soviet of workers' deputies which had just been set up under the presidency of Nikolai Chkheidze, assisted by Kerensky, son of Vladimir Ulyanov's protector, containing a majority of Mensheviks (Bogdanov, Lenin's friend until their break; Chkheidze; and Mikhail Skobelev), Menshevik sympathizers, internationalists, and a Bundist, among others.

The Duma Committee and the Soviet both located under the roof of the Tauride Palace give an indication of the unexpected character of this revolution. The Duma was the emanation of the liberal bourgeoisie that had associated itself with the popular movement in order to avoid sinking with the monarchy. The masses turned toward the Duma; the masses who had made the revolution handed power over to the Duma because they had no leaders on whom to confer it. No doubt the Soviet, which came into existence at the same time, was more representative of those masses. But had the Socialists dominating it not always repeated that the revolution must at first bring the bourgeoisie to power? By trusting in the bourgeoisie, the revolutionary crowd was faithfully following Socialist teaching. But, and here lay its great weakness, the liberal bourgeoisie was not the origin of the power that it held but the representative of forces that had given it authority and therefore considered themselves entitled to supervise and even direct it.

The Provisional Government that was set up by the Duma Committee and the Soviet Executive was headed by the former president of the Zemstvo Union, Prince Lvov, and contained some remarkable personalities: the historian Pavel Miliukov as minister of foreign affairs, Kerensky as minister of justice, and Alexander Guchkov as minister of war. This cabinet, on which the Soviet immediately imposed its conditions, was made up of a majority of liberals. Kerensky soon became the member most accepted by the people, who considered him a moderate Socialist who was also close to the Soviet. He had one foot in each body and in March 1917 seemed to be the rising star of revolutionary Russia.

The Provisional Government immediately had to define its position on the crucial problem of the continuation of the war. The position was all the more difficult to arrive at because the army had been disorganized by the revolution, by the famous "Order of the Day No. 1" which had established complete equality between officers and soldiers. The army no longer had rules of operation, and it was therefore difficult to see how it could continue to fight the war. How could a society that wanted peace be made to accept an interminable war?

By March 4, Foreign Minister Miliukov had presented a note to the Allies, declaring that his government was determined to respect the international obligations contracted by the former regime and that it would continue the war until the end. Russian war aims thus remained unchanged. The organ of the Soviet, *Izvestia*, published an article on March 14 which responded, in its way, to Miliukov's note. It was an appeal to the peoples of Europe to make peace, but it remained imprecise and urged no one to make a "shameful" peace.

When the Georgian Menshevik Irakli Tsereteli returned from exile, he suggested that the Soviet adopt a more precise position: Make war while simultaneously fighting for peace.[4] The slogan "Peace without Annexations or Indemnities" then became the program of the moderate left. Under the pressure of public opinion, Miliukov made the following declaration on March 27: "The aim of free Russia . . . is the establishment of lasting peace on the basis of the right of peoples to self-determination." Thus for a brief period of time, the Provisional Government and the Soviet seemed to share the same view of the goal to be reached. The return of Lenin shattered this ephemeral unity.

HOW TO GET BACK TO RUSSIA?

Sukhanov may have been surprised by the coming of the revolution, but the exiles were even more so. In Geneva, London, and New York where they had settled, they were far from imagining that the event they had dreamed of, which was always put off, would one day occur. In Zurich, where he was living at the time, Lenin paid close attention to the activities of the Swiss socialists, in whom he placed a good deal of hope. He gave lectures to watchmakers in La Chaux-de-Fonds, and he wrote articles; in a word, he envisaged everything but what happened in his own country. Suddenly he was told of the inconceivable, the end of czarism and the triumph of the revolution. He was so astounded that he rushed to get the Swiss newspapers to confirm the truth of the news he had just heard. From then on he was obsessed by a single idea: He had to return to Russia as soon as possible to take part in the revolution about which he still knew little, but for which he was already developing plans to shape its direction. His vision of the future took form as soon as he heard the news. In a meeting that took place in Zurich, Angelica Balabanov heard him hammering out with all the strength of his inner conviction: "Unless the Russian Revolution develops into a second and successful Paris Commune, reaction and war will suffocate it."[5] She went on to express her surprise: "I had been trained, like most Marxists, to expect the social revolution to be inaugurated in one of the highly industrialized, vanguard countries, and at the time Lenin's analysis of the Russian events seemed to me almost utopian."[6]

Lenin's principal preoccupation was to find a way to return to Russia. In order to do this, he would have to go through Sweden, and therefore go through either Allied or German territory. He first thought of asking for help from England, where he had many Socialist friends, but he soon understood that his defeatist ideas could only frighten the Allies for whom keeping Russia in the war was essential. He knew that they would have no reason to want him to return to Russia in order to advocate a separate peace or defeat, whereas the Provisional Government had from the outset declared its fidelity to the alliances that had been made. On the other hand, what made his return to Russia undesirable to the Allies had some attraction for Germany. Having considered and reconsidered all the possible solutions, he soon arrived at the conclusion that he would not be able to return to his country without appealing to Germany.

The thoughts that troubled him were shared by the leaders of the Central Powers. They had long hoped that a separate peace would make it possible for them to focus their entire war effort on the Western Front. But by 1916 they had had to give up that illusion. First the tsar, and then the Provisional Government made it clear that they would not sign a treaty contrary to the commitments made before 1914. Lenin's ideas about the war were well known and attractive to the Central Powers because, in 1915, a strange figure, Alexander Helphand, known as Parvus, had presented them to the German foreign ministry.[7] At the time he prepared, as the German archives show, a memorandum/program entitled "Preparation for a General Strike in Russia," in which he referred to the defeatist view of Lenin (war ⇨ defeat ⇨ revolution). The plan seemed interesting enough to the German authorities for the secretary of the treasury to allocate "two million marks for revolutionary propaganda in Russia" on March 7, 1915.[8] To be sure Lenin had few direct contacts with Parvus before 1917, and he received nothing from the subsidies provided. But Parvus was then working with Hanetsky who was very close to Lenin. Lenin was in constant correspondence with Hanetsky, ignoring Trotsky's warnings about his ties to "Doctor" Parvus (a usurped academic title) whom he accused of being nothing but a "paid German agent."

In March 1917 Lenin's prejudices against this dubious figure suddenly disappeared. Any contact was acceptable for negotiating with Germany the right to cross its territory so that he could return to Russia. Martov, as impatient as he to return home, had come up with a rather similar plan that he thought likely to persuade the German authorities to help him. If they allowed Russian Socialists to go through Germany, when they arrived, the Russians would secure in exchange from the Provisional Government the release of a certain number of German and Austrian prisoners.[9] This plan did not interest Berlin, and it was rejected. The proposal would in fact have had no effect on the continuation of the war, whereas the presence of Lenin advocating the immediate cessation of hostilities and revolution would be a substantial contribution to German interests. This was the sense of statements from Gisbert von Romberg, the German consul in Berne, and from Parvus. They managed to persuade Berlin to accept Lenin's request, not Martov's. The motive behind the agreement that was reached was clearly the German intention to use Lenin to propagate defeatist ideas. The proof lies in a telegram emanating from the German foreign ministry: "His Imperial Majesty has decided this morning that the Russian revolutionaries will be transported through Germany and will be supplied with propaganda material so they are able to work in Russia."

The negotiations, in which the Swiss socialists Robert Grimm[10] and Fritz Platten participated, were directed by Lenin, but prudent as always, he was represented at every stage by Zinoviev. Lenin set as a condition that the train used would enjoy extraterritorial status, in order to avoid any accusation of cooperation with Germany. This demand, which gave rise to the legend of the "sealed train," was accepted. Germany also released substantial credits intended to finance pacifist and revolutionary propaganda and, thus equipped, Lenin was able to carry out his planned return.

The Bolsheviks left Zurich on March 27, 1917. Lenin and Krupskaya were accompanied by many of their loyal friends, with Inessa Armand in the first rank, and including Zinoviev and his family, Radek who was to discover Russia for the first time, and a few Bundists. Aware of the unfortunate impression that this journey organized and protected by the Germans risked creating among European socialists, Lenin had asked the French Zimmerwaldists to approve it publicly. The same request addressed to Romain Rolland was dismissed contemptuously. The departure from Zurich was dramatic; while supporters who had escorted him to the station intoned the *Internationale,* hostile demonstrators called the travelers traitors.

Later a second train following the same route would bring to Russia Martov and exiles who were close to him: Axelrod, Balabanov, Lunacharsky, Grimm, and Grigory Sokolnikov. The last two joined the Bolsheviks as soon as they arrived.[11]

At this point it is necessary to point out that none of the parties involved in the affair was deceived about the terms of the bargain. For the German authorities, Lenin was a trump card that they could use to disorganize the Russian regime. In order to provoke revolution, he was going to advocate peace and foster the disintegration of the army. As for the rest, the future would decide. In

1917 Germany had a pressing need to concentrate its forces on the Western Front. The United States was about to enter the war, and Germany had to be in a position to win the war as soon as possible, or at least to secure some decisive victories, which was unlikely as long as the conflict continued on two fronts. Lenin, for his part, was clear about the reasons for the interest and assistance with which Germany had suddenly provided him. He knew that without this help (including financial help) he would be able to do nothing, neither return to Russia, nor provide his party with the resources necessary to seize power. And, as Angelica Balabanov showed, the seizure of power was his only goal.

On his return he was forced to recognize that his party was far from sharing his views.

THE APRIL THESES

Lenin's return to Petrograd was apparently triumphant. Exiles had been returning for weeks, all of them welcomed by large delegations from the Provisional Government and the Soviet celebrating their arrival. Lenin's reception was extraordinary. In his detailed account, Sukhanov writes: "The Bolsheviks, who shone at organization, and always aimed at emphasizing externals and putting on a good show, had dispensed with any superfluous modesty and were plainly preparing a real triumphal entry."[12] Among the reasons for the Bolshevik effort to give this welcoming committee unusual splendor, Sukhanov points out the need to erase the negative effect of the return through Germany and to prevent a campaign of criticism that was already getting underway.

Military music, banners of all sorts, several delegations, nothing was lacking that day at the Finland Station, and it might have been thought that the usual ceremony would take place without a hitch. When the train pulled in, Lenin was the first to get off. He faced Chkheidze, who gave the welcoming speech "in the name of the Petersburg Soviet" of which he was the president, "and of the whole revolution," and added: "[W]e think that the principal task of the revolutionary democracy is now the defense of the revolution from any encroachments either from within or from without. We consider that what this goal requires is not disunion, but the closing of the democratic ranks. We hope you will pursue these goals together with us."[13] During this speech Lenin remained impassive, as though the words were not addressed to him. He glanced in every direction and fiddled with the enormous bouquet of flowers with which he had been burdened, while appearing to hear nothing. As soon as Chkheidze had finished, Lenin turned his back on him and spoke forcefully: "Dear comrades, soldiers, sailors, and workers! I am happy to greet in your persons the victorious Russian revolution, and greet you as the vanguard of the worldwide proletarian army. The piratical imperialist war is the beginning of civil war throughout Europe. . . . The worldwide Socialist revolution has already dawned. . . . Any day now the whole of European capitalism may crash. Long live the worldwide Socialist revolution!"

Then, leaving his listeners stunned, he walked off as the *Marseillaise* was played, got into an official car that a duly mobilized crowd attempted to stop, applauding and asking for more speeches, and he went to Bolshevik headquarters.

They had requisitioned the Kzhezinskaya Mansion for their exclusive use; it was the former home of a gifted ballerina for whom Nicholas II had felt some attraction long ago, before his marriage. When he arrived at the mansion where his allies were waiting, he rushed to the balcony, delivered a brief harangue interrupted by applause, but also by some hostile shouts that were quickly stifled by an efficient group of supporters, and finally joined the Bolshevik leaders.

He had been greeted by a large number of militants, workers, and young society women curious to catch a glimpse of this Lenin who was still little known in Russia but of whom so much evil had been said. After brief introductory remarks by Zinoviev and Kamenev to which the audience paid little attention because they had not come to listen to subordinates, Lenin finally addressed his admirers. For two full hours, carried away by the joy of being back in Russia after seven years of exile, of finding himself among his friends, he lavished on them, in his entirely personal oratorical style that "hammered, assaulted the listener," a completely unambiguous speech. As he had done at the Finland Station, he immediately returned to his favorite theme, the transformation of the war into a civil war, and he condemned in plain language the attitude adopted by the Soviet up to that point, asserting that the "soviet democracy advocated by Tsereteli and Chkheidze can lead neither to real peace [through civil war] nor to revolution. . . . The Soviet led by opportunists, social-patriots, can only be a tool for the bourgeoisie. In order for it to serve world revolution, it must be conquered, it must be proletarian!"[14] Two conclusions flowed from this: the refusal to support the Provisional Government and the need to impose on the Soviet a Bolshevik majority if not Bolshevik domination. Lenin's supporters listened to this speech for which they were not at all prepared in stupefaction. The revolution had led them to dream of Socialist unity, not of division, whereas Lenin had just told them that only supporters of the Zimmerwald Left positions were authentic revolutionaries.

During the weeks following the collapse of czarism, the Bolsheviks, lacking their leader, had not been inactive. As early as February 26, with Petrograd in ferment, Shlyapnikov, Zalutsky, and Molotov had drawn up a manifesto that was published by *Izvestia*, the newly created organ of the Petrograd Soviet. Molotov and Shlyapnikov had begun working to restore a Bolshevik organization in the capital in 1916, and at the time they constituted the Russian Bureau of the Central Committee. Their manifesto adopted a modest tone; when it appeared on February 28, the new government was not yet stabilized. The manifesto therefore simply called for the formation of a "Provisional Government of the Revolution" and for reforms of a democratic nature: the calling of a Constituent Assembly elected by popular vote, an appeal for peace among proletarians, and the confiscation of large estates. When he had read this manifesto while still in Switzerland, Lenin had been pleased to see the proposal to call for proletarian solidarity in order to achieve peace, which he considered proper, although it was of little concern to him.

Soon thereafter, with freedom of the press established in Russia, *Pravda* had reappeared under the editorship of Molotov and immediately adopted the positions of the manifesto. It was nevertheless not easy for the Bolsheviks to choose a clear political line, in particular with respect to the Provisional Government. Should it be supported, or, as Molotov thought, opposed? On March 13, three veterans of *Pravda* who had lost control of it because of their Siberian exile, Stalin, Kamenev, and M. K. Muranov, returned to Petrograd and immediately resumed control of the party organ. The position they then adopted for the paper had nothing to do with the one that Lenin was to defend.[15] Kamenev, who was a brilliant journalist, wrote that in wartime an army could not be asked to lay down its arms. Even though this defensist position was to turn out to be a minority one, *Pravda* had thus adopted a moderate attitude toward the Provisional Government, avoiding any attack on it or on its intention to continue the war. In the end the editors of *Pravda* had cautiously decided to wait for events to take a clearer course before sharpening their own analysis.[16]

The dominant element in their approach was the certainty that the February Revolution was a bourgeois revolution and that the Provisional Government could therefore legitimately claim to represent it and to speak of peace while taking revolutionary interests into account. Another component of the Bolsheviks' approach was their desire for unity, and hence the possibility, Stalin declared, of a reconciliation among everyone who accepted the principles of Zimmerwald and Kienthal. The distance between their "conciliatory" views and Lenin's positions was so great that in March, when Lenin, who was still in Zurich, sent them articles called "Letters from Afar,"[17] which anticipated *The April Theses* calling for the overthrow of the Provisional Government, Kamenev and Stalin decided to censor him. They published only the first of the letters in *Pravda*, after cutting out its attacks on the Provisional Government.[18]

Lenin's blunt remarks on his return were hardly in accordance with the moderate behavior and the desire for unity of his supporters. But even more than his speech of the first day, his meetings on the next set off an uproar. There was a meeting of Socialists of all tendencies at the Tauride Palace on April 4 for the purpose of proclaiming unity. Lenin took an opposing view with great violence. He read a handwritten text to the Socialists that was a complete program for moving to a new phase of the revolution; more seriously he argued for the immediate application of his plan. Its principal elements were the following: the immediate cessation of all war efforts; the end of support for the Provisional Government and the transfer of all power to the soviets; the abolition of the regular army, replaced by people's militias; the confiscation of landed estates and nationalization of the land; and the control of production and distribution by the soviets.

On an assembly that had been called in a spirit of reconciliation, Lenin's speech had the effect of a hurricane destroying everything in its path, and it outraged the majority of the participants. Lenin was acting like a provocateur, they thought, not like a clear thinker, and protests came from all sides. Bogdanov declared, "This is the raving of a madman!" I. P. Goldenberg, a historic Bolshevik, shouted, "Lenin has now made himself a candidate for one European throne that has been vacant for thirty years–the throne of Bakunin! . . . It's ludicrous to speak of unity with those whose watchword is schism and who are placing themselves outside the Social-Democracy of their own accord!"[19]

Tsereteli, one of the best Menshevik orators, hastened to condemn Lenin, but Lenin's thinking was so foreign to him, so removed from reality, that he became entangled in his own arguments and his response fell flat. In the end Lenin had, to be sure, drawn insults and jeers, but the meeting did not produce a structured critique of his position. This is what saved him, and what would later give him his strength. The Provisional Government thought that he was finished in the eyes of the Social Democrats and hoped that his excessive language, added to the episode of the return to Russia with German help, would alienate his supporters, as well as public opinion. The French ambassador to Russia, Maurice Paléologue, recounts in his *Memoirs* that Miliukov "happily told" him that in his opinion Lenin would never get over the humiliation he had suffered at the meeting.[20] And the leaders of the Provisional Government, who had at first feared Lenin, even hesitating to allow him to return (but in the fevered Russia of February, such a refusal was unthinkable), began to dream. Lenin was a finished man, they thought. Only one of them did not harbor this illusion, that is, Kerensky, who was convinced that Lenin would soon make a comeback. The fact that so few shared his lucidity helps to explain the weakness of the liberal bourgeoisie in power in the face of the man who was to destroy democracy a few months later.

First Lenin had to impose himself on his own party, which was not an easy task. *Pravda*, to which he brought his speech that became known as *The April Theses*, was reluctant.[21] The text was not in agreement with the positions that the paper had adopted. But Lenin was more obstinate and a better tactician than any of his associates. On his return, along with the faithful Zinoviev, he had forced his way into *Pravda* and installed himself on the editorial staff. With arguments and threats, he got his way, and *Pravda* published his speech on April 7, with the title "The Tasks of the Proletariat in the Present Revolution." It was, however, preceded by a note from Kamenev emphasizing that it committed no one but Lenin, and adding: "It is unacceptable to us, because it assumes that the bourgeois revolution is completed and advocates the immediate transformation of that revolution into a socialist revolution."

Bolshevik opposition to Lenin's positions was so strong that the following day the capital's Party Committee met to debate them. The final vote was devastating: thirteen against, two in favor, one abstention. Similar condemnations arrived from the provinces, which suggests the difficulty Lenin would have in winning the party over to his views.[22] He was nevertheless not discouraged, and he very carefully prepared for the All-Russian Bolshevik Conference which was to meet ten days later.

On that occasion, their were two factors in his favor. First was the presence of rank-and-file Bolsheviks, who were disoriented by the hesitations that had been shown so far by the people leading the party in his absence, particularly on the question of the war. They were suddenly facing a decisive leader, who spoke with clarity, and whose strength of will was impressive.

Even more important, revolutionary Russia was troubled by Miliukov's about-face on the war. Although his note of April 3 seemed in agreement with the Socialists' desire for peace, in his view it had been only a momentary concession to their pressure. On April 18 he went back on his preceding declaration in another note to the Allies in which he strongly reaffirmed Russian war aims. The hope for peace seemed to be slipping away, and Miliukov was accused of duplicity. The immediate reaction was the organization of demonstrations in the capital with the slogan, "Miliukov resign!"

It was against this background of crisis that the conference assembled 149 delegates elected by nearly eighty thousand members.[23] In opposition to Lenin, Kamenev proposed that the party stick to the line established in March, and "keep an eye on" the Provisional Government. Rykov, for his part, declared: "The initiative for the socialist revolution does not belong to us." But Lenin was supported by the immovable Zinoviev, and also by Bukharin who had opposed his positions on the national question in 1915 (he was hostile to the idea of self-determination), but who shared his conviction that the revolution should be immediate. Finally, Stalin was suddenly converted to his views. Stalin's support of Lenin led to his being a member of the Central Committee elected at the close of the conference, with a number of votes exceeded only by those given to Lenin and Zinoviev.

While the conference continued its work, the crowd was demonstrating in the streets. The troops, which the Provisional Government hesitated to deploy against the demonstrators, seemed in any event hardly inclined to follow any such orders. Events seemed to be confirming Lenin's views and strengthening his dominant position. The final votes indicated that he had been able to persuade the party and to impose his authority over it. In the resolution on the war, he was supported by an almost unanimous assembly (seven abstentions). In his call to prepare for a transfer of power to the soviets, he won 122 votes. On the other hand, only seventy–one backed the resolution on the immediate advance of the Socialist revolution. Lenin had also fought for abandonment of the term "Social Democrat," a synonym of treason according to him, in favor of the term "Communist." The conference refused to follow him on this point, just as it decided, against Lenin's wishes, to create a working group of Bolsheviks and Mensheviks with a view toward restoring unity. The Socialists had not given up the dream of reconciliation.

Lenin had thus won on the essential points, but not completely. The Central Committee elected at the conclusion of the conference, made up of nine members and five alternates, reflected the ambiguity of his victory. Among the nine full members were four of his supporters–Zinoviev, Sverdlov, Ivan Smilga, and

Stalin (although there were some reservations about him because he had rallied to Lenin so recently). Against this group of five—including Lenin, elected with 104 votes—were those he called the "old" Bolsheviks—Kamenev, Victor Nogin, Dmitry Milyutin, and G. F. Fedorov.

Lenin's greatest success no doubt lay in the fact that at the conference the party had adopted the slogan "All power to the soviets." By proposing this slogan in April 1917, Lenin was in fact presenting a modified version of his own ideas. Earlier in the year, while he was still in Switzerland, he had broached the subject of the soviets in a lecture, but had treated it in a few brief sentences and shown little interest in the institution. He had gradually come to understand its importance and in his first "Letter from Afar," he had described it as "a government of workers representing the interests of the proletariat and of the poorest segment of the population."[24] Lenin's changing perception was a foretaste of the slogan of *The April Theses* and of the equivalence he was to establish between the Soviet and the Paris Commune, authorities that both originated in the "direct initiative of the popular masses, an initiative that came 'from the bottom' of society." In assimilating Commune and Soviet and referring to Marx, Lenin was providing a solid historical basis for his argument. This did not prevent his conception (he expressed himself with utmost clarity on this point) from being that of a Soviet penetrated by the party, an expression of the will of the party. But the party did not have very coherent ideas about the political representation of society. Its program, adopted in 1903, and still unchanged in 1917, considered the Constituent Assembly elected by universal suffrage as the representative body of popular sovereignty. During the April conference, the participants still placed the Soviet and the Constituent Assembly on the same footing, without attempting to set up a hierarchy between the two bodies in terms of power. After October the disagreement between Lenin (who was still cleverly silent on this delicate point) and the party as a whole would become apparent. But in the months following the April conference, Lenin's party, along with all the other Socialist organizations, relentlessly attacked the Provisional Government for its delay in organizing elections intended to bring the Constituent Assembly into being.[25] This did not prevent the Bolsheviks from proclaiming at the same time and ever more loudly: "All power to the Soviets!"

THE ALLIANCE WITH TROTSKY

Following the April conference, changes occurred rapidly, transforming the situation in Russia and within the party.

The first change was the formation of a coalition cabinet replacing the government of Prince Lvov which had fallen because of the crisis provoked by the Miliukov note. The note in fact had merely been a spark in an already volatile situation. Russia was then suffering from dual power, or rather from the difficulty the Provisional government had in confronting the Soviet. The only

Socialist in the preceding government, Kerensky brought out by his presence, by the ambiguity of his position, by his maneuvers between government and Soviet, how difficult it was to locate the center of power. Thus, as a consequence of the crisis, a coalition government was formed in early May. Prince Lvov remained as prime minister, but six Socialists representing the Soviet entered the government, two SRs, two Mensheviks, and two Popular Socialists. Lvov no longer represented anything.[26]

It was the reconciliation with Trotsky that opened a new phase for the party. Trotsky returned to Russia early in May. The day after his arrival, he spoke before the Soviet, where no one had forgotten that he had been president in 1905. He immediately adopted the positions put forth by Lenin, calling on the deputies to turn over all power to the soviets and to waste no time in transforming the democratic revolution into a proletarian revolution. There no longer seemed to be anything dividing Lenin and Trotsky, except that Trotsky was associated with the internationalist Social Democratic organization (the *Mezhraiontsy* or interdistrict group) which was intent on retaining its independence from Bolsheviks and Mensheviks. Lenin was eager to draw Trotsky into his camp, and Trotsky, eager to be involved in action as soon as possible, was aware that the leader of the Bolsheviks was the most likely to set it in motion.

It was Lenin who took the first step by attending a meeting of the *Mezhraiontsy* as soon as Trotsky had arrived in the capital and proposing that he join the editorial staff of *Pravda* and the committee charged with preparing the party congress. If unity was not established immediately, this was because Trotsky was still hesitant to rally to the Bolshevik flag. He thought that Bolshevism had outlived its usefulness and that the time had come to establish a new party. His hesitation expressed his discomfort, but also his pride. If he were to join Lenin, would he not be recognizing that the Bolsheviks were in the right? He preferred to keep his distance, hoping that Lenin would accept his arguments. But Lenin, consistent and persuaded that events would impel Trotsky to come around, refused to dissolve the party that he had created for the purpose of one day seizing power. Nor did he intend to change its name. He saw that success was at hand and thought that it was not the time to change anything about the party. He was ready to welcome Trotsky into it, and he was also willing to bide his time.

In the following weeks, a meeting of the Zimmerwald group was held in Petrograd to decide whether the Russian Socialists should take part in the Socialist conference scheduled in Stockholm for the purpose of discussing peace. The participants were divided into those in favor of attending and those in favor of a boycott.[27] Trotsky was even more violent than the Bolsheviks in his denunciation of a planned conference intended to bring together Russian Socialists, already involved in the revolution, and a number of European Socialists who were still convinced of the necessity of supporting their respective governments. He had no words that were harsh enough to denounce the "conciliators," as Lenin allowed him to occupy the forefront and play the role of intransigent Socialist. Surprised to see him adopt such an extreme position, Angelica

Balabanov asked Lenin what was still holding Trotsky back from joining the Bolsheviks. Lenin's reply is revealing of the ambiguity of the relations between the two men: "Now don't you know? Ambition, ambition, ambition."[28]

Lenin's attempts to co-opt others were not limited to Trotsky. Martov, who had returned to Russia at the same time, was offered an analogous proposal aiming to incorporate into Bolshevism those Mensheviks who were in agreement with Martov in defending an internationalist position and the desire for peace. It was at this time that the coalition government was formed that included two Mensheviks, but the Menshevik Party as a whole was reluctant to approve that participation because of the "defensist" positions of the government. Martov arrived just in time for the Menshevik conference to debate participation and showed violent hostility to the presence of members of his party in the new government. To Lenin, he seemed to be an important ally, because Martov's intellectual prestige was still substantial. But it had to be recognized that emigration had made him lose a large part of his political influence. For, despite Martov's opposition, the Menshevik conference did approve the entry of members of the party into the coalition and promised the government unconditional support. Forty-four voted for participation, eleven against, and thirteen abstained. Martov had simultaneously lost a battle and any hope of taking leadership of the Menshevik Party. Although he was isolated, he refused to rally to Lenin.[29] By 1917 he had formed a very negative opinion of his former friend. He no longer saw in him anything but a cynic whose single passion was for power. And he confided in Tsereteli, shortly after his return: "In Lenin's eyes, neither peace nor war are of any real interest. The only thing that counts for him is the revolution. And the only true revolution is the one that will allow the Bolsheviks to take power."

It is easy to see that this judgment made any reconciliation between the two men inconceivable. But in the end it mattered very little to Lenin that his overtures were rejected, because the Bolshevization of public opinion was proceeding slowly but surely. At the time, in fact, he had valuable assets not available to his opponents.

First of all he had control of a press whose financial resources (deriving in part from money supplied by Germany) were incomparably larger than those of the other parties. With these resources Lenin was able from the moment of his return to develop a multifarious press addressed to various social and national groups. By the summer of 1917, *Pravda* was printing 90,000 copies. The total print run of party papers was 320,000 copies. Of the 41 papers, 27 were published in Russian, the others in Georgian, Armenian, Lithuanian, Latvian, Tatar, and so on. But the Bolshevik newspapers, and this was their strong point, were not addressed solely to linguistic communities, but also to particular social groups, for example, women and soldiers (there were even individual papers for sailors, front-line soldiers, and so forth). In addition the Bolshevik presses printed a substantial number of pamphlets. For all these publications, the party had a printing press that had cost 260,500 rubles. Volkogonov, who carefully verified this information, pointed out that the dues of members, even though their numbers were increasing at the time, could not have financed this purchase.[30] The result was that Lenin had at his disposal an incomparable tool for propaganda.

The press was not enough, and the Bolsheviks found another means of influencing the working class in factory committees. The unions were, in fact, dominated by the Mensheviks, and it was thus important to reduce their influence. Lenin encouraged the formation of factory committees, within which the Bolsheviks engaged in intense propaganda. To be sure these committees were not easy to manipulate, because they sprang from workers' spontaneous initiatives which the Bolsheviks had been obliged to cheer on. Although remaining suspicious of these anarcho-syndicalist movements that he had always denounced, Lenin understood that it was better to use them to fight the authority of the Mensheviks among workers and thereby to assume as much control as possible over a working class showing a strong tendency to organize itself as it saw fit. Always pragmatic, if not opportunist, Lenin decided to get what advantage he could from these movements.

"WE ARE READY TO TAKE OVER THE GOVERNMENT"

After barely two months in Russia, Lenin had good grounds for satisfaction. The situation was rapidly changing, confirming the decline in governmental authority. The coalition government had expressed its intention to reach a peace with neither indemnities nor annexations, but peace was not forthcoming and discontent was growing in the army. The entry of the United States into the war, the government explained to the people, changed its nature, making it no longer a war among only imperialist states, and was a promising step toward the peace wished for by Russia. But society was deaf to these speeches and observed that the war and its suffering were continuing. Agitation in the cities, carefully encouraged by the Bolsheviks, but also disorders in the countryside, demonstrated the government's increasing isolation. And conferences and congresses of peasants and workers, all intent on putting forth their demands, helped to create a stormy atmosphere in which the Bolsheviks always played their role.

It was in this context of political radicalization that the First All-Russian Congress of Soviets was convened in June. The Bolsheviks were far from controlling it; out of 822 voting delegates, they counted only 105 representatives, far outdistanced by the Socialist Revolutionaries with 285 delegates, and the Mensheviks with 248. There were many delegates not yet members of any party, waiting to see how the balance of forces would turn out. The Bolsheviks undertook a significant effort to persuade the hesitant.

In an overheated Tauride Palace filled with many soldiers, an incident was created when Tsereteli, the minister of posts and telegraphs, asserted: "There is no political party in the country today that is able to say: 'Give power to us, and leave.' There is no such party." Lenin rose and answered, emphasizing each word, each syllable, using his immense powers of persuasion: "There is [such a party]. . . . It is ready at any moment to take over the Government."[31]

His speech, entirely focused on the war and the government's inability to bring it to an end, was interrupted by hostile shouts and derisive laughter, but also punctuated by applause from the soldiers and sailors who had invaded the Tauride Palace. It is their overwhelming presence that explains the apparent lack of success of Kerensky's speech, even though it was marked by unanswerable irony and logic. He spoke directly to Lenin: "You advise us to imitate the French Revolution of 1792. You want to drag us into a complete disorganization of the country. When you have succeeded in destroying us with the help of the reactionaries, you will have prepared the way for a dictator!"

Applause and votes did not run in parallel. Between Lenin and Kerensky, it was Lenin who had achieved a real triumph, thanks to the soldiers who were present. But when it came time for the vote expressing the existing balance of forces, Kerensky won out. The delegates voted a motion of confidence in the Provisional Government and rejected the Bolshevik resolution demanding an immediate transfer of state power to the soviets.

Before adjourning the congress decided (this resolution was important for the future) to institutionalize itself, to meet every three months, and to elect an All-Russian Central Executive Committee (VTsIK or CEC), which would be the permanent body for the soviets acting between plenary sessions. Of the 250 members elected to the CEC, only thirty five were Bolsheviks. Control of the Congress of Soviets thus slipped out of Lenin's grasp despite his efforts and his own speech in favor of soviet power, and even despite the formidable pressure exerted by the soldiers and sailors present, who had unceasingly applauded Bolshevik arguments, shouted down Lenin's opponents, and given the meeting the flavor of an extreme leftist assembly.

Although he remained weak within the Congress of Soviets, Lenin was not weak in the streets, and he decided to make an immediate demonstration of that fact. On June 9, leaflets emanating from the Bolshevik Party and from factory committees called for a "peaceful" demonstration on the following day, but the slogans suggested that it would be far from peaceful: "Down with the Tsarist Duma!" "Down with the Ten Minister Capitalists!" "All Power to the All-Russian Soviet of Workers', Soldiers' and Peasants' Deputies!" "Bread, Peace, Freedom!" Some regiments—the troops of the Petrograd garrison were virtually under the control of the Bolshevik military organization supervised by Lenin—had announced that they would participate in the demonstration armed.

Appalled, Chkheidze alerted the All-Russian Congress, evoking the blood-bath that was likely to result from such a demonstration of strength by the Bolsheviks, while Tsereteli accused Lenin's supporters of fomenting a coup d'é-tat. Curiously, Lenin was absent from the Tauride Palace on that day, and was thus unable to react to the anxious appeal of delegates exhorting him to give up the demonstration. It was finally canceled; the Bolsheviks accused the government of having fabricated the supposed plot in order to be able to disarm the workers and weaken the garrison. But the evidence points to the fact (and the investigation proved it) that the Bolsheviks were counting on the demonstration leading to a coup d'état. All the preparations had been made for installing a new government as soon as the coup had succeeded.

The Soviet met the next day to analyze the lessons of events. The Mensheviks and their principal spokesmen, Dan and Martov, asked that strict rules be set concerning the conditions in which demonstrations could take place. Only the Soviet would be empowered to authorize them, and armed demonstrations would not be tolerated, barring exceptional permission given by the Soviet. The Bolsheviks attended the debate without reacting. This was all the easier for them to do because when Tsereteli asked the assembly to go further than Dan had proposed and disarm them, as well as the groups they were manipulating, in order to prevent the rapid destruction of legality, it was Martov who opposed him, declaring that it was unthinkable to "disarm the working class." The final decision followed Dan's proposal, but spared the Bolsheviks from the grave threat hanging over them of being forced into illegality. At that point they were not sure enough of themselves to confront that danger. They might have shown some gratitude to Martov, who had defended them and presented them as revolutionaries who might be a little agitated and uncontrollable, but were legitimated by the popular support they enjoyed; but they did nothing of the kind. Tsereteli's attempt to outlaw them had failed. In a little while, the Mensheviks would learn that Tsereteli's prophecy was closer to reality than they had wanted to believe.[32]

By the next day, Lenin had resumed the initiative. Indeed, *Pravda* declared that, as far as the Bolsheviks were concerned, the Soviet had no standing to control or authorize demonstrations, and that they would under no circumstances ask its permission to demonstrate when they wished. Lenin was determined to take advantage of the favorable situation to carry out another operation. He had to wait only a few weeks for the opportunity to present itself, or so he thought.

A FAILED PUTSCH

On June 29, Lenin went with Krupskaya for a few days' rest at the dacha of his friend Vladimir Bonch-Bruevich in a village in the Finnish countryside. Was this a rest or a necessary retreat? No doubt he was exhausted by the incessant activity in which he had been engaged since his return, and his nervous condition, which Krupskaya carefully attended to, was not of the best. A stronger motive than a desire for rest might explain this departure from the capital, namely, caution. In the final days of June, Lenin knew that the Provisional Government was preparing a file against him containing evidence of his treason. While the return through Germany was well known and was still the subject of harsh criticism, this was about to be supplemented with evidence of the financial dealings of Hanetsky and Parvus, that Lenin had been aware of these maneuvers, and that it was German money flowing abundantly into the Bolshevik coffers that had made it possible for them to give such unprecedented scope to the defeatist campaign their leader had been advocating since 1914.

The moment of these revelations, in which the French intelligence services had cooperated, was particularly unfortunate.[33] Two weeks earlier, on June 16, Kerensky had launched an offensive on the Southwestern Front, and had decided that, in order to support the offensive, it was going to be necessary to return to Russia the divisions that had been sent to France. He was hoping through this final effort to break the spiral of Russian military failures and to demonstrate to the Central Powers that they could not count on a separate peace. The Bolsheviks had to admit that, at the front, but also in society as a whole, patriotic fervor was not entirely dead once belief in success was revived, and the first operations in Galicia turned out to be encouraging. But a brutal German counteroffensive ruined these hopes in the space of a few days. It then remained to recognize the disaster and count up the futile deaths, the wounded, and the prisoners. Above all, it remained for Kerensky to pay the price for a decision that was now considered pure madness. He was held responsible and lost a good deal of his authority. This disgrace struck him at the precise moment when the July putsch was to require of him a decisiveness that he had never shown and a prestige that had now been seriously eroded.

This is not the place to present a detailed account of the failed putsch, but it is appropriate to summarize its major elements. We should begin by recalling two important aspects of the situation in the capital in the summer of 1917.

First was the increased activity of the anarchists, who had taken over the villa that belonged before the revolution to former Interior Minister Peter Durnovo, located on the Vyborg district. It had become their headquarters and, according to Sukhanov, worried the Soviet as well as the Provisional Government, who were both convinced that it was stacked with weapons and bombs that could be used at a moment's notice. But no one dared to intervene or even investigate. In June the anarchists had seized a printing plant, giving the government a pretext for taking action. It attempted to evict them from both the printing plant and the Durnovo villa, which gave the anarchists grounds for mobilizing the population of Vyborg to defend them. In the end the result of the incident was to transform the Vyborg district into an armed camp where anarchist workers and sailors joined in considering that the "majority" (government and Soviet together) was in the camp of the enemies of the revolution. It remained to translate this conviction into open warfare.[34]

The unrest in the Vyborg district was joined by growing unrest in the city's barracks, where the Bolsheviks were fostering the soldiers' discontent. The June offensive had provoked strong feelings because the soldiers were afraid they would be sent as reinforcements to the Galician front. The Bolsheviks in turn were worried that the Provisional Government would take advantage of the situation to rid the capital of troops that had been won over to their ideas. It was in this troubled context that the news of the defeats suffered at the hands of the German and Austrian armies added to the growing discontent the certainty that the government was totally incapable of carrying out its mandate.

On July 3 a veritable insurrection began in Petrograd, which lasted for three days, put an end to the first coalition government, and demonstrated how indecipherable the political situation in Russia remained. The insurrection was preceded by the government's decision to put an end to the activities of the Bolsheviks, whose maneuvers among the troops, in a state of near mutiny against the orders sending some of them to the front, it considered to have gone beyond all bounds. Making use of the file on Lenin's treason, the government decided to arrest the Bolshevik leaders. This decision, about which Lenin was informed while it was still under discussion, probably explains his decision to seek temporary refuge outside the capital.

On July 3 workers' demonstrations and soldiers' processions were organized in the capital and, for the next two days, spread through the streets; besieged the Tauride Palace; took some politicians hostage, including Victor Chernov; and demanded that power be turned over to the Soviet. Despite its disarray the Provisional Government took various repressive measures. It banned *Pravda*, brought loyal troops into the capital, and finally ordered the arrest of three Bolshevik leaders, Lenin, Zinoviev, and Kamenev.

These July days (everything was over by July 6) were the outcome of efforts by three groups of actors, Bolsheviks, demonstrators, and government. The actions of each group are surprising in their lack of decisiveness, uncertainty, and in the end a kind of abdication.

The Bolsheviks, deprived of their head (Lenin did not leave his refuge until July 4), were led during those uncertain days by a newly established troika, Zinoviev, Kamenev, and Trotsky, who had clearly rallied to Lenin at this point. Trotsky in fact appeared to be the leading figure in the crisis, speaking at every opportunity and demanding that power change hands at the most heated moments of the insurrection. The Bolsheviks acted on two fronts: they spoke to the rioters, giving instructions that were often later contradicted; and they operated within the Soviet, which contained a workers' section that they attempted to use as a spearhead.

The second force during these days was made up of the workers and soldiers who had been converging on the centers of power since July 1, awaiting directives from the Bolsheviks on how to continue their movement, which the Bolsheviks claimed was spontaneous. But, considering it more closely, they had carefully stirred it up for weeks, if not provoked the movement themselves. July 3 was the decisive day. The insurrection then appeared impossible to halt. Workers and soldiers, who had invaded the streets of the capital, seemed more determined than ever. There was scattered gunfire and a moderate amount of looting. Workers and soldiers converged on the Tauride Palace, seat of both Provisional Government and Soviet, with banners bearing the slogans: "Down with the Ten Capitalist Ministers!" and "All Power to the Soviets!" Kamenev leaped up on to the speaker's platform in front of the Soviet and cried out: "We never called for a demonstration, but the popular masses themselves have come out into the streets. . . . [O]ur place is with them. Our task now is to give the movement an organized character."

The Bolsheviks thus seemed on the point of seizing power with the help of the insurgents. But they did not, and they continued to give out contradictory instructions. The following day, however, it seemed as though Lenin's supporters had decided to take action. All night, they had debated the forms of action at party headquarters, while the government, aware of the danger, had brought in military reinforcements. At dawn everything changed again. Bolsheviks, along with some deputies, were sent to barracks and factories to persuade soldiers and workers to refrain from any action.

After a long period of equivocation, the Bolsheviks had thus decided that the time for decisive action had not yet come. The orders and counterorders given to the demonstrators indicate their indecision. On July 4, for example, *Pravda* was printed with a strange first page juxtaposing a large censored space with an article calling for moderation. What is the explanation for these hesitations, the most striking illustration of which was Lenin's behavior on July 4, when the government seemed paralyzed and the crowds ready for anything as long as they had some real leadership?

A partial but necessary explanation lies in the revelations about Lenin's treason that were about to be made public. By July 4 Kerensky had given the order to release the documents that demonstrated it, but the government was still hesitating over the urgency of the publication. During the course of the same day, it thought that it was in a position to curb the riots and make the Bolsheviks into outlaws, and it was already thinking about the trial that would permanently remove them from political life. For that reason it made public only a small fraction of the documents incriminating Lenin, keeping the bulk of them for the projected trial; after offering them to the newspapers, it withdrew them.[35] In fact there was total disagreement on the issue between the minister of justice, P. N. Pereverzev, who wanted to publish the documents in full, and the majority of the Soviet, who were indignant over the treatment he wanted to inflict on Lenin. Even Tsereteli, despite his dislike, helped to block publicity about the affair. All newspapers kept it quiet, except for *Zhivoe Slovo*, which published an article entitled "Spies: Lenin, Hanetsky, and Company." This publication, which was widely read, had disastrous consequences for Lenin. The Russian people, including the soldiers who had been won over to Bolshevism, certainly hungered for peace, but they were not ready to accept the idea of a peace bought and paid for by the enemy.

The Bolshevik counterattack was certainly swift. On July 5 Zinoviev spoke before the Soviet:

> A monstrous slander has appeared in the press and is already having its effect on the most ignorant and backward strata of the masses. There is no need for me to explain to you the meaning of this piece of baseness. . . . It is bound up not only with the interests of our revolution, but also with the entire European working-class movement. . . . [We] ought to take the most resolute measures to rehabilitate Comrade Lenin and suppress all the conceivable results of this slander. I've been charged to come here in the name of the Central Committee of our party.

This strong declaration was unable to conceal the Bolsheviks' disarray and anxiety. It is probable that, aware of the effect produced by the revelations, they had concluded (Lenin more than anyone) that it was impossible to seize power under the circumstances. This was the source of their urging moderation on the insurgents.

The government seized the opportunity to recover the initiative, which was facilitated by the reaction taking shape in society. Elements hostile to the revolution or to the Bolsheviks wrecked the *Pravda* offices and laid siege to Bolshevik headquarters. The government chose this moment to disarm the mutineers and to restore some control over the barracks. At the same time, it ordered the arrest of the Bolshevik leaders.[36]

Although Lenin and Zinoviev were able to hide in time and then flee to Finland, Kamenev, Trotsky, Lunacharsky, and Kollontai were arrested. In prison, they joined Hanetsky, sent there for the affair of the German money. In his book Sukhanov notes that Lenin's flight did not help to improve his image: "Lenin of course may have prized. . . . his freedom of political action. But in a prison of the time could he have been more hampered than in his underground retreat?" He goes on to say that the arrested Bolsheviks acquired martyrs' haloes, whereas the slander hanging over Lenin "heightened the odium of Lenin's flight a thousandfold. . . . Any other mortal would have demanded an investigation and trial even in the most unfavorable conditions."[37]

In Sukhanov's view Lenin's moral stature was forever changed by his flight and the abandonment of those who had fought beside him. Indeed his behavior in this instance was far from praiseworthy. He paid more attention to his own safety than to the revolutionary project during the putsch and to solidarity with his associates afterward. This behavior was in accordance with his view of the party. He had identified himself with the organization that he had founded too much to imagine for a moment that his decisions were not legitimate. He saw them as the decisions of the entire party, because he was its leader and its embodiment.

Incidentally Lenin's decision was disapproved by many Bolsheviks, and he had to argue with them to justify it. On July 7, when he had taken temporary refuge in the apartment of Sergei Alliluyev (a friend of Stalin's who would later provide him with a hiding place), the subject was debated by Lenin, Krupskaya, Stalin, Ordzhonikidze, Nogin, and a few lesser known Bolsheviks.[38] Nogin, one of the earliest Bolsheviks, who had been close to Lenin since 1903 and had been elected to the Central Committee in April, advocated his surrender and attempted to persuade him at length. What tipped the balance in favor of flight was the arrival of Elena Stasova, another longtime loyal Leninist, who announced that the government was propagating information that could be the basis for a prosecution: Lenin was said to have been not only a German agent but also a paid Okhrana agent. "Don't go to prison," Stalin cried out, "they'll kill you!"[39] Lenin, already inwardly convinced, decided to go along with that advice rather than following that of Nogin and Ordzhonikidze. During the following week, a letter signed by Lenin and Zinoviev was published in *Proletarskoye Delo* (Proletarian Cause) that was the last word on the affair. They proclaimed their refusal to be arrested without a complete guarantee of equitable judicial treatment.

In the aftermath of the putsch, characterized more by the hesitation of the crowds and the Bolsheviks than by the decisiveness of the government, the latter nevertheless seemed to have the upper hand. Lenin and his party were faced with a disaster that left the field open to the Provisional Government, the Mensheviks, and the SRs. The revolutions now seemed to have entered on a clearer path, with the absence of the Bolsheviks from the political stage and the discredit into which they had fallen suggesting that some stability might follow the perpetual threat of radicalization.[40]

A DIFFICULT RECOVERY

As a consequence of the July events, the first coalition government fell in the days following the storm. Prince Lvov resigned, this time for good, and Kerensky assumed leadership of a cabinet with a Socialist majority, becoming simultaneously prime minister and minister of war and the navy. He brought into the cabinet such Socialist revolutionaries as Boris Savinkov and Lebedev, and even some Kadets. This coalition, however, was attractive to no one. To strengthen his authority, on July 18 he appointed General Lavr Kornilov as head of the Russian armed forces. But the authority that had been reestablished constantly came up against Lenin and the Bolsheviks, and the harassment to which it was subject prevented it from carrying out its initial plan to make public, in a complete and definitive way, the affair of the German funds. The government was assaulted by criticism from the Soviet which challenged the need for the arrests, that had indeed been numerous, but especially continued to defend Lenin. Martov showed himself to be the fiercest critic of the government's action; he constantly repeated that Lenin was doubtless an unscrupulous intriguer, but certainly not a traitor. Tsereteli followed his lead. Thus disavowed, the government was gradually obliged to give up its investigation of Lenin's treason. This first victory by Lenin required no action on his part; he won it simply because those of his adversaries who seemed to be the most lucid felt the need to come to his assistance.

The Bolshevik Party reorganized at its Sixth Congress, held from July 26 to August 3.[41] It was a remarkable congress, attended neither by Lenin, who was in hiding, nor by Trotsky, who was in prison, but nevertheless dominated by the personalities of the two men. It bore the symbolic name of unification congress which, in such a troubled time, clearly indicated the desire of all Bolsheviks to resurface. It was also the result of well-organized delegate elections, in which nearly one hundred seventy thousand members had participated, one-fourth of whom were in the capital. The 267 participants were not only declared Bolsheviks, but also representatives of the interdistrict group to which Trotsky belonged, and of various internationalist currents that had until then been careful to preserve their independence. All were eager to achieve unity, because they sensed that they were confronting mounting reaction in the face of which they needed to come together.

The unity that was achieved in his absence was nonetheless Lenin's victory. This was how he had always seen it, with all those who claimed to be Socialists coming under his flag, with no conditions.

The leadership elected at the congress consisted of 22 members. Lenin had the largest number of votes (133 out of 134 voting participants), followed by Zinoviev (132), and Trotsky and Kamenev (131). This Central Committee was very heterogeneous, bringing together people from varied backgrounds and opposing tendencies. Lenin, Zinoviev, Kamenev, Trotsky, Bukharin, and Sokolnikov had long lived as émigrés, whereas Stalin, Rykov, Felix Dzerzhinsky, Shaumyan, Sverdlov, and Muranov were men of the interior, accustomed to prison and to long stays in Siberia. At one time or another, most of those elected had entered into conflict with Lenin, either about party disputes, the war, or, as for Bukharin, the national problem. Some had been Mensheviks, like Kollontai, or had long been hostile to Lenin, like Trotsky, who had not joined him until that summer, a reconciliation to which the Sixth Congress gave an official form.

The congress also sanctioned two internal organs of authority, the presidium, where those who were present held seats (Stalin, Sverdlov, A. Lomov, M. S. Olminsky, and K. K. Yurenev); and the real ruling body which included Lenin, Trotsky, Zinoviev, Kamenev, Lunacharsky, and Kollontai, then confined in Vyborg prison and owing a good deal of her prestige to her captivity.

Stalin, who presented the Central Committee's report in Lenin's absence, acted as spokesman for the leader in hiding. He declared that from now on, relations between the government and the revolution were summed up in Lenin's famous formula: "*Kto kogo?*" (Who will get the better of whom?), and concluded: "Before July, a peaceful transfer of power to the Soviets was possible. But that is no longer the case; the peaceful phase of the revolution is over. The period of rupture and explosion has arrived."[42] Lenin was absent, but his ideas were spiritedly defended by the man who was already intent on presenting himself as Lenin's most faithful representative. Stalin also spoke on a question that was very troubling to the party, although no one dared to raise it openly: Should Lenin have submitted to a trial in order to clear himself of the accusation of treason? Or was he right to have fled? Stalin's answer was equivocal. If the government had offered him all necessary guarantees of security and equity for a possible trial, it would have been better to appear; but in the absence of those guarantees, the most basic prudence dictated flight.[43] Stalin was violently criticized for these remarks, which were considered too mild by Dzerzhinsky, N. A. Skrypnik, and especially Bukharin, who ridiculed the idea that a "bourgeois court could be equitable." No matter, Stalin's position was nonetheless revealing of a certain disavowal of Lenin's flight which had provoked a deep sense of discomfort among many loyal followers.

It is also important to mention two events during this congress which went almost unnoticed at the time but were to count in the future.

First was the near disappearance of the slogan "All Power to the Soviets!" replaced by a still vague slogan, but one emphasizing the radicalization underway: "The revolutionary dictatorship of workers and peasants."

Martov's faction also sent a message of congratulations and support to the Bolshevik congress and affirmed its solidarity with the party of Lenin in the struggle against the coalition government. Although he was exiled and discredited,

Lenin could nonetheless take pleasure in seeing longtime opponents gathering around him. These often unexpected gestures of support helped to soften his isolation.

As the congress was coming to an end, Lenin, who was in hiding in Razliv, a village northwest of Petrograd, was informed that his secret refuge had been revealed. He had been spending peaceful days in the company of Zinoviev, working on short articles and reading in preparation for a major theoretical work, *The State and Revolution.* When he learned that he was at risk, he decided to seek refuge in Finland. He traveled there under a false identity and with a forged passport; Zinoviev did the same. Lenin's appearance had undergone a radical transformation; clean shaven and wearing a blonde wig, he was unrecognizable. His inseparable companion reversed the process, shaving his head and letting his beard grow.

Thus metamorphosed, following an epic journey during which they were almost captured, had to swim across a river, and masquerade as railway workers, the two companions finally arrived in Helsinki. Lenin found shelter with the chief of the city's police, a refuge that was unmatched for safety.

Meanwhile the situation in Petrograd was continuing to deteriorate. The coalition government lasted for only two weeks and was replaced by another, still dominated by Kerensky, who decided to summon a State Conference in Moscow. He hoped that its two thousand participants would succeed in formulating proposals that would make it possible to ensure the stability of the regime. Although the press gave the conference considerable publicity before its opening, no one knew precisely what purpose it was intended to serve. All parties were to be represented, and the usual debates over participation or boycott briefly preoccupied them. The discussions were unimportant, because the conference almost immediately turned into a fiasco.

Things then happened very fast. The society was waiting for responses to its demands—the end of the war and agrarian reform—whereas Kerensky and his government stubbornly continued the war and postponed the reforms until a Constituent Assembly could be called, the election of which they were in no hurry to organize. The government temporized on every subject. Since the failure of the Bolshevik putsch, Kerensky had moreover been obsessed with fear of a coup from the right. It was in order to forestall such a possibility that he had appointed Kornilov, characterized by General Alexei Brusilov as having "the heart of a lion and the brain of a sheep." At the same time, he feared the putschist inclinations of his new armed forces chief. Neither man trusted the other, and both had hidden agendas. For these reasons, recognizing the failure of the State Conference and of all proposals to preserve the country from disorder, Kornilov crossed the line into rebellion.[44] In order to deal with the revolutionaries' increasing pressures on the army, as well as with the German troops who were threatening the capital, he demanded that the government resign and that he be given plenary powers. Kerensky immediately dismissed him. The general responded by marching on Petrograd at the head of his troops on August 27. In the face of this threat of a coup, all the parties of the left—

Bolsheviks, Mensheviks, and SRs–mobilized, organized the masses, and declared that their priority was to block the conspiracy. Their efforts were unnecessary: Kornilov's troops showed little fighting spirit and that was the end of it. On September 12 Kerensky was able to have Kornilov arrested. In appearance, he had won.

In the end, this failed putsch had two consequences. First, it demonstrated that the government was now nothing but a phantom, unable to rally the country around itself and to preserve the power that had come out of the February Revolution. Its political hesitations had led it into a series of dead ends. Had it been faced with a more resolute opponent with more social support–Kornilov received no help from society in general–Kerensky would probably have fallen from power at the time. In addition the failed putsch had a miraculous effect for the Bolsheviks. It brought them back onto the Russian political stage and at the same time was a unifying factor for the left as a whole. The Bolsheviks in the end came out of this ordeal, in which they had played a minor role, as the major victors. In the aftermath of the putsch, Sukhanov analyzed its effects: "The peril was at hand. By now it was not only the central Soviets of the capital and the leaders of all the others that were in Lenin's hands. . . . But the army in the field! And the garrisons in the rear! All this . . . meant a brimming over of all real power and State sovereignty . . . into the hands of the Bolshevik 'outsiders' firmly united with the masses."[45]

At the same time, the swift Bolshevization of the country forced the other socialists–Mensheviks and SRs–to move to the left in order not to be left behind. It was becoming clear that bourgeois democracy was moribund.

THE EVE OF BATTLE

Russia was inexorably sliding toward another revolution, but the now paralyzed Kerensky barely reacted. The Provisional Government survived in a fourth coalition, in which he remained prime minister, that was formed on September 24. This government's authority was minimal, because power had definitively been cut in two between the Soviet and the government. From September 4, the Petrograd Soviet had been under the presidency of Trotsky, who had just been released from prison. As soon as he was elected, he took the floor to declare that he was not taking the place of Chkheidze, but that it was Chkheidze who had usurped his. Having been president of the Soviet in 1905, Trotsky was thereby emphasizing the continuity of the revolutionary movement. At the same time, he made efforts to present a still liberal image of the Soviet, asserting that although its task was to lead the revolution to final victory, the Soviet "will never oppress the minority." A few weeks were enough to demonstrate the illusory nature of proclamations of the kind. Trotsky further asserted that the government no longer represented anything but itself, that it no longer made sense to have any link to it. He expected from the Second Congress of Soviets, which was about to convene, the establishment of an authentically revolutionary government. In fact, in the wake of the putsch, the Soviet had secured the release of all the Bolsheviks arrested in July, and the Bolshevik Party was again in a strong position everywhere, which it showed by becoming demanding.

From Finland, Lenin had attentively followed both the putsch and the shifts of thinking in the barracks and factories over the following days. He soon understood that the power that had slipped from his grasp in July was now within reach. He now had to avoid tactical mistakes, and with Zinoviev's help he drew up a plan of action and concrete propositions for the immediate future. In a first stage following the failure of the putsch, Lenin's plan consisted of deriving the maximum advantage from the crisis that had just come to an end by definitively weakening Kerensky and showing that only the Bolsheviks were in a position to radically change the balance of forces. For this purpose he put forth what he called his "partial demands": "demand from Kerensky the arrest of Miliukov; distribute weapons to the workers; also demand the dissolution of the Duma, the establishment of workers' control over the factories, the immediate distribution of land, the suspension of all bourgeois newspapers, and so on." But Lenin's strategy in the days immediately following the putsch remained cautious. The lines of action that he sketched out for the use of the Party Central Committee, he explained, were an "indirect means of taking action." For the plan to be effective, the demands presented to Kerensky would have to be backed by the rank and file. The Bolsheviks therefore had the task of persuading workers and soldiers to speak in favor of them and to harass the dying government until Kerensky collapsed under the battering from the streets. Lenin also addressed these directives to public opinion in repetitive articles in *Rabochy Put* (Workers' Path) which had taken the place of *Pravda*, banned since the July days.

Following Lenin's instructions the Bolsheviks gradually took control of political bodies in the capital and in the provinces. For example, on September 25 elections to the Executive Committee of the Petrograd Soviet, previously under Menshevik control, gave two-thirds of the forty-four seats to the Bolsheviks, five to the Mensheviks, and none to the Menshevik-Internationalists who had been in the majority at the beginning of the revolution. The Bolsheviks had won a majority in Moscow six days earlier. Aware of the strength of the Mensheviks and the SRs in various political bodies, Lenin had proposed a compromise to them through an article published in *Rabochy Put*. This article suggested that if the Soviet broke with the bourgeois parties, if the Petrograd Soviet and its local counterparts were given supreme authority, and finally if freedom of agitation was accepted with no limitations, then the Bolsheviks were ready to support the Soviet. At the very moment that he was proposing this compromise to the other socialists, Lenin commented: "This offer has probably come too late, and the time when a peaceful development of the revolution was possible is already past."

In his Finnish refuge, he moved very quickly from an attitude of caution to more radical proposals. He was seized with impatience. After advising it to revive the slogan "All Power to the Soviets!" (which was done in *Rabochy Put* on September 14), he wrote to the Central Committee that the time had come to take power. In this case, he wrote secret letters rather than public articles. "The Bolsheviks must seize power"[46] was the heading of the letter dated September 12–14, supplemented by directives on "Marxism and Insurrection" written on the same dates.[47] Martov summed up the situation at the time in these terms: "There are now only two ways of forming a government. Either the act of a citizen placing a ballot in the ballot box, or the act of a citizen loading his gun." Lenin's position had no more ambiguities: he had chosen the second way.

He demonstrated this radical position on the question of participation in the Democratic Conference called by the government in anticipation of the November elections which were supposed to establish the Constituent Assembly. Out of this conference was supposed to come a Pre-Parliament, and positions diverged within the Bolshevik Party on the attitude that should be adopted toward it. Stalin and Trotsky favored a boycott, but the majority followed Kamenev and Rykov, who supported participation. Lenin exploded: "You should immediately besiege the conference site and arrest all that jail bait. Otherwise, you are nothing but weaklings."[48]

Bukharin later reported that Lenin's reaction, contained in a letter to the Central Committee, left its members dumbfounded. After a debate on what action to take, they decided to forget the incident and to destroy the letter, the violence of which, going so far as to threaten anyone who disobeyed the absent leader, was unacceptable to them.

This is an example of the strange climate then prevailing inside the Bolshevik Party. There was a majority in favor of a wait-and-see position, anxious not to repeat the mistakes of July. On the other hand was Lenin, eager for immediate action and furious that he was not listened to. He was even more furious that his letters to the Central Committee, all of which expressed the urgency of an insurrection, were suppressed by that body and were not published in the party press. The tenor of some of them was not revealed until 1921. Lenin was so exasperated that he threatened the Central Committee that he would resign and go in person to explain to the rank and file that the party was fearful, that it refused to have confidence in a working class that was ready to undertake the final assault.

This was not the first time that Lenin had come up against the caution of the party. But in September, he had a potential ally of great authority, Trotsky. Trotsky had transformed the Soviet into a veritable bastion of the Bolshevik Party, and this success had encouraged him to believe, as Lenin did, that the situation was ripe for a radical political change. Although he was not in complete agreement with Lenin, this did not have to do with the problem of the seizure of power, for which he thought the conditions were already established, but only with its timing.

Lenin wanted to wait no longer. He thought in terms of urgency and strategy. In his view, waiting was "a crime and a danger," because reaction was always to be feared. The urgency also had to do with the fact that he saw increased agitation in the capitalist countries, particularly in Germany, where mutinies had broken out in the army, he wrote, and where the support of a proletariat ready to act would not fail the Russian revolution. Lenin was also haunted by a problem of revolutionary strategy. Leaving the decision to the Congress of Soviets, as Trotsky proposed, would mean diminishing the historic role of the party, subordinating it to the Soviets. They had been Bolshevized, not only in Petrograd and Moscow. In the course of the month of September, the Soviets of Ivanovo-Voznesentsk, Saratov, and many other cities had passed into the hands of the Bolsheviks. Because the authority of the party over them was established, it was up to the party to act.

Waiting in a peaceful place removed from revolutionary agitation was now intolerable for Lenin. He felt the need to be near not only the revolutionary center but also the Bolsheviks, in order to put pressure on them. In late September he left Finland and moved, still in hiding, to Vyborg, accompanied by the inevitable Zinoviev. From there he sent to *Rabochy Put* an article entitled "The Crisis Is Ripe," in which he proclaimed: "We are on the eve of a world revolution."[49]

The party would no longer be able to avoid Lenin's presence and his pressure. The distance between Vyborg and Petrograd was not great. In a few days, he decided to join his associates and to set in motion, with Trotsky's help, the final phase of his plans, the one that would give meaning to his lifelong battle and thus to his entire life, the seizure of power.

Chapter Nine

ALL POWER TO THE BOLSHEVIKS

IN THE EARLY DAYS OF OCTOBER, PETROGRAD HAD SEVERAL political centers, and the actors of the revolution were constantly running from one to another. There were first of all the two official centers of the "dual power." After the July days the government was headquartered in the Winter Palace, on the banks of the Neva. At the same time, the Soviet had left the Tauride Palace and taken possession of the Smolny Institute, a favored school for noble girls before the revolution. On October 7 the Pre-Parliament, or more officially the Provisional Council of the Russian Republic, had been solemnly installed in the Marinsky Palace. Kerensky had in fact proclaimed the Russian Republic on September 1. Each of these centers had its own predominant political characteristics. The government coalition excluded the Bolsheviks and preserved the previous balance between SRs and liberals, while the Soviets of Petrograd and Moscow were at the same time dominated by the Bolsheviks, who also had full authority over the *Ispolkom* or Executive Committee of the Soviet. The Pre-Parliament, consisting of 308 delegates, had a majority made up of SRs (120) and Mensheviks (60); the Bolsheviks had a minority of 60 delegates sometimes supported by 20 Left SRs. Facing them, a delegation of 75 from the Constitutional Democratic or Kadet Party had little influence on debates, indicating the shift to the left that had taken place in Russian political institutions.[1]

The delegates to this Pre-Parliament had been chosen by the political parties, and they generally were hesitant about the purpose of the body. There were some notable absences: above all Plekhanov, prevented from participating in events by age and illness, and Lenin, the warrant for whose arrest was renewed every week and who remained discreetly in hiding. Despite the Bolshevik debate about the boycott, Trotsky was present and launched a veritable declaration of war against the established authorities at the opening session, calling on Russia to immediately give all power to the Soviets. His diatribe unleashed an indescribable uproar, punctuated with reminders of Lenin's treason and the notorious "sealed train," and with shouted insults. Trotsky himself was called a "bastard," and in this tumult, the Bolsheviks definitively left the Pre-Parliament, thereby indicating to the other socialists that they were breaking with existing institutions and with them. Sukhanov fully understood their gesture: "There was

153

only one road for them out of the Pre-Parliament—to the barricades. If they cast away the 'electoral ballot,' they must take up the rifle."

While continuing its official existence, the Pre-Parliament henceforth held no further interest. And the political competition was reduced to that between the organizations of the dual power.

LENIN'S IMPATIENCE

Lenin observed the unfolding of events from his place of hiding and was worried by some of them because he was afraid those events would have unfavorable consequences for his plans. The election of the Constituent Assembly in particular seemed to him to pose a threat. Long delayed, it had finally been set for November 12. At first sight, it might be thought that the vote would produce an Assembly mirroring the Soviets, favorable to the Bolsheviks, but he suspected that things would turn out otherwise. The Soviets were elected in cities by workers. But the largest proportion of the population were peasants and supporters of the Socialist Revolutionaries, who were impatiently awaiting the elections in order to come to power. An Assembly elected by popular vote, enjoying unquestionable legitimacy, would become the only real representation of the people. This election would prevent the Bolsheviks from speaking, as they constantly did, in the name of the people. And it would be difficult to snatch power away from that kind of Assembly.

Moreover, Lenin had long refrained from expressing support for the proposal for a Constituent Assembly. The slogan he had launched in April and fiercely defended since then, "All Power to the Soviets!" left no room for the authority of an assembly elected by the country as a whole. For months Bolshevik statements on the subject had been remarkably duplicitous. Lenin refrained from mentioning it, while the rest of the party forcefully proclaimed: "Long live the power of the Soviets in the name of the Constituent Assembly!"

In October, with the elections approaching, this duplicitous language became untenable, and the Bolsheviks endeavored to show how much Lenin cherished the Constituent Assembly. On October 4, *Rabochy Put* wrote: "Lenin has never been against the Constituent Assembly. From the very first months, along with our entire Party, he unmasked the Provisional Government which was delaying its calling. If our revolution succeeds, we will see in practice a perfect association between the Republic of Soviets and the Constituent Assembly." This article, unsigned but brilliantly argued, was probably written by Zinoviev, who was still at Lenin's side, and was a witness during the period underground to his doubts and adaptations to a situation that caused him great anxiety.

Indeed, in addition to the prospect of elections, Lenin was worried by the German threat hanging over the capital, out of which he thought Kerensky might be able to come up with ways of weakening the Bolshevik position. Already in the Baltic provinces, the German troops were a short distance from

Petrograd and appeared to be in a position to capture it in the early days of October. If the danger were to become more definite, Kerensky was then thinking of transferring the government to Moscow, and he put in place a plan for evacuating the capital. At the same time, he left it up to the *Ispolkom* to arrive at its own position. Lenin saw this as a plan intended to surrender the capital to the Germans, along with the working class and the institutions dominated by the Bolsheviks. He suspected Kerensky of wanting in this way to settle the Bolshevik problem, with German help, and thus to stay in power. Duly instructed by Trotsky, the *Ispolkom* declared that nothing could be decided without its participation, challenging in particular Kerensky's instructions to send reinforcements taken from the capital's garrison to the precarious Baltic front.

Finally, Lenin was confronted with the problem of the next Congress of Soviets. He wondered whether it might not form a counterweight to an as yet nonexistent Constituent Assembly. In fact a Congress of Soviets elected principally in cities could also serve as a body that would legitimate the Bolsheviks' claim to be the true representatives of the society. If not that, it could cover and legitimate a coup fomented by them in order to seize power. At this point the Bolsheviks came up against two difficulties. The other Socialist parties were reluctant to convene a Congress of Soviets which they sensed would weaken the Constituent Assembly or render it pointless. On the other hand, they were worried at the prospect of a Bolshevik majority in the Congress, whereas they felt capable of winning the November election. The Soviets that the Bolsheviks consulted expressed a similar reluctance. There too the Constituent Assembly on the point of being elected had widespread support. Since February a veritable myth of the Constituent Assembly had grown up in Russia, which had become all the more seductive as its convocation had been constantly postponed *sine die.* The decision to summon it, announced by Kerensky after the July days, had revived hopes, and everyone was awaiting the moment, even in the Bolshevized Soviets of the capital.

The Bolsheviks were not prepared to accept any opposition, either from their opponents or from those they considered under their control. Overriding various objections they gave to the *Ispolkom*, over which they exercised control, the task of announcing that the Second Congress of Soviets would meet in Petrograd on October 20. Then the date was changed and definitively set for October 25.

The way in which the Congress was constituted was hardly in conformity with the rules of representation. Fearing that they would be a minority, the Bolsheviks manipulated the preparations to such an extent that even the *Ispolkom* was disturbed, and *Izvestia* denounced them. The quotas for representation—one delegate for twenty five thousand electors—were ignored. Sometimes the Bolsheviks simply eliminated districts, and sometimes they gave a few hundred people abusively called "districts" the right to elect a delegate to the Congress. The other Socialist parties exposed the maneuvers, but it was too late to stop the electoral machinery and take away from the Bolsheviks the powers that they had arrogated to themselves.

MUST POWER BE SEIZED BY FORCE?

For Lenin there was no doubt about the answer: the time had come to set off the insurrection and to seize power by force. By the end of September, he was writing to his colleagues: "Having the majority in the Soviet, the Bolsheviks can and should seize state power." The observation was accompanied by concrete instructions: "Without losing an instant, we should organize a command post for insurrectional detachments, distribute our forces, send our surest regiments to the most important points, occupy the telegraph and telephone exchange . . . set up our headquarters there, and connect it by telephone to all the factories and all the regiments." Far from responding to these orders, the Bolsheviks had attempted to persuade Lenin to remain in Finland in order to escape from the police. But, listening to his intuition alone, he decided to come closer to the theater of operations, and it was then that he took up hiding in Vyborg. From there his messages proliferated, tirelessly demonstrating to his supporters that they could wait no longer. The reasons for his impatience were clear. He had thought about the Bolshevik defeat in July and realized that it was hardly likely that he would enjoy broad support among the masses, a belief held by the majority of his companions. The conclusion he drew from this analysis was in accordance with the convictions that he had always held, namely, that "professionals" would make the revolution by means of a carefully prepared insurrection. He was convinced that they should paralyze the centers of power and not wait for it to fall into their hands through a popular uprising.

Lenin's imprecations against those in the party who wanted to wait came one after the other. On October 7 he wrote, "If the Bolsheviks are taken in by the trap of constitutional illusions, faith in the convocation of the Constituent Assembly, waiting for the Congress of Soviets, and so on, they will become veritable traitors to the proletarian cause."[2] And, no longer able to stand giving orders from a distance, coming up against the unwillingness or hesitations of his colleagues, he turned up in Petrograd on October 10, still wearing a wig and clean shaven, with a bald and bearded Zinoviev in tow, both of them highly amused by their disguises. He attended a meeting of twelve members of the party's Central Committee, held in Sukhanov's apartment, in his absence and without his knowledge, at which, as his memoirs indicate, Sukhanov took strong offense.[3] In any event the essential point was that Lenin intended to drag the Central Committee into the decision to set off the insurrection before the meeting of the Congress of Soviets.

On the necessity of launching an armed insurrection to seize power, Lenin could count on a powerful ally in the person of Trotsky, who considered the situation ripe for a takeover by force. The two men continued to disagree about the date.

Lenin demanded an immediate insurrection, that is, before October 25. In support of his position, he asserted that the internal situation was ripe, that the masses would follow the Bolsheviks as soon as they had seized power from the government. Moreover he put forth the possibility of a world revolution breaking out in the wake of the Russian revolution.

Although Trotsky was equally persuaded of the necessity of a takeover by force, he nevertheless wanted to wait for the meeting of the Congress of Soviets, which would confer legitimacy on the uprising.

Lenin confronted opposition from the faithful Zinoviev, Kamenev, Nogin, Mikhail Uritsky, and Rykov, who were all against an insurrection. For them the action was premature. The Bolsheviks risked defeat, whereas the Congress of Soviets and well-prepared elections to the Constituent Assembly could give them the means to come to power peacefully.

The final vote dividing the two camps of the Central Committee was in favor of Lenin's position, which succeeded in persuading all who had hesitated, except Zinoviev and Kamenev. The latter refused to support the decision and resigned from the Central Committee. Even so the resolution that Lenin had gotten from the other members of the Central Committee, although it asserted that armed uprising was on the agenda, was not very precise about the date and more or less linked the uprising to the Congress of Soviets. The idea was that the uprising would come very shortly before the Congress convened, and the Congress would then confer immediate legitimacy on the uprising. The day after the meeting, the two who had opposed the decision wrote a letter to Bolshevik organizations challenging it, which constituted a violation of party rules of discipline. On October 16 they reaffirmed their opposition before a meeting of the full Central Committee. Finally, on October 18, Kamenev and Zinoviev published a letter in Gorky's newspaper *Novaya Zhizn,* in which they described the insurrection as a "desperate act." A furious Lenin, who was again in hiding, wrote to the Central Committee demanding that the "strike-breakers" be kicked out of the party. But Kamenev had already submitted his resignation to the Central Committee. As for the other members of the Central Committee, even those who had come around to Lenin's position, they were far from unanimous in their support of him. Hence Lenin's letter was published in the Party organ *Rabochy Put,* but it was accompanied by a discordant note from Stalin: "The brutal tone of comrade Lenin should not conceal the fact that, fundamentally, we are in agreement."

Lenin's "Letter to the Comrades" was published in three installments from October 19 through October 21.[4] On October 20 the Central Committee met without Lenin but with his instructions and his letter of invectives against those whom he called "criminals." Kamenev's resignation from the Central Committee was accepted, but Lenin's demand to expel his two opponents from the party was "omitted" by the Central Committee. They were simply ordered to make no more public declarations about their opposition to decisions made by the majority of the party. In any case things were happening so quickly that the members of the Central Committee were more intent on preparing for the insurrection than on exploring their differences.

A MILITARY TOOL FOR THE INSURRECTION

Whether they favored or opposed armed action, all the Bolsheviks were aware of their relative weakness. They knew that despite their propagandizing of military units, the majority of soldiers were not prepared to follow them. They therefore needed an effective military instrument before they could think of taking action. This instrument was the Military Revolutionary Committee (MRC), established on October 9, on the eve of the meeting of the party Central Committee. At the outset this body had in fact been proposed by the Mensheviks in the Soviet for the purpose of organizing the defense of the capital at a time when there was fear of a German offensive. On reflection the Bolsheviks had understood the benefits they could derive from the plan, and during the debate they presented a resolution defining their own conception of a committee of defense (defense against "internal" as well as external enemies), enumerating the bodies that should be represented on it and the powers that it would have. If this Bolshevik resolution is read carefully, it becomes clear that in their view the creation of the MRC was in itself already a veritable coup d'état. The legal organs of power were kept at a distance from the MRC in favor of the Soviet alone. The Executive Committee or *Ispolkom* was to concentrate in its hands all military authority, that is, in fact, to appropriate complete power. Commenting on the Bolshevik resolution, Sukhanov recounts the conditions in which it was finally adopted by the plenum of the Soviet. In the course of the debate, a Menshevik representative declared that "the projected Military Revolutionary Committee is nothing but a revolutionary staff for the seizure of power." This drew an immediate stinging response from Trotsky, asking whether he was speaking in the name of Kerensky or of the Okhrana, which provoked tumultuous enthusiasm in the hall and helped to secure passage of the resolution by an overwhelming majority.

The revolutionary tool now existed, and it was in the hands of the Bolsheviks. In it they held an effective means of isolating the government from the military forces and could perfectly legally give instructions to those forces. As a result those who were worried by the increasing power of the Bolsheviks expressed their fears, but few of them had a precise sense of what Lenin was preparing and what he was capable of doing. On October 18 Gorky published an alarmist article: "Rumors are being spread more and more insistently about a Bolshevik coup. . . . The Bolshevik Central Committee has done nothing to confirm the rumors of a coup, though it hasn't refuted them either. . . . It is its duty to refute them, if it really is a powerful and freely acting political organ capable of directing the masses." The anxiety expressed by Gorky was shared by the chief of staff of the Petrograd region who repeated various rumors running through the capital. In a report to Kerensky, he had noted that the Bolsheviks were preparing a "demonstration of protest against the Government." It "would have a peaceful character, but nevertheless the workers would come out armed."

The question then arises, as it did for Sukhanov, of how to explain the surprising passivity of Kerensky in the face of such warnings. His response at the time matches what he said in conversation a half century later: he did not believe that Lenin would be able to bring his plans to fruition.[5]

An examination of Kerensky's behavior throughout the period running from April to October 1917 reveals two attitudes characterizing all his choices. In the first place, it is obvious that for a long time he underestimated Lenin, although he considered him a dangerous agitator. Sukhanov calls his attitude "naïveté and childishness." In Kerensky's constant determination to rely on shaky institutions while he believed he was offering real resistance to Lenin, there was unquestionably a large degree of naïveté. When, in October 1917, the head of the government still hoped that the Pre-Parliament and the announcement of the (oh so belated) elections to the Constituent Assembly would be enough to pacify Russia, he showed himself to be immensely less clearheaded than men such as Dan and Martov who had continually warned him about the disturbing authority that the MRC was arrogating to itself. For his part Martov had understood from the outset that the MRC would block the government from any direct contact with the army, and that, even before the Bolshevik seizure of power, it gave them full authority over the soldiers. What could a disintegrating government do if it no longer had any armed forces? Kerensky avoided asking himself that question to the very end.

There is another explanation for his attitude, which the American historian Richard Pipes has developed at length and is just as plausible. Kerensky, he explains, feared above all a coup from the right.[6] During the dramatic July days, and he was persuaded of the same thing in October, he had thought that the right was using Lenin as a bugbear to justify a coup and perhaps even an attempt to restore the monarchy. Indeed this explanation complements the preceding one. Both indicate Kerensky's blindness in the face of Lenin and his schemes. Because he underestimated the Bolshevik leader's thirst for power and the effectiveness of the resources he put into operation to attain his goal, Kerensky left Lenin free to the very end to mobilize the most active elements of the army and the working class, while he directed his own efforts of resistance against those on the right whom he suspected of plotting against him. Most important, at no time was he really troubled by the establishment of the Military Revolutionary Committee. The Mensheviks, even though they were more lucid in their fears of Lenin, sometimes helped to foster this naïveté. During a debate in the Central Executive Committee intended to decide on measures for the defense of the capital, referring to the activity of the Bolsheviks, Dan ingenuously asked that they say whether they intended to seize power, to which the Bolshevik spokesman David Ryazanov of course replied: "Dan knows that we are Marxists and do not prepare uprisings."

The credulity revealed by a dialogue of this kind, as surprising as the reluctant attitude of Kerensky, explains why Lenin's determination, at the opposite pole from his caution in July, was unshakable in October.

THE "CREEPING" INSURRECTION

By October 21, the situation in the capital gave evidence of Bolshevik preparations for the seizure of power. Lenin sent the following message to Smilga, chairman of the Committee of Workers, Soldiers, and Sailors of Helsinki: "It is ridiculous to waste time voting on resolutions and amendments when we should be preparing to overthrow Kerensky. The most important question is obtaining weapons. . . . As for your role, it is to insure that we have the cooperation of the Finnish army and the Baltic fleet."[7]

By the following day, operations were underway. The MRC decided to place the Petrograd garrison officially under its authority, informing it that it would have to deal henceforth only with orders from that body, and would be responsible only to it. Informed of this coup d'état, the chief of staff turned to the Soviet, the body that had theoretically created the MRC, which was already entirely controlled by the Bolsheviks, and demanded that it immediately denounce the instructions given to the garrison if it wanted to avoid an open conflict with the government. Kerensky, duly informed, but still as unaware of the real strength of the Bolsheviks, still believed in the possibility of taking advantage of these first steps toward a coup d'état to take action and finally annihilate his enemies. He was still calculating in October on the basis of the balance of forces that had prevailed in July. He deliberately ignored the arrival in Petrograd of a Lenin who was determined this time to carry his plans out to the end.

On the same day, the Soviet held an emergency session in the Smolny Institute. The Bolsheviks had taken pains to invite leaders or representatives of the regiments stationed in the capital. It was to them that Trotsky spoke to inform them that the staff had refused to submit to the authority of the MRC, and he declared:

> [T]he Staff of the Petrograd military area has failed to recognize the Military Revolutionary Committee. . . . By this very fact . . . the Staff has made itself the tool of counter-revolutionary forces. . . . Soldiers of Petrograd! The defense of revolutionary order . . . is incumbent on you, under the leadership of the Military Revolutionary Committee. No orders to the garrison, not signed by the Military Revolutionary Committee, are valid.

War had thus been declared on the government and the military staff, and Kerensky had to decide on a response, which turned out to be feeble and inappropriate. He called on the Don Cossacks commanded by General Petr Krasnov, who had been stationed at a short distance from the capital. But the Bolsheviks were on the watch, and the movement of Cossacks ordered by the government was immediately blocked. On the evening of October 22, Kerensky then called on the students of the military schools, who, having been subjected to intense Bolshevik propaganda, were reluctant to obey orders from a government that was already being called illegitimate. It was only two days later, on October 24, that some young officer cadets took up guard positions at various strategic locations in the capital. However, they were dispersed, and defense of the Winter Palace was handed over to a battalion of female shock troops. From that moment on, troops called up as reinforcements took the precaution of asking that orders given them by the government be confirmed by the Soviet. Once they took that step, it was a simple matter for the Soviet to tell them not to move, which explains why, despite the still imposing military resources it might have had available, the government was able to mobilize only a very small part of them.

While Kerensky was wasting time giving orders that were followed with reluctance, the preparation of the coup d'état continued. On October 23, in a debate with his colleagues, Lenin had finally won them over to his point of view: the insurrection could no longer wait; it had to be carried out before the opening of the Congress of Soviets on October 25.[8]

At the moment when the insurrection was set in motion, the MRC contained two members of the party Central Committee, two representatives of the Left SRs, four representatives of the soldiers of Petrograd, and, above all, among the most active figures, Trotsky leading the whole operation, as well as Dzerzhinsky, Vladimir Antonov-Ovseyenko, M. M. Lashevich, Vladimir Nevsky, and N. I. Podvoisky. The men gathered around Trotsky during those decisive hours were Bolsheviks who had followed different trajectories, but who were all logically led to come together at the Smolny Institute on the night of October 24.

Antonov-Ovseyenko, in the first place, was particularly suited to take care of the military aspects of the coup d'état. A career officer trained in the cadet school of the capital, he was more capable than anyone else of indoctrinating his juniors, the aspirants of 1917. What he was doing in October he had already attempted in 1905 when, as a member of the RSDLP and a participant in the subversive activities of the army in which he was an officer, he had provoked a mutiny in two regiments stationed in Poland. A Menshevik until 1914, and then a member of Trotsky's group of internationalists, he was very close to Trotsky. His military past and his exploits in 1905 had given Antonov-Ovseyenko the reputation of being one of the most competent experts for organizing an insurrection. Nevertheless his relations with Lenin were strained. As a Menshevik he had vehemently attacked the Bolsheviks and called their leader and his party "corruptors." The role assigned to him in the "troika," leading the insurrection, was due both to Trotsky's support and to his extraordinary military skill.[9]

Felix Dzerzhinsky was quite different; he was a member of the Polish gentry who had been won over to Social Democracy at an early age, was first close to Rosa Luxemburg, but had later moved away from her and sided with Lenin. From that point on, in 1911, Dzerzhinsky had been an ally of incomparable loyalty, supporting Lenin on every occasion on which the party was divided and especially every time Lenin found himself in the minority. How could he not appreciate such a supporter? Indeed, in the October 16 debate, when the Central Committee was reluctant to follow him on the problem of the insurrection,

Dzerzhinsky had violently opposed Zinoviev and Kamenev, helping to tilt the balance in Lenin's favor. Quite naturally appointed to the MRC, on October 24 he had the heavy responsibility of keeping watch on all the movements of the Provisional Government.

Podvoisky and Nevsky, who were both a few years younger than Lenin, had together established the party military organization in the capital in the late summer of 1917. The former became president of the MRC and after the revolution devoted himself to army matters.

Lashevich, finally, was just a worker, and hence later not inclined to climb the rungs of the Party hierarchy. But in 1917, he had excellent credentials for playing the role assigned to him, because, as a noncommissioned officer, he had succeeded in bringing his entire regiment over to the revolution.

It can thus be seen that the tool for insurrection was not merely a formal structure but was made up of genuine specialists.

In the course of October 23, both the Bolsheviks and the government had made a number of decisions tending to make the situation irreversible. The MRC had sent delegates—the first military political commissars—to all units in the garrison and widely distributed a communiqué stipulating that "all power now belongs to the Military Revolutionary Committee. Troops must obey Committee orders transmitted by commissars." A military detachment under the command of a commissar was also sent to the *Pravda* printing plant, which had been closed on government orders, and had it immediately reopened. On the other side, orders and counterorders came one after another. Kerensky decided to ban Bolshevik newspapers in order to block their propaganda. Always equally concerned to close the door to reaction, he also banned two right-wing papers, depriving his action of any practical impact. He also considered ordering the arrest of the members of the MRC who, with their call for army disobedience, had just provided him with an excellent pretext for doing so. But the minister of justice was opposed, alleging that such an act could be considered a provocation.

Always unsure of his prerogatives, Kerensky then decided to ask the Pre-Parliament for its agreement to repressive measures. This step is a clear illustration of the strange situation in which Russia found itself. The MRC had already declared itself the legal holder of power. At the same time, Kerensky was asking a garrulous assembly to give him the authorization to take the "energetic measures" necessary for the restoration of order. Martov, the Menshevik leader, whose political intelligence was undeniable but who often lacked clearheadedness, had the Pre-Parliament pass a resolution asking the government to carry on a democratic policy in order to prevent civil war. Martov gave no indication of how this was to be done. The Pre-Parliament would have been in favor of a Committee of Public Safety, but this notion remained a purely theoretical one. Besides, there were no forces on which such a body could rely, because the garrison was beyond government control.

While all these debates, prognostications, and proposals were going on, the first act of open insurrection was unfolding. A small group of sailors, led by a commissar, occupied the government telegraph agency. Because it was poorly guarded, the seizure took place without damage, and there ensued a rather comic flurry of activity. Informed of the event and of the small number of sailors occupying the telegraph agency, Kerensky sent a small detachment of military cadets who dislodged the occupiers and recaptured the premises without a struggle. The telephone lines to the Smolny Institute were immediately cut, and the Bolsheviks were isolated from their supporters outside.

This sequence of events suggests that with a little decisiveness the irreparable might have been avoided. But the government victory did not last very long. On October 24, the die was cast on the other side, and the Bolsheviks were assured of definitive victory.

SUCCESS OF THE INSURRECTION

Everything was decided on October 24. The two enemy forces had decided to bring things to a head. Somewhat encouraged by the recapture of the telegraph agency and convinced that, without telephone contacts, his opponents were now in difficulty, Kerensky announced that he was taking action. With military cadets deployed throughout the city, he ordered the Cossacks, who had finally arrived, to fight the Bolsheviks, and he telegraphed the commander of the Northern Front to have him urgently send troops to help. Orders were given to raise the bridges on the Neva to prevent reinforcements from coming to the aid of the Bolsheviks. At the same time, Lenin was planning the insurrection, ordering that the uprising begin during the day, or at the very latest, the night of October 25. The campaign plan was established by the MRC. Late on October 24, Lenin put on his wig and went in disguise to the Smolny Institute, where he spent the night with the members of the MRC, especially Trotsky, the principal organizer of the operation, who was in charge of its successful execution.

The first step was to restore access to Petrograd and neutralize all the forces suspected of intending to defend the government. Soldiers commanded by commissars lowered the Neva drawbridges. During the night troops occupied the districts around the Finland Station and then moved toward the center of the capital. All strategic points and seats of power were quickly taken by force: railway stations, bridges, telephone and telegraph agency, state bank. At the telephone agency, the Bolsheviks paid the government back; after restoring their own lines during the day, they cut off lines to the Winter Palace. The government in turn was isolated and unable to follow developments.

A particularity of the October 25 insurrection is that it had essentially been accomplished beforehand, in the course of the preceding days when the MRC was establishing control over the army. The portion of the insurrection for which Lenin gave the signal on October 24 hardly resembled an uprising, because it took place in a surprisingly calm atmosphere. When confronted by Communist detachments, the cadets guarding strategic points controlled by the government turned out to be unable to offer any resistance. They were ordered by the commissars leading the revolutionary detachments to withdraw, and they obeyed. No shots were fired, and the city imperceptibly fell under Bolshevik control.

As Sukhanov correctly pointed out, the most important moment in an insurrection comes when the existing authority has been defeated and the seat of power passes into the hands of the insurgents. But during the night of October 24–25, no one was concerned with the Winter Palace or with Kerensky or his ministers. Lenin himself, who had been dreaming of this seizure of power throughout his life, who could finally relish the moment, found it more urgent to publicize his success than to decide on the fate of his predecessors. He ordered that bells be rung at ten in the morning, and he set to work on the proclamation that would be read in every city and broadcast on crackling and often inaudible radios at the front and to the most distant confines of Russia:

To the Citizens of Russia. The Provisional Government has been deposed. State power has passed into the hands of the organ of the Petrograd Soviet of Workers' and Soldiers' Deputies, the Military Revolutionary Committee, which heads the Petrograd proletariat and the garrison. The cause for which the people have fought, namely, the immediate offer of a democratic peace, the abolition of landed proprietorship, workers' control over production, and the establishment of Soviet power–this cause has been secured. Long live the revolution of workers, soldiers, and peasants![10]

This manifesto was signed by the MRC. Its content and composition were, however, entirely the work of Lenin, who went on a few hours later to harangue a constantly growing crowd at the Smolny Institute. Sukhanov describes the scene at around three o'clock when he arrived: "I went straight . . . into the great hall . . . Trotsky was chairman. . . . an unknown, bald, clean-shaven man was standing on the platform making a heated speech. But he spoke in a strangely familiar, loud, hoarse voice. . . . Eh–Lenin! He had appeared that day, after a four-month stay underground."[11]

A few moments earlier, Trotsky, who had just read Lenin's manifesto to the crowd, had said: "We were told that the insurrection would provoke a pogrom and drown the revolution in torrents of blood. So far everything has gone off bloodlessly. We don't know of a single casualty. I don't know of any examples in history of a revolutionary movement . . . which took place so bloodlessly." At three o'clock in the afternoon of that day, Trotsky was right–Lenin's revolution was showing a peaceful face. No one could yet imagine that it would cause torrents of blood to flow and that Trotsky's blood would join it one sunny day in August 1940.

The mood in those hours of triumph was not merely optimistic but close to utopian. Lenin declared to his listeners: "The oppressed masses themselves will form a government." In the capital, aside from those constantly running back and forth between the Marinsky Palace and the Smolny Institute, no one knew that the political order had just been overturned. Stores were open, and many people were on the streets. Louis de Robien, an attaché at the French embassy and an eyewitness to the revolution, wrote in his diary for November 7 (October

25 on the Julian calendar in use in Russia): "The city is apparently quite calm. You cannot even see the usual trucks with their cargo of *tovarisch* striking heroic poses."[12]

The question of government, however invisible the existing one had become, had yet to be settled. The Bolsheviks had everywhere proclaimed their accession to power, or more precisely that of the Soviet that they dominated, but the Provisional Government still existed and, further, the Second Congress of Soviets was about to begin. Then where did legal power lie?

Lenin decided that the Winter Palace should be stormed before the Congress began its work. But could this be done without danger? The Bolsheviks were afraid that Kerensky, who had gone to seek for help from the command of the Northern Front in Pskov (an expedition made necessary by the silence that had greeted his pleas), would return to the capital with reinforcements. The ministers were barricaded in the Winter Palace, without protection. Although Sukhanov asserts that the troops charged with defending the seat of government were insufficient in number and not very warlike, when the assault finally came, the women of the Battalion of Death demonstrated genuine courage. Nevertheless fervor for participating either in the insurrection or in the struggle to defend the government was lacking on either side. This is a surprising aspect of these revolutionary days. The capital garrison had two hundred thousand men subject to constant pressure from the Bolsheviks, but barely one-tenth of their number participated in the struggle. On the other side, the military cadets on which Kerensky counted so heavily were highly inclined to return to their schools as soon as they were asked to in the name of the revolution. As for the regiments who were supposed to have remained loyal to the government, they were in no hurry to fly to its assistance. This explains the calm that prevailed in Petrograd until the final assault.

On October 25 a cautious approach was no longer possible. Lenin feared the sudden arrival in the city of the reinforcements called for by Kerensky and was not totally convinced that the troops who had come over to his side would be able to hold them off. However, he could not come before the Congress of Soviets while a government, even a ghostly and invisible government, was still in existence. The myth of the successful revolution presumed that power was concentrated in a single place. It was in fact its duality that had a few months earlier doomed the power that had come out of the February Revolution.

That afternoon he therefore gave the order to attack the Winter Palace and to put the entire Provisional Government under arrest. In the meanwhile Trotsky was attempting to put off the opening of the Congress of Soviets, whose delegates, gathered at the Smolny Institute, were growing impatient, not understanding the reason for these delaying tactics. Everyone was waiting for Lenin, but he refused to appear until the Winter Palace had been taken. He was camped out in a nearby room, lying on a makeshift bed, waiting for the event finally to happen.

In the end the MRC sent an ultimatum to the occupants of the Winter Palace: They had to surrender immediately or the attack would be launched, and the palace would come under fire from the cruiser *Aurora*, which had come under MRC control three days earlier and was lying at anchor opposite the palace, and from the Peter and Paul Fortress, also under MRC control. When the ultimatum was rejected, the assault began at eight o'clock, and it was swift and violent. Its defenders were awaiting the reinforcements that Kerensky had gone for; seeing that none were coming, they gradually scattered or surrendered. The women of the Battalion of Death were the last to resist, with some degree of courage, but they were too weak to hold off the assault. The Bolsheviks, under the command of Antonov-Ovseyenko, finally entered the Winter Palace around midnight, arrested the members of the government, and abandoned the building to an excited crowd, many of whom were drunk, who pillaged the palace and committed rapes and murders.

When he was brought news of the victory, Lenin leaped up and hurried to the hall where the Congress was in session. He was so impatient that he almost forgot to remove the wig that he had again been wearing out of caution. The only thing making his satisfaction incomplete was that Kerensky had not been arrested. He had fled after vainly attempting to get help. The other ministers had been taken to the Peter and Paul Fortress in an atmosphere of violence which, by the next day, would begin to replace the calm that had prevailed until then.[13]

The Winter Palace had already ceased to exist as a political entity. All the attention and energy of the Bolsheviks was now directed toward the Smolny Institute, where the Second Congress of Soviets was in session.

THE SECOND CONGRESS OF SOVIETS

A few hours before the capture of the Winter Palace, it had been necessary to formally open the Congress.[14] Trotsky's efforts to delay the moment had had to give way before the impatience of the delegates.

The Menshevik Dan opened the proceedings. But the election of the presidium soon demonstrated that the Bolsheviks enjoyed unchallangeable authority; fourteen of the twenty-five members elected were Bolsheviks, including Lenin, Trotsky, Zinoviev, Kamenev, Rykov, Nogin, Kollontai, Antonov-Ovseyenko, Lunacharsky, Muralov, and Ryazanov. The makeup of the Congress also indicated their preeminence; of 650 delegates, 360 were Bolsheviks, who would be joined by close to one hundred SRs. A Bolshevik, Kamenev, was of course named to preside over the Congress. A few hours later, he was able to announce triumphantly the fall of the Winter Palace and to read out earnestly, to the applause of some of the delegates, the list of ministers arrested and taken to prison. One of the Left SRs rose to protest against the arrest of Socialist ministers, but Trotsky brutally replied that there was no time now for such trifles. The revolution had swept away the old order, and the former ministers had suddenly become outside the law. The Mensheviks and SRs, who were in the minority, decided to leave the Congress, leaving the Bolsheviks in a much more comfortable position by increasing their relative strength in the assembly and removing from debate orators whose talent might still create an impression by denouncing their abuses of power. This was the case for Martov, who was outraged to hear Trotsky condemn the opposition to end up on "the garbage heap of history."

Between two sessions of the Congress, Lenin had gone off to draw up the decrees demonstrating the complete change of the political system that he would present to the second session. Kamenev opened the session by announcing the abolition of the death penalty and the liberation of all political prisoners that the Provisional Government had arrested. It is true that at the same time the prisons were beginning to welcome new "guests," the vanquished of the revolutionary days. Then Lenin read a long document made up of three sections to which we return: the decree on peace, the decree on the land, and the decree announcing the formation of a new government.

The reading of the first of the three decrees unleashed enthusiasm, and Lenin completed it to the sound of the *Internationale* intoned by all the delegates, who then passed the decree unanimously.

The assembly was less enthusiastic when it heard the decree on land. To be sure, it was adopted, and the only signs of reservations were eight abstentions and one negative vote, but in the atmosphere of nearly religious fervor that had taken hold in the Smolny Institute, under the suspicious gaze of the Bolsheviks who were constantly applauding, these hesitations already suggested a certain courage on the part of those expressing them.

The time came to decide on the question of the government. At the outset there was the question of what it was to be called. How could they arrange for its name to express the novelty of the revolutionary phenomenon, the "new world" into which Russia had made its entry? Lenin was particularly sensitive to the problem. When he had arrived at the Smolny Institute to present his decrees, he had triumphantly declared, "Let us greet the first day of the Revolution," a day that meant for him a total break with the past. Encountering Kamenev during these feverish hours, Sukhanov had asked him: "Are you going to set up ministers and ministries, as in a bourgeois society?" Kamenev replied: "It'll be a government by Boards, like during the Convention. The chairmen of the Boards will constitute the supreme organ of Government." This formulation was not adopted, but the term minister was dismissed from the outset by Lenin, who decreed: "Anything but minister."[15] Trotsky then thought of calling the members of the government "commissars" and the government the "Council of People's Commissars." Sukhanov notes that this suggestion seemed unfortunate to some of his friends, because "commissar" evoked police activities. Perhaps the Bolsheviks had unconsciously made that choice because they sensed that their power would have a strong need of taking on those forms.

Lenin's announcement of the formation of the government was not made in complete calm. The delegates who had protested against the Bolsheviks' hasty methods before walking out of the Congress had left a thorny question hanging which would, in the course of a few days, give rise to an important conflict. This was the matter of the total power that the Bolsheviks were intending to arrogate to themselves. To be sure, Lenin declared that he was talking of a "provisional government" intended to lead Russia until the Constituent Assembly was elected, but the composition of the government that he proposed, made up entirely of Bolsheviks, could only outrage the other Socialist parties.

In the beginning Lenin did not want to be part of the Council of Peoples Commissars (or *Sovnarkom*) and proposed that Trotsky be its leader. Trotsky declined the offer, and Lenin, under pressure from his closest comrades, had to accept the position of premier without portfolio.[16] The government was made up as follows: Rykov at interior; agriculture went to Milyutin (the author of a brochure on agriculture, he had accumulated a long record of arrests and sentences to imprisonment and exile before 1917); at labor, the trade unionist Shlyapnikov; military and naval affairs were given to a board consisting of Antonov-Ovseyenko, one of the leaders of the Petrograd insurrection, Lieutenant Krylenko, who had assisted him, and the sailor Pavel Dybenko; industry and commerce were given to a Muscovite, Nogin; education went to the brilliant intellectual, Lunacharsky; justice to G. Lomov (also known as Oppokov) who could boast of having studied law; finance to I. Skvortsov; supply to I. Teodorovich; and posts and telegraphs to Glebov (Avilov).

There were particularly noteworthy appointments to two other cabinet posts. Foreign affairs was given to Trotsky. This was a theoretically prestigious position, but one that needed fundamental restructuring in light of Lenin's views in the area. For this reason Trotsky had in fact been given a subordinate position. As for the position of commissar for nationalities, an innovation of the October Revolution, it could go only to Stalin.[17]

Two figures who were missing from this government deserve mention: Zinoviev and Kamenev. Of course, in meetings of the Central Committee on October 10 and 16, they had strongly opposed Lenin's desire to set off the insurrection. But they had finally been won over, and they had moreover been loyal followers who had never abandoned Lenin during the hard years of solitude before the war. Wondering about the causes for their absence from the government, Sukhanov suggests a different explanation: "[F]or tactical reasons it was advisable to cut down as much as possible on the number of Ministers of Jewish origin (the sole exception was Trotsky)."[18] Lenin had also decided to appoint Zinoviev as editor of the newspaper *Izvestia*, which was to become the government's official organ, and Kamenev as chairman of the Central Executive Committee (*Ispolkom*), a position he in fact occupied for a very short time.[19] The government was to be responsible to this Executive Committee, which supervised the activities of the commissars and had the power to dismiss them.

By the evening of October 26 then, everything in Russia was in the hands of the Bolsheviks. However, as Trotsky had pointed out, authority established in Petrograd did not imply success everywhere, and the struggle that unfolded in Moscow after the October 25 insurrection in the capital gave evidence of the resistance that the Bolsheviks were yet to encounter.

During the debates over the timeliness of an insurrection in the former Russian capital, the Bolsheviks had been rather inclined to support Zinoviev and

Kamenev. The proclamation of the successful revolution in Petrograd silenced their doubts, and, following the model that had already been tested, they immediately set up a Military Revolutionary Committee, with which the SRs, who had established their own Committee of Public Safety, refused to cooperate. Under Bukharin's leadership, the Moscow Bolsheviks decided to storm the Kremlin in order to signify their control over the city. They were unsuccessful at first, but then were saved by the arrival of reinforcements won over to their cause, while the Committee of Public Safety of the "Socialist Revolutionaries," which had at first believed they had won, collapsed.

Summed up in this way, the Bolshevization of Moscow seems to have been a simple matter. However, the account would be incomplete without noting the fact that, to win victory over an enemy determined to carry on a defense, the Bolshevik forces had to fight in every street and bombard houses (causing significant damage), and finally won out only because of the reinforcements that had come to their aid.

Fighting was also often fierce elsewhere; although cities ended by giving way before Bolshevik power, the countryside and the peripheral regions (we come back to them) remained generally closed off.

The Second Congress of Soviets was adjourned on October 27. It had been the shortest of all. The atmosphere in the capital had already become less peaceful than it was on the first evening of the revolution. On October 26, the MRC had sent sailors to the printing plants of newspapers it considered hostile to the new order and had ordered the seizure and public burning of all available copies. The imperial administration had never carried out such destruction, and these brutal measures, bringing about the destruction of the entire "bourgeois" press in a few hours, made an unfavorable impression on both many ordinary inhabitants of the capital and on the Mensheviks and Social Revolutionaries who were not part of the government. With arrests, often decided by the MRC, on the increase, Martov came before the Bolshevik Central Committee to demand a return to legality and the release of the Socialist ministers. He received no response. In general the Bolsheviks were inclined to answer that victory had indeed been won, but they were surrounded by many dangers. The country was far from having been won over to their cause, and, nearby, Kerensky, who had fled, was suspected of attempting to gather troops in the country to launch a counterattack. They therefore felt entitled to proclaim a veritable state of siege.

Although victorious, the Bolsheviks remained watchful, knowing not only that they had to implement the program Lenin had proclaimed at the Second Congress of Soviets, but also that they had to survive.

Л Л Л

The history of the revolution between February and October can be broken down into two periods. From the February Revolution until the summer, various political solutions, various adjustments in the line followed by the Provisional Government still seemed to be possible. Despite the pressure that Lenin began to exert on the government and the Soviet from the moment he returned to Russia, the chances his party had to attain power were tenuous. This was all the more true because, after the February Revolution, many of his companions who had returned from exile were tempted to accept the existing political situation, the bourgeois revolution, and to participate in leadership of the country. Of course power was marked during this period by the existence of two centers of authority, government and Soviet. But this was not the essential point. What society expected from the Provisional Government, and not at first from the Soviet, because it was the government that had the legal capacity to decide and to act, was a response to its strongest aspirations: peace and agrarian reform. The weakness of the Provisional Government, which gradually made it lose its legitimacy, consisted of its inability or unwillingness to provide the expected responses to the two pressing demands of society.

The intention expressed by Miliukov, and then by Kerensky, to adhere to existing alliances, which meant continuing the war, came up from the outset against the aspirations of a society hungry for an immediate peace.

The response to the land problem proposed by successive governments up to October was no less opposed to popular demands. The problem was referred to the body that could legitimately make a decision, the Constituent Assembly. But for months governments delayed elections to bring the body into being, by this very procrastination undermining some of the prestige it enjoyed in the country, and at the same time discrediting themselves.

The deep disappointment brought about by an attitude so contrary to popular hopes was at the origin of two developments that can be seen by the summer of 1917. First of all, society, understanding that it could expect nothing from the government, turned away from it to seek answers in other bodies, chiefly the Soviet, to which in a few months the public gave its confidence, thereby conferring on the Soviet its own legitimacy. But, beginning in the summer, this frustrated society also decided to ignore official authorities and find its own responses to its aspirations in concrete circumstances. Increasing desertions at the front from that time on and confiscation of lands and estates in the countryside by peasants on their own authority signaled this spontaneous action of society with no reference to constituted authority. These initiatives on the ground in turn created irreversible situations to which the authority created in October 1917 would have to accommodate itself.

Lenin, whose political instincts are undeniable, soon grasped the importance of the developments that had taken place in Russia between February and April 1917. He launched the slogan, "All Power to the Soviets!" because he recognized from the moment of his return that the Petrograd Soviet and its sister institutions throughout Russia were in the process of acquiring legitimacy at the expense of, and not alongside, the Provisional Government, and that that legitimacy might one day be harnessed by the Bolshevik Party.

Was the victory of the Bolsheviks therefore inevitable? Could it be predicted by the summer of 1917, and could it be asserted that the masses were falling irresistibly into the Bolshevik camp? No. Society was closer to the other Socialist parties during this period, even though it considered them to have been compromised by participation in the coalition governments. The peasant majority in Russia expected a response to its expectations from the SRs, and the Mensheviks retained genuine authority in the working class. The Bolsheviks' failed attempts at seizing power by force had not added to their prestige. But, in these circumstances, Lenin was strongly assisted by Kerensky. From the summer of 1917 to October, the Russian political stage, so fertile in events, was in fact dominated by an invisible confrontation between the two men. Lenin had perceived and analyzed Kerensky's two principal weaknesses, one linked to his character, the other to his inability to make a correct analysis of situations. Kerensky had an irresolute temperament, unable of consistently carrying out a plan. At the most difficult moments, he hesitated, changed his opinion, temporized, and added to this indecision a certain cynicism in his relations with others. This was true with General Kornilov, whom he used and deceived, which definitively lost him the sympathy of the army. He was also incapable of making a clear analysis of complex and changing situations. For example, he was always obsessed by the fear of being confronted with a counterrevolution intended to restore the monarchy or to carry the army to power, and he constantly turned his attention and his actions against this imaginary opponent, and underestimated Lenin's capacity to profit from his attacks on the right. Similarly, until October, Kerensky underestimated the Bolsheviks' ability to recover after their many failures. When he became aware of his mistake, he had already lost the battle.

Confronting Kerensky's political blindness, Lenin played his role much more cleverly. To be sure, he also made mistakes, particularly in July 1917. But there was one point on which he never blundered during these difficult months, and that was in his perception of Kerensky. He was always able to detect his opponent's errors in judgment or action and to integrate them into his own political strategy.

The "Kerensky card" turned out to be the perfect trump for Lenin, despite the minority position of the Bolshevik Party. To this should be added the card offered him by his Socialist opponents, notably the Mensheviks. Convinced that they were more popular and more solidly established in the working class than the Bolsheviks and therefore stronger, they underestimated Lenin just as much as Kerensky did. They too did not pay enough attention to his strategy of "entryism" into the Soviets and then into the army.

In the end his rivals all had the weakness of not paying enough attention to the speeches and writings of Lenin. Had they listened and read, they would perhaps have better perceived or foreseen an important aspect of the October Revolution, the role of "professional" revolutionaries and, following their mentor, their enthusiastic manipulation of institutions.

PART FOUR

THE END OF THE DREAM
(1917–1924)

Chapter Ten

FROM THE DEATH OF THE STATE TO THE REVOLUTIONARY STATE

IN OCTOBER 1917, CAPTAIN JACQUES SADOUL, MEMBER OF THE French military mission in Petrograd, decided to send his minister, Albert Thomas, a daily report on the Russian Revolution unfolding before his eyes. Of course he was not a perfectly dispassionate witness, and his sympathies lay with the side of the victors. But he was a sharp observer, and his remarks are invaluable for an understanding of the course of events. On October 31, a few days after Lenin's success, he noted:

> The streets are perfectly calm. Unbelievably, during the week of bloodshed, thanks to the iron fist and the powerful organization of the Bolsheviks, public services (trolleys, telephone, telegraph, mail, transports) never stopped operating normally. Order was never better kept.
>
> Only officials and the bourgeoisie are sulking. The ministries have little to do. But Trotsky will rigorously force them to carry out their duties. . . . Everyone will learn that the Bolshevik insurrection is able to break down any resistance.[1]

Sadoul suggests here what was the principal question at the end of October. Lenin had been prepared to win the insurrection that he had wanted so much, but how were the Bolsheviks going to organize power thereafter throughout the country, overcome resistance, and fulfill expectations.

WHAT KIND OF STATE FOR THE REVOLUTION?

Although Lenin had always been passionately concerned with the seizure of power and had defined the rules and means for carrying it out in many writings, the aftermath of the revolution left more room for uncertainty in his analyses. On the eve of seizing power, while he was in hiding in Finland awaiting the opportune moment to resurface, he finally turned to this problem and composed *The State and Revolution*, a work whose subtitle sheds a good deal of light on its intentions, "The Marxist Theory of the State and the Tasks of the Proletariat in the Revolution."[2] Although it was written in haste, it is not entirely a circumstantial work, because Lenin had been considering this problem from the beginning of the year and, as was his custom, he had read a great deal and taken notes that provided the material for two preparatory notebooks. "Marxism on the State"[3] and "Sketches and Notes for the Book *The State and Revolution*."[4] From these systematic readings had come a strange and ambiguous work that is open to several readings.

To begin with Lenin argues against the writers whose analyses of the state he wants to dismiss and whose thinking lay behind the Russian revolutionary movement. He forcefully challenges the federalist views of the anarchists (Proudhon, Bakunin, Kropotkin), as well as the anarchist myth of rebellion replacing any form of organization. He also attacks orthodox Marxists (Kautsky, Plekhanov) and Reformists (Bernstein), all of whom he accuses indiscriminately of having betrayed Marx: "A gulf separates Marx and Kautsky," he writes, "over their attitudes towards the proletarian party's task." He adds this definitive condemnation: "Kautsky, the German Social Democrats' spokesman, seems to have declared: I abide by revolutionary views. . . . Still, I am going back on what Marx said as early as 1852, since the question of the tasks of the proletarian revolution in relation to the state is being raised."

All of Lenin's targets in the book were wrong either in denying the importance of the state or in granting it, in the course of the revolution, a status different from that in Marx's analysis.

This condemnation is formulated in the concluding portion of the work, and it is worth considering its central subject: the state in the revolution and afterward, as Lenin has derived it from Marx and Engels. In his view as well, the state, an instrument of oppression of one class by another, must be abolished; counting on its withering away would be futile. "The current . . . conception of the 'withering away' of the state," he writes, "undoubtedly means obscuring, if not repudiating revolution." The state must be abolished by violence, which is the only thing capable of opposing the violence of the ruling class. In *What Is to Be Done?* Lenin had already clearly explained the necessity of revolutionary violence and armed struggle in order to ensure the victory of the proletariat. Here, even though the emphasis placed on violence as such is not as strong and the term is less frequent, the discourse is nonetheless a discourse of violence: "special coercive force for the suppression of the proletariat by the bourgeoisie" and "dictatorship of the proletariat" are not peaceful expressions. Quoting Engels, in an argument in which he attempts to demonstrate that it is mistaken to reduce his view to that of the "withering away of the state," Lenin specifies: "[T]he same work of Engels's, whose argument about the withering away of the state everyone remembers, also contains an argument on the significance of violent revolution." Appreciation of its historical role is transformed in Engels into a veritable panegyric on violent revolution; the role of the revolution is to "break" the state machine, to "destroy" it, to "demolish" it. We could go on at length with an inventory of the vocabulary that Lenin uses to describe the thinking of Marx and Engels that is all associated with brutal notions whenever he deals with the state that the revolution must suppress.

Beyond this justification of indispensable revolutionary violence for the purpose of abolishing the existing state organization, Lenin, still referring to Marx, proposes the state model of the Paris Commune: "The Commune is the form 'at last discovered' by the proletarian revolution, under which the economic emancipation of labor can take place."

In the end, and again relying on Marx and Engels, Lenin gives a dual vision of revolutionary strategy toward the state. "Before" the revolution, the state, an organization for domination by the exploiting classes, can neither be reformed nor used for revolutionary purposes; it must be destroyed, swept away. "After," once the proletariat has won its victory, the revolutionary state exists for a time—and this is where the Commune serves as a reference—while simultaneously preparing for its withering away. Lenin advances cautiously in his description of this state that is destined in the end to disappear. What he describes is principally the operation of the state in the phase of the dictatorship of the proletariat, when it exists and functions in unprecedented ways. The reason for the persistence for a time of the state after the triumph of the proletariat—in this work, Lenin refers very little to the party; the masses play a central role—is the need to destroy permanently any inclination toward resistance by the exploiting classes who are not immediately resigned to disappearing from the stage of history. It is their resistance that explains the need for maintaining a state. But with what powers?

The Paris Commune is there as a model. It represents the power of the majority, that is, of the proletariat exercising a veritable dictatorship over the former exploiters who are now a minority. This power does not resemble traditional power, in particular because what has always characterized the state, control over the means of force—army and police—escapes it. The people in arms have become the army, and they exercise police powers. Deprived of these two pillars, the state cannot exercise violence against the people; on the contrary it depends on the people. The same thing is true of all administrative and managerial functions; everything will be carried out by officials coming from the people, elected and subject to recall by the people. The state will have no authority over those who ensure its operation. Lenin explains: "All officials, without exception, elected and subject to recall *at any time*, their salaries reduced to the level of ordinary 'workmen's wages.'" This is in complete accordance with the model of "[t]he Commune," which, Marx wrote, "made that catchword of bourgeois revolutions, cheap government, a reality, by destroying the two greatest sources of expenditure—the standing army and state functionarism."[5]

Who will this new kind of state official be? Everyone, because no particular knowledge is required to ensure the operation of this simplified state: "A beginning can and must be made at once, overnight, to replace the specific 'bossing' of state officials by the simple functions of 'foremen and accountants,' functions which are already fully within the ability of the average town dweller."

The slogan "the state can be run by a cook" comes out of this view, which excludes, because it assumes that all proletarians are interchangeable, the possibility of the emergence of a new ruling stratum of bureaucrats tempted to divert state power to their own benefit. Similarly, Lenin derives from this constant mobility of social actors the conviction that all the social flaws engendered by the will to hold on to power—such as criminality and all forms of delinquency, as well as economic inequalities—would automatically disappear: "[F]reed from capitalist slavery, from the untold horrors, savagery . . . people will gradually *become accustomed* to observing the elementary rules of social intercourse."

One democratic principle that Lenin dispenses with in short order is the separation of powers. The Commune is a condemnation of traditional parliamentarism, which he calls "venal and rotten to the core," and it brings about a synthesis of the executive and legislative. Indeed, Marx had written: "The Commune was to be a working, not a parliamentary body, executive and legislative at the same time."

This utopian work with an anarchist flavor poses a series of problems. In the first place, there is the question of the relationship between this view of the proletariat identified with the state ("the state . . . [that is,] the proletariat organized as the ruling class," Lenin writes, and "the fulfillment of the role of the proletariat in history is the dictatorship of the proletariat, political domination by the proletariat") and the view of the party which Lenin had always insisted was not identified with the proletariat, but was its guide, the possessor of the knowledge that it needed in order to fulfill its role. What has happened to the party in this view of the ruling proletariat? The question is barely mentioned, nor does Lenin indicate how the proletariat is supposed suddenly to have acquired the innate class consciousness that he had always claimed it did not have. The party built to take power, made up of "professional" revolutionaries (a professionalism on which Lenin had always insisted), is the antithesis of proletarians capable of anything and of a state in which no particular competence is any longer required.

Elsewhere in the work, Lenin brings together contradictory views in a very ambiguous manner. He emphasizes the importance Marx attached to the "centralized" state against anarchist views; to "[n]ational unity [which] was not to be broken, but, on the contrary, organized by the communal constitution." He goes on to say that "Marx purposely used the words: 'National unity was . . . to be organized,' so as to oppose conscious, democratic, proletarian centralism to bourgeois, military, bureaucratic centralism." He presents a vision of society that is also perfectly organized and centralized: "The whole of society will have become a single office and a single factory, with equality of labor and pay. But this 'factory' discipline, which the proletariat, after defeating the capitalists . . . will extend to the whole of society, is by no means our ideal, or our ultimate goal." It is only a step. The final stage is the development of communist society, at the conclusion of a "protracted . . . process," toward a future whose outlines are impossible to see both for Lenin and Marx.

Lenin thinks that he has dealt with this difficulty by recognizing it, but the reader of *The State and Revolution* is left in the greatest perplexity. How is it possible to reconcile the anarchic vision of the proletariat that Lenin proposes on the basis of the model of the Commune (it is everything and takes on everything, it can elect and recall at any time, it is both legislative and executive) with his organizing vision in which "centralization," "unity," and "factory discipline" are the key words for the state that he describes? How is it possible to move from this strong organization to the absence of any organization? By what kind of decision? Through continuous development? Thanks to proletarian spontaneity? Through the will of those who, at a particular moment, in the "single office" and the "single factory," are in the command posts?

In the end the obscurity hovering over the final stage is of no help in encouraging adoption of Lenin's logic.

The question that finally needs to be asked is the place of this utopia in the intellectual trajectory of Lenin. To be sure this unfinished work was written in a feverish state, because Lenin was living in hiding and in the expectation of the insurrection that he was advocating. (The work remained unfinished. On November 30, 1917, Lenin wrote an afterword intended for the next edition. It was published as a pamphlet in 1918.) But he had gathered the materials for it over a period of several months, which indicates his strong interest in the subject. Perhaps the best answer to the question lies in a parallel between the development of the work and the course of events.

When Lenin undertook an examination of the works of Marx and Engels on the state early in 1917, he certainly had his gaze fixed on a Russia dealing with military reverses; but, most important, he was anticipating a world revolution. His planned book was probably not intended only for Russia. Late 1916 and early 1917 was, in fact, a strange period in the history of the war. Peace proposals were coming from all sides. "The Central Powers proposed peace negotiations on December 12, 1916; Wilson offered a peace plan on December 18. The Russian socialists did the same in March 1917, followed by the Dutch and Scandinavian socialists. Not wishing to be left behind, Pope Benedict XV launched a proposal in August."[6] Lenin thought that these calls for peace would encourage pacifist currents in civil society as well as in the armies, and he believed that the phase of disintegration of political systems on which he had been counting since the beginning of the conflict was fast approaching. An attempt to analyze the future of revolutionary societies, whose advent he foresaw in Western Europe, thus seemed to him to be necessary. When he wrote the work, which is so incompatible with the rest of his writings and difficult to situate in the development of his thinking, he was addressing a Russia that had been in the throes of a revolution for several months. It is thus easier to understand the meaning of the work, intended primarily to discredit the arguments of those he considered his principal opponents in Russia, that is, the Socialists who were open to the idea of a coalition.

Above all Lenin intended to provide a legitimating argument for the Bolshevik seizure of power. The utopian view of the Commune—an entire people holding power—was certainly easier to justify than a party alone seizing it. It hardly mattered that the model of the Commune, whose existence was so ephemeral, was not very persuasive. The essential point for Lenin was to call on Marx and this brief revolutionary adventure, and to place under those auspices, revered by all Socialists, the adventure on which he was about to set out.

In remaining nearly silent about the name and the existence of the party, was Lenin being hypocritical, or was revolutionary fervor leading him to surrender to a utopian vision? It is difficult to accept the second possibility without reservation. It is most plausible to suggest that, before acceding to power, Lenin felt the usefulness of having available a theoretical work referring to the "fathers of Marxism" which would justify from the outset the elimination of everyone who did not follow him and also legitimate his authoritarian conception of power.

In *The State and Revolution*, Lenin's contempt for parliamentary procedures and for elections (except for the system of permanent election of officials of the Paris Commune) is expressed without disguise, as is his rejection of the separation of powers. However, these bluntly formulated positions have the virtue of matching statements by Marx. As for the problem of the incompatibility of his anarchist view of proletarian power, and the centralist view of the power of the party, it is obvious that Lenin was postponing its resolution to the aftermath of the seizure of power. Indeed he had explicitly declared his adhesion to the formula attributed to Napoleon: *"On s'engage et puis on voit."* His attitude throughout the October Revolution, when he had to overcome the hesitations of his associates who asserted that a Socialist revolution in Russian conditions was premature, was a confirmation of his unshakable decision: we have to take action, and then we'll see.

If the book seems at first sight incoherent, if it can be read with an anarchist or authoritarian slant, depending on one's inclination, it is nevertheless obvious that Lenin was able to give it internal coherence by offering not two distinct readings, but a reading corresponding to two historical periods: the period of transition, in which a mixture of anarchist views and a will toward organization will dominate; and the very long-term vision of the withering away of the state, which he carefully refrains from locating in time, and the content of which he does not discuss. The work as a whole is a utopia which was never to be implemented to any degree. However, if we take into account Lenin's character and the other writings contemporaneous with this work, everything suggests that the utopia was not a moment in the development of his thought, but simply a component of his strategy for the seizure of power.

THE STATE AND REVOLUTION IN THE FACE OF REALITY

The most immediate problem, which Lenin thought he had settled with his speech to the Congress of Soviets, was that of the exercise of power, that is, the problem of government. In accordance with his habit of using his party as the principal instrument for all his plans, he had at the outset established a government that excluded the other Socialist parties. But on this point he had to confront the indignation not only of the Socialist Revolutionaries and the Mensheviks, but also of his own camp. On November 1, Sadoul wrote to his minister: "A crisis is taking shape. Kamenev, the most parliamentarian of the maximalist leaders, is frightened by the splendid isolation of the Bolsheviks. Like Zinoviev, Rykov, Shlyapnikov, Ryazanov, and most of his comrades, he thinks that only a socialist coalition government would be able to preserve the conquests of the third revolution."[7]

The crisis that broke out in the party was foreseeable at the Congress of Soviets, where the delegates had voted with an overwhelming majority for a resolution offered by Martov calling for the opening of the government announced by Lenin to the other Socialist parties. This vote, coming in an assembly dominated by the Bolsheviks at the very moment when Lenin and his Party had just seized power, is revealing about the state of mind of the Bolsheviks. Indeed, one of them, Lunacharsky, had strongly supported Martov's proposal in the ensuing debate. This general outcry against Lenin's "monopolistic" views is easily understandable. Many of his companions had reluctantly rallied to the insurrection, and their doubts persisted. Many "old Bolsheviks," even after the seizure of power, continued to consider it a manifestation of reprehensible political adventurism. This was true for Bogdanov, Krasin, and Gorky, among many others. Because power had been won in unfavorable circumstances, they thought it necessary to attempt to preserve it by bringing in all the Socialists. The dream of unity, which was so foreign to Lenin, had not been given up by his comrades, who reiterated their belief that union among Socialists had never been so necessary. Only Trotsky supported Lenin with no qualms, and told Captain Sadoul of his confidence in the use of authoritarian and repressive measures to preserve Bolshevik power. Although he had come over to Lenin only recently, he was his strongest supporter in the crisis.

The major figures of Bolshevism were not the only ones who played a role in this crisis. The powerful Executive Committee of the railwaymen's union, Vikzhel, intervened to demand that the Bolsheviks give up the monopoly of power and accept the idea of a coalition. To demonstrate its determination, it announced that unless negotiations between the Bolshevik Party and the parties excluded from the government got underway immediately, all rail traffic would come to a halt.[8] The threat had some force because, despite Sadoul's admiring remarks about the Bolsheviks' capacity to keep the public services running in a time of revolution, the situation had deteriorated in the course of a few days. By October 28, strikes had broken out in public services and banks. Civil servants who had not taken part in the insurrection, but who manifested passive sympathy for the changes underway, were shocked as early as October 26 by the Bolshevization of the country. Lenin was thus confronted by silent but effective pressure from "white-collar" workers, vigorous pressure from the railwaymen's union, and the doubts of his friends.

Few of his supporters agreed with his position. Aside from Trotsky, he was supported only by Stalin and Ordzhonikidze. This was insufficient for him to reject any dialogue. When he was obliged to accept the principle of a dialogue, he was persuaded that he was making a formal concession, while determined to make no real concession in the end.

When he learned on October 29 that the revolution in Moscow was turning into a bloodbath and he was confronted with the paralysis of the administration in Petrograd, he was forced to give in. A meeting was organized under the auspices of Vikzhel, bringing together Bolsheviks—Lenin, Trotsky, and Stalin did not attend—and representatives of various organizations of the left. The purpose of the meeting, held under the explicit threat of a rail strike, was "the construction of the authority of the state."[9] Kamenev was a member of the Bolshevik delegation as president of the Central Executive Committee of the soviets, elected at the conclusion of the Second Congress and dominated by the Bolsheviks (66, as compared with 39 Left SRs and 10 "independents"). During the meeting, Kamenev threw all his weight in the balance in favor of the coalition. An implicit consequence of his proposals was clearly admitted on the following day: any coalition agreement would involve the elimination of Lenin and Trotsky because of their intransigence which would doom any coalition government to failure.

Lenin had certainly understood that he risked being sacrificed for the sake of compromise, and for his part took steps to consolidate his authority over the party. On November 1 he declared to the Central Committee that the Bolshevik negotiators were "miserable cheaters," and he concluded with a statement that excluded any concessions: "There is no question of negotiating with the socialists. Our slogan is: no compromise, and a completely Bolshevik government."

It was important for Lenin not to come into open conflict with his interlocutors, because of the substantial risk of a crystallization of the alliance that would eliminate him, but he sought to provoke a response from the party that would deprive apparent concessions of any meaning. This task was given to his spokesman, V. Volodarsky, who conveyed his proposals to the Central Executive Committee of the soviets.

Lenin, said Volodarsky, accepted dialogue, and particularly the expansion of the Central Executive Committee (CEC), to include representatives of unions, peasant soviets, and the armed forces. He also acquiesced to the principle of subordination of the government to the CEC. This was an ambiguous compromise. Of course, from the non-Bolshevik point of view, this proposal involved no change in the government; but the opening of the CEC to forces close to other parties and the supreme authority attributed to it were attractive to the Socialists, who thought they would thereby be able to control the Bolshevik government. For Lenin the essential was preserved, that is, the monolithic government. He thought he would gradually be able to strengthen the influence of the party in the CEC. Above all he needed to gain time.

The Bolsheviks on the CEC did not discern this hidden agenda, and the agreement was passed by thirty-eight to twenty-nine. Vikzhel considered the measure insufficient and called for a pure and simple withdrawal of the Bolsheviks from the government. To sidestep the difficulty, Kamenev proposed that Lenin be removed and replaced by the Socialist Revolutionary Viktor Chernov.

This was too much for Lenin, who summoned a meeting of the Central Committee and demanded that all negotiations on the formation of a coalition government be broken off. When it came to a vote, he was obliged to recognize that he was under severe challenge; against ten opponents he was able to secure only three favorable votes, including, of course, Trotsky's. To rescue the situation, Trotsky then advocated a midway position, a continuation of negotiations with the Left SRs alone, taking this concession to be a final attempt to resolve the crisis. The participants agreed, and in his writings on Stalin, Trotsky notes that, although Stalin said nothing in the debate, he ended by siding with Trotsky.

Lenin was determined to pursue the confrontation to the end, and he seized the opportunity to demand submission from the minority. The ultimatum was signed by ten members of the Central Committee, one of whom, Alexei Bubnov, relates this characteristic example of Lenin's methods. Lenin drafted the text, then he "called each member individually into his office, presented the text to them, and demanded that they sign it."[10]

Lenin followed up this assertion of power, placing in the minority a group of Bolsheviks who were close to the aspirations of the party as a whole, with another decision that deeply shocked them. In the past the Bolsheviks had committed themselves to respect freedom of the press; they contrasted this commitment to the closing of their own papers decreed by the Provisional Government at moments of crisis. Lenin had then exalted freedom of the press, explaining that it existed only on condition "that the opinions of all citizens could be expressed."[11] Less than three months later, he forgot this article entitled "How Is the Success of the Elections to the Constituent Assembly to Be Assured?" Once power had been achieved, he was hostile both to the free press and to the Constituent Assembly. It was then that the decree limiting freedom of the "counterrevolutionary press" was issued. When the Bolshevik Yuri Larin denounced this measure before the CEC, he provided a new opportunity for Lenin to revile "those who infringe Party discipline." The CEC rejected by only two votes Larin's motion calling for a condemnation of the decree on the press. A large number of Bolsheviks were thus voting against the Sovnarkom and therefore against Lenin. The time to choose had arrived. Lenin ordered the opposition to accept the positions of the Central Committee. Some preferred resignation and open protest. Kamenev, Zinoviev, Rykov, Milyutin, and Nogin resigned from the Central Committee; the last three also gave up their cabinet posts, and Kamenev left the chairmanship of the Central Executive Committee, to which Lenin immediately appointed Sverdlov. The five men published a letter justifying their action in the official organ of the Sovnarkom, *Izvestia*. Once again they said that they were convinced of the necessity for a government open to all Socialists, and they expressed their intention to call on society against the authoritarianism of the "group dominating the Central Committee."

There was unquestionably a split in the party, but Lenin could not tolerate a split. He excluded and "purged," and arranged to come out of the crisis in a stronger position. This is far from *The State and Revolution* and the approach to power drawn from the Paris Commune. Lenin was assisted in this conflict by the division of the Socialists. The moderate Socialists, demoralized by his brutality, had stopped attending sessions of the CEC, preferring to wait for the calling of the Constituent Assembly in order to reopen the question of the government. In November 1917 the Socialists still believed that Lenin would have to give way before an assembly elected by universal suffrage. His only remaining interlocutors were the Left SRs, inclined to accept his proposals, which turned out to be very clever. To be sure they had attacked Lenin's intention to monopolize power, but he was soon able to win them over with offers and advances. In fact he offered to have them participate in the government and to enlarge the CEC to include new representatives, particularly peasants. After several days of intense negotiations, the agreement suggested by Lenin was accepted on November 15. The only participants were the Left SRs; the remainder of that party and the Mensheviks were excluded. Some Socialist Revolutionaries then entered the government, including Izaak Steinberg, who was appointed commissar of justice.

To appease the railwaymen's union, Lenin accepted the request that it had presented and proposed giving the post of commissar of transport to one of its members, Krushinsky, who was in addition a Left Socialist Revolutionary. Because Krushinsky had played an important role in the confrontation with the Bolsheviks, Lenin was aware of the risk that he might turn out to be an uncontrollable minister, but he had to accept the union's demands in order to neutralize it. He found the solution by appointing as vice-commissar under Krushinsky his own brother-in-law, Mark Elizarov. Because Elizarov was an engineer and member of the union, the Vikzhel accepted the appointment. Each of the three participants in this bargain—Lenin, Elizarov, and the union—had a hidden agenda: with the presence of his brother-in-law in the commissariat, Lenin was certain of having a reliable agent capable of influencing the titular commissar and through him the railwaymen's union; Elizarov hoped to be able to maintain a balance between the two camps, and indeed expressed that intention; as for Vikzhel, after fulfilling Lenin's wishes, it thought it would be able to exercise unchallenged authority over the commissariat of transport and the government.

Of all of them, the one who was most reassured in his calculations was Lenin, for whom the coalition was only a temporary concession, and the presence of non-Bolsheviks in the Sovnarkom could only be ephemeral. It was urgent not only to put off strike plans but also—Lenin counted on his brother-in-law for this—to manipulate the preparation of the railwaymen's union congress scheduled for early December, in order to eject the existing leadership, in constant opposition to the Bolsheviks, and to secure the election of a conciliatory union leadership, if not one totally subservient to his views. "Enlarging the government," as we have seen, meant to him something entirely different from a genuine concession to those who wanted parties and groups besides the Bolsheviks involved in power.

Under color of a political opening, Lenin's maneuver also reached the CEC which, during this period, was taking the place of a still nonexistent legislature.

The November 15 agreement had in fact provided for this enlargement, and Lenin opened the 108-member body to large contingents of peasants, soldiers, and union representatives. The result of this apparent concession was an increased centralization of power. The membership of the CEC was increased to 366, which made it totally ineffective, all the more because the mass of newcomers, peasants and soldiers, increased the heterogeneity of views and demands. Another consequence was that the Bolsheviks did not carry much weight in comparison to the Left SRs, to whom the peasants felt particularly close. No matter; every assembly had a presidium, and this one was reorganized on December 12, with the Bolsheviks arrogating twelve seats to themselves, as opposed to seven for the Left SRs. And the presidium was the body that held real power. The CEC, too large, too difficult to bring together, in which it was even more difficult to have a serious debate, experienced the fate that often strikes overpopulated assemblies, absenteeism and empty speech-making. As a result its meetings grew infrequent, and the legislative proposals that were supposed to be submitted to it by the Sovnarkom were no longer. Sitting every day, the Council of People's Commissars found it more expedient to exercise executive and legislative power simultaneously. In *The State and Revolution*, Lenin had emphasized Marx's sympathies for this arrangement. He had increased the size of the CEC so that it would become impossible for the Sovnarkom not to exercise both powers. In this respect it can be said that his utopian work had become a reality in the space of a few weeks.

This act of political prestidigitation did not escape the attention of the Bolsheviks' partners, the Left SRs, and they were outraged. But their participation in the government made them accomplices of a practice that they condemned, and their protests were therefore without effect.

In any event, in December 1917, while Lenin was strengthening his power, everyone who disagreed with his methods was impatiently waiting for the election and convocation of the Constituent Assembly to restore to Russia political activity more closely corresponding to the existing balance of forces.

LIFE AND DEATH OF THE CONSTITUENT ASSEMBLY

The convocation of a Constituent Assembly had been a major hope of Russian society ever since the fall of the czarist system. The elections were promised but always put off, which had hardly contributed to the popularity of the governments that had succeeded one another between February and October. Aware of the deep disappointment of public opinion, Lenin had of course declared that the vote should take place, and, taking power after the date had already been set, he had committed himself to carrying it out. However, this commitment was not very convenient for him, and he discussed with his associates ways of getting out of it. He suggested as much to Trotsky, who objected that he could not act like the Provisional Government without danger, to which Lenin answered bluntly: "Nonsense. It is facts that are important, not words."[12] Lenin finally had to give up his intentions, because the other political parties, particularly the Socialists, who were counting on these elections to reduce the power of the Bolsheviks, had been engaged in a very active electoral campaign since the beginning of November. The Socialist Revolutionaries in particular had been traveling throughout the countryside, mobilizing the peasants. The result was a very high level of voter participation, particularly in the countryside, lower in the cities, although even there it was close to 60 percent. For practical reasons, the elections, set by the Provisional Government for November 12, in fact continued through November 26. It is worth noting that women voted. Lenin had briefly thought of lowering the voting age from twenty to eighteen, hoping to have a more malleable body of voters. But it was too late to change the system. His various plans (call off the elections or change the body of voters) arose from the very accurate sense that the vote would confirm the fact that the Bolsheviks lagged behind the Socialist Revolutionaries.

The results of the voting, remarkable in its seriousness and the degree of conscientiousness of the voters, and, except for a few incidents, completely fair, matched Lenin's worries. The Socialist Revolutionaries drew seventeen million votes, or 40 percent, and the Bolsheviks less than ten million, or 24 percent. The SRs were further strengthened by the success of their Ukrainian counterparts, who received five million votes, or 12 percent, which brought the total share of Socialist Revolutionary votes above 50 percent. On their side the Bolsheviks could add to the votes that they had received only the half million, or 1 percent, of their Left Socialist Revolutionary allies. For the Mensheviks, on the other hand, the election was a disaster; with less than 1.3 million votes, they did not even reach three percent. The liberal parties, led by the Kadets (or Constitutional Democrats), despite their near exclusion from political life, managed to gather a little more than three million votes, or 7 percent of the total. They had good newspapers and enjoyed a broad audience among all those who rejected the Bolsheviks. It was not a remarkable success, but after the October coup, it was not a disaster either. Principally elected in the large cities, the Kadets still represented a hope for a fraction of urban society.

The result of the elections, translated into seats in the Assembly, could hardly be reassuring to Lenin. Of the 703 seats, the SRs obtained 419, or 60 percent; the Bolsheviks 168, to which were added the 40 seats of the Left SRs; the Kadets 17; the Mensheviks 16; and 90 seats went to parties representing the national minorities. The composition of the assembly that had been elected clearly showed that a political change had occurred in the Russia that the Bolsheviks believed they dominated. Two-thirds of the members of the assembly that came out of the popular vote—a vote exercised in conditions of social mobilization that attested to the importance attributed to it by the people—were not Bolsheviks, who were now faced with a body that was completely beyond their control and hostile to their power. Until then, Lenin had succeeded, through his maneuvers of "enlargement," in swamping and reducing to a state of impotence the Congress of Soviets and then the Central Executive Committee. With the

Constituent Assembly, he could not act in the same way. There then came to the fore the question that he had adopted from Chernyshevsky: What is to be done?

The question was all the more acute because a Union for the Defense of the Constituent Assembly had just been set up. Its establishment tended to indicate that society was aware of the challenge with which the Bolsheviks were suddenly confronted. This union, consisting of representatives from all the parties, except the Bolsheviks and Left SRs, and from many unions and associations, presented itself as the successor to the Committee for the Salvation of the Motherland and the Revolution, which had been established a month earlier to oppose the Bolshevik takeover of the totality of power. The same problem thus arose again after the election of the Constituent Assembly: The non-Bolshevik parties and many unions were both terrified and exasperated by Lenin's will to power, but in late November 1917, they had a real political means of keeping him in check, the newly elected assembly. The important thing was to prevent its dissolution, because Lenin's opponents were clearheaded enough to sense that this was his hidden intention.

The Provisional Government, which had set the date of the election before it was overthrown, had also decreed that the new assembly's inaugural session would be on November 28. The Union for the Defense of the Constituent Assembly decided to mobilize society in order to protect the meeting of the assembly on the appointed date. It sent out the order to hold a session even though the representatives had not yet been officially convened, and only a small number of them were in a position to reach the Tauride Palace. Demonstrators in favor of the assembly had come in large numbers to protect them, but a meeting with no real status, limited to a few dozen delegates, and therefore far from the required quorum, could only turn into an abortive show of force.

During this time Lenin was not inactive. He had already proposed to the Sovnarkom to postpone the opening of the assembly on the grounds of the extreme difficulty of bringing together all the delegates. Simultaneously he attacked the Kadet Party, which a decree issued on November 28–the day of the first confrontation over a possible meeting of the Constituent Assembly–banned as a "counterrevolutionary party." The Kadets were accused of fomenting the overthrow of the government on behalf of the bourgeoisie and using the Constituent Assembly for that purpose. An order to arrest its leaders accompanied this outlawing of a party that had just had some success in the elections. The accusations made against the Kadets–plotting against the authorities–were in addition sufficiently imprecise to be extended if necessary to all the Socialists opposed to the Bolsheviks.

This November 28 decree was a test that revealed the inability of the parties that had won the elections to ward off the coup that Lenin was preparing against the assembly. By this point, moreover, Lenin had put in place in the streets and in the future meeting place of the assembly a force of men that would allow him to carry his plans to their conclusion. The director of the operation in the field was Sverdlov. During the period of internal crisis in the Bolshevik Party marked by the opposition of many leaders to the monolithic government imposed by Lenin, Sverdlov had been the confidant who had supported with no hesitation the radical position of the head of government. It was because of this so "Leninist" attitude that he had replaced Kamenev at the head of the CEC and continued as chairman of the secretariat of the Central Committee, a post that enabled him to control the entire organization of the party. Georges Haupt, the eminent historian of the Second International, wrote of him:

> Lunacharsky drew a striking psychological portrait of the brown-haired man, who was short and had a pronounced Semitic appearance, and was the first to dress entirely in black leather, which was to become the uniform of the commissars. The trait that struck Lunacharsky in all the great revolutionaries, their calm and equilibrium in the most trying circumstances, reached in Sverdlov "impressive and almost monumental" dimensions. As for his role and his place in the Party, Lunacharsky defined them in this way: Whereas Lenin and a few others were in charge of ideological leadership, the contacts between them and the masses, the Party, the Soviet apparatus, and finally all of Russia were taken care of by Sverdlov.[13]

It was this special role as central agent of the party that Sverdlov was to put at the service of the battle that Lenin was still carrying out behind the scenes against the Constituent Assembly, which he wished to block at all costs. Sverdlov called the Bolshevik delegates together in Petrograd and organized them into a compact and coherent group prepared to follow whatever strategy they were given. Then he sent them out to factories to present systematic criticism of an "unnecessary" assembly. When this propaganda came up against the reservations of workers who remained in favor of the assembly that they had elected, it was quickly dropped, and Sverdlov thereafter concentrated his efforts on the delegates themselves. They were collectively placed under the authority of a bureau emanating from the Central Committee charged with supervising the Bolshevik parliamentary faction. This bureau was led by two very different men: Bukharin, who was obsessed by the idea of world revolution, had come into conflict with Lenin on the questions of the state and national minorities, but had supported him since 1915 in his conviction that Russia had to be defeated; and Sokolnikov, whom Lenin saw as totally loyal, who had supported him unquestioningly during the insurrection, had defended the notion of a homogeneous government, and shared his aversion for the Constituent Assembly. Given this leadership, the Bolshevik delegates were prepared to defend Lenin's position and constantly repeated that the existence of the body was acceptable only if the delegates could be recalled at any time by a decision of the government.

On December 12 Lenin took a public position by publishing his "Theses on the Constituent Assembly" in *Pravda*.[14] The idea he set out was unqualified: The Constituent Assembly had no reason for existence insofar as the parliamentary stage had already been superseded. Society, he asserted, is in perfect agreement with the government, whereas the Constituent Assembly to which bourgeois parties have been elected represents a different stage of social consciousness. Revolutionary Russia cannot regress, and accepting the Constituent Assembly, expression of a prerevolutionary social consciousness, would be a historic retreat.

These arguments matched the ideas that Lenin had been defending for months. In late July he had written "About Constitutional Illusions," in which he bluntly asserted that in a revolutionary period, the "will of the majority" did not count; "what is important is a minority that is better organized, more aware, better armed, able to impose its will on the majority, and win."[15]

Lenin was not lacking in resources to impose his convictions. In early December he had leaders of the Union for the Defense of the Constituent Assembly arrested, including the Right Socialist Revolutionary Nikolai Avksentiev, and ordered the arrests of Viktor Chernov and Tsereteli. The time had come for the Right SRs to react, but they did nothing, persuaded that once it convened, the Constituent Assembly would assert itself over the minority Bolsheviks and demonstrate their illegitimacy. The hopes they placed in the Constituent Assembly were strengthened by the support, limited as it was, given by the Left SRs, who were opposed to abolition of the assembly and made its convening a condition of their support of the Bolsheviks.

Lenin had to give in on this point, but he was already preparing the last act. The announcement that the Constituent Assembly would convene on January 5 was accompanied by a solemn warning from Zinoviev, who, after his rebellion against the homogeneous government in November and his resignation from the Central Committee, had hastily returned and resumed his responsibilities.[16] Kamenev waited a few more weeks before following him on the path of submission to Lenin. By the time the convocation of the Constituent Assembly was announced, the Bolsheviks were reunited, and Zinoviev warned the delegates that the survival of the assembly would depend on its docility: it would have to begin by recognizing the legitimacy of the government and agreeing to be subordinate to it. For further security Lenin announced that the Third Congress of Soviets would meet on January 8, so that the two assemblies would be confronting one another.

The days preceding the meeting of the Constituent Assembly were feverish for both sides. The Mensheviks and Right SRs worked out their programs. They also very carefully prepared the organization of the session. The work they were doing was complicated by arrests and by the fact that the most prestigious figures who were still free were forced to live in hiding. Bolshevik revolution and liberty did not go together, even during this period when Lenin was attempting to cover with the mantle of legality the coup he was preparing against the only democratic institution in Russia.

The Right SRs did not merely draft a program; some of them recalled that terrorism was one of their forms of struggle and decided that the best way of dealing with the problem presented by Lenin was to act against him as they had in the past against the czar. A tyrant, even if he was a Bolshevik, remained for them a tyrant. On January 1, as he was going to the Smolny Institute with the Swiss Socialist Platten and his sister, Lenin's car came under fire. He escaped from the bullets only because Platten pushed him to the back of the car, but the attack indicated open warfare between Lenin and the Right SRs.

As his opponents were working to develop a democratic program, Lenin was drafting the one the delegates "would have to" adopt, which was first ratified by the Central Committee two days before the opening of the Constituent Assembly. Entitled "Declaration of the Rights of the Working and Exploited People," it was a kind of constitutional charter that would later be incorporated into the Constitution of the RSFSR (Russian Soviet Federated Socialist Republic).[17] Thus, the Constituent Assembly, theoretically charged with deciding the path that the country would follow, had no choice, it was explained, but to adopt the political program of the government in place, or else face immediate dissolution. The blackmail was clear.

It was accompanied by police measures intended to prevent any popular movement in favor of the elected assembly. Determined to liquidate it, Lenin not only did not rely on support from society, but he also had no confidence in its passivity. Despite limitations on press freedom, arrests, and a Bolshevik propaganda campaign of unprecedented harshness, he still feared an outburst from the people who wished to believe in an assembly that had been so long awaited. This is why, on January 4, Uritsky, head of the Petrograd Cheka, declared a state of siege and deployed well-trained Latvian troops. The Tauride Palace was surrounded by sailors, and Uritsky gave orders to all officials there to obey only the palace commander, who was under his authority. The mechanism that was to neutralize the Constituent Assembly was thus fully organized the day before it met.

From his point of view, Lenin had not been wrong to place the new assembly in a state of siege, because during the night columns of peaceful demonstrators tried to take up positions around the Tauride Palace in order to not leave the delegates at the mercy of Uritsky's troops. There was already some firing and a few casualties before dawn. As the assembly was about to open on January 5, the atmosphere was anything but calm, and it required a good deal of courage on the part of the non-Bolshevik delegates to pass through the ranks of aggressive sailors raising their fists and singing the *Internationale*, when they were not hurling insults at anyone who did not represent Lenin's party.

Inside the palace, Lenin's friends immediately set the tone. The oldest representative, who had come to the rostrum to open the session in accordance with parliamentary tradition, was immediately pushed aside by Sverdlov, on the grounds that the Central Executive Committee had authorized him to preside. He began by reading the declaration drafted by Lenin the day before, and the Left intoned the *Internationale*, with raised fists. The atmosphere was far from the calm dignity of parliamentary debate. Then came the election of a chairman. Two SRs were candidates, but they came from different sides: Viktor Chernov was supported by all but the Bolsheviks and their allies, whereas Maria

Spiridonova, who had joined the terrorist wing of the SRs in her early youth and had been sentenced to death in 1906, was the candidate of the Left SRs and the Bolsheviks. Chernov won by 246 votes against 151 for his rival, and immediately undertook to persuade his colleagues of the necessity for working together. This calm speech, intended to be conciliatory, seemed irrelevant to everyone, because it paid no attention to what was going on outside: Troops were surrounding the Tauride Palace and keeping at a distance a mass demonstration of people wanting to defend the Constituent Assembly; there was shouting, fighting, and gunfire.

Inside the walls of the palace, the atmosphere was just as unruly. Shouts and insults burst from the Left, while Chernov's supporters were appalled to hear him deliver a speech that barely mentioned the threat that the Bolsheviks posed to democracy. It was only with Tsereteli's passionate speech that the questions of Bolshevik violence, the monopolization of power, and the *fait accompli* that Lenin had opposed to the wishes of the electorate were raised. Despite the outcry Tsereteli managed to get to the end of his speech, which had reinvigorated the camp of the SRs, Mensheviks, and Kadets. When Fedor Raskolnikov, leader of the Kronstadt sailors during the October insurrection, presented to the assembly what he asserted ought to be its program—Lenin's "Declaration of the Rights of the Working and Exploited People"—it was rejected, by 237 votes against 146, and the program developed by the Socialists was adopted.

The situation was clear. The assembly was hostile to the Bolsheviks, as were a large number of the people in the streets. But all the instruments of power—government, army, and the like—were in Lenin's hands. That being the case, he said, what was the point in keeping the assembly? He had imperturbably attended the beginning of the session, then ostentatiously left at the point when the delegates were really going to begin their work. The rest of the Bolsheviks and the Left SRs also made a spectacular exit.

Chernov seized the opportunity to bring to the floor and have adopted a series of proposals of decisive importance: nationalization of the land, establishment of the Russian Federated Democratic Republic, and calls to the Allies for a general peace treaty. The Constituent Assembly was unquestionably responding to the society's expectations. The debate was all the more remarkable because it was constantly troubled by the pressures, intrusions, and interruptions of the guards posted by Uritsky, and the public he had installed in the galleries, all similarly manipulated by the Bolsheviks. There were repeated shouts from the galleries, and the guards, calling for the session to be adjourned, threatened to cut off the electricity or to clear the premises by force. But the deputies, who were aware of the threat of dissolution hanging over the assembly, were determined, despite the deplorable conditions and their own exhaustion, to leave a trace of their work for history, if not for the Russia of the present.

At four in the morning, worn out, they adjourned the session and agreed to reconvene a few hours later. When they returned to the Tauride Palace, the soldiers prohibited their entry. Posted on the door, they could read the government decree approved by the Central Executive Committee that dissolved the

Assembly. This decree was printed in *Pravda*, whereas the newspapers that reported the Constituent Assembly's debates were immediately seized and destroyed. Lenin had won.[18]

Addressing the CEC that evening, Lenin identified democracy with the counterrevolutionary forces, and set against it the popular will expressed in the Soviets. He was repeating an argument he had already made: at the time of the Soviets and the revolutionary people, the Constituent Assembly, expression of the capitalists, the owners, the bourgeoisie, was nothing but the symbol of a dead past. He went on to say that the slogan chanted in the streets–"Long live the Constituent Assembly!"–really meant "Down with the power of the Soviets!" It was thus not possible, if the Soviets were to be preserved, to allow the Constituent Assembly to survive; the future of the revolution and the will of the people were dependent on its dissolution. We know that Lenin had always been hostile to the idea of convoking the Constituent Assembly; he mistrusted the voters, despised the parliamentary idea, and constantly sought ways of keeping it from coming into being, even after the vote. The use of force made it all the easier for him to do it in because his opponents had few resources and did not dare to call openly for popular support. Lenin's victory was the consequence of his desire to destroy the Constituent Assembly, but also of the moral weakness of the Socialists: the country had come out in their favor, in the crucial hours the city attempted to support them, but they had unquestionably lacked resolve.

The death of the Constituent Assembly was accompanied by violence in Petrograd. Bolshevik sailors murdered two Kadet deputies, Alexei Shingarev and Fyodor Kokoshkin, which provoked Lenin's amusement when he learned that his opponents were denouncing such excesses: "Let them protest," he said, "they are not fit for anything else." And he commented on the situation to Trotsky: "You haven't started a civil war but a war against the Socialist Revolutionaries."

The success of Lenin's strategy was ratified over the course of the following days when the Third Congress of Soviets met in the same place that the assembly had sat, the Tauride Palace.

On January 9, the day before the Congress opened, Petrograd held a solemn funeral for those who had died in clashes with the army because they had been coming to support the Constituent Assembly. Gorky saluted their memory in *Novaya zhizn'*, recalling that the dream of a Constituent Assembly had been harbored for nearly a century by the Russian people and that, to defend the dream that had become a reality, workers had been massacred. The dying Plekhanov declared: "Their dictatorship is not one of the laboring people, but the dictatorship of a clique. And precisely for this reason they will have to resort more and more to terroristic methods."[19]

Unlike the Constituent Assembly, the Third Congress of Workers' and Soldiers' Soviets was in Lenin's view the true parliament of the people, designed to ensure the legitimacy of his power. This congress had nothing of a parliament nor of a body capable of deliberating with seriousness. This was true first because of the large number of participants, nearly two thousand, not all of whom were the "delegates of the Soviets" that had been announced. In fact, on January 19, the third day of the congress, it was expanded to include the Congress of Deputies of Peasant Soviets that had been hastily convened. A large number of soldiers were also seated, as well as union representatives, factory committees, and the like, who had not initially been a part of the delegations. As for the choice of delegates, it had been carefully controlled by the Bolsheviks; some had even been designated outside any decision by any Soviet. In short, the representative character of the assembly was highly doubtful. The number of its members made it a mere recording body for Bolshevik proposals. Under these circumstances it is not at all surprising that the document presented to the Constituent Assembly by Raskolnikov that had been rejected was happily passed twice, first by the Soviet of Workers and Soldiers and then by the expanded assembly.

The congress listened with attention to Lenin and Sverdlov, with admiration to Trotsky, whose oratorical talent impressed everyone who heard him, and with complete indifference to Martov when he attempted to alert his audience to the terrorism into which the Russian government was lapsing. But the time had passed when Martov could make himself heard; in the Tauride Palace he could count on only a handful of sympathizers.

The congress passed all the measures presented to it. It began by electing a new Central Executive Committee, totally dominated by the Bolsheviks. Then it decided that the term "provisional" that had qualified the Sovnarkom from its formation would disappear and that no further reference would be made to the defunct Constituent assembly. The contest was over: Lenin had set his power under the legitimating banner of a Congress of Soviets that he controlled and had erased from history the inconvenient assembly elected by a people that rejected him. To carry out this plan that he had harbored for so long, he had had to overcome his often reluctant associates, discredit and eliminate his opponents, and use, successively or simultaneously, deception, manipulation, and violence. He had put at the service of the project that had dominated his entire life a political genius that should not be underestimated and an incomparable cynicism that often shocked even his close associates. But by late January 1918, the state of Soviets existed, its government was no longer provisional, and no popular will could oppose him, because he had abolished its institutional expression.

Democracy was certainly dead. But isn't that exactly what Lenin wanted? It remained to resolve an urgent problem whose constant postponement had cost the life of the czarist regime and its successor: to put an end to a war that the people abhorred.

THE TREATY OF BREST-LITOVSK

The first act of the Bolshevik government had been to publish the Decree on Peace, which had been an invaluable indication of the order of priorities that

Lenin had established and of his political views in general. The document also came out of his vision of the war as he had constantly expressed it since 1914.

Always hostile to the war, he had used the slogan "Immediate Peace!" against the Provisional Government after February 1917 in order to weaken it, while paying no attention to the practical means of bringing it about. From February to October, peace was for Lenin only a weapon against his opponents, something that would help to bring him to power. But beginning in October, the time of slogans had passed, the Bolsheviks were in turn confronted with the concrete problems of peace, and they could no longer be satisfied with mere declarations of intent. The appeal of October 26 proclaimed their desire for a "peace with no annexations or indemnities," based on the disappearance of multinational states and colonial empires. Lenin was perfectly aware that this peace program that would sever the territories of the Central Powers and put an end to the colonial power of Russia's allies was unacceptable to all parties. But the appeal was not addressed to governments. He was calling on the peoples to make peace over the heads of their governments and against them.

If the Decree on Peace was very important, this was because it constituted a negation of the classic diplomatic process designed to put an end to a conflict and because it proposed a procedure indicating the existence of a new political order. In launching his appeal, Lenin was challenging the traditional international society based on governments and relations between states and relied on communications between governments; he was addressing an international society of a new kind in which the actors were the peoples. To be sure the workers' movement had harbored a similar ambition, although it was limited to workers and did not extend to society as a whole. The failure of the movement to mobilize the working classes of the countries of Europe against the war in 1914 had demonstrated that national solidarity within states could be immensely stronger than class solidarity. In October 1917, Lenin, who had always denounced the failure of the workers' movement (blaming it in fact on the reformism of its leaders), adopted as his own the dream of solidarity of the working class to make it the foundation of his politics. He hardly cared whether his appeal for peace was heard by governments. He did not want to convince them but rather the peoples whom he exhorted to resolve the problem of war by following the example of the Russian people, that is, by removing the question of peace from the governments by overthrowing them. He thus counted on establishing in practice the link between war and revolution that he had so often discussed in theory in his writings. The Decree on Peace was simultaneously a call for revolution. In it Lenin revealed his intentions. In taking power he intended to deal not only with the fate of Russia; starting from revolutionary Russia, he had the purpose and believed he had the resources to overturn the order of the world.

His appeal also defined the nature of the Soviet state as he intended it to be. It was totally different from the traditional states known to international society; it would be the first link in a new chain of states born from the world revolution. Trotsky fully shared this vision. When he was appointed commissar of foreign affairs, he himself called his office ephemeral. His only mission was to settle the problem of peace, and once that was done, he said, he would "shut up shop." There would be no need for an office and a minister of "foreign" affairs for revolutionary peoples sharing the same fate in a unified world that had been reconciled by the triumph of the proletariat. Hence, Lenin's appeal for a "peace of the peoples" referred to an unprecedented kind of state.

The call for a new order along with peace had not been heard by those to whom it was addressed. In every country the soldiers had continued the fight to defend their nation. On the home front, despite some disturbances, revolutions had not overthrown the governments of the belligerents. Only the governments of the Central Powers had paid attention to the Decree on Peace, because they saw it as an opportunity to sign a separate peace that would free them from the obligation of keeping troops on the Eastern Front. Hence, the Decree on Peace, conceived by Lenin as an instrument of war to spread the revolution, was to lead to an entirely different result.

In fact it led to long and difficult negotiations with the intention of signing a separate peace between the representatives of the Central Powers and the new Soviet state. The peace that Wilhelm II had expected from his cousin Nicholas II was to be offered to him by Lenin. But wasn't this what the German government had counted on in helping Lenin return to Russia in 1917 and financing his movement? The Soviet state was thus to make its entry onto the international stage as a state of the usual kind. Its interlocutors saw nothing new in it, only that the participants in the negotiations had changed.

Although it immediately set the Central Powers in motion, Lenin's call for peace was diversely interpreted by his own companions. These different views must be taken into consideration, because all of them touched on the future of the revolution and therefore conditioned the development of the Soviet state. Three positions emerged at the time, all of them tied up with the possibilities for concrete action that their advocates perceived. Each one was embodied by one man, Lenin and Bukharin at the two extremes, and Trotsky in the middle.

Lenin began with the situation of his country and derived from that the consequences for its foreign policy. He noted that Russia had accomplished the revolution that he had passionately sought and swept away the "old world." He nevertheless recognized its extreme weakness and felt the need for a reprieve. Russia no longer had an army on which the regime could rely to defend the new system against two enemies: from the outside, its opponents in the war, and from within, the forces attempting to overthrow the revolutionary order. Not only did it no longer have an army, but the new institutions were uncertain both in content and in practice. Everything in Russia depended on a few determined men. Even so, Lenin was only half convinced of the support of his close associates; the repeated crises in the leadership of the party made him aware of the relative precariousness of his position. Was it possible in these circumstances to conduct simultaneously an internal struggle to save the system and an external war? Lenin was persuaded that this was illusory and that he had to devote all his efforts to the internal front in order to keep the revolutionary state from being swept away. The class enemy was the one threatening his entire achievement, and any compromise with that enemy was unthinkable. This enemy had been defeated, removed from power, but not destroyed, and it was immensely dangerous; if the war went on, it would be given a reprieve. It was imperative for Russia to choose its goal: end the war and struggle against the internal enemies, or continue the war against the external enemies.

In his way of posing the problem (anticipating the future), Lenin established a total equivalence between the "class enemy"–everyone in Russia who did not support the Bolsheviks–and the external enemy. He was therefore to declare war without mercy, leading to the destruction and liquidation of all his opponents–individuals, parties, and social groups–against that "class enemy." War is by definition without mercy, based on a simple proposition, the eventual disappearance of the loser. Lenin chose that priority without hesitation; he wanted to save the revolution, which he saw in terms of war without mercy and elimination of the other. In the effort to save the revolution, obligations entered into toward the Allies or the desire not to increase the power of German imperialism carried little weight because, in the final analysis, he asserted, if the revolution in Russia was saved, then German imperialism would also be swept away.

Lenin was here emphasizing an idea that would be a constant in his thinking: Revolutions should not be gratuitous acts without consequences, merely destined periodically to remind peoples of a distant goal and then to become the subject of glorious memories, like the Paris Commune. In order to change the world, it was necessary to cling to the revolutions that had been made and accept their reality, and not sacrifice them to some obscure desire for perfection. In saying this Lenin was not yet thinking of asserting the preeminence of the Bolshevik Revolution; he was simply stating that it should be the "spark" that would light the flame of other revolutions. The value of the Russian Revolution lay for him in the mere fact of its existence.

It was therefore necessary to save the Russian Revolution for the coming world revolution, and in order to do this to make peace at any price, even on Berlin's conditions involving annexation of all occupied areas and increased territorial and economic power for Germany. Lenin defended this idea in "Theses on the Question of a Separate and Annexationist Peace" written in January 1918 and in the ensuing debate in the Central Committee on January 7.[20] Bukharin was then leader of the opposition. A passionate internationalist and as clear-headed as Lenin about the tragic situation of Russia, he nevertheless did not accept the conclusions drawn by the president of the Sovnarkom. He agreed of course that the Russian army no longer existed, but, he argued, signing a treaty would amount to agreeing to strengthen imperialism, leaving the proletariat at its mercy and thereby ruining the chances of world revolution. As a way out of this dilemma, Bukharin proposed to appeal to the revolutionary consciousness of all the Russian people. In the face of an advance of the German armies, it would then be an army of partisans, a people in arms to defend the revolution, and not a state, that would replace the regular army that had been destroyed. And how could other proletarians in uniform agree to combat these proletarians fighting in the name of the revolution?

Trotsky, whose office made him responsible for peace negotiations, hesitated between Bukharin and Lenin. He agreed with Lenin about the danger of continuing the war while internal opposition was growing and threatening to sweep away the Bolshevik regime. Like Lenin, he understood that it would be hazardous to sacrifice the Russian Revolution to Western workers' movements who were passively witnessing its developments and the mounting dangers it was confronting. At the same time, he shared Bukharin's fear of discouraging the Western proletariat from ever entering on the path of revolution if it were abandoned to a Germany that had been made more powerful by what it had seized from Russia. Like Bukharin, he thought he could rely on the class consciousness of the workers. But, in the end, he could not come to a decision between Lenin's and Bukharin's arguments. At times he was inclined to believe that peace would have a shock effect on the German proletariat and impel it to follow the path of revolution. At other times he shared Bukharin's fear that peace would lead to a crushing of the proletariat. His uncertainties were expressed in the position that he finally adopted, "neither war nor peace," and the Central Committee, meeting on January 8, agreed that he should attempt to hold to that line.

The course of negotiations in Brest-Litovsk reflected these divisions in the Bolshevik leadership. They had begun on November 18, when the Russian delegation, at first headed by a close associate of Trotsky's, Adolf Abramovich Yoffe, and including Kamenev, had come to negotiate an armistice. In observing its efforts to stir up soldiers at the front as well as prisoners, the Germans began to wonder about the real intentions of the Russian government. Was Russia in fact seeking peace or did it simply want to gain time?[21] The attitude of Trotsky, who took the head of the delegation in late December, strengthened the Germans' doubts and led them to harden their positions. The idea of a peace "with no annexations or indemnities," presented by Russia and which Germany seemed at first ready to discuss (closing up the Eastern Front was certainly worth it), was abandoned once the Germans had gotten a complete picture of Russian weakness. They then decided to make a separate peace with the Ukraine (signed on February 9) and to annex all the Russian territory that they were occupying.

In the face of these demands, the division among the positions of Lenin, Bukharin, and Trotsky could only become more acute, and the Central Committee was rather inclined to support Trotsky against Lenin, who argued in favor of acceptance of immediate peace, whatever the conditions. Armed with this support, Trotsky returned to Brest-Litovsk and applied himself to dragging out the negotiations until he was presented with an ultimatum. He had to accept the German conditions with no discussion or delay, or else negotiations would be broken off and the German offensive would resume.

Confronted with these harsh demands, Trotsky left Brest-Litovsk on February 10. The discussion was over and the German offensive resumed immediately, even threatening the capital. The Central Committee was once again torn between Lenin, who wanted to sign without further delay, and Trotsky, who had decided to stop the fighting and to demobilize the whole army, or what was left of it.

Captain Sadoul then wrote to his minister: "*Coup de théâtre*: Trotsky has not signed the treaty but declared that the state of war has come to an end between Russia and the Central Powers."[22] In what Sadoul calls the "fantastic conclusion to the negotiations," Trotsky was still supported by Bukharin, and their position won agreement from the Central Committee when it met on February 17 by a majority of one vote. But the German advance on the following day was so swift that Trotsky understood the foolishness of maintaining the slogan "neither war nor peace." It had not stopped the German troops or provoked an uprising of the proletariat in the West, but had left Russian territory wide open to the enemy. He then changed sides and joined Lenin, while Bukharin stubbornly rejected a return to the negotiating table. The majority was reversed, and seven votes supported a separate peace against the desperate advocates of rejection. The Germans were immediately informed of the acceptance of their conditions, and a delegation later returned to Brest-Litovsk to sign a treaty that was extremely costly in terms of territory and wealth, but also for the cohesion of the regime. In order to secure the agreement of his colleagues to a *diktat*, Lenin had had to threaten to resign from the Central Committee. Everyone had rejected the idea, but a number of those who remained opposed to the solution advocated by Lenin resigned from their positions. Trotsky turned over his commissariat and the duty of signing the treaty to Chicherin, he wrote, with "an immense sigh of relief." This time the delegation was headed by Grigory Yakovlevich Sokolnikov, and included Yoffe and Karakhan. Bukharin, who had never become reconciled to the idea of "betraying the Western proletariat," resigned dramatically from all positions and brought left-wing Bolsheviks with him.

The treaty signed on March 3, 1918, made Russia give up immense territories, including Poland, Finland, and the Baltic countries; and the Ukraine became independent. With these territories, Russia lost a substantial portion of its population, as well as vast economic resources. Except for Turkestan and the Caucasus, practically nothing remained of the empire that had been built up over three centuries, whereas German territory was greatly expanded.

Lenin had imposed his views after hard struggles, but his opponents did not stop defending their positions. The treaty had to be ratified, and the Fourth Congress of Soviets was called for that purpose for the middle of March. It was preceded by a special Party Congress, the Seventh, from which Lenin asked for support in return for a secret resolution granting the Central Committee the power to "annul at any time all the peace treaties signed with imperialist and bourgeois governments."[23] This resolution, which made the Central Committee of the Party the privileged actor in the foreign policy of revolutionary Russia and denied in advance the validity of agreements reached, followed directly from Lenin's position underlying the Decree on Peace. He did not believe in relations between states, the party alone should decide according to circumstances, and he did not feel bound by government agreements that could in no way be imposed on the party of the working class.

Even though the Congress of Soviets, which met on March 14, contained a Bolshevik majority, it was more difficult to silence than the Central Committee.

Lenin and his close associates were violently criticized by a minority on the "left," led by Bukharin, Kollontai, Ryazanov, and Dybenko, who were opposed to ratification. Bukharin summed up the matters at issue. Peace of course momentarily saved Russia, or rather the Bolshevik regime, but it condemned world revolution to death. Lenin had chosen the national interest over the internationalist view of the revolution. But Lenin rejected this accusation and replied by also brandishing the argument of world revolution. The Treaty of Brest-Litovsk, he said, was only a reprieve; it would not be applied because revolution would spread, all the more because the Russian Revolution, having been preserved, would serve as a point of departure and a model: "We put the entire matter in the hands of the Bolsheviks," he went on, "because the revolution is ripening in all countries, and when all is said and done, and not at the very beginning, the international socialist revolution will come!"

Like Bukharin, Lenin foresaw world revolution, but their revolutionary strategies depended on different choices. When they spoke of peace, they were disagreeing over a question that went beyond peace; their dispute had to do with the definition of the principal force of world revolution. Was it the Bolshevik Party or the world (that is, Western) proletariat? Was it acceptable to sacrifice the Russian Revolution, which had already taken place, to the still hypothetical future of Western revolutionary movements, or did their success have to be linked to the survival of the Russian Revolution?

In his choice, Lenin remained faithful to what he had always thought and wished for. A party man, skeptical about the revolutionary consciousness of any proletariat, he relied entirely on the revolutionary tool that he had forged that had made it possible for him to take power in Russia. He could not possibly have confidence in the proletariats of the West who did not have a comparable tool and whose weakness and opportunism had made possible the fighting of proletarians in a world war for the benefit of their governments. Like his opponents, he was convinced that the Russian Revolution could not survive alone and the world revolution had to break out in order to save it. Neither Lenin nor his opponents thought it possible to confine the revolution within the borders of a single country. They all looked to the outside world and asked themselves the same question: How can we help bring about the revolutionary explosion in Europe?

When the debate was over, Lenin's position had won out. The Congress had agreed to ratify the treaty by 724 votes against 276, and 118 abstentions. The opposition came principally from Left Socialist Revolutionaries and left-wing Bolsheviks. (In 1918, a group was established in the party, including Bukharin, Radek, Pyatakov, Uritsky, and Bubnov, known as Left Communists. This group opposed the Treaty of Brest-Litovsk, wanted to turn the war into a "revolutionary war," and called for a policy of radical economic measures, in particular the total nationalization of the economy.) In the face of what they considered a disaster, the Left SRs decided to break off the appearance of coalition and to resign from the government. In the meantime the government had been moved from Petrograd to Moscow in order to preserve the center of power, and in order to save the system, Lenin considered going as far as necessary, even to the edge of the Urals. Sadoul noted, "The Bolsheviks are ready, if necessary, even to abandon European Russia," unquestionably a sign of a deep sense of helplessness.[24] Once the treaty was signed, the substantial increase in the power of Germany was clear. Despite countless difficulties, Lenin did not share the widespread pessimism. He had retreated to Moscow and was finally heading, as he had wanted to from the outset, a homogeneous government.[25] He would be able to set himself to work on the immediate task of organizing that state, which was not really a state, but on which depended the future of world revolution.

Chapter Eleven

HOLDING POWER AT ALL COSTS

A STATE DIFFERENT FROM ALL KNOWN STATES, A TRANSITIONAL state, the Bolshevik state nonetheless had to organize itself if it wanted to last. The obsession that Lenin had harbored for so many years of how to take power gave way to another: how to keep power. The answer to the question was not simple, because the Bolsheviks were opposed by the political parties that they had removed from all positions of authority but that still existed and by a large part of the country (neither provincial centers nor the countryside had been won over), and they were facing a dreadful military situation. The Germany armies threatened to move on the capital at any moment, and from the remnants of the imperial army would arise attempts to overthrow the Bolshevik regime. For Lenin it was out of the question to weaken his power by compromises, as he had shown by dissolving the Constituent Assembly and rejecting the idea of a coalition government; it was even more out of the question to give up power because of the difficulties. He had to hold on, and to do that he had to have access to the tools necessary for the exercise of authority.

THE INSTRUMENTS OF POWER

As soon as power was conquered, Lenin put in place a governmental structure, the Sovnarkom. At first, this was a rather empty shell, because real authority, as Lenin had worked to ensure, lay with the Soviets.

Two large Soviets dominated Russian life in the winter of 1917–1918, the Petrograd and Moscow Soviets. But throughout the country, others had sprung up. These bodies were initially characterized by two kinds of heterogeneity, between one another, and within each one. The most prestigious, the Petrograd Soviet, considered as the bearer of the revolution, experienced swift changes after October, presaging those that would take place elsewhere. A Soviet of workers' deputies, it was expanded at the behest of the Bolsheviks to include soldiers, who were more subject to the influence of Lenin's Party than the workers, and then to include peasants, an expansion that had two consequences. The constant increase in the number of participants made its meetings inefficient, and its growing internal heterogeneity left the initiative to the most active elements, who were the most manipulated by the Bolsheviks, that is, the soldiers. Whereas at the outset the Soviets (particularly the Petrograd Soviet) were dominated by the Mensheviks and the Socialist Revolutionaries, the systematic "entryism" advocated by Lenin neutralized them, and the non-Bolshevik Socialists tended to desert them, leaving the stage to Lenin's followers. In Moscow, the Soviet at first seemed more able to resist Bolshevik pressure, but the party soon sent its representatives there and to provincial Soviets in order to centralize and make uniform procedures and actions.

By late November the Soviets had received the order to report their activities to the Council of Commissars of the People, and the commissar of internal affairs, Grigory Petrovsky, became a kind of supervisor of these assemblies that were theoretically the holders of revolutionary legitimacy. A twofold movement thus gradually took place: the internal Bolshevization of the Soviets was hastened where the Bolsheviks could impose themselves, and, at the same time, the central government, regardless of its weakness, established a hierarchical link that gradually subordinated all the Soviets to it.

One difficulty remained. When they took power, the Bolsheviks had neither administrative experience nor institutions making it possible to manage the country. The commissariats were buildings with almost no furniture; the commissars had neither assistants nor contacts with the rest of the country. On the other hand, the Soviets were established everywhere, and they had ties to the population, particularly in rural areas where the Bolsheviks had little influence. Quite naturally Lenin put into operation the slogan he had proclaimed months earlier: "All Power to the Soviets!" But after October this was in entirely different circumstances and with a totally different meaning. For a time the Soviets were to be the instrument of power for the Bolsheviks.

The months immediately following the revolution were thus characterized by an increase in the power of the Soviets and an apparent fading of the party. This transfer of administrative power to the Soviets was a central element in Soviet life in late 1917 and early 1918. In a few months, the most active party leaders migrated to the Soviets, and the party was being emptied of its militants.

Financial difficulties were another cause of the strengthening of these bodies. Operating in the field, the Soviets mobilized existing resources and party organizations often came to depend on their goodwill.

The flourishing of their authority was demonstrated principally by the confusion of powers that took root at the time: the same men at the top of the system embodied indiscriminately the state of the Soviets and the party. This was the case for Lenin, founder of the party, who was head of the Sovnarkom; it was even more true for Sverdlov, who was secretary of the Party Central Committee and at the same time chairman of the Central Executive Committee of the Soviets. Hence, in the early days, the distribution of authority between the party and Soviets, and between Soviets and the government seemed unclear.

However, a decisive instrument of the new regime was already taking shape, the one that Lenin had generously attributed to society in *The State and Revolution*: the power of repression. Its birth was practically simultaneous with the birth of revolutionary power, and would soon be justified by Lenin as necessary for the revolutionary exercise of terror. His old friend V. Adoratsky reports that as early as 1908, when he questioned Lenin about the fate of the defeated after the seizure of power, he answered: "We'll ask the man, 'Where do you stand on the question of the Revolution? Are you for it or against it?' If he is against it, we'll stand him up against the wall. If he is for it, we'll welcome him into our midst to work with us."[1] And he frequently quoted Marx, for whom "revolutionary terror was indispensable to the birth of the new order." There was nothing surprising then in the fact that within the Military Revolutionary Committee a "military investigation commission" of five members was established, first mentioned on November 1, which soon made itself known for abuses. But Lenin found this body inconsistent and inefficient. He hesitated among several titles and, on December 7, set up an "All-Russian Extraordinary Commission for Struggle against Counterrevolution, Sabotage, and Speculation," which tragically entered history under its acronym *Cheka*. It was promptly put under the leadership of its inventor Felix Edmundovich Dzerzhinsky, who had been very active on the MRC during the October insurrection. He had not always had peaceful relations with Lenin and, while supporting him in October, had opposed him during the peace negotiations, going so far as calling for his dismissal. For the Bolsheviks, Dzerzhinsky had become a symbol of revolutionary purity, but the left-wing socialists detested him, because they were aware of his cruelty and his talent as a manipulator. In fact, Lenin found the figure very attractive. Austere to the point of losing his humanity (he had volunteered for terrorist work), he mirrored in many respects the merciless "new man" that Lenin had encountered in his adolescent reading.

The press did not report the decree establishing the Cheka, and its functions were very vaguely defined.[2] Although certain documents published at the time suggest that the new body was supposed to carry out investigations in order to prevent sabotage and counterrevolutionary enterprises and to hand the accused over to a court, the commission in reality enjoyed from the very beginning of its existence unlimited powers of investigation and repression. On October 27, 1917, the Second Congress of Soviets had without debate abolished the death penalty, but the Cheka used it at will without reporting its decisions to any other body. Indeed, Lenin had deplored the inherent naïveté of the original decision: "How can one make a revolution without executions?" On another occasion he asked: "Is it impossible to find among us a Fouquier-Tinville?" And he had no qualms about ignoring the decision abolishing the death penalty. From the outset, he gave Dzerzhinsky the resources to carry out his duties in conditions guaranteeing the effectiveness of the Cheka. Although administrative services of the people's commissars were still nonexistent, the Cheka, which began its work with 120 employees, had more than thirty thousand a year later.

As a careful reader of Marx's analysis of the Paris Commune, Lenin had placed another institution under the control of the people in *The State and Revolution*, the army. In this case as well, the development of Lenin's ideas and their entry into operation were almost immediate. Shortly after his resignation from the commissariat of foreign affairs, Trotsky had become commissar of war, but in this instance he did not suppose that he would soon have to "shut up shop." In 1918 the Russian army had disintegrated; all that was left were the Red Guards, with neither hierarchy, nor discipline, nor military know-how. Everything had to be built from the ground up. An avid reader of Clausewitz, but of Jaurès as well, Trotsky had borrowed a good deal from both to forge his own view of war and the army. To begin with he agreed with Jaurès's notion of a popular militia and derived his first idea from that, one day to create a people's army. Although he rejected as a matter of principle the idea of a standing professional army, he was to implement that option in practice, asserting that the people's army belonged to the realm of the future, when Russia would be rid of all the remnants of the former social system and would have overcome its backwardness and consolidated Soviet power so that it would no longer be under any threat. Called on to establish an army at a time when civil war was in the offing, he saw that as a further reason to forget the dream of a people's army in favor of a military instrument of the traditional kind.[3]

In Trotsky's view the organizing principles of this army were very similar to those of all the armies in the world. In the first place, he thought that the army should be a permanent institution obeying precise hierarchical rules of command. Election of officers, which had contributed to the disintegration of the army since the revolution, was abandoned in favor of their appointment from the top down on the basis of military competence rather than political criteria. Discipline, which had also been condemned in the blaze of revolutionary passion, resumed its constraining role and was no longer subject to discussion. Competence and training had to be sought where they could be found, in the officers of the former empire, military specialists who had been so recently scorned and dismissed by their troops and were suddenly asked to rejoin the army being formed. To be sure Trotsky made room in his creation for a category that was to become famous, the political commissars,[4] but in 1918 he had a precise idea of the respective roles of officers and commissars that avoided any interference of the political official into strictly military matters. He explained this in June 1918 in a speech to the First All-Russian Congress of Political Commissars: "Officers are fully responsible for military operations, commissars are charged with maintaining morale and loyalty." A little earlier, addressing the party organization in Moscow, he summed up the major principles of military morale in three words, "work, discipline, order." No army could fail to recognize itself in those words.

Of course, despite his new position as commissar of war, Trotsky did not forget that the framework of his program was shaped by the revolution and its future. He explained this on many occasions: the effective tool was the army of the present, the one that would be able to save the revolution. He also thought about the future and asserted that when the state withered away, the army would become the people's army and would be fully democratized. By thus projecting himself into an indefinite future, he made his peace with Jaurès. In the meanwhile he claimed that the army of the revolution, despite appearances to the contrary, would not be an army of the standard type. As he was forging its first elements, he thought that what already differentiated it was its underlying spirit. Even though officers held authority, and hierarchy and discipline set up visible barriers between them and their troops, all of them were inspired by the conviction that they were working for a common future in which equality among men would be the rule. The new army consisted principally of workers and peasants; the union established between them prefigured the future community ready to sacrifice itself for a shared ideal. And the officers themselves, although they had been trained by those of the old army, would also come from the peasantry and the working class. Thus the class army which was at the source of the Red Army would become, with the abolition of classes, the army of the proletariat.

These guiding principles, frequently proclaimed by Trotsky, did not, however, lead him to fall into the illusion of a strategic confusion between the political and the military. The officers of the old regime recruited by the Red Army had a tendency to seek rehabilitation by advocating the development of a proletarian military strategy. Trotsky vigorously condemned this view and calmly asserted that Marxism was of no help in matters of strategy. It was better to forget it. Military doctrine, he said, was a question of knowledge and accumulated experience; there was no room for ideological speculation in this area. He concluded: "You do not play chess by consulting Marx, nor do you make war by referring to him."

Beyond principles, the implementation of concrete measures occurred all the more swiftly because events compelled the Bolsheviks to defend themselves against the rebellion of Czech war prisoners in Siberia. They had been captured by the imperial army when they were part of the Austro-Hungarian forces and had been freed by the Provisional Government to fight alongside the Russians. After the signature of the Treaty of Brest-Litovsk, it was decided that these forces, recognized by the Bolsheviks as "autonomous troops" whose independence was guaranteed by the Allies, would be repatriated through Vladivostok and, in the meanwhile, they should under no circumstances become involved in Russian political life. When they did, it was for accidental reasons. They periodically came into conflict with local Bolshevik authorities who attempted either to enlist them as allies or to seize their weapons. This situation lasted until the day when Trotsky had the idea of integrating them into the army he was establishing. Wishing only to return home, the Czech detachments revolted, placing very weak Soviet authority in danger in Siberia and the Urals. Captain Sadoul summarized the crisis: "While the affair is troublesome for the Allies, it is extremely dangerous for the Soviets. They are confronted by 25 thousand volunteers, who are brave and disciplined men. [These men] are occupying a region in which there are many Czech prisoners who will not fail to join them."[5]

Furthermore, the situation was becoming tense elsewhere, particularly in the Ukraine, and it was imperative for the Bolsheviks to have a real army to deal with it. Trotsky had already appealed to the Allies, principally the French, for the urgent dispatch of military experts to the Bolsheviks.

On April 11, Sadoul noted: "It was at my insistence that the Bolsheviks asked France for a contingent of forty officers. . . . They wanted to have many more, and a much larger number would indeed be necessary to inspire confidence and induce sound military elements to return to the army." He described with a strong attempt at objectivity the difficult conditions under which the Russian army was being organized:

> The work of military reorganization is progressing slowly. The trans-fer of a part of the commissariat to Moscow, while some offices remain in Petrograd, and the dispersal of different command posts in the center of Russia have multiplied the difficulties. . . . The manag-ing personnel of the commissariat, at first purely Bolshevik, has grad-ually been joined by professionals. The best technicians were not the first to return, and a certain number of major positions are in the hands of inadequate and barely loyal men. . . . But Trotsky is really demonstrating perfect political impartiality and a desire to use the professionals and judge them only on their competence.[6]

The picture sketched by Sadoul is impressive. Trotsky was full of goodwill, he noted, but very ignorant of military matters. As a young man he had even evad-ed military service. He listened attentively to advice, recruited former officers, and had recourse to the services of Allied officers. But with the matter of the Czech Legion, the need to make swift and radical decisions was clear. Workers in large cities aged twenty-one and above were mobilized for six months. Then a decree restored compulsory military service, while a second decree issued at the same time (June 1918) compelled all officers of the dissolved army to join the Red Army. The call for volunteers was replaced with the obligation to par-ticipate in defense and with the threat of severe sanctions against anyone attempting to avoid that duty. As a result the political commissars took on greater importance, insofar as Trotsky was convinced that he could not rely on the loyalty of officers who were no longer serving out of choice. A staff school was established to train the officer corps. In a few months, the Red Army was thus established, but it was heterogeneous and badly led. "Give me people who know how to obey," Trotsky had said when he took office, but it was difficult to restore a principle of obedience that had been thrown overboard a few months earlier. In order to succeed, he would have to use threats and force toward the army that was taking shape.

Hence, by the summer of 1918 it was necessary to recognize the death of the dream of a "Commune." Barely created, still unsure of its organization, the Soviet state had restored the two pillars of traditional power, the army and the police, which were dependent on the central authority and outside any control by the Soviets and the rank and file. The elements of a strong and centralized power were in place, while the organization of political power remained uncer-tain and had little assurance of lasting.

To be sure the Bolsheviks sometimes expressed their discomfort at this rapid development of the system. Just as Trotsky described a future army in harmony with social transformations, so Zinoviev expressed in 1918 the conviction that the Cheka, an emergency institution, would disappear as the withering away of the state progressed. In both cases these remarks of 1918 had more to do with the desire to conceal the gulf between prerevolutionary ideology and the reality of the aftermath of the revolution than with a real intention to work toward the swift disappearance of the police and the army. Lenin, who had vigorously protested against the abolition of the death penalty advocated by Kamenev, had the military model rooted in his mind, as all his writings indicate. His vocabulary had always had a military inspiration. Whereas at the beginning of the century, he had thought of the party by referring to the army and had adopted a military pattern in order to shape his party (in particular for the principles of centralism, hierarchy, and discipline), after the revolution, when Russia no longer had an army, the party then became the example imposed on the army. Unlike Trotsky or Zinoviev, Lenin never gave way to vain regrets over the institutions of power that were taking shape; at no point did he evoke the final stage when those institutions would disappear. Indeed, the increasing police power followed the logic of the slogan that Lenin had used as an epigraph to *What Is to Be Done?* on the need to "purge" the party. The practices that took shape in 1918 unquestionably came from the view of authority and control that he had set forth in 1902, a view from which he had never departed.

PROMISES AND RETREATS

Before seizing power Lenin had made numerous commitments to the peasantry. Because he had little influence over it, and because, as a disciple of Marx he knew that a revolution in which the peasants did not join the chorus of rebels was doomed to failure, by April 1917 he had promised them what they so vehemently demanded, land. In fact, there was nothing innovative in his slogan; it was simply adapted to the swift development of the situation in the countryside. When he seized power in October, the peasants had anticipated his victory and had already taken possession of the land. The old dream of the "great distribution" was in the process of becoming reality. On October 26 Lenin presented the Decree on Land to the Congress of Soviets. It abolished large landed property without compensation and placed the land at the disposal of those who cultivated it. To be sure he explained that the Constituent Assembly was to develop an agrarian reform, but because the framework of that reform was defined in the earliest decrees emanating from the revolution, the Constituent Assembly would have little opportunity to supply innovations or additions. In fact the Decree on Land conferred legal status on the situation that the peasants had created since the summer of 1917. It gave them immediate satisfaction and thus won them over to the Bolsheviks. It simultaneously created a paradoxical situation; the revolution called itself Socialist and, at the same time, one of its first decisions consisted in ratifying the principle of property in the countryside. It took both Lenin and the peasants little time to recognize this contradiction and draw the appropriate conclusions.

But for the moment, the peasants, armed with the Decree on Land, concluded that the "Black Repartition" (*cherny peredel*) should continue, and they appropriated the available land, the tools to cultivate it, the cattle, and the means of transport (carts and the like) useful for rural life. On December 9, 1917, *Izvestia,* the official organ of the government, commented on the "Black Repartition" in progress: "The peasants have understood nothing about the Decree on Land. They are beginning to plunder the herds and materials in the region [of Samara]. The Soviet had to send detachments to restore order."

The autonomous revolution in the countryside was all the more remarkable because it contradicted the development occurring in the working class at the same time. To understand what was happening among workers, it is necessary to return to the views set out by Lenin when he was on the point of seizing power. At that moment he knew that Socialism could not yet be realized in Russia, and in the last article he wrote before the October Revolution, "The Threatening Catastrophe and How to Fight It,"[7] he started from the idea that capitalism could be brought down merely by workers' control of production, and he proposed five economic measures of "revolutionary democracy":

1. Fusion of all banks into one whose operations would be controlled by the state; as an alternative, nationalization of the banks
2. Nationalization of the largest cartels (oil, coal, metals)
3. Abolition of commercial confidentiality
4. Forced "cartelization" of all industries, trades, and so on
5. Quasi-obligatory grouping of the whole society into organizations of consumers to control production and consumption networks

These measures were not Socialist, and Lenin explained: "Nationalization and confiscation of private goods are distinct measures. The ownership of capital concentrated in banks is certified by written documents. None of these certifications is changed or invalidated by the nationalization of the banks." He went on: "The principal advantage of the nationalization of the banks is to facilitate the provision of credits to small businessmen and peasants."

At the time he thus presented nationalizations as measures intended to rationalize economic life and to facilitate the life of small businessmen, who would have access to the capital they needed, and not as a destruction of private property. Similarly, with respect to cartelization, Lenin explained that "it does not take a kopeck from any owner," and he compared the proposed measures with those in force in the societies of Western Europe. What he wanted, he said, was to bring the capitalists to cooperate with the government arising from the revolution. In addition, he intended, through the control that would be exercised over them, to prevent them from sabotaging the economic policies of a revolutionary government. In the end what Lenin envisaged on the eve of the revolution was the establishment of a "state capitalism" which would constitute a transitional phase toward Socialism. He defined his perception of the future in these terms: "Socialism is nothing but the stage immediately following monopoly capitalism."

The transitional Socialism described in this article was perfectly compatible with peasant property. After seizing power Lenin took one further step. He established workers' control over business. This provision, adopted after the Decree on Land, fell far short of the aspirations of the working class, because it implied that business owners would remain in place, and it often fell short of changes that had actually taken place. Workers had the feeling that they were the architects of Lenin's victory, they saw themselves as owners of their workplaces, and they expelled the owners. They could not accept the idea of merely exercising control when they had expropriated the owners on their own authority. But the "Declaration of the Rights of the Working and Exploited People" of January 1918 confirmed Lenin's views and obviously fell short of the expectations of the working class.[8] The declaration indicated Lenin's intent to slow down a movement of expropriations resulting from the spontaneous will of the workers. It was only on June 28, 1918, that the decree on the expropriation of heavy industry was finally issued. By that time the owners who could be expropriated had already been kicked out by the workers or had fled on their own from businesses where the hostility and sometimes violence of the workers made it impossible for them to continue to resist.

From October 1917 until late June 1918, in the name of the single principle of the Socialist revolution, two opposing social and legal situations thus coexisted in Russia. In the countryside Lenin's government had recognized from the outset peasant aspirations for ownership and had given them legal status; in the industrial world, it had on the contrary closed its eyes for months to a revolutionary situation, the voluntarist action of the working class, and the only legal framework it had attempted to provide was that of workers' control. In this contradictory behavior, we encounter once again the pragmatism that Lenin demonstrated throughout his life and that brought him constantly to subordinate the principles to which he claimed allegiance to the demands of reality. In the minority in the countryside, subject to competition from the Socialist Revolutionary Party, he wanted to be the one who had responded as early as October 1917 to the traditional aspirations of the peasants, thereby hoping to steal a march on the SRs and reap the peasants' votes in the coming elections. The attempt was futile; the peasants embarked on the organization of the countryside in their own way, taking advantage of the decree granting them ownership. Nevertheless they did not turn their backs on the party that had always represented their interests, and the elections to the Constituent Assembly confirmed their loyalty to the SRs. Lenin had always seen the peasantry of his country as a symbol of its backwardness and Asiatic tradition, and this behavior confirmed his unending distrust of the Russian countryside. He knew that the peasants had participated in the revolutionary movement between April and October 1917 only in order to win a victory for their individualism and desire for ownership, and not at all from adhesion to Socialism.

The break would be brutal, and the peasants would pay a fearsome price for their two illusions, trusting Lenin's speeches and believing that their aspirations had been accepted once and for all.

Lenin's relations with the working class developed in the opposite direction, although that did nothing to provide any real improvement to the workers' lot. Beginning in the summer of 1918, when the Bolshevik government was under attack from every direction, the workers were at Lenin's side defending the revolution. The alliance was precarious. In the early 1920s, the workers tried to emancipate themselves from a Party that intended to lead them according to the principles set forth in *What Is to Be Done?* The attempt by workers to find their own means of action was at the time another problem for Lenin; he was once again able to measure the distance between society, whether worker or peasant, and its governing bodies. The solitude of the Bolshevik regime, which Lenin frequently imputed to the betrayal of the Western proletariat, which was not at all eager to follow the Russian example, was primarily his own solitude in his own society.

Finally Lenin's promises at the dawn of the revolution were also addressed to the nations of what had been the Russian Empire. After asserting during the war their right to self-determination, Lenin acted toward them as he had toward the peasants. In order to win them over, he recognized their national aspirations without the slightest reservation. As in the case of the peasants, his words had consequences on the periphery of the country, all the more because the political disintegration of the empire and of the Provisional Government encouraged inclinations toward independence. Addressing the All-Russian Congress of Soviets on October 26, Lenin read the Decree on Peace, the first declaration on the problem of the cessation of hostilities with the Central Powers, but also on the problem of annexations and therefore of the dying empire. It said that "every incorporation of a small or weak nation into a large or powerful state without the precisely, clearly, and voluntarily expressed consent and wish of that nation, irrespective of the time when such forcible incorporation took place, irrespective also of the degree of development or backwardness of the nation forcibly annexed to the given state, or forcibly retained within its borders, and irrespective, finally, of whether this nation is in Europe or in distant, overseas countries" was to be condemned. The Decree on Peace specified that this also applied to the annexations of the Great Russians, that is, to the Russian Empire. On November 2, the Declaration of Rights of the Peoples of Russia, coauthored by Lenin and Stalin, the commissar for nationalities, defined the four principles guiding the new regime in its relations with the peoples who had been annexed:

1. The equality and sovereignty of the peoples of Russia
2. The right of nations to self-determination, up to and including separation and the formation of nation-states

3. The liquidation of all national and national-religious privileges and restrictions
4. The free development of national minorities and ethnic groups inhabiting the territory of Russia

Thus, like the peasants, nations were suddenly legally authorized to choose their fate. In this case as well, Lenin had secured a respite, long enough to seize and consolidate power, and he thought he had gained the support of the periphery of the empire, which had been in great turmoil for months. For most nations, as for the vast majority of peasants, Lenin's decrees were considered to be definite commitments, not clever maneuvers related to a strategy aimed at establishing priorities among problems and first of all consolidating his power. In this case as well, the actors in this tragedy soon became aware of the misunderstanding, which came out into the open and, at the moment of truth, led them into terrible confrontations.

CONSTRAINTS: CIVIL WARS AND NATIONAL WARS

In signing the Treaty of Brest-Litovsk, Lenin had counted on gaining a reprieve (*peredyshka*) in order to consolidate his power while he waited for the Russian revolutionary spark to set Europe ablaze and bring to his country the support of the Western proletariat. The hope was soon dashed. Far from settling problems, the treaty opened a new and frightful period for Russia, marked by war on three fronts: civil war, foreign intervention, and national wars.

When he took power, Lenin had promised peace, land, and bread. From the outset he was confronted with the problem that had undermined the power of his predecessors since 1914, the hunger that alienated the population from those in authority. This population had continued to hope that one government or another would be able to provide it with the means of subsistence. It had not forgotten (only five years had passed since 1913) that before the war its conditions had been improving. The conflict had certainly put an abrupt end to that tendency toward progress, but the decline in material conditions in the years from 1914 to 1917 was nothing in comparison to what Russia experienced from 1918 on. The principal factors contributing to the disaster were the political situation of Russia after the peace treaty and the situation of the peasantry.

The Treaty of Brest-Litovsk had deprived the country of one of its richest regions, the Ukraine, which produced wheat and contained 90 percent of the sugar industry and 70 percent of the iron ore. After briefly attempting to stay out of the conflict on their territory between the Soviet regime and the White armies (led at first by General Kornilov, who was killed in battle, and then by General Anton Denikin), the Don Cossacks rose up against the Bolsheviks. Where the Bolsheviks gained ground, they immediately established a system of terror, requisitioning goods and arresting and shooting whoever came into their hands. The entire Don, under the authority of their Ataman, Petr Krasnov, escaped from Bolshevik control. In the east, the revolt of the Czech Legion had taken on significant proportions. After capturing various towns in the Urals–Novo-Nikolaevsk, Kurgan, Omsk, and Samara–their detachments reached Kazan, where they joined the Volga peasants who had also rebelled. There was widespread and fierce fighting among Cossacks, Czechs, peasants, and Red Guards, and in a number of cities–Tula, Kostroma, and Saratov–workers also joined the rebellion.

The regime reacted with increased violence against this storm of opposition. Trotsky gave his nascent army orders to repress presumed enemies without mercy and to increase the use of exemplary capital punishment. Arbitrary executions proliferated, of "Whites" captured in battle and peasants, but also of soldiers and officers who showed insufficient zeal. The army was growing; by the fall of 1918, it numbered nearly one million. And as it came under increasing control of the political commissars, the army was stirred to greater cruelty by their extremist orders.

The growing terror settled nothing, particularly not the immediate problem of hunger. The disorganization of the country had spectacular effects on transports, namely, on the distribution of food supplies. The Russian rail network which, as both the Russo-Japanese War and the World War had demonstrated, had always been inadequate to connect the various parts of a vast territory, was now in addition partly destroyed. Whereas in 1913 Russia had 18,000 locomotives able to transport 10 million tons of merchandise, in 1918, only 7,000 or 8,000 were left, and their carrying capacity was one-third of what it had been five years earlier. Agricultural production often remained in place and rotted. Even when it could be transported to cities, trains traveled so slowly and in such deplorably unsafe conditions that when merchandise arrived it was often unusable. Or else, trains did not arrive because they had been attacked and looted on the way. Furthermore, peasants were little inclined to sell anything at all. Lenin's slogan, "Land to the peasants!" quickly turned, as we shall see, to class warfare in the countryside; the desperate peasantry turned inward, while people in cities were dying of hunger.

The situation in urban centers deteriorated as a result of two phenomena: unemployment and the return of soldiers and prisoners. Retooling of the war industries proceeded with difficulty. Deprived of the resources of the Donbass region and of access to raw materials because of transport difficulties, factories used up their inventories and closed their doors. The workers who had been called to the revolution to build a "new world" found themselves out of work, while prices were climbing at an accelerated rate and a black market sprang up. By returning soldiers to civilian life, the Treaty of Brest-Litovsk further aggravated the situation. One and one-half million severely wounded soldiers, often handicapped for life, and three million prisoners returned to cities that could provide them with neither work nor food. Sometimes they decided to return to the countryside where they swelled the ranks of the discontent.

The spring of 1918 was terrible for the entire society but especially for the cities. In Petrograd, 70 percent of the population was out of work, and there were interminable lines to get barely a pound of bread. The increasing unpopularity of the Bolsheviks is hardly surprising. An election for the local Soviet took place in Sormovo in April 1918, which resulted in a Menshevik and Socialist Revolutionary majority. The political parties that Lenin had deprived of electoral victory in the Constituent Assembly understood that the time had come to go on the counterattack, facilitated by the isolation of the Bolsheviks and their inability to respond otherwise than by violence. The non-Bolshevik elected majority of the Constituent Assembly still embodied the hopes of social consciousness.

In Moscow the Constitutional Democratic Party tried to set up an opposition organization that would be able to rally the many who were discontent. The Union for the Renewal of Russia brought together right-wing Socialists and left-wing Kadets, who adopted the program of an immediate convening of the Constituent Assembly. Boris Savinkov, a prestigious figure in the Socialist Revolutionary Party, for his part created the Union for the Defense of the Fatherland and Freedom; he called on officers to join him and tried to create a veritable structured and secret organization, with centers in Moscow and the provinces, with a view to overthrowing the Bolshevik government. No doubt these organizations were weak because they were scattered, in competition with one another, and particularly because they often proposed out-of-date programs, ranging from the restoration of the monarchy to the convocation of the stillborn Constituent Assembly. In the chaos into which Russia was sinking, these programs provoked little response, but they helped to show that the regime established by Lenin was precarious and that forces were rising against it everywhere, demonstrating that the legitimacy in which it clothed itself was entirely self-conferred. Increasing opposition also manifested itself to the left of the Bolsheviks, where the anarchists found Lenin's seizure of power no more acceptable than did the moderate parties. Anarchist groups, swollen with bands of the hungry, brandished black flags and launched the slogan of "Rebellion against the Commissars!" May and June 1918 saw the proliferation of armed conflicts, and Tsaritsyn (later Stalingrad, and then Volgograd), Samara, Saratov, and a number of other cities were the theater of bloody uprisings that the Bolsheviks crushed with unparalleled cruelty.

Beginning in March, famine and the disorganization of the economy and often of government institutions were joined by the preparation and outbreak of the counterrevolution and foreign intervention.

Part of the army, essentially officers, was distressed by a peace that was considered "shameful." Restored to civilian life and then called on to command Trotsky's army, a large number of them refused and attempted to set up their own military organizations to seize power from the Bolsheviks. There were combinations of the most diverse movements. White armies politically hostile to the Bolsheviks, armies of "beggars," peasants made desperate by the violence of the Leninist regime, betrayed hopes, and the civil war imposed on the countryside by the party, often came together with anarchists. The fragments of the imperial army (one-half million men) formed the White armies, led by ambitious generals who rejected the revolution, or the peace treaty, or both. The fifty thousand members of the Czech Legion gradually came under the command of French officers and constituted an efficient army that was joined by Russian volunteers.

Administrations grew out of these new forces coming together. In Omsk, a government of western Siberia, with a conservative slant, was established. In Samara, there was a government led by the Socialist Revolutionaries which established ties with the Ural Cossacks, who had also revolted. In the south, General Denikin put together a volunteer army, partially equipped by the British government and assisted by a British military mission. The allied intervention, however discreet it may have been, brought appreciable support to those who wanted to put an end to the Bolshevik regime. Since March 1918, French and British troops had been landing in Murmansk, then in Arkhangelsk, and, finally, in the summer in Vladivostok. By April, Japanese troops had penetrated into the territories of the Russian Far East.

This picture of chaos in Russia would be incomplete without the inclusion of national secessions reducing the reach of the authority of Lenin's government. In the Ukraine, the Germans had first signed a separate peace treaty, thereby tearing the Ukraine away from Russia. Then they dismissed the Ukrainian government, the Rada, which they suspected of hostility, and installed General Paulo Skoropadsky, who restored the Hetmanate, a prerevolutionary institution that was certainly not likely to adopt revolutionary ideology. Supported by the German high command and the large landowners, Skoropadsky made the Ukraine a possible base for intervention against the Bolshevik regime. Central Asia was no more favorable to the Bolsheviks. It had been in revolt against the empire since 1916, and governments hostile to the central authorities were established, for example, the republic of Kokand, which was proclaimed in 1917 and collapsed in February 1918 under the blows of the Bolsheviks, whom its defenders considered a new avatar of Russian domination. At the same time, popular resistance was growing throughout the Ferghana Valley, known as the movement of the Basmachis ("barefoot"); this was a veritable peasant guerrilla organization that made life difficult for Lenin and his successors for years. The same hopes and the same will to fight inspired the peoples of the Caucasus. Everywhere, governmental bodies or national resistance movements counted on England to protect their struggle against Bolshevism, which they considered nothing but imperialism in disguise.

Among the organized counterrevolutionary troops, national revolts, and foreign armies of intervention, there were also indefinable groups, known as Greens, who belonged to no camp. In the general disorder, they sowed panic wherever they passed and sometimes managed to seize entire cities.

THE REBIRTH OF THE POLITICAL OPPOSITION

In the summer of 1918, the situation of the Bolsheviks seemed hopeless. Their field of action was constantly shrinking, as their opponents increased in number and gained territory, challenging their right to hold power, refuting it in the name of various forms of legitimacy—the monarchy, the popular will expressed in the elections to the Constituent Assembly, and finally the increasing poverty and chaos that the Bolsheviks had fostered and were incapable of overcoming. Even where they were in control of the situation, particularly in the recently established capital of Moscow, their power was undermined.

The Socialist Revolutionaries were fully conscious of this weakness. In May 1918 their National Council had demanded the convocation of the Constituent Assembly. The silence of the Bolsheviks on this point (for Lenin, that assembly had never existed and the call for a popular vote was pure "cretinism") drove them to take action. In July they organized uprisings in Moscow and Petrograd. Terrorist tactics then took the place of the call for social representation. The SRs fighting against the Bolsheviks were no longer only the Right, opposed from the outset to the coup d'état, but also the Left SRs, who had been faithful allies to Lenin until the summer of 1918. They turned against him in June and demanded from the Congress of Soviets a radical change of policy: immediate dissolution of the Red Army and the Cheka, and abolition of the brigades for the requisition of grain in the countryside. Lenin loftily ignored these requests, and the SRs then decided that the hour of confrontation had come.

Yakov Blyumkin, a Left SR, assassinated the German ambassador, Count von Mirbach, accused of embodying German militarism and defending the interests of his country in Russia. The story of the "sealed train" was in everyone's mind, and Mirbach was considered by Lenin's countless opponents as the man who was manipulating him for the greater good of Germany. They followed this exploit with the arrest of Dzerzhinsky and the assassination of Moisei Volodarsky and Uritsky. The choice of these two targets was significant. In the aftermath of the revolution, Volodarsky had been one of the most resolute opponents of a coalition government. Charged with preparing the elections to the Constituent Assembly in Petrograd, he had defined his task in this way: "Either the Assembly will have a Bolshevik majority, or we will have to make another revolution." Mikhail Uritsky had no better a reputation among the SRs, who had seen him at work in the dissolution of the Constituent Assembly, when this "commissar of the Assembly" helped to throw out the delegates by force, before organizing terror as head of the Petrograd Cheka. By assassinating them, the SRs were attacking opponents hated by society at large. Their deaths outraged only the Bolsheviks.

Emboldened by these exploits, they seized the telegraph center and called the population of the capital to insurrection. But Russia had been dominated since April 1917 by the powerful personality of Lenin. It was unthinkable, in this final battle to liberate their country from Bolshevik terror, that the SRs would forget the man who had so passionately desired the revolution, but had uncompromisingly imposed on it his own conception of total power. Lenin was therefore to be their next target. He had already escaped from an assassination attempt in Petrograd in January. His sister Anna, so quick to relate all the remarkable moments of her brother's life, had been silent on the incident. Captain Sadoul was also indifferent to it, and it is reasonable to conclude that at the time it did not trouble many people. On the other hand, the assassination attempt carried out by Fanya Kaplan on August 30 caused a great stir and had lasting consequences.

The facts may be simple to summarize, but the affair is not as clear as has long been thought. On August 30, Lenin held a meeting at the Mikhelson Factory located in the old quarter of Moscow. After explaining to the workers, who were expecting something besides fine words, that democracy was a snare and that they had to work better and harder in order to destroy the enemies of the regime (the speech was principally directed toward the glorification of class struggle), Lenin left, and as he was walking toward his car, shots were fired which hit him this time. Two bullets wounded his neck and shoulder, and his health was for a time seriously affected. The would-be assassin was a young woman, Fanya Efimovna Roitman, also known as Dora Kaplan, the daughter of a Jewish schoolteacher in the province of Volhynia, who had joined the anarchists at an early age and had already been involved in terrorist activities. Her move from anarchism to the Socialist Revolutionary movement was the result of her meeting in a detention camp with the legendary figure of the terrorist branch of the SRs, Maria Spiridonova. Interrogated at once, Dora Kaplan raised no difficulties in recognizing that she had indeed fired the shots, and declared that she had acted alone, in order to liberate Russia from its oppressor and to place the country back on the path of revolution. She was executed after a few brief interrogations and without trial. The man who was ordered to "shoot her down" (the mission was presented to him in these hardly juridical terms), the Kremlin Commandant Pavel Malkov, was later not shy in displaying his qualms of conscience. Executing a woman was in itself not a pleasant task. The conditions of the execution were in addition particularly sordid. It took place only a few days after the assassination attempt, on September 4, in a garage with an automobile engine running to muffle the sound of the shots, and in the presence of the "'proletarian poet' Demyan Bedny . . . for the sake of 'revolutionary inspiration.'"[9]

Those are the facts related by historians. Angelica Balabanov, who visited Lenin in the country house where he was completing his convalescence, noted that he balked at dwelling on the Dora Kaplan case. She suggests that the execution had been so distasteful to him that he wished to remain silent about it precisely because it punished an act directed against him. If the victim of the attack had been another people's commissar, the execution would have left him indifferent, she writes. Later, when she complained to him about the execution of a group of Mensheviks, Lenin replied: "Don't you understand that if we do not shoot these few leaders we may be placed in a position where we would need to shoot ten thousand workers?"[10] Balabanov concludes that Lenin was merely expressing a necessity.

However, the execution of Dora Kaplan, which put an end to a life devoted to terrorism, was not as clear as Soviet history long wanted the world to believe. General Volkogonov, who studied the entire matter attentively and sought out all the details in the archives, expressed doubts about the veracity of the official account. From his investigation he concluded that the only established fact about the event was the assassination attempt, but that the rest amounted to a "mystification." In his view Dora Kaplan was probably not the person who fired the shots, but her links with the Socialist Revolutionary Party were used by the Bolsheviks. Until recently supported by the Left SRs, the Bolsheviks had no clear idea as to how to move from the break to the elimination of these troublesome allies who were suddenly calling for a return to legality. If Volkogonov is right to call into question the official version of events, the assassination attempt attributed to Dora Kaplan came at a providential moment to allow the Bolsheviks to get rid of all the SRs and to cast their demands into the category of "counterrevolutionary wishes."

State terror could now be unleashed.

THE TRAGEDY OF THE PEASANTS

The specter of famine had hung over Russia throughout the war, but it was particularly strong after the summer of 1917. The Provisional Government had early on taken authoritarian measures to ensure that food supplies reached cities and the army. Special committees had been put in place on the local level and in the capital to prohibit speculation and attempt to rationalize the sale and delivery of food, particularly grain, in order to avoid critical situations. As early as May 1917, a ministry of food supplies had been established for that purpose and placed under the leadership of a right-wing populist, Alexei Peshekhonov. He soon came into conflict with Viktor Chernov who intended to preserve the authority of the peasant committees and thus opposed the control exercised over them by the food supply committees. By the summer of 1917, because of institutional rivalries and the desire of the peasants to see a government policy in conformity with rural interests, the bulk of the harvests remained in the countryside or became the object of illicit trade outside government control. Further, the rural population was increased by city dwellers attempting to avoid hunger, as well as by soldiers who, in anticipation of peace, wanted to participate in the distribution of land. When he came to power, Lenin thus inherited an extremely critical situation, characterized by irregularity in food supplies and habits of autonomy among peasant bodies. He was taken unawares, not having foreseen such a crisis.

The people's commissar in charge of the problem, Ivan Teodorovich, was a moderate man who refused to use violent methods against the peasantry. From the outset his attitude brought about a debate and an institutional division. As soon as he was appointed, the adjunct commissar in Petrograd came out in favor of punitive operations against the peasants. But in Moscow, where the Bolsheviks were inclined to advocate conciliation, the opposition to violent methods was pronounced. The All-Russian Committee for Supply, established in December 1917, was the site of confrontations between supporters of the two positions among the presumed experts in agrarian problems, because the entire debate revolved around the peasants and the means of inciting—or forcing—them to feed the country. It was at this point in the discussion that Lenin intervened, on January 14, 1918, when he spoke before a mixed audience of deputies to the Petrograd Soviet and members of the local food supply committee. He had come up with the solution, and he set it out bluntly. It was necessary, he said, to establish detachments made up of ten to fifteen soldiers and workers, organize several thousand of them, and send them into the countryside with the power to put any peasant not submitting to their demands before a firing squad. This was the first time that such a radical proposal had been made by Lenin (at least openly). He appalled his audience, even though they had already suggested having recourse to the Cheka against "saboteurs," and forcing peasants to provide food supplies, but had not yet envisaged relying on organized terror against one segment of society.

The Third All-Russian Congress of Soviets, which met from January 10 to 18, proposed a more moderate solution than the one suggested by Lenin, turning the responsibility of dealing with the crisis over to a Soviet of food supply workers. This Soviet delegated its powers to an executive of thirty-five members, twenty-one of whom were Bolsheviks, Lenin had made sure of that. This body reported directly to the Sovnarkom, not to the Supreme Economic Council. From this complicated organization it emerges that, unable to convince his colleagues to use terror directly against the peasantry, Lenin tried to set up a body packed with Bolsheviks under his own authority that would have the task of providing food supplies by any means necessary. In practice the executive had no authority and the matter was a dead letter, which explains the issuance of a decree on February 15 announcing that Trotsky was appointed "director of food supplies," heading a special commission created for the purpose. Not having been informed of his new mission, Trotsky did little to carry it out.

This constant and disorganized establishment of new bodies, all charged with resolving the crucial problem of food supplies for cities and the army, indicates the Bolsheviks' lack of preparation for dealing with a problem that they had severely underestimated before seizing power. In this first stage of their rule, from October 1917 to May 1918, they were obliged to recognize the scale of the difficulties and the fact that the regions able to provide food supplies to the country were more and more slipping from their grasp. With the Ukraine lost, there remained Siberia, to which many missions were sent, and the countryside of Central Russia, where peasants were manifesting increasing resistance, which the still occasional requisitions merely strengthened further. The regime, which had carried over from the Provisional Government the principle of a state monopoly over the grain trade, was still hesitating between two policies designed to secure grain supplies: a "commercial" approach to be implemented by local committees and a violent approach based on the requisitions that Lenin had decided on in January. He was supported in his desire to seize crops from the peasants rather than negotiating their purchase by the Bolshevik organizations in Petrograd, still full of militant fervor. It was from there that the first detachments of workers and sailors from Kronstadt were sent out into the countryside to carry out "forceful" requisitions. They took place while the official slogan remained respect for peasant property. They therefore seemed all the more illegal and out-rageous to the peasantry, who held fast to their suspicion and hostility toward the Bolshevized city. The social unity that Lenin had believed possible in October was quickly turning into a conflict of interests. Although the policy of friendly relations with the peasantry had not yet been abandoned, an antipeasant class struggle was being established behind the scenes.

During this period of tension, when nothing had yet been definitively settled, the peasantry counted on its own organizations and the Socialist Revolutionary Party to defend it. The peasant organization that enjoyed the confidence of the rural population was the All-Russian Congress of Peasants' Deputies, which had met for the first time in May 1917. At that time it had set up an executive com-mittee designed to maintain contacts among rank-and-file organizations between congresses and to prepare future meetings. On the eve of Lenin's coup, this executive had decided that the Second Congress would take place after the meeting of the Constituent Assembly, and it was by reason of this decision, made in ignorance of Lenin's plans, that the peasant leaders had left the Bolsheviks masters of the field. The October 25 coup d'état had been ratified by a Congress of Soviets made up of workers and soldiers, with no peasants as such, although the soldiers were often of rural origin; Lenin was able to lay claim to the support of all of Russian society before the peasantry had spoken. Aware of the mistake they had made, the peasant leaders called a special meeting of the Congress of Peasants' Deputies on November 10 in order to define their own views after the change of regime. Summoned in haste, with very rough criteria for representation, this Congress was dominated by the Left SRs, three times more numerous than the moderate SRs, and included a Bolshevik delegation. The flamboyant personality of Maria Spiridonova, who was elected chairman, dominated the assembly and helped to push it to the left. Those in attendance were principally concerned to maintain the independence of peasant organiza-tions and the positions cherished by the SRs, that is, to support the idea of a coalition government. At the same time, the Congress decided to send repre-sentatives to the Central Executive Committee, which thereby added to its 108 original members 108 representatives of the peasantry, along with 100 repre-sentatives of the army and 50 union delegates. In the view of the peasant lead-ers, this change, which has already been mentioned, would give the CEC the character of a veritable parliament of the various categories of the population and would thereby be given the capacity to carry weight in debates against the government. This decision, which at first sight appeared to weaken the govern-ment, could not really cause Lenin any concern. The unwieldiness of the CEC took away any real force it might have had. In addition the increased presence within it of the Left SRs, through peasant representation, presented an advan-tage for him: his opponents could no longer accuse him of imposing a monop-oly of Bolshevik power. The appearance of a coalition was strengthened, but he still needed to exercise more control over peasant organizations.

The Second All-Russian Congress of Peasants' Deputies (the early November meeting was not part of the official numbering) met from November 26 to

December 11 and was marked by confrontations between the extremism of Maria Spiridonova and Viktor Chernov's desire to maintain the independence of peasant organizations. There were two primary divisive subjects. First, the moderates led by Chernov insisted that the Constituent Assembly should be convoked with extreme urgency and that its "constituent" power be respected by the Bolsheviks, a strong subject of irritation for Lenin, who was hardly inclined to take the demand seriously. For that reason his speech at the Congress was greeted with boos that Spiridonova could not manage to suppress. The other subject of division was the idea of the union of the peasant congress with the Congress of Workers' and Soldiers' Deputies, advocated by the Bolsheviks and supported by the Left SRs, but opposed by the centrists behind Chernov. Spiridonova managed to put off the question to the Third Congress, which was scheduled for February 1918 but actually met in mid-January, and organized a subtle manipulation. She proposed that the representatives to that Congress, instead of being elected by the rank and file, should be the same as those to the Second Congress, whose mandate would be extended to the Third. Having thus set up a scenario that ignored the rules of democratic representation, the Left SRs and the Bolsheviks arrived in force at the Third Congress of Peasants' Deputies that opened on January 13.

On the day of the first meeting, the political conditions were favorable for the annihilation of any wishes for peasant autonomy. With the Constituent Assembly dissolved, the Bolsheviks were in a position of force; the Left SRs were now for them nothing but weak allies compelled to follow them or to experience the fate of the Socialist Revolutionary Party, whose electoral victory had been canceled by Lenin. It was not surprising that, addressing the Bolsheviks, Spiridonova made a real mea culpa, declaring that the SRs had been wrong to hang on to "the historically obsolete myth of the Constituent Assembly." Not allowing the Congress to debate the rest of the agenda, she pushed through a unanimous vote for union with the Congress of Workers' and Soldiers' Deputies. The autonomy of peasant organizations was at an end.

The delegates to the Third Congress unanimously passed the "Declaration of the Rights of the Working and Exploited People" that the Constituent Assembly had refused to ratify, and asked that the CEC draw up the Russian Constitution on the basis of that document. The Congress also voted in favor of the law on socializing the land, which was intended to give concrete content to the "Decree on Land" of October 26.

On this last point, the representatives of the peasantry, including all the SRs, and the Bolsheviks were in serious disagreement, although the terms of the disagreement were not yet very explicit in January 1918. A few months later, the terms of the conflict were to become comprehensible to all parties. For the SRs, "socialization" of the land was in accordance with their traditional views: It implied that power in the Socialist society in the process of being organized would belong to its various component groups and would emanate from the rank and file. The peasantry would have to organize their own life and decide on its orientations. For the Bolsheviks, the objective was the "nationalization" of the land; its consequence would be the insertion of the countryside into a global economic program in which the privileged actors would be the industrial sector and the working class, with peasant labor being called on to support progress. This general economic program assumed the granting of absolute authority to the central government as the vehicle of a common vision.

Lenin had never been unaware of the misunderstanding between him and the peasantry, but he was prepared to adopt for the time that was necessary laws that would win over the peasants and make it possible for him to feed Russia. The "Decree on Land" and the law on the socialization of land were of little concern to him; he thought the texts of the laws were of little account in comparison to the way in which they would be interpreted and applied. He commented on the conflict, while refusing to inflate its importance, by saying: "It's enough if we find a way of arranging the populist idea of socialization to suit our purposes."[11] The SRs, on the other hand, took it for granted that once the law was passed the Bolsheviks would be obliged to respect it; this is why they insisted that the Third Congress of Soviets pass it.

The law was therefore adopted. The essential component of the government's mission was to foster collective agriculture, much more likely than individual cultivation to contribute to economic progress. It intended to develop collective farms, to give them priority in the redistribution of land. The SRs had gained a partial victory in this legal battle, but they were not aware of the fact that while they were imposing their views in the text of a law, Lenin was already creating the conditions for a mobilization of peasant labor in the service of the industrial development of the country.

In this phase, during which the government did not dare attack the peasantry head-on, it concentrated its efforts not only on the problem of food supplies, but also even more (and here it was consistent in the measures taken) on the penetration of the rural world by proletarian elements, a foretaste of the coming class war. Under various names—"agitators," "commissars," "instructors"—the government encouraged workers and soldiers to go to the countryside, sometimes for requisitions and sometimes to train and supervise the peasants. Of course they had little legal power, and once they came to a village, they operated on their own in the absence of any central authority supervising their activities. But the role played at the time by these refugees from the cities—endowed, they believed, with the status of "proletarians on mission"—should not be underestimated. A significant fraction of them came from the two capitals, that is, the revolutionary centers. They left cities where people were dying of hunger and found themselves in the countryside among peasants who were already being called "saboteurs" and "speculators." They were expected simultaneously to find out what was happening in the village, to supervise, and to prepare the peasants through propaganda for the goals of the socialization of the land, that is, for collective agriculture. For these poorly educated envoys, who were convinced of the superiority of the city over the country, there was a great temptation to abuse their authority over the peasants, to which they often succumbed. Testimony about their excesses was frequent in every region of Russia. But their proselytism and their abuses had no effect but to create a climate of deep suspicion in the villages. In general they were unable to accomplish their two primary tasks, to arouse sympathy for the Bolsheviks to the detriment of the SRs and to bring the local Soviets over to the Bolshevik side. The consequences of their presence and activities in the countryside were far from what Lenin had hoped; the rural world was not becoming Bolshevik, and the institutions of local power (the rural Soviets) remained weak and could not serve as a lever for the activity of the central government. Lenin, who had never believed in the need to treat the peasantry with consideration, saw in this a confirmation of his conviction that the peasants, whom he thought with a few exceptions to be bearers of the "bourgeois spirit," would contribute to the progress of the Socialist system only under compulsion. The policy shift of May and June 1918, which inaugurated the period of War Communism and class warfare in the countryside, was in complete conformity with his views on this point.

WAR COMMUNISM

In May 1918 Lenin had no more cause to hesitate. The Treaty of Brest-Litovsk had certainly freed him from the war, but it had also had negative consequences for Russia stemming from the enormous losses of territory and economic potential that had been inflicted on it. The Fourth All-Russian Congress of Soviets, which met from March 14 to 16 and ratified the treaty, had already given a signal of the need to modify economic policy. The Supreme Economic Council (VSNKh), established in November 1917 and placed under the chairmanship of Alexei Rykov in March 1918 so that he might reorganize it into the sole and effective architect of Bolshevik economic policy, set the new policy in motion.

This appointment of the head of the VSNKh, however, gave no warning of the coming shift in policy. Rykov had always called into question the capacity of a predominantly agrarian country like Russia to carry out a Socialist revolution, and his peasant origins did not predispose him toward launching an all-out war against the rural world. His weakness of character, however, brought him to give way before stronger personalities who were determined to change the economic policy that had been followed until then. Milyutin and Yuri Larin therefore became the real leaders of the VSNKh. Both were fervent supporters of economic centralization and rigorous planning. Larin, who had originally been a Menshevik, was in addition an unconditional admirer of industrial concentration and of the methods that had governed the organization of the war economy in Germany. Richard Pipes is correct in reminding us that he was known as the "Russian Saint-Just." This is an indication of the fanaticism that Larin was to display in arguing for and then applying the idea of a "turn to the left."

The political debate on this turn, which did take place, occurred against the background of the Treaty of Brest-Litovsk, which had deeply divided the party between the realists behind Lenin and the Left led by Bukharin, which Larin represented up to a point with respect to economic questions. In late April,

Lenin wrote a long article entitled "*The Immediate Tasks of the Soviet Government,*" which *Izvestia* published in full.[12] This article, which had the support of the Party Central Committee, was debated by the CEC on May 3, where it was opposed by Bukharin in the name of the Left, before finally being adopted. Immediately thereafter Lenin hammered the point home by publishing a virulent pamphlet, *On "Left-Wing" Infantilism and on Petit-Bourgeois Tendencies,* in which he set out a moderate view of the possibilities for the immediate transformation of Russia.[13] Bukharin and the Left were in despair over the Brest-Litovsk compromise, because they once believed that the Russian Revolution had to be carried to its conclusion by breaking with capitalism. This would be achieved by nationalizing banking and industry, abolishing all private business, setting up a fully planned economy, and nationalizing agriculture. In response to this position Lenin's answer was an argument for state capitalism. For him a period of transition was necessary, designed to provide Russia gradually with the productive forces and the capital that it still lacked. Of course Lenin insisted on the need for dictatorship and repressive power in order to keep this compromise system from lasting for very long. But once again his pragmatism brought him to intermediate solutions which seemed to him best suited to Russia's social conditions. He intended to hold on to the reins of political power without concessions, but he wanted to have the economy and the society develop at the pace that was possible, not according to the utopian rate advocated by the infantile leftism that he denounced.

However, it was the Left's position that won out. There were many reasons for this. Prestigious figures in the party—Bukharin, Radek, Pyatakov, Kollontai—urged the adoption of leftist solutions. Workers in the cities were exasperated by their living conditions and demanded that the peasantry be compelled to submit to the general interest. Finally, everything in the internal situation of Russia in the spring of 1918—famine, social despair, rising criminality, symbolized by gangs of wandering children prepared for anything—suggested that the compromise of the preceding months was no longer tenable. Lenin gave in to this pressure, perhaps because the need to pacify a turbulent population seemed the most urgent thing, but primarily because, since October, the working-class rank and file had never followed the instructions for limited nationalization. Workers had unofficially collectivized their enterprises, thereby contributing to the chaos. Even though they had become the managers, unemployment was rising, and prices were going up by approximately 30 percent per month. Money was losing all value, and the currency in circulation was insufficient, which made it possible for Bukharin to assert that the era of the monetary economy had passed.

How could Lenin respond? His appeals to foreign investors were unlikely to attract very many of them, in light of the economic disaster, the state monopoly on foreign trade decreed on April 22, and the disregard he himself had shown for the foreign debts contracted by his predecessors. What remained was the solution of the Left, which involved violence.

The countryside was the first target of the new policy. The government undertook to force the peasants to feed the population of the cities, to work for them by turning over all their harvests. The period of hesitation when negotiations and violence had alternated was over; all that remained was unbridled violence. Sverdlov declared to the CEC: "We must attack the problem of the villages. We have to create in them two warring camps, stir up the poor against the kulaks. If we are able to divide villages into two camps, to inflame civil war, then we will accomplish the same revolution in the villages that we have in the cities." This warlike language was not simply propaganda; it pointed to a precise program (the destruction of the peasantry through terror), a specific target (the kulaks), and the tool (the poor).

The reality was quite different from these words, because the majority of the population in the Russian countryside was made up neither of kulaks nor of the poor, but of middle peasants, which meant that a very large part of the peasantry turned out to be the designated enemy. A decree of June 11 created the official institution of the class struggle in the countryside, the Committees of the Rural Poor (*kombedy*). At first they were not clearly defined. For some they were supposed to be provisional bodies intended to enlarge the Soviets, and to begin by cooperating in the requisition of harvests. But, from a more radical perspective (which many remarks indicate was that of Lenin), the *kombedy* were in fact to bring the class struggle to the countryside and to compel all landowning peasants (the *kulaks*) to surrender definitively to the will of the authorities. The radical line won out in the field, and the *kombedy* became the agents of a terrorist policy that led to a veritable genocide of peasant society. The "poor peasant," the great myth of this sinister period, was set in opposition to the contrary myth, the kulak, seen as powerful, a hoarder of food, and an agent of the counterrevolution. His twin brother was the "bagman" (*meshochnik*), the speculator who traveled from the country to the city to sell foodstuffs at prohibitive prices. He was the symbol of the "prosperity of the rich peasants," contrasted in this primitive imagery to workers' poverty. Through this division of the rural world, the government hoped to recover the confidence of the working class and associate with the workers a fraction of the peasantry, the poor (*bednota*), the number of whom it overestimated.

Measures indicating the "turn" came one after another. A people's commissariat of food supplies (*Narkomprod*) was established, intended to eliminate all private trade in food, which was totally forbidden by a decree of November 21, 1918. The members of the *kombedy* were given the incentive of free grain which they sold, and punitive expeditions proliferated in the countryside, reinforced by detachments of workers. The method did not, however, seem to be sufficient; the *kombedy* were not set up everywhere, even though the poor were everywhere summoned to plunder those who were not as poor as they. Middle peasants resisted and put pressure on their fellows, who did not rush into the ranks of the committees that were supposed to embody Soviet power in the countryside. Requisitions took place with violence, in pitched battles where no quarter was given, and detachments sent to the countryside were free to shoot peasants who resisted their demands, or merely to set an example.

In late 1918 Lenin was forced to recognize that organized violence by the rank and file had not been enough. He established a planned system of requisition quotas in the villages and collective responsibility of the peasants for their fulfillment. To be even more persuasive, on August 11, 1918, he sent precise directives to the Communists of Penza on the way of "putting down" peasants who had rebelled against the measures applied in the countryside:

The interests of the entire revolution require . . . [that one] give an example.

1. Hang (hang without fail, so the people see) no fewer than one hundred known kulaks, rich men, bloodsuckers.
2. Publish their names.
3. Take from them all the grain
4. Designate hostages.[14]

This letter was followed by countless messages of the same kind; confronted with social resistance, Lenin could think of nothing but ordering measures of terror. Three weeks later, in a memorandum to Nikolai Krestinsky, then secretary of the Central Committee, he proposed the secret formation of a commission to take emergency measures "to prepare the terror."[15] And it was indeed unbridled terror that was unleashed, a subject to which we return. It is appropriate to note here that it brought about a strong peasant resistance, both against a policy of requisitions designed to break down the peasantry by starving it, and against the terror itself. The violence of despair against Leninist violence: Russia had become a country in which an unprecedented state terror was being carried out. Forging ahead regardless of consequences, the government broke totally with the peasantry; in February 1919, it decreed that all land was state property and that the use of the soil must be collective. Peasants were required to join communal *(kolkhoz)* or state *(sovkhoz)* farms; five thousand of these farms were set up at the outset, but they drew only the most destitute and unfortunate peasants. To the others there remained resistance with the energy of despair.

Moreover, the civil war in the countryside did not produce the expected economic effects. Food shortages remained just as large, and the cost of each product remained exorbitant. Peasants had accepted neither the grain tax imposed in October 1918, nor the outright requisitions without compensation of January 1919. Deprived of machinery that factories were no longer producing, furious at being treated as enemies, they cut down on planting. By 1919, cultivated land was only 85 percent of what it had been in 1913, and it fell to 60 percent by the end of 1920. It is therefore not surprising that a barter economy took on large proportions in Russian life, in which foodstuffs were the most precious commodities. A movie ticket cost one egg in 1919; Shaliapin asked for two hundred kilos of flour to give a concert. Price increases express the general madness; if 1913 is given the value 100, by 1918, prices had already climbed to 1,285, and in July 1919, they reached 10,000. Bukharin and Evgeny Preobrazhensky, the Left Communists despised by Lenin, were delighted by these mad prices and by barter; they thought that with money having lost all meaning, Communism was imminent. Until it was reached, one might just as well give up the use of any currency. These arguments in no way reduced the suffering of the urban population. Epidemics of typhus and cholera ravaged the cities, factories closed, and the working class fled to the countryside or into the army, wherever it could. In 1917, Russia had three million workers; they had been cut in half by early 1920. Did the state of the dictatorship of the proletariat still have a proletariat?

War Communism accompanied general economic arrangements with disciplinary measures intended to preserve what could still be salvaged of the working-class world. Beginning in April 1918, industrial and commercial enterprises were forbidden to engage in any transactions; soon thereafter transmission of wealth by inheritance was prohibited. Private property no longer existed. The state took charge of all components of economic life through four measures: nationalization of all the means of production (except for the land which, as we have seen, came under another policy); nationalization of all the means of exchange; centralized planning of the economy; and abolition of the monetary economy.

War Communism also involved the rigid regulation of human activity. Already in early 1918, by imposing a system of food rationing dividing the urban population into four and later eight categories, ranging from the most militant workers to the retired and the members of the old elite, the government was outlining the real contours of its social vision. The workers themselves were not exempt from rigor whenever efficiency was at stake. The working day was increased to ten or eleven hours. In January 1919, workers were no longer authorized to leave their jobs. The following year absenteeism was subjected to heavy penalties. Labor law became a tool for the enslavement of a working class that thought only of fleeing factories and cities. In the end workers were treated almost as badly as peasants, with the sole difference that the former remained officially supporters of the government whereas the latter all fell into the category of class enemy. In addition the working class was subjected to a policy of mobilization that was a reflection of a war economy: mobilization at the workplace and mobilization in the army that Trotsky was establishing in which the unemployed were forcibly enlisted. The death penalty was restored in June 1918 to provide a legal basis for executions, but Dzerzhinsky's men, spurred on by Lenin's insistent words—"Hang! Shoot!"—had not been hesitant to hand out capital punishment at will even before laws had given them that right.

In the space of two and one-half years, the dictatorship of the proletariat had taken on a well-defined face: dictatorship of the party and of its secular arm the Cheka over society as a whole, by means of unlimited terror. Even so the government was not assured of being in control of the situation.

THE RED TERROR[16]

Terror took many forms in the course of this period. By the summer of 1918, the means used against class enemies in the countryside—arrests, executions without trial, large-scale hostage taking organized by a decree of September 4, 1918–had been strengthened by the establishment of concentration camps to which were sent without legal procedures everyone the government suspected of hostility toward it, along with various categories that were "condemned" in advance: "priests, White Guards, kulaks, and other dubious elements," as Lenin, always concerned with precision, defined them. The most notorious of these camps, established a few short months after the glorious October Revolution, was set up in the monastery on Solovki Island. But the system was very soon organized, and camps proliferated.[17]

Bolshevik zeal did not stop there. Lenin, who had never been able to stand having his authority questioned, decided to have the Menshevik leaders arrested in July 1918. The SRs followed quickly, after Dora Kaplan's assassination attempt. On September 5 a decree officially established the Red Terror, a mass terror that freed the Cheka from any legal concerns.

In July 1918 the assassination of the imperial family took its place in a policy aimed at liquidating anything that might possibly interfere with the activity of the Bolshevik government. Exiled in the depths of the Urals in Ekaterinburg, the czar and his family had since the Bolshevik seizure of power been subjected to countless privations and humiliations. Their supporters prepared plans of escape that were as absurd as they were ineffective, and constant rumors circulated, further worsening their conditions. Although Trotsky had expressed the wish that a trial like the one that Louis XVI went through during the French Revolution take place to decide the fate of "bloody Nicholas," Lenin had very early expressed his inclination toward summary justice: "Exterminate all the Romanovs, a good hundred of them." This was the proposal acted on the night of July 16, 1918, when a detachment of Chekists, including five Latvians, led by Yakov Yurovsky, member of the Cheka and of the Ural Executive Committee, assassinated the members of the imperial family and the servants that had remained with them. At almost the same moment, in conformity with the aim of general extermination of the Romanovs expressed by Lenin, all the other members of the family who were in Perm and Alapaevsk were massacred. None of those who were within reach of the Bolsheviks escaped death.

But the will to exterminate was not accompanied by acknowledgment of the murders. When Trotsky asked Sverdlov about the circumstances in which the decision had been made, Sverdlov answered: "We decided it here. Ilyich was convinced that we couldn't leave the Whites a symbol to rally around." Lenin, for his part, attempted to have people believe in the murder of Nicholas II alone, sensing that the assassination of adolescents would provoke horror, even in a time of horrors. It was not until 1919 that the government acknowledged that no member of the imperial family had been spared. The lying statements about a coldly decided murder clearly correspond to the attitude of concealment that Lenin adopted in dealing with the terror. Most of his directives–"Kill, shoot, deport, and so on"–were given secretly. He took pains to preserve in all circumstances the image of a man who was concerned about others. The myth of the "good Lenin" was beginning to take shape.

Although the murder of the imperial family fits into the Red Terror, it is only the best-known incident. To it should also be attributed the "decossackization" decided in January 1919, which organized the physical elimination of a significant segment of the Cossack community, the abolition of all its rights, and the confiscation of all its wealth, a veritable genocide.[18] To this should be added the liquidation of peasant rebellions by means of an implacable civil war, the abolition of political parties and opposition newspapers, and finally the murder or deportation of anyone who did not fit into the "proletarian" framework. Lenin had even turned his purging fury against prostitutes. The balance sheet of this Red Terror, inseparable from War Communism, has already been drawn up. It is important to point out that ignorance on this point, long pleaded by advocates of the system, was willful almost from the beginning. Indeed, S. P. Melgunov's *The Red Terror in Russia* was published in 1925, and anyone who read it would have known.

Л Л Л

Although she was very attached to Lenin, Angelica Balabanov notes in her memoirs:

> As official reports arrived, confirming the extent of the Terror, I grew more and more disturbed. Revolutions, I knew, were not accomplished without bloodshed, and the suppression of counterrevolutionary activity was both inevitable and fully justified on the part of the revolutionary regime. Russia was compelled to defend itself not only against the assaults of world capitalism but against thousands of conspirators and reactionaries within its own borders. But was wholesale slaughter necessary? Was not the Terror expanding beyond its legitimate bounds?[19]

Although Angelica Balabanov adopted the arguments of the Bolsheviks to justify the Terror then in progress, she nevertheless displayed a certain dismay in the face of the repression that had come down on "thousands of conspirators and reactionaries," while the victims of the Cheka already numbered in the tens if not hundreds of thousands. She also justified the tragedy, although in her vocabulary it was Russia, not Lenin and his associates, who was killing to save itself. The consequences of this period are of blinding clarity. A government engaged in unbridled violence imposed itself on an entire country that was treated as an enemy. The non-Bolshevik Left, the liberals, the peasants, the Whites, the national minorities, all tolerated the government established by Lenin only because the Terror compelled them to. On seizing power in October 1917, Lenin had from the outset forged the tool intended to supervise and control society:

the Cheka. With the help of this tool, which produced and imposed its own legal rules, the power seized in that month from an exhausted Provisional Government was maintained until the late 1980s, for more than seventy years, against an increasingly rebellious society. Lenin won out in the course of those few years when his ambition, as he had clearly stated, was not to imitate the Paris Commune, whose existence had been so brief, but to ensure the perpetuity of the power that had been seized in 1917. But at what a cost and for what a future?

Chapter Twelve

WORLD REVOLUTION OR REVOLUTION IN ONE COUNTRY?

LENIN'S LIFE HAD BEEN ENTIRELY DEVOTED TO THE PASSION for revolution. He had forged its tools, organized the seizure of power, and as head of government after October he desperately fought against the forces threatening his work, determined to accept any compromise necessary to save it. His authority throughout this history cannot be questioned. But there were two areas in which he had even more decisive influence: foreign policy and the national minorities policy that was in part dependent on it. In organizing his party, deciding to make the revolution, and governing, he was often challenged, and his colleagues did not always accept his choices. He had the last word on almost everything in the government, of course, but Trotsky was the founder and head of the Red Army at a time when the civil war conferred particular authority on his decisions. In foreign policy, on the other hand, no one could challenge the correctness of his views. Although he had been obliged to accept his colleagues' positions temporarily during the Brest-Litovsk negotiations, he had been strengthened by the course of events. On national questions, the positions he had been working out since 1914 would in turn be quickly confirmed by the turbulence on the periphery of the Russian state. This explains why the policy adopted toward the external world was the one that Lenin favored. Nonetheless it went through fluctuations and radical shifts over the course of three years.

A FOREIGN POLICY TOOL

The Decree on Peace had, we recall, implicitly asserted the replacement of relations between states by revolutionary relations between peoples. When he was appointed people's commissar for foreign affairs, Trotsky had ratified this view, saying that once the war was over he would "shut up shop." At first Trotsky's commissariat did not have much of an organization. Taken up with other matters and having dismissed or driven away the former employees of the ministry, the competent diplomats, he left the offices in charge of his second in command, F. Zalkind, who always carried a huge pistol and had installed machine guns on the premises. Once the Treaty of Brest-Litovsk had been negotiated, Trotsky resigned from his position. The new commissar, Gyorgy Chicherin, immediately changed the atmosphere of the administration, replacing the amateurism of its beginnings by a professional conception of foreign policy. It is true that Chicherin was a professional diplomat, familiar with the outside world, well versed in foreign languages, and remarkably gifted for negotiations. He had long been in opposition to Lenin, who had been delighted to win his support, because he was aware of his qualities and his usefulness in this position. Chicherin gave the foreign policy of the Bolshevik state a respectable and reassuring face for the rest of the world. But in everything, as he clearly stated in his memoirs, he executed the policies drawn up by Lenin. He was assisted from 1921 on by Maxim Litvinov, who succeeded him in 1930, and was as different from Chicherin as it was possible to be. But for a few years, they pooled their talents to develop an effective Bolshevik diplomacy.

The commissariat of foreign affairs that Chicherin took over in the spring of 1918 was not, however, an organization with clear objectives. From the beginning its role was ambiguous; for example, in December 1917, it was given substantial funds for "the needs of the revolutionary movement." Soon thereafter the *Narkomindel* (its Russian acronym, by which it will henceforth be designated) was expanded with the addition of a "section for international propaganda" under the direction of Radek. This section essentially had the task of propagandizing prisoners of war of the Central Powers and German soldiers at the front. It was then taken away from the Narkomindel and placed under the direct authority of the All-Russian Central Executive Committee. The dual purpose of the commissariat thus emerged from the beginning: to promote the revolution, but also, for a time, to provide a breathing space for the new Bolshevik state. The course of events would force Russian diplomats—or rather Lenin, the man really in charge of policy—to shift constantly between the two objectives.

AN AMBIVALENT POLICY

Having seized power in circumstances that were not very propitious for the establishment of socialism, Lenin justified his action by the conviction that this was only the first revolution, the spark that would inflame all the proletariats of Europe. As surprising as it may be, his faith on this point was complete. Since the beginning of the century, no one had been more critical than Lenin of the opportunism of the Western proletariat, and no one had so greatly deplored the failure of the workers' movement in 1914. His pessimism about this corrupt proletariat was equaled only by his voluntarism. When he decided to plunge into the revolutionary adventure in October 1917, he coldly asserted that by doing so he would draw other countries into the revolution. He did not keep up this sudden optimism for long, for when the time came to negotiate a peace treaty, he opposed Bukharin's revolutionary convictions with a much more realistic view of the situation. He wanted to negotiate because he no longer believed that the Western proletariat would fly to the assistance of the Russian revolution. This suggests something of the ambiguity of Lenin, who usually analyzed situations with coolness and clarity but forgot everything he knew and had understood once he felt or decided that power was within his reach. At that point voluntarism won out over any kind of lucidity. He was then compelled to deal with reality (as with Brest-Litovsk), but at the same time maintained his goal of unleashing world revolution. Trotsky was closer to him than might appear, and in his role as chief of foreign policy made statements as ambivalent as those of Lenin. Hardly had the Bolsheviks taken power when he violently attacked the "ruling classes of Europe" for not having understood that the Decree on Peace had been "promulgated by a *State* representing many millions of people." Although they had rejected relations between states, when they wanted to persuade the outside world, Lenin and Trotsky immediately invoked the "state" power of the Russian revolution.

The Sovnarkom had given the Narkomindel funds for "revolutionary" propaganda and established an office for their proper use. But the negotiators of the Treaty of Brest-Litovsk accepted without batting an eyelid clause 2 of the treaty, which stipulated that "each contracting party will refrain from any agitation or propaganda against the government, the state, or the military institutions of the other party." Did this not amount to the abandonment of all revolutionary aims? Bolshevik commentary on the subject was not without duplicity. Chicherin constantly reiterated: "We respect this article, and if any organization in our country were to violate it, the Sovnarkom would react immediately." At the Seventh Party Congress that met from March 6 to 8 to debate ratification of the treaty, he calmly explained that the Russian government had already violated the clause at least forty times. Sverdlov was even more precise, declaring to his colleagues that article 2 needed to be interpreted: "It means, of course, that the Russian government, the Sovnarkom, will have to refrain from propaganda activities; but that hardly matters, because the Party will do what the Sovnarkom has promised not to do."[1]

The party then took charge of the small groups of prisoners of war that Radek's section had been organizing into "national" groups of propagandists given the task of spreading Bolshevik ideas among their compatriots. These small groups were given the name "foreign sections of the Russian Communist Party" and attached to the Party Central Committee, and the office directed by Radek was abolished. Radek then worked directly in liaison with the Central Committee. Propaganda activities were certainly not abandoned, but their transfer from state bodies to the party allowed the former to claim that it was respecting the treaty.

This equivocal policy provoked a veritable scandal in Moscow on April 16, when the "All-Russian Congress of Internationalist Prisoners of War" opened. "There are about four hundred delegates," wrote Jacques Sadoul. "One can imagine the horrified surprise of the German government. The internationalist prisoners have in fact already expressed their complete solidarity with the government of the Soviets and their intention to fight by its side in order to provoke the revolution outside the borders of Russia."[2]

Yoffe's activities in Germany were in the same vein. Yoffe, who had been an implacable opponent of Lenin's position favoring a resumption of the Brest-Litovsk negotiations, and had then been entrusted with reopening the negotiations and had brought them to a conclusion, deeply believed in the chances of a revolution occurring in Germany within a very short time. This was the reason for his being sent to Germany as the first Russian ambassador in May 1918. Yoffe devoted his service principally to helping the revolutionary forces, politically but also financially, and his embassy became a real center for revolutionary activities.

Lenin was concerned about the possible cost for such activities, because Germany was still powerful. Addressing the Central Executive Committee on May 14, 1918, he recommended that it adopt a more cautious attitude: "Russia is surrounded by enemies." Not yet prepared to defend itself, it would have to look for compromises, as at Brest-Litovsk, not a confrontation in which it was doomed to failure. This is why he decided to open trade negotiations with Germany. In addition to Yoffe (a veritable Janus, negotiating an agreement with a government and simultaneously preparing a revolutionary movement against it), they were conducted by Larin, one of the advocates of War Communism, Sokolnikov, and Vyacheslav Menzhinsky, the successor to Dzerzhinsky at the head of the GPU (the name given to the Cheka in 1922), who was in 1918 merely the consul general in Berlin. On August 27, in spite of the chaotic state of Russo-German relations, three codicils to the Brest-Litovsk Treaty were signed in Berlin: a political agreement, a financial agreement, and, most important, confidential agreements in the form of notes dealing with Russo-German relations in the Baltic States and Georgia, as well as with ways of removing Entente forces from northern Russia.

These secret notes are very revealing about the development of Lenin's views. They are the first indication of his adherence to the secret diplomacy that he had always attacked, but that he accepted when it turned out to be of use to Russia. Less than a year after the Decree on Peace and the solemn proclamation of a new form of international relations, Lenin returned unhesitatingly to the traditional paths of diplomacy. In any event this secret agreement had no consequences, because Germany was already on the point of defeat. This imminent collapse of Germany explains why Lenin had been able to conduct such an ambivalent policy without too many obstacles, negotiating with the enemy and at the same time allowing Yoffe, one of the negotiators, to multiply his underground revolutionary activities.

This policy was also inspired by deep anxiety about the survival of the regime. Lenin had witnessed the growth of French and British hostility toward him, as the initial curiosity of the English turned into the determination to destroy the Bolshevik regime. The activities of Russia's former allies between June and August 1918 left no room for doubt. The English landed at Murmansk and then jointly with the French at Arkhangelsk, while the Americans joined them in the north, and the Japanese took positions in Vladivostok. In southern Russia, the White troops of General Denikin were also receiving increasingly active support from the Allies. In this very dangerous period, cooperation with a Germany still at war became a last resort for Lenin to fight off the mortal threat that the Allies posed to his regime. If he had not given up the idea of playing the revolutionary card, this was because he was aware of the growing weakness of Germany, and dreamed of unleashing the German revolution, the one that in the eyes of every Bolshevik ought to be the *real* revolution in a country destined to take leadership over the movement.

FINALLY, REVOLUTION IN GERMANY!

In late September 1918, Germany admitted defeat and asked for an armistice. Lenin then recovered his revolutionary enthusiasm and saw this as a confirmation of his hopes. The defeat of Germany meant that the time of the revolution had come. His own premature and unorthodox revolution was now justified because he would be able to help the German proletariat complete its task. He immediately expressed this conviction: "Finally, the proletariat of the entire world will recognize that we were right to base all our activity on support of the world proletarian revolution." And he asserted that before the next spring, Russia would mobilize an army of three million men to assist the world revolution.[3] He sent a congratulatory letter to the Spartakists "who have saved the honor of the German workers' movement," and another to Liebknecht on his release from prison.[4] (The Spartakus group, led by Rosa Luxemburg, Leo Jogiches, and Karl Liebknecht, brought together the German Communists determined to oppose the war; it represented the left wing of German Communism.) He then declared, "Thanks to us, the creation of a world proletarian state is in sight." And he wrote *The Proletarian Revolution and the Renegade Kautsky*, in which he reiterated that "his" role had been and remained to prepare for world revolution.[5]

Hence, Lenin witnessed happily the rush of events in Germany. The kaiser abdicated on November 9, 1918; the following day, the German delegates left to sign the armistice at Compiègne, while in Berlin councils of workers and soldiers set up a Council of Representatives of the People under the chairmanship of the Socialist Friedrich Ebert. Lenin hailed the event with an address to a crowd gathered in front of the Kremlin. Most important he seized the opportunity to declare the Treaty of Brest-Litovsk null and void and to launch an appeal to the workers of the formerly enemy countries, Germans and Austrians, for the establishment of a new international order. It seemed that October 26, 1917, had returned.

However, relations between Lenin and the unfolding German revolution were not idyllic. Radek, who had hastened to Germany to come to the assistance of the revolutionaries, soon found himself forced into a difficult dialogue with them. From the outset Lenin wanted to make a gesture to show Russian solidarity with revolutionary Germany, and offered to send two grain convoys to a country where hunger was the daily lot of the people, a gift of the no less starving Russian people. To his indignation he received the answer that America had already offered food aid to Germany and that that was sufficient. Lenin took this rejection as a snub and considered it to be a betrayal. Did the German proletariat prefer the generosity of American capitalists to the fraternal help of Russian proletarians?

Lenin was also concerned about the influence, during what he called the "Kerensky stage" of the German revolution, of his old adversary Kautsky and of Rosa Luxemburg, both of whom, despite their differences, had adopted a very critical attitude toward the Russian revolution, as well as toward any possible revolution in Germany. Rosa Luxemburg believed that, in order to succeed, a Socialist revolution had to be driven by a mass party, which did not yet exist in Germany. In no way did she accept the Leninist idea of the party "leading the masses."

The "Kerensky stage" of the German revolution did not lead to a new October. In January 1919 the recently created Communist Party was banned, and the two Spartakist leaders, Rosa Luxemburg and Karl Liebknecht, were arrested and killed. Next it was the turn of Leo Jogiches to be shot down, like Luxemburg and Liebknecht, while "attempting to escape," a frequently used pretext. The dominant figure of the German Communist Party then became Paul Levi. Soon thereafter Radek was sent to prison. The German revolution collapsed with very little struggle.

This was not really a surprise for Lenin. He had moved swiftly from enthusiasm to a kind of disappointment. His vision of coming revolutions was entirely dependent on the Russian model, but he had been compelled to recognize that Germany was far from imitating that model. No doubt, in both cases, defeat had put an end to the existing political system, and German society, like its Russian counterpart, exasperated by the war and desperate living conditions, had turned against the leaders whom it accused of being responsible. But in Russia, Lenin had decided that he would compel an angry society to follow him into revolutionary adventure, whereas none of the Socialists in Germany, from the Reformists to the Spartakists, approved that form of adventurism or thought of driving a hesitant population to go beyond its opposition to the war. Lenin had momentarily believed that the world revolution was going to break out because the Russian example would be enough to bring other peoples to it. In a letter of January 29, 1919, to the Menshevik historian, Nikolai Rozhkov (whom he ordered Stalin to deport in 1922),[6] he wrote: "The civil war in Germany and the struggle precisely along the lines of soviet power . . . against the counterrevolutionary Constituent Assembly . . . [have] shown . . . that you cannot get by anywhere without a civil war. The intelligentsia will have to arrive at the position of helping the workers precisely on a Soviet platform."[7] The failure of the German revolution brought him to a consideration that was not new to him: the world revolution needed an instrument, the Third International, the idea of which he had in vain attempted to impose during the war. On January 21, 1919, he wrote a letter to the workers of Europe and America, in which he noted that although it had as yet no *de jure* existence, the Third International had already begun to exist in reality.[8] Its baptismal certificate dated from the transformation of the Spartakist movement into the German Communist Party. The party was indeed the decisive instrument for the great revolutionary upheavals. Through all the years and ordeals, Lenin had held firm to his faith in the party, not in the masses of whom he said little.

1919: THE YEAR OF ALL THE DANGERS

Having begun with the failure of the German revolution and the murder of Rosa Luxemburg, one of the major figures of the European revolutionary movement, the year 1919 was to be for the young Soviet state, the year of all the dangers. War Communism and the total collapse of the economy completed the work of turning the population against it. The combination of civil war and foreign intervention reduced the range of the Russian government to an increasingly threatened space. The survival of the state was Lenin's primary preoccupation, and the failure that had occurred in Germany confirmed the fact that the European proletariat would not come to the aid of Russia. This is why he greeted favorably the invitation by the great powers for a meeting of all those fighting in Russia, Whites and Reds, on the Prinkipo Islands in the Sea of Marmora. In order to be helped by the states of Europe, and not by the proletariat that was passive in the face of the danger confronting Russia, Lenin was prepared to recognize Russian debts, and also prepared to grant concessions such as mines to the Allies in exchange for an indispensable breathing space for his country.

The planned conference never took place because of opposition from the Whites, who were supported by France. Ties were gradually broken between Russia and the states of the West. The division between two worlds, at the heart of Lenin's program as it was expressed in the Decree on Peace, was taking shape, but it was not revolutionary Russia that was challenging the capitalist world. On the contrary the capitalist world was isolating Russia and supporting the internal opponents of the regime in order to bring down the Soviet state. Lenin then had to acknowledge that "Russia was living in a system of states," within which cohabitation between it and the others could not last. Who would perish?

In 1919 the answer seemed clear: Soviet Russia could hardly survive. At two points, its end even seemed imminent. In the spring the armies assembled in Siberia by Admiral Alexander Kolchak began an offensive into the heart of the country. A few months later, in September, General Denikin's troops advanced toward Moscow, while troops from the Baltic States under General Nikolai Yudenich tried to capture Petrograd.

This second offensive, which threatened to take both capitals from the Bolsheviks, was the more formidable. Denikin had battle-ready troops under his command, led by experienced officers able to impose discipline on them. He even had some civil organizations dependent on him in the territories that he controlled. The probable reason for his eventual defeat in early winter lay in his intransigent attitude toward national aspirations. His perspective was "Russia strong and indivisible," an ideal difficult to defend when all the nationalities of the empire had one ambition, to separate from Russia. Denikin's arrogance, not only toward aspirations to independence, but also toward the vision of autonomy fostered by the Kuban and Don Cossacks, put a gulf between him and those remarkable fighters, who might have done wonders alongside the Whites against a still inexperienced Red Army.[9] By placing too much emphasis on "Great Russia," he discouraged those natural allies, but also the Poles who might have been able to give him assistance. In a similar way, Admiral Kolchak, steeped in the same "Great Russian" vision, might have benefited from Finnish aid during his march on Petrograd. The Finns asked only that he recognize their independence, but Kolchak refused.[10] The obstinacy of the White leaders in refusing to recognize that the empire no longer existed and the abuses committed by their troops in the zones that they controlled (the civil war was dreadful on both sides, but the Bolsheviks were able to create a significant response in Europe to their enemies' abuses, while of course keeping silent about their own) did not predispose Western public opinion in their favor.

For his part Lenin had long been able to recognize the virtues of the slogan of national self-determination. This strategy was really "his," and he made much use of it during the civil war, always reiterating that self-determination was a matter for the peoples who claimed it. His practice with respect to self-determination, to which we return, nevertheless showed that this was for him a temporary strategy of limited use. But it served to distance the nationalist from the camp of the Whites, even when the Bolsheviks and their system held no attraction for them. It is true, as Lenin, unlike the White generals, had clearly understood, that the nations of the former empire wanted primarily their independence, and put off into an indefinite future the problem of their relations with the Bolsheviks.

In the spring of 1919, confronting the military danger of the White advance, the total international isolation of Russia, which the other powers refused to treat as a normal state, and the German disaster, Lenin had to bring himself to recognize that the two aims of his action, ensuring the survival of the state that he had founded and spreading the revolution, imposed a policy combining the two, rather than favoring each in turn as he had done since October 1917. The solution therefore lay in the establishment of a new International, the Third, which would provide him with a way of establishing connections with the proletariat of the West through the intermediary of parties that would mobilize it; it would also, he hoped, provide him with a tool likely to accelerate the course of revolution. Above all (his future strategy in the International was already taking shape), he would have a propaganda channel in capitalist countries that would make it possible for him to shift public opinion in a direction more favorable to Russia. He thereby hoped to break down the wall of hostility encircling his country.

THE COMINTERN: LENIN'S INTERNATIONAL

Although the difficulties he encountered from every direction drove Lenin to create the Third International in 1919, he had never stopped thinking of the idea since 1914, and he had set it out in his *April Theses*. In the immediate aftermath of the seizure of power, there were other urgencies, making peace and consolidating his power, and he had little time for putting in place the party of the world revolution. But in the spring of 1919, the question was back on the agenda, not only for the reasons already mentioned, but also because Lenin perceived the threat of a revival of the Second International, which he detested. The British Labour Party proposed that a conference be held in Berne to restore the sleeping International to life. The conference took place in the absence of several Socialist parties and was largely devoted to denouncing the "dictatorial" methods prevalent in Russia, and hence to condemning Lenin. But, writes Angelica Balabanov, "[i]t was the signal for the immediate launching of that new Third International for which Lenin had fought at Zimmerwald and Kienthal and which now . . . he was in a position to push through."[11]

The birth of the Third International is revealing about the confusion that prevailed in Russia in 1919 between the state and the Party. Lenin, who was then president of the Sovnarkom, decided to call a congress in Moscow in January for the purpose of founding the organization. The letter of invitation was addressed to thirty-nine groups or parties considered by the signatories to have a place in the new International. The letter was signed by Lenin and Trotsky in the name of the Central Committee of the Russian Party, and by various foreign communist leaders then living in Russia.[12] In his excellent *Histoire de l'Internationale communiste*, Pierre Broué analyzes this summons in detail.[13]

Two remarks suffice here. First, Lenin was indeed at the center of the proposal. In view of the congress, he had drafted "theses" on "Bourgeois Democracy and the Dictatorship of the Proletariat,"[14] whereas the manifesto announcing the establishment of the Comintern was written by Trotsky. Also, and here the confusion between state functions and the program of world revolution is obvious, the commissar of foreign affairs, Chicherin, went on the radio on January 24 to call on the foreign parties to meet in Moscow. It was he who made the letter from Lenin and Trotsky public. In early 1918 his commissariat, the Narkomindel, had already undertaken to lay the groundwork for a Zimmerwald conference calling for peace; it did not take place in the official form proposed, because the Treaty of Brest-Litovsk had made it obsolete. This initiative taken so early in the new regime clearly shows that the idea of establishing a new International was already a part of the normal activities of the Narkomindel. Chicherin's call on the radio in 1919 thus confirmed the bond that existed in Lenin's mind between the institution for foreign policy and revolutionary organization.

Second, the invitation was addressed to the Socialist parties of Europe and North America, and, except for the Japanese Socialists, no party representing non-European or still colonial regions, with which Lenin was so concerned, was invited. In January 1919 he thought that the expansion of the revolution was a matter for Western societies. It took only a short time to persuade him to look as well toward the societies that were then called "backward."

The nascent International met in Moscow from March 2 to 6, 1919.[15] Fifty-one delegates participated, most of whom were entitled to vote, with about a dozen having only observer status. The largest number of delegates represented Russia (eight) and the parties of national groups that had belonged to the empire until 1917 (Latvians, Armenians, and so on), and "foreign sections" of the Communist Party. The bulk of the delegates, whatever their national affiliation, lived in Russia. This was the case for the Swiss representative, Fritz Platten. Some members of the Russian Party spoke in the name of foreign parties; for example, Khristian Rakovsky was present as a delegate of the Balkan Revolutionary Federation. By force of circumstance, the congress was therefore dominated by the Bolsheviks—Trotsky, Zinoviev, Bukharin, Stalin, and Chicherin, assisted by two delegates with observer status, V. V. Vorovsky and V. V. Obolensky—but above all by Lenin, elected to the presidium at the outset, along with the German Hugo Eberlein and the Swiss Fritz Platten.

The problem that first arose for the participants in this forum was to define its nature: congress, as Lenin wanted, or conference, as the Germans particularly wished, because they were worried that, given the weakness of Communism outside Russia, the International would become an institution under Russian domination. Lenin could respond to these concerns by pointing out that the forum had adopted German as the working language and that the Russian edition of the proceedings of the meeting would be nothing but a translation of the German edition. Except for Stalin, the Russian delegates had excellent command of German, and all their speeches were made in that language. Despite these initial hesitations about the nature of the meeting, Lenin's will was on display from the outset: a huge banner was stretched on the wall behind the presidium bearing the inscription "Long live the Third International!" From the outset as well, Lenin decided that the Zimmerwald movement would be dissolved and replaced by the Third International. Its bureau would immediately transfer to the new organization the functions and documents belonging to the body that since the war had begun to supplant the Second International.

After two days of hesitation, during which those in favor of treating the meeting merely as a conference fiercely defended their position, the participants unanimously decided to accept Lenin's proposal, and the conference then became the First Congress of the Communist International. The reasons for this unanimous agreement have not yet been fully elucidated. Angelica Balabanov, who was deeply shocked by the sudden and unceremonious dissolution of the Zimmerwald group, attributes it to the spectacular arrival in the midst of a conference session of an Austrian delegate named Karl Steinhardt (alias Grüber), who presented to the Congress the electrifying picture of a proletariat that was everywhere on the verge of revolution, and stated that the International had to bear this in mind.[16] Pierre Broué challenges this interpretation and accepts the idea that even Lenin and Trotsky were at first hesitant. However, considering the preparation for the meeting and Lenin's speech, it can only be concluded that he had made a very definite decision to provide the Russian revolution with an instrument capable of protecting his work and encouraging expansion of the revolution based on the Russian model. In his speech Lenin forcefully emphasized the necessity for the dictatorship of the proletariat and the rejection of any compromise with the bourgeoisie and parliamentarianism. The man who had so constantly worked for a centralized and powerful party could not accept a simple body for international liaison among Socialist parties that was hardly in conformity with the principles that he had established. He forcefully reiterated the point that the Russian model was the one that had succeeded, and it therefore should be followed.

Before adjourning, the First Congress established the Comintern's rules of operation, broadly imitating those of the Russian Communist Party. An Executive Committee was appointed, with the leadership consisting of Lenin, Trotsky, Zinoviev, Rakovsky, and Platten, and Angelica Balabanov as secretary. Describing the circumstances of her appointment to a position that she did not want, Balabanov sheds some very useful light on Lenin's relations with other members of the party. As she was explaining her reluctance to him, Lenin "interrupted me. Closing one of his eyes as usual, when he wished to speak categorically, he replied: 'Party discipline exists for you too, dear comrade. The Central Committee has decided.' (When Lenin had decided something before the Central Committee had ratified his decision, he usually anticipated their action in this fashion so as to avoid superfluous discussion.)" Lenin had demonstrated his intentions throughout the four days of the congress, demanding that his Italian-Russian comrade join in the suicide of the Zimmerwald movement and that she announce on her own authority the affiliation of the Italian Party to the Third International. All these demands were covered by the convenient authority of the Central Committee, but as Balabanov mischievously notes, behind this "authority" lay only Lenin's own will and his intransigent view of party discipline.[17]

It is therefore difficult to imagine that he had suddenly hesitated to establish this Third International, plans for which had obsessed him since 1914 and that he had tried to impose at Zimmerwald and Kienthal, because he was the target of criticism from Eberlein, the colorless representative of a Spartakism that had lost its most prestigious leaders. Indeed, Eberlein later asserted that his opposition to the immediate establishment of the International had been at the direction of Rosa Luxemburg. According to Eberlein, when she learned of Lenin's plan in her cell a few days before she was killed, she gave him the mandate to have the formal establishment of the Comintern delayed until a more propitious time. And for his part, her companion Leo Jogiches, who had organized the Spartakist League with her, was reported to have recommended to the representatives of the German Communists that they leave the Congress if the decision was made to establish the Comintern immediately.

Among the objections put forth by Eberlein during the debates, the principal one, which was incidentally quite to the point, was that the representative character of the delegates was highly dubious and the Congress was to be dominated by Russian Communists. It had in fact been impossible to reach a number of parties and organizations in time for them to send representatives to Moscow, and getting to Russia at a time when a "cordon sanitaire" surrounded its borders was extremely difficult.

Although this criticism could not be challenged, there was one point on which Lenin insisted in order to mollify German concerns, his desire not to make Moscow the seat of the International. If the First Congress had been held in Moscow, he explained, this was because of the exceptional circumstances. It would have been impossible to hold the meeting anywhere else because it would have been immediately broken up by the police. But, he went on (and Zinoviev, appointed head of the Executive Committee, reiterated it at the Eighth Congress of the Russian Communist Party held practically in the immediate aftermath of the founding Congress of the Comintern, from March 18 to 23), the Bolsheviks hoped that the Third International and its executive could be moved as soon as possible to another capital, Berlin or Paris. This move would be the signal of the territorial expansion of the revolution in Europe.

This intention to confer on the International a universal, or at least European, character is easy to understand. Although he was persuaded in 1919 of the necessity of forging an effective revolutionary instrument, one in harmony with the views that had guided the formation of his own party, Lenin was nonetheless, as he had always been, a convinced internationalist. Praising the virtues of the Russian model did not at all make it into a *Russian* model. On the contrary he was eager for the revolution to go beyond the borders of his country, to ensure the survival of the Russian revolution, no doubt, but principally so that the revolution could finally take on its true face and become international and proletarian. His desire to save his work in Russia in 1919 was rooted in a project of world revolution. It was the *spark* that he intended to preserve, not a specifically Russian event. The transfer of the Comintern to Western Europe seemed desirable to him for symbolic reasons, to be sure, but also for reasons of efficacy. Moreover, he was aware that the Russian state (existing, as he had acknowledged, in a system of states the disappearance of which he had hoped for, an outcome that he did not foresee in the very near term) needed to appear to other governments as a respectable institution, not as a simple agent of the revolution. Although the interests of world revolution and the imperatives of Russian security were inseparable, Lenin knew that it was better not to make this too apparent to the rest of the world. The safety of Russia depended on it.

It is true that in the spring of 1919 it was not conceivable to install the Comintern concretely anywhere but Moscow. At the very same time, the Soviet state, isolated and threatened by the greatest internal dangers, suddenly saw hope rise again beyond its borders. Was world revolution again on the agenda? Then the Comintern could help to speed it up.

THE AWAKENING OF THE PROLETARIAT?[18]

On March 21, 1919, after the conclusion of the First Congress of the Comintern, but while the Eighth Congress of the Russian Communist Party was still in session, a miraculous piece of news came to the Bolsheviks who felt that they were under siege: revolution had just broken out in Budapest.

It was to be sure an unusual revolution, which brought to power a coalition of Socialists and Communists among whom the dominant figure was Bela Kun, an old acquaintance of Lenin's, who had just been released from prison and was attempting the experiment of a Soviet Republic. Like Lenin, although he was much less gifted than his mentor, Bela Kun thought that the revolution had to be dynamic and go beyond the borders of the country in which it started, and he launched an appeal for insurrection to the neighboring proletarians of Bohemia and Slovakia. Domestically, he would imitate the Russia of War Communism and combine nationalization of industry and land with prohibition of commerce and Red Terror. It is not surprising that in the space of 143 days, this Soviet Republic lost all support and collapsed. But in March 1919, it was a sign that the "spark" had managed to spread the flame of revolution. Lenin, although he showed some concern about the interpretation of what seemed to him to be something of a putsch, nevertheless felt the rebirth of hope.

On the other side, the Western governments panicked; the shadow of Bolshevism was spreading over Europe, said Lloyd George.

Anxiety on one side and hope on the other were confirmed less than one month later on April 13, when a Soviet Republic was set up in Bavaria. What had happened in Munich seemed to mean that the German revolution so long awaited had finally arrived. Chicherin immediately hailed the event and proclaimed that Russia was directly linked to this Soviet Republic: "Any blow against it will be a blow against us." Who was speaking, the head of Russian diplomacy or a spokesman for the Comintern? The intertwining of the two programs, governmental and revolutionary, had never been tighter. A few months later, the commissar of foreign affairs explained that the Comintern was the "foreign policy of the proletariat." This was a return to the views of the Decree on Peace.

The time of disillusionment was near. The Bavarian Republic lasted for only two weeks. Its end on May 1 might seem symbolic of the helplessness of the German proletariat, broken by a terrible war and not very inclined to change the world. The following month, a failed coup d'état in Vienna showed how difficult it was for Communist leaders to lead workers to take decisive action. In August, Bela Kun's Soviet Republic was unable to withstand the combined attacks of Rumanian troops, supported by the Allies, and domestic opposition. Within five months the revolutionary awakening of Hungary, Bavaria, and Austria had led to disasters that were added to the one that German Communism had suffered at the beginning of the year.

Lenin, who had taken great care to warn the parties tied to the Comintern against revolutionary attempts that were only badly prepared putsches (while Zinoviev was imprudently urging this course of action), returned to his original position, that organization was the preliminary step that had to be emphasized. He decided that the moment had come to play another card, that of the frustration of the German people at the extremely harsh conditions of the Treaty of Versailles. The Germans learned of the clauses of the treaty in the summer of 1919, and Lenin immediately profited from the fact. Through the voices of their heads, Chicherin and Zinoviev, the two sister institutions, Narkomindel and Comintern, set up a cross fire consisting of two arguments: "Versailles is another Brest-Litovsk" and "[o]ppressed proletarians and oppressed peoples [Germany at Versailles and Russia] have the same battle to fight." We can see emerging here an analysis affirming the solidarity of "peoples" mistreated by capitalist interests. It would lead to a rapprochement between the Bolsheviks and defeated Germany (and not only the Communist elements in Germany) early in 1920. The aid discreetly given by the Red Army for the rebuilding of the Reichswehr, and even the very positive attitude of the Comintern in 1923 (through the voice of Radek) toward Leo Schlageter, who had blown up a bridge to protest against French occupation of the Ruhr, entered into this strategy. Acknowledgment by the Comintern of the value that the national battle could have in certain circumstances and its relation to the socialist battle, what was for a fleeting moment known as the "Schlageter line," could already be discerned in the conclusions Lenin drew from the Treaty of Versailles.

He then discovered another means of action designed to restore vitality to the German, and more generally the European, revolutionary movement. It was necessary, he thought, to bring the Comintern closer to the communist groups active in the various countries. A Comintern Secretariat for Western Europe was set up in Berlin under the direction of Yakov Reich (known as Comrade Thomas) and Adolf Wrszawski (alias Bronski). They were joined by the German communists Paul Levi, August Talheimer, and Willi Munzenberg. In the background during the establishment of this outpost, Karl Radek, who had been in Moabit prison for months, acted as advisor to the German Communists, and although this was not officially stated, represented Moscow both to them and to the Secretariat. Despite his forced absence, Radek had been elected to the Central Committee of the Russian Party at the Eighth Congress in March, and after his release from prison and return to Russia in late 1919, he was immediately appointed as secretary of the Comintern. At the same time, Lenin entrusted Sebald Rutgers, who had represented the Dutch Communists at the founding congress, with the mission of setting up a bureau of the Comintern in Amsterdam and calling a Communist conference in that city. The conference was held in February 1920, and the Comintern sent as a delegate Mikhail Borodin, on the staff of the Narkomindel and the Comintern, who had just returned from a mission to the United States on behalf of the International. (In 1923, he was to serve as an adviser to the Kuomintang in China.) Clara Zetkin led a delegation of the German Communist Party in Amsterdam. The meeting, which was interrupted by the police, lasted for only two days and had no results, but the proof had been given that the Comintern was beginning to exist.

If to these attempts to loosen the vise squeezing Russia, we add the opening of a bureau of the Comintern in the Ukraine, where the Bulgarian former

Menshevik Rakovsky had been appointed president of the Sovnarkom, and we note that the bureau was under Balabanov's authority, we can see the importance given by Lenin to these various openings onto the outside world. He explained this to Balabanov when, after her appointment, she complained to him about having to leave Moscow: "[I]n the current battle, the Ukraine is our principal objective." Despite the difficulties, the Comintern was thus taking on more personnel, spreading its locations, and above all increasing its resources. It is worth noting in passing that many of those who were sent abroad were given subsidies by an old acquaintance who was a specialist in party finances, Yakov Hanetsky.

The existence of bureaus of the International abroad also presented the advantage, when problems or crises arose in Communist parties, such as the one that divided the German party in the fall of 1919, of providing Lenin with the means of exercising influence on the spot through an intermediary. In the German conflict, for example, Radek, who was better informed about the local situation because of his time in prison along with almost all the German Communists, was able to help Lenin become aware of the need to support cautious positions. At the time a certain revolutionary optimism prevailed in Moscow, whose most fervent spokesman was Bukharin, and Lenin hesitated over the position to adopt. Should he urge the German Communists to unite in order to form a true mass party, or should he support the small existing Communist Party. Debates in Germany in late 1919 suggested that a rebirth of the revolutionary movement was possible. Clara Zetkin was even afraid that the Amsterdam bureau would supplant the Berlin secretariat at the moment, she argued, that the German Communists were about to take action. And, indeed, on March 13, 1920, two German generals organized a putsch and installed a nationalist government in Berlin led by "Chancellor" Wolfgang Kapp. The attempt failed because a general strike brought it to an end; the unions were the real forces of opposition. The Comintern had not had the time to react. It nevertheless sent congratulations and good wishes for success after the fact to the German workers, while contradictory commentaries proliferated. Had the German Communist Party not been overcautious in accepting the idea of a Social Democratic government in the event of a victory over the putsch? This was the accusation made by Radek and Bela Kun, whereas the more sensible Lenin supported the moderation of the Communists, considering their strategy adapted to the moment, that is, to their weakness and their divisions. Once again Lenin had projected onto foreign events the image of the Russian revolution and thought he saw in Kapp's putsch a replay of the Kornilov affair. "October," if this analysis was correct, would no longer be a distant prospect for the German revolution.

THE SECOND CONGRESS OF THE COMINTERN

Renascent hope in Germany served as a backdrop to preparations for the Second Congress of the International, called for the summer of 1920. The mood in the Kremlin was generally optimistic. Kolchak and Denikin had been defeated. The domestic military threat was over, or almost over. In Copenhagen, Litvinov was negotiating an agreement with England for the repatriation of prisoners that would be signed on February 12, 1920. On February 2, the peace treaty between Poland and Estonia had been signed, and Tallinn could be used as link for Russian foreign trade that Lenin's envoys abroad were attempting to reorganize. The Russian state was gradually resuming its place on the European stage. Finally, during the Ninth Party Congress in March 1920, Lenin launched an appeal for the restoration of peace and normal commercial relations among states.

Thus hardly had the year 1919 come to an end, a year that had been marked by the total isolation of Russia, compelled to place all its hopes in the prospect of world revolution, than the tone changed, and Russia proclaimed its intention to play the game of a world made up of states with different systems. Chicherin tirelessly expounded the theme of the indispensable coexistence between the communist and capitalist worlds. Radek went even further in asserting that Russia would refrain from engaging in revolutionary agitation in states with different systems, as long as those states in turn did not attempt to support the counterrevolution.

The idea of "peaceful coexistence" was indeed present in Leninist language in 1920. Armed with this optimistic vision, in April 1920, Lenin wrote his last major work, *Left-Wing Communism, an Infantile Disorder,*[19] in which he suggested a break with the relatively sectarian line advocated by the Comintern in 1919. The establishment of the International had sealed the defeat of reformism; in 1920 it was appropriate to choose reasonable strategies, adapted to particular circumstances. Lenin cited the history of Bolshevism as an example, punctuated with compromises with various political forces in order to better prepare future success. Of course he did not totally condemn leftist radicalism, but he argued for a strategy making use of unions and parliaments that was favorable to the progress of the mass movement.

The work nevertheless reveals some contradiction in Lenin's thinking in 1920, a year in which the situation in Europe was changing. On the one hand, he maintained that the success of the Russian revolution implied that the line followed had been correct and concluded that the same process would inevitably take place everywhere. The Bolsheviks owed this success to their party and its iron discipline, but also to the masses who had supported them unfailingly. To attain victory they had engaged in compromise, but the only legitimate compromises were those imposed by circumstances. It was up to other parties to carefully evaluate the objective conditions of their actions. In addition Lenin emphasized the indissoluble link between party leaders and the masses. In his view, to speak of dictatorship of the leaders or dictatorship of the masses would express complete mental confusion, because the revolutionary universe was made up of both. But in making this argument, Lenin forgot that the masses of the most advanced European countries already had long experience in the workers' movement. This was the source of the contradiction with which he was struggling. He exhorted the Communists of other countries to take into account "their" social conditions and "their" history, but at the same time he asked them to look at themselves in the mirror of Russia in order to define the strategies that would bring them to the revolution.

His polemic nevertheless had its effect. The Amsterdam bureau, which was under leftist influence, argued that workers should refrain from participating in union and parliamentary activities. The International's sanction was immediate: the bureau was abolished, and all its functions were transferred to the Berlin secretariat. The decision was made by the Executive Committee, with no debate of any kind in the Second Congress.

It is true that in the spring of 1920 Russia was facing another threat that confirmed Lenin in his intention to offer the outside world the image of a state not engaged in revolutionary destabilization. Poland was on this occasion the source of Russian concern. As long as the White generals threatened the overthrow of the Bolshevik regime, Józef Pilsudski, head of the independent Polish state and commander in chief of his country's armed forces, had maintained a cautious neutrality between the two camps. He had been born in the Russian part of Poland and feared more than anything that a victory by the Whites would mean a return of the Russian Empire. He had also been a Socialist early in the century (he had founded *Rabotnik*, the Socialist Party newspaper) before adopting an openly nationalist position and taking the leadership of a movement in favor of independence. Hence, the Bolsheviks were no closer than the White generals to his views, although while the Whites held the upper hand, he had thought it wise to allow them to wear each other out fighting and to support neither side. Once the Whites had been defeated, Pilsudski, fully aware of the Bolsheviks' weakness, decided that the moment had come to take advantage of the situation. By supporting the foundation and consolidation of independent states carved out of the former empire—the Baltic States, the Ukraine, Belorussia—he hoped to establish around the Soviet state a barrier of buffer states that would compel Russia to adopt a cautious attitude toward its neighbors rather than persevering in its old aggressive stance.

Any understanding between Pilsudski and Lenin was impossible, because the former wanted it to be based on the independence of the Ukraine, a possibility that the latter rejected. Chicherin attempted to forestall the danger by arguing to Pilsudski that he would be playing into the hands of Germany, which was only waiting for a Polish movement supported by France to join forces with Russia, providing it with a possibility for revenge.[20] His warning proved futile, and Polish troops, allied with the troops of the Ukrainian Hetman Semyon Petliura, launched an attack against Kiev, which was captured in May. Confronting the Polish and Ukrainian troops, the Red Army was led by a young general, Mikhail Tukhachevsky, who had been recruited from the czarist officer corps. The victorious advance of the Polish army gradually slowed. The Ukrainians fighting with it were not at all persuaded of the need for the alliance. Even though the Ukrainian peasantry was hostile to Bolshevism, it was equally hostile to the Poles, whom it identified with the large landowners who had dominated the country before the revolution. Polish territorial claims and the old enmity between Poles and Russians revived Russian national feeling, and many former czarist officers joined the Red Army in order to fight the Polish enemy. Strengthened by experts and morally inspired by what was becoming a national war, the Red Army went on the offensive in June, gradually forced the opposing troops to retreat, and reached the borders of Poland in late July.

Lenin was now confronted with an unprecedented problem. Should he stop there or continue the triumphal march in order to attempt to establish in Poland a regime that would come out of the revolutionary uprising that the Russian advance, in his view, could not fail to provoke?

Up to that point, Lenin had always been cautious in foreign policy. Confronted with such a decisive challenge, he understood that the Polish problem had two aspects: Because it was a war, it raised questions of international relations; but it might also be the first link in a revolutionary chain, and it thereby shifted from the international sphere to a matter of strategy for the world revolution. In July 1920 Lenin moved from caution to enthusiasm and chose the revolutionary solution. In his view the matter went beyond Poland. He foresaw that as the war between states became a revolutionary war, it might make it possible to go through Poland in order to join up with the German proletariat, which could not fail to rise up in turn when it knew that the Red Army was advancing in its direction, or so he hoped. In July 1920 Lenin adopted the dream of war changing into revolutionary war, a position that Bukharin had held in late 1917 and that Lenin had rejected as utopian.

The circumstances, of course, were different. Russia had triumphed in the civil war and had shown its strength against the White troops and the Polish and Ukrainian armies. How could the Polish proletariat, and the Germans after them, not rise up at the call of the Red Army, the army of the first proletariat that had succeeded in making the revolution? Was the coincidence between the historical opportunity that had suddenly appeared and the imminent meeting of the Comintern Congress not also a fateful sign? With the success of the "march on Berlin," the Communist parties meeting in Moscow would be able in turn to decide to join the revolutionary movement.

For Lenin the decision of July 1920 was in a way a repetition of the one he had made in 1917. The "spark" that he had ignited at the time was, he believed, in the process of setting the world ablaze, and this is why he ordered the Red Army to advance. He was convinced that the Polish Communists were numerous and powerful and that an internal uprising was imminent. A few advisers of Polish origin urged him to be cautious, pointing out that Polish national feeling would win out, even in the proletariat, over class solidarity. But he refused to listen and insisted that the Red Army move as quickly as possible to the German border. He also decided to establish in Poland, under the protection of the Red Army, a Provisional Polish Revolutionary Committee, led by Bolsheviks of Polish origin, Dzerzhinsky, founder of the Cheka; his adjutant Iosif Unshlikht; and Julian Marchlewski, who was to be its chairman.

Against this background, the Second Congress of the Comintern opened in Moscow on July 21. It lasted until August 7, while the Red Army under

Tukhachevsky's command entered the suburbs of Warsaw. It is easy to imagine the atmosphere of victory and high hopes. Everything about this Congress was different from the one in 1919. The First Congress had had few delegates, and their representative character was dubious; the 1920 Congress had 217 delegates representing 37 countries and 67 organizations. These delegates from abroad could see that the Russian state had been consolidated, if only from the lavishness of their reception. The Congress began in the Tauride Palace in Petrograd, and was then transferred to Moscow, where sessions were held in the Kremlin. Also in contrast to the First Congress, the international aspect was given pride of place, with four languages being used—German, Russian, French, and English—although the Russian leaders continued to use German.

The Congress was opened by Zinoviev, but was dominated by Lenin, who spoke on most subjects, and by Bukharin and Radek. Quite naturally, Lenin turned immediately to the Polish situation and agreed with the proposal of the German delegate Paul Levi, asking the Congress to call on the workers of all countries "to oppose through strikes and demonstrations any aid to Poland or any attack on Russia."

Taking place at a moment when the worldwide success of the revolution seemed to be near, the Second Congress of the Comintern, unlike the First, was less inclined to identify the cause of the revolution with the cause of Russia, and largely dealt with possibilities and strategies for the world revolution. To help bring it about, it was advisable to turn the Comintern into a veritable Party of the Revolution. This was the origin of the "twenty-one conditions"—nineteen in the original version—imposed on all Communist parties, which made the International into a centralized and hierarchical organization, whose discipline was an inflexible rule, all of which was unquestionably reminiscent of the Leninist conception of the party.

After the adoption of these twenty-one conditions, the International had indeed become Lenin's creation; he had finally succeeded in aligning all Communist parties with the one he had founded two decades earlier. Seen at the outset, even though this was not Lenin's intention, as a relatively flexible body serving as a "common home" for parties adhering to the same principles and objectives, one year later the Comintern became a veritable party with worldwide influence through its national bureaus. More than anything else, party discipline became the governing principle in every context, and national parties or sections could not deviate from the rules and strategy established by the International. As Lenin had indicated in the epigraph to *What Is to Be Done?* "purging" if not expelling parties contravening what the International had decided or would decide was the corollary of universally accepted discipline. The Comintern was the embodiment of will and unity; it possessed knowledge and spoke the truth—the consciousness of the world proletariat—and therefore imposed discipline and excluded those who violated it.

The history of the International was to show the price to be paid in many countries and many circumstances for this centralization of the Communist movement. The participants in the Second Congress, having expressed little opposition to the principles of organization proposed to them, passed them by a near unanimous vote.

On this subject, as on the others discussed, Lenin's positions were ready in advance, an indication of the decisive role he played in preparations for the Congress, despite the heavy burden of his work as head of government.[21] But it was the future strategy of the Comintern that most engaged his energies, and on this question, Zinoviev could not serve as his spokesman. He focused particularly on the crucial question of the international situation, a subject about which he was the principal speaker, seconded by Bukharin. Debates on the national and colonial problems took place for the most part in committee, but they were so impassioned that they often attracted larger attendance than plenary sessions. It is true that Lenin had devoted a long preparatory document to the question.[22]

The First Congress of the Comintern had barely considered these problems, but in 1920 the International welcomed to its assembly not only European revolutionaries, but also some participants from Asia, suggesting the spread of its field of action. The revolution had spread to Russian colonial territories, and Lenin, who had anticipated these developments in his writings as early as 1916, intended to have the International incorporate them into its strategy. The debate set up a confrontation among three positions, two of which had until then almost never been expressed in a meeting of European Communist parties.

The first position was a classic one, consisting in asserting that the revolution, the product of class struggle, had its center in Europe, and that the International had to give it primacy in its strategy. This position was supported by the Italian delegate Giacinto Serrati. He reacted violently to Lenin's report, presented at the first session, which asserted at the outset his conviction that "world imperialism will collapse only when the revolutionary offensive of the exploited and oppressed workers within each country . . . joins with the revolutionary offensive of hundreds of millions who have until now been outside of history."[23] Serrati forcefully rejected this view, asserting that Lenin's position was dangerous for the Western proletariat.

The real debate placed Lenin and Serrati in opposition to the representative of the Indian communists, M. N. Roy, who was determined to demonstrate that the Western revolution could not be accomplished without the contribution of Eastern movements, and that "revolutionary nationalism would lead to the fall of European imperialism."[24] For him, the key to world revolution was to be found in the East.

Lenin was thus challenged by Serrati for the excessive importance he attributed to the changes under way outside Europe, but he was just as determined not to accept Roy's position that wished to give preeminent importance to Eastern revolutions, thereby challenging the entire Marxist conception of class struggle. Between Serrati and Roy, Lenin defended an intermediate position that was supported and adopted by the Congress as a whole.

The confrontation between the Russian and the Indian–Serrati's extreme Eurocentrism carried much less weight in the debates, even though it reflected the unspoken assumptions of most European Communists–was already an indication of the problems that Lenin would have to face in his own country. Although most participants viewed the debate as principally an intellectual one, for Lenin it had a very concrete content. As head of the Soviet government, and not only as founder of the International, he had to find allies for his country outside Europe, able to attack the colonial powers hostile to him from the rear. He knew, and he said so, that in the dominated countries, these allies were the bourgeoisie who were in the vanguard of the national struggle, and not, as Serrati and Roy, temporarily in agreement, wanted to have him say, the proletariat, which he knew did not exist, or the still unorganized masses. Lenin's thinking on the colonial question was extraordinarily consistent, from the Stuttgart Congress in 1907 to the Second Congress of the Comintern in 1920. He had long understood that even the Communists of the colonizing states would not follow him in his intention to derive support from the nationalist movements of the colonized countries. His confrontation with Serrati made this clear yet again. Until illness struck him down, he would fight in the International, at the Third and Fourth Congresses, against what he considered a manifestation of a "colonialist" spirit in some European Communists.

Although Lenin advocated a strategy linking the revolutionary and national movements of Europe and the East by relying in the case of the East on the social forces capable of leading them, he nonetheless assumed that once revolutions had taken place in backward countries, they would follow the Russian model. In his view the stage of capitalism could be avoided, and the establishment of Socialism be immediate by means of a Soviet-style organization, the underpinnings of which would not be the workers, who were still not numerous enough in those countries, but the peasants and generally all the "workers," that is, all the "exploited."

In defending this realistic vision of societies outside Europe, Lenin was once again reinforcing the legitimacy of the Russian revolution and of the model that it offered. Once again it was the man governing Russia as much as the revolutionary who spoke; the two roles were inseparable in his view.

Two further remarks should be made on the basis of a simple examination of the work of this Congress.[25] The first has to do with Lenin. A statesman struggling to make a place for Russia in the community of nations, he had not hesitated to play the role of master of ceremonies at the Second Congress of the Comintern. To be sure he had done the same thing in 1919. But the First Congress had been a discreet meeting, with no international repercussions. In 1920, on the other hand, the barrage of propaganda around the meeting was substantial, and government leaders had their eyes fixed on this forum promising the end of the world that they ruled. The Lenin who played a starring role at the meeting was for the rest of the world no longer a mere head of government, but a revolutionary proclaiming his intention of destroying the existing order everywhere and depriving great states of their empires.

In 1920 this attitude indicated Lenin's belief in world revolution. He was head of government only until the advent of the world Soviet state. But he made no distinction between his function of the moment and his grand design. In

1921, on the other hand, when it seemed that the prospect of world revolution had receded, Lenin became discreet, and the head of government prevailed over the herald of great upheavals. At the Fourth Congress, the last that he was able to attend, Lenin was merely an almost silent witness, but that in no way prevented him from preparing positions and writing about the subjects that were to be debated. In 1920 he was eager to take charge of the organization and to take responsibility for defining revolutionary strategies. Thereafter he was just as eager to make ever clearer distinctions between the Soviet state, whose safety could only be ensured to the extent that it acted like a state, and the "global" revolutionary program.

The second remark that needs to be made has to do with the importance assumed by the Russian model within the Comintern in 1920. This importance is perhaps related to the moment at which the Comintern was organized, adopted rules of operation, and became a lasting institution, which was not yet the case in 1919. At the time when the Second Congress began, Russian military successes in 1920, domestically and in Poland, suggested not only that the Russian revolution had been successful but also that it was in the process of developing into a world revolution. To compel it to spread, Lenin forced all the Communists to rally behind the flag of a Comintern that was in a sense an extension of his own party. Of course he did this so that the revolution would go beyond the borders of his country, not to impose on everyone an exclusive model and the domination of the Russian Party. But when the dream of "global" revolution had faded, all that remained was the Russian model and the submission of all parties to a Comintern under Russian authority. Involuntarily Lenin had played the role of sorcerer's apprentice.

When the Congress was over, the delegates dispersed with the conviction that revolutions were imminent. Russian troops were in Warsaw. The aid that the Poles hoped for had not come. The Allies, who had been called on to help, were silent. In Danzig, German dock workers prevented the delivery to Poland of equipment that had been paid for. However, an uprising suddenly took place in the capital, where Polish Socialists set up workers' battalions and appealed to national solidarity against the slogan of class solidarity propagated by the Red Army. The demoralized Polish troops were galvanized by this awakening of civilian resistance, and the counterattack began from all directions. It was so powerful that in less than a week Tukhachevsky's Red Army was surrounded by General Vladislav Sikorski's troops, who took tens of thousands of Russians prisoner, while the remainder of the routed Red Army fled in every direction. The troops led by General Semen Budenny were no more successful, and the disintegration of the Russian army prompted the Poles to advance toward Moscow. Lenin had only one way out, acknowledgment of the disaster, a request for peace, and the surrender of territory to secure an immediate cessation of combat.

Yoffe, who had already been active at Brest-Litovsk, had to negotiate this humiliating peace. The armistice was signed on October 12, and then the Treaty of Riga on March 18, 1921. Huge portions of Belorussian and Ukrainian territory reverted to Poland, but the bulk of the Ukraine remained within the borders of the Soviet Republic.

In conversation with Clara Zetkin, Lenin analyzed the causes of this failure: "When they saw the Red Army, the Poles did not recognize it as a fraternal army, but saw it as the enemy. The Poles acted not as revolutionaries but as nationalists." And he blamed himself for having momentarily succumbed to a culpable optimism despite Radek's warnings. He was all the more regretful because he was precisely the one who had always seen, against the majority of Communists, the importance of national solidarities and the need to integrate them into all his calculations. Clara Zetkin pointed out that the price had been heavy; any chance of provoking a revolution in Germany had been destroyed by this episode. Aware of his mistake, Lenin attributed another one to himself; the lack of success, he thought, had saved not only independent Poland but also the Europe of Versailles and the treaty that had created it.[26]

The signature of the treaty at least made it possible for him to devote all Russian military efforts to the liquidation of the last bastions of the civil war. General Peter Wrangel's army had to retreat to the Crimea and then embark in panic for Turkey. With Southern Russia restored to Soviet control, there remained a final enclave, the Republic of the Far East that the Soviet regime had tolerated for a time because it served as a barrier to Japanese forces. By late 1921 Russia felt strong enough to block Japan from any presence in Siberia, and it therefore had no more need of this buffer state. By late 1922 the Republic of the Far East was occupied by Russian troops and incorporated into Soviet territory.

THE EAST: REVOLUTION BY PROXY

Once the delegates to the Second Congress had returned home, the Bolsheviks had to look reality in the face; Russia was, to be sure, the fatherland of the revolution, but it was alone of its kind and doomed to stay that way. Under these circumstances, could it survive as a revolutionary state? Lenin had never considered this possibility, and in that fateful month of August, he refused to accept it. He had long ago seen the problem of revolution in worldwide, not solely European, terms. The time seemed to have arrived to put that conviction to the test, to go beyond even his own previous analyses, to adopt the positions of the Indian delegate Roy, and to attempt to overcome the passivity of the Western proletariat, by fighting in the rear with the masses of the dominated world. For, in Lenin's view, the defeat in Warsaw was not only the consequence of a strategy guided by optimism, but also the Polish proletariat was responsible because they had acted according to the dictates of nationalism. The German proletariat had done likewise, impassively witnessing the advance of the Red Army in its direction, while not making the slightest attempt to profit from the situation, when it should have staged an uprising and drawn the Poles into its movement in order to link up with the Red Army. Lenin's only recourse was to revert to his original intuitions and turn toward the "rear" of the Western proletariat. The

Second Congress had included in its program the need to continue the dialogue between Lenin and Roy; the Congress of the Peoples of the East in Baku was to provide the opportunity.

In fact this was not the first meeting of its kind. In November 1918 Stalin had held in Moscow the First Congress of Muslim Communist Organizations, and at its conclusion had set up a Central Bureau of Muslim Organizations of the Russian Communist Party (*Musburo*). The intent at the time was to bring together and establish some order among scattered organizations. One year later, in November 1919, the Second Congress of Communist Organizations of Peoples of the East, held along the same lines, had been opened by Lenin, who had also presented a very important report in which he explained: "We Russians have begun a task that will be completed by the English, French, or German proletariat. But we realize that they will be unable to triumph without the help of the laboring masses of all the oppressed colonial peoples, those of the East first of all. We must understand that by itself, the vanguard [the Western proletariat] cannot accomplish the transition to communism."[27] And the resolution on the Eastern question began in this way: "The Congress considers that the problem of world socialist revolution cannot be resolved without the participation of the East."

The Congress of the Peoples of the East called in Baku in September 1920 at the behest of the Second Congress of the Comintern thus followed the line set out by Lenin in 1919. The participants in the Second Congress of the Comintern had seen no drawbacks to the proposed congress; in fact, they had paid little attention to the matter. They thought that revolution was imminent in Europe, and they were eager to return home to participate in it. They were unconcerned by debates that would take place at the edge of the Soviet state about what seemed to them a marginal problem. The atmosphere at the Baku meeting from September 1 to 9, 1920, was entirely different. The first reason was that the participants were generally not the same as those who had crowded into the luxurious halls of the Kremlin. The delegates to Baku were primarily from the East. The delegates numbered 1,891–235 from Turkey, 192 from Persia, 8 from China, 8 Kurds, and 3 Arabs; the others were all from non-Russian regions of the former empire, that is, Central Asia and the Caucasus.

The former subjects of the Russian Empire—especially the inhabitants of Turkestan—had the historic experience of colonization. They had just gone through the revolution in colonial conditions.[28] Unlike the European Communists, they had little experience of Marxist debate, but they intended to testify about the experience they were in the process of living through, the revolution in the colonies and the respective roles of and relations between the colonizers and the colonized. For them it was an opportunity to compare that experience with the purely theoretical ideas, removed from reality, held by Western Communists. From the outset they summarized their vision of the problem in a harsh formulation: "The contempt of the communists who, maintaining a mentality of rulers, look on Muslims as their subjects."[29]

Confronting these self-assured and demanding delegates, the leadership of the Comintern was represented by Zinoviev, whose only thought was how to save the Russian revolution from its isolation and who felt oppressed by the thought of having to forget revolution in the West; by Bela Kun, the Comintern apparatchik, and Radek, both haunted by the failed revolutions in Europe; by Georgy Safarov, an informed observer of the revolution in Turkestan and an adviser to Lenin on these problems; and by Mikhail Weltman (known as Pavlovich), who had been a Menshevik before the revolution, but whom Lenin had drawn into his orbit because he was an orientalist and the party needed to devise a strategy for the East and institutions designed to implement it. For all of them, the Baku Congress was a last chance. Their mission was to mobilize the Easterners, who knew little of Marx and Lenin, but who intended to carry out a revolution that was for them identical to national emancipation.

The misunderstanding between the two groups was great. The representatives of the Comintern were only a small handful of men, but they made up the entire presidium of the Congress, with Zinoviev in the chair. They dominated the hall, and they had behind them the authority of the Comintern, which had just crowned itself in Moscow the "World Party of the Revolution." Except for Safarov, who was clear about the political force they were facing, they thought they were in a position to mobilize these masses to serve their purpose—world revolution, that is, above all revolution in the West—and intended to define the ways of bringing this about.

At the outset things seemed simple. When Zinoviev opened the Congress and concluded his speech by launching an appeal to "holy war against imperialism," the enthusiasm of the audience was indescribable. "Jihad!" they shouted in response, to be sure adding in passing "Long live the International!" but above all "Long live the rebirth of the East!" Nevertheless when the delegates from the East took the floor in turn, they emphasized the specificity of the East and its particular circumstances. They asked that revolution in the East be given pride of place in the strategy of the Comintern. Did the stagnation of the revolution in the West not mean that the immediate future lay outside Europe, in the movement of emancipation transforming their regions? To the great dismay of the Comintern representatives, what emerged from the debates was a total reversal of their views. For the "communists" of the East, history was being displaced into their regions, and it would be the success of their revolution that would one day make possible the rebirth of the hope for revolution in Europe. Didn't Russia itself, a country at the crossroads of Europe and Asia, illustrate that change in perspective? The revolution had taken shape in the most backward country of Europe, and it should turn toward the East in order to survive by means of the expansion of the movement that it had begun.

These ideas, awkwardly presented by orators whose existence had never been suspected by Zinoviev and his colleagues—Narbutabekov, Ryskulov, and the like—had already been set forth by the Tatar Mirsaid Sultan Galiev, who had written in 1919 that although it was proper for the Russian revolution to rely on world revolution, to claim that that support was to be found in the West was a source of failure.[30]

Confronted with this desire to displace the revolution's center of gravity (a foretaste of many later shifts, such as the strategy of encircling the cities by the countryside, and the Chinese notion that "now, the revolutionary wind is blowing from the East"), the leadership of the Comintern in the presidium of the Baku Congress refused to ratify these positions and pushed the adoption of positions that were in retreat from those of the Second Congress of the Comintern. The speeches by Radek, Bela Kun, and Pavlovich emphasized the *secondary* position of the liberation movements of the peoples of the East (which in Lenin's view were integrated into world revolution) whose principal purpose was only to support and strengthen world revolution. In no case did they accept it as an alternative to revolution in the West. From this attitude of the Comintern derived a strategy intended to bring the conditions of the struggle in the East as close as possible to those prevailing in the West. Although they were unable to ignore totally the specificities of revolution in the East, the Comintern leaders emphasized at Baku that the acknowledgment of those particularities was only temporary and limited. They thereby distanced themselves from Lenin's recommendations. But their retreat is easy to understand; in these nine days of debate, they had discovered that the movement of national revolution that was growing in the East was escaping from their directives, that there was no common objective between Communism of the West and Communism of the East, and that their interlocutors harbored the dream of total emancipation from the West, capitalist or Communist, if not of revenge against it.

The name of Mao Tse-tung was still unknown to the Comintern, but the name of Sultan Galiev made an impression on its representatives in Baku. Galiev completed his theoretical analysis between 1923 and 1928 in asserting the fundamental and irreducible difference between the West in which the oppressed constituted a class, the proletariat, and the East in which the oppressed were nations, entirely proletarian because they were subject to oppression. He concluded that the emancipation of the East could in the end be achieved only by replacing the oppression imposed on all classes by the West with the dictatorship of the proletarian "nations" of the East.[31]

The rejection of the positions of the Eastern Communists by Zinoviev and his colleagues implied (in conformity with the conclusions of the Second Congress of the Comintern) the need for a single strategy, defined by the Comintern and stringently imposed on all its members, without the slightest deviation.

Л Л Л

Lenin, who had remained in Moscow, already knew that Russia was alone in keeping the revolutionary flame alive. From this point on, without saying it explicitly, he accepted the consequences of this recognition. With the revolution confined to one country, that country had to give itself the means to survive. As a result the state had to be given priority. As head of government, Lenin would henceforth devote himself to the state, strengthening it and ensuring its safety in every realm. He would henceforth give priority to his role as head of government in both domestic and foreign matters. It is easy to understand why he was from then on less visible in the Comintern. It was not for lack of interest, but because the Comintern ceased being a real World Party of Revolution to become a transmission belt for the national interest of the Soviet state.

A final abortive attempt at revolution in Germany in March 1921, adventurist rather than carefully planned, finally convinced Lenin of the need to place all his efforts and all the efforts of the Communists at the service of the Soviet state. But, before anything else, he had to restore to that state a space, a human dimension, and resources that the revolution had caused it to lose. The time had come to reconstitute Great Russia, to put an end to the self-determination that had, of course, served the revolution, but that in 1921 threatened to put the Soviet state in danger.

Chapter Thirteen

AFTER SELF-DETERMINATION, THE STATE RECONSTRUCTED

FOR YEARS LENIN HAD THOUGHT ON HIS OWN ABOUT THE national problem, against the majority of the workers' movement and failing really to interest the Bolsheviks in the subject. When he returned to Russia in April 1917, he forced his party to accept the most iconoclastic of his propositions, the right to secession as a component of revolutionary strategy. The problem was debated at the Seventh Congress of the Party in Petrograd from April 24 to 29, and gave rise to a very sharp dispute. Stalin presented the report on the national question; he supported Lenin's position, the right of national minorities to separate from Russia, but he made some qualifications. National minorities were not obligated to make use of the right, and it should be exercised principally in light of the interests of the proletarian revolution. From the outset he declared that as far as he was concerned, he would be opposed to the separation of Transcaucasia. The remark was tragically confirmed a few years later by his dealings with his Georgian compatriots. Pyatakov and Dzerzhinsky vehemently opposed the idea of granting the right of separation to national minorities who would use it, said Pyatakov, against and not in support of the proletariat, and he proposed a motion condemning the right to self-determination. Lenin had to use all his authority to secure the rejection of Pyatakov's motion and a vote in favor of Stalin's resolution, which in the end was passed with 56 votes in favor, 16 against, and 8 abstentions.

The positions adopted included four points: the right to secession; broad regional autonomy for national minorities not separating from Russia; guarantees of minority rights by law; and unity of the party.

Some points, on the other hand, were left vague. When might the right to self-determination be exercised, when peace came or when the interested parties decided? Above all, to which national minorities did the right apply?

Despite these silences and the Bolsheviks' reservations, the adoption of Lenin's ideas was to transform the bases of Russian political life.

THE WEAPON OF SELF-DETERMINATION

The future of the national minorities was among Lenin's principal concerns when he took power. The Declaration of Rights of the Peoples of Russia was issued on November 2, 1917, immediately after the Decree on Peace and the Decree on Land. It defined the fundamental principles imposed on the party by Lenin and implicitly raised two questions, the borders of the Soviet state and its organization.

On January 12, 1918, The Declaration of the Rights of the Working and Exploited People, adopted by the Third Congress of Soviets, reaffirmed the principle of self-determination, but explained: "All national minorities have the right to decide whether and on what grounds they may participate in the federal government and other Soviet federal institutions."

Thus, from the very beginning of the new regime, Lenin had included in his vision of the national problem, in parity with the right to self-determination, an option that he had earlier rejected, the federal link.

At the same time that the direction of national minorities policy was modified in this way, Lenin created the instruments intended to implement it. The government included a commissariat for nationalities (*Narkomnats*) under the leadership of Stalin, with two associates.[1] In the beginning this commissariat was a simple liaison authority charged with coordinating eight departments or sections led by representatives of the nationality concerned. These sections were created as concrete problems appeared. The first to be set up were the commissariat (they had this title at the time) for Poland, in November 1917, followed by commissariats for Lithuania, Jewish affairs, and Muslims.

By 1918 the Narkomnats was coordinating the activities of eighteen sections whose leaders made up a bureau, also under Stalin's authority, which often entered into conflict with him, attempting to oppose his centralizing vision with the demands of the national rank and file. The developing antagonism between center and periphery persuaded Lenin of the need to change the Narkomnats to prevent it from being changed into a "Parliament of Nationalities." The June 9, 1918, reform did not abolish any sections, but no longer guaranteed their representation in the bureau, which was reduced to nine members and placed under the joint authority of the Party Central Committee and the Sovnarkom, both of which would ratify its decisions and arbitrate internal conflicts.

The rather frequent changes in the organization of the commissariat should not be allowed to conceal their underlying basis, a shift in the relations of the regime with the nationalities. In the beginning its function was to associate the nationalities with the policies of the new regime in order to win their support. This explains the two anomalies in the pattern of representation, the Jewish and Muslim sections, although neither Jews nor Muslims had ever been considered nationalities by the Marxists. But in 1918 political reality drove Lenin to that solution even though it was very much against his principles.

Lenin soon recognized the use that nationalities were attempting to make of the commissariat. It was a place to defend their national demands and provided the possibility of organizing within this framework a "common front" of nation-alities against the central authorities. Lenin therefore took action, and Stalin, charged with imposing central authority, prepared a large number of reforms, all of which tended to place increased powers in the hands of the central com-missariat, to make it the architect of relations among nationalities in order to block their growing solidarity, and finally to chip away ceaselessly at the pre-rogatives of the national sections. When the USSR was established in 1924, the commissariat for nationalities disappeared because the federal state considered itself the sole organizer and guarantor of national rights and believed that all problems posed by nationalities had been definitively settled.

A fairly precise doctrine of the exercise of self-determination went along with the federal principle accepted in article 2 of the Declaration of the Rights of the Working and Exploited People, which replaced earlier ambiguous and often contradictory statements. The January 12 declaration specified that *all* workers could exercise that right in the Congress of Soviets, which thereby became the body of last resort. The first Russian Constitution, unanimously adopted by the Fifth Congress of Soviets on July 10, 1918, sheds light on Lenin's thinking and the interpretation of federalism that events had brought him to accept. The body of the Constitution was made up of the January 12 declaration and the measures organizing the Federal Republic. Reading these documents gives rise to two observations. The words "federal" or "federation" are used very sparingly. "Federation" appears only in Chapter I, article 2. There is, to be sure, talk of the "federal" organization of various entities, but this deals principally with decen-tralization. In the end the federalism of 1918 seems to have been reduced to the voluntary nature of the coexistence of peoples and the assertion that, in the Soviet state, all nationalities are equal before the law. For Lenin, who had exer-cised control over a special commission of the Central Committee charged with combining two constitutional proposals, one from a commission chaired by Sverdlov, the other developed by the commissariat of justice, federalism was a concession to reality that should be limited to what constituted its basis, "the interest of the working classes," as he explained. Further, and this is the most sig-nificant point, this concession was "transitory," "making it possible for the work-ers to rise above national conflicts."[2] Lenin summed up his program in these terms: "The federation is a step toward voluntary fusion."[3]

This realistic vision, entirely directed toward the resolution of immediate problems, is easy to understand. In early 1918 Russia was in complete chaos, and the spontaneous self-determination of the nationalities was contributing to that chaos in no small measure.

SELF-DETERMINATION AT THE GRASS ROOTS

By launching the slogan of the "right of peoples to self-determination," Lenin had hoped to maintain control over its practical implementation. But the nation-alities of the empire did not wait for his help in deciding their fate. They were all the more determined to act by themselves because they had the support of foreign states, and the universal response to their desire for emancipation led them to give it a more radical cast.

Lenin had offered self-determination but hoped that it would not be used. This illusion gave way before the instantaneous disintegration of the empire, and when the Bolsheviks came to power, they realized that their authority extended over a Russian territory that had been amputated of areas that were economically and strategically decisive for its survival. None of the nationalities paid attention to the practical details of self-determination, which the Bolsheviks in any event had difficulty defining. They simply declared their intent to separate from Russia.

The first two who took that step were the Polish and Finnish nations.

In October 1917 Poland was practically independent; the war and the German occupation had created that de facto situation, which Lenin was compelled to accept with no precondition or debate. In 1920, as we have seen, he went back on that independence, when he thought he could unleash revolution and establish a Soviet state in Poland.

Finland decided to follow the same path. Lenin hesitated to accept because he thought that a revolutionary situation existed in the country—Russian troops were still stationed there and were able to support the Social Democratic Party. But in the fall of 1917, he did not dare force a nation into union for fear of provoking anxiety elsewhere. The solution of a revolution "provoked" in Finland would have had the support of a majority of his colleagues, but he finally imposed on them respect for the right to self-determination and sent Stalin to Helsinki on November 14 to indicate official recognition of the Mannerheim government and of independence, which the Sovnarkom ratified by decree on November 17, 1917.[4] This recognition was not without ulterior motives, and Lenin noted: "We will conquer Finland, our union will be based on the solidarity of the exploited." The reconquest that Lenin contemplated was swift. On January 15, 1918, the Red Army, whose departure from their territory the Finns had not been able to obtain, lent a hand to a coup by the local Socialists, who were close to the Bolsheviks. A Council of Representatives of the People was installed in power in Helsinki under the leadership of Kullervo Manner. It contained fourteen ministers, among whom was Otto Kuusinen at education, who founded the Finnish Communist Party a few months later, became one of the central figures of the Comintern, and always remained a close "companion" of the USSR. On March 1, 1918, this government proclaimed the Socialist Republic of the Workers of Finland and signed a treaty of friendship with the Soviet state.

Lenin was triumphant: the "coup of Helsinki" that he had announced to the congress of railway workers a few days before it happened was, he thought, a justification for his strategy.[5] Acceptance of self-determination had demonstrated to the nations that Russia respected its commitments, but immediately thereafter, the "self-determination of the workers," as this manipulated revolution was christened, demonstrated that the working class was able to decide its own fate.

This revolutionary "model" was to have extraordinary success in Eastern Europe in the aftermath of the Second World War. In the meanwhile Lenin saw it as the proof that his approach was correct and that the revolution was spreading. However, the Finnish "model" of 1918 had only a brief existence. The Mannerheim government, which Russia had recognized on December 17, 1917, did not capitulate and called for help from Germany. Within a few weeks, Germany intervened, the Socialist Republic was annihilated, and its leaders fled to Moscow.[6]

The collapse of the Finnish revolution opened the dark series of revolutionary failures—Germany, Hungary, Bavaria, Austria. The restored independence of Finland, thanks to German help, was full of lessons for other nationalities, who understood that it was not enough to trust Lenin's commitments, but that it was also advisable to have access to the protection of other states in order to escape from plans for reconquest masked by the convenient pretext of the "will" of the working class.

The turbulent history of the Baltic countries illustrates this complicated interplay involving simultaneously national wills, Lenin's plans, and foreign interventions. In Estonia and Latvia, Soviet governments were installed, swept away by German military advances, and finally replaced by national governments. In Lithuania, a pro-German government took power in February 1918, and was left without support by the German defeat. The question for Lenin was how to settle these problems in a way that would avoid giving Russian policy the trappings of imperialism. Wouldn't the solution tried out in Finland be the one to apply everywhere? After the departure of German troops, it was attempted in Estonia, where Lenin backed the formation of the Commune of Workers of Estland, which the RSFSR recognized officially on December 7, 1918, and provided with financial and military assistance. At the same time, the Sovnarkom presided over the establishment in Latvia of a "government of workers', peasants', and *streltsy* (riflemen's) deputies" recognized and assisted by Russia like the "Commune of Estland." Its president, Pyotr Stuchka, founder of the Latvian Communist Party, later worked on the Executive Committee of the Comintern.

It was indeed close associates or even agents of the Bolsheviks whom Lenin used to organize "workers' self-determination." Should it be called self-determination or revolution? In any event the action of the Russian government was decisive. But as in Finland, it came up against other states that were unpersuaded by these manipulated revolutions. The British fleet in the Baltic supported the return to power of national governments in Estonia and Latvia, and the White general Nikolai Yudenich was to use the Baltic States as the base for his attacks against the Bolsheviks. After his defeat Lenin understood that reviving revolutions in the Baltic countries would not only conflict with national feeling but also would provoke Great Britain. The moment for revolution in the Baltics had passed swiftly, and British protection guaranteed real self-determination for those countries, that is, independence.

Lenin thought he had found a solution in Lithuania thanks to the departure of the German troops. He then supported the formation of a provisional revolutionary government presided by Vikenty Mitskevich (Kapsukas) and recognized it on December 22, 1918. In February 1919 he sponsored the union of Lithuania and Belorussia and the installation of a single government in Vilnius. The maneuver seemed to be a wise one, in part because Belorussia, where the Bolsheviks were active, was uncertain of itself, hesitating between Moscow and Warsaw in the name of old historical links. Lenin had understood that this was a real opportunity, the possibility of implementing the celebrated self-determination leading to union. Supported by Russia, the Belorussian Bolsheviks called for that union, and Lenin intended to make it a model. Belorussia was not incorporated into Russia, but on January 31, 1919, it was established as a sovereign Soviet Republic, tied "to the elder brother, the Russian state, by close federal bonds in the economic and political realms." The establishment of an independent republic of Belorussia was a decision easy for Lenin to make insofar as Bolshevism was well established there: the Bolsheviks had won 60 percent of the votes for the Constituent Assembly, as against 25 percent elsewhere. The Bolsheviks swiftly set up structured Communist organizations, a process favored as it happens by a political void. This decision had the substantial advantage, because the greater part of the population was favorable to Russia, of creating a real "sister republic."

Lenin also urged union with Lithuania, imposed in February 1919, when Lithuania was dreaming of independence. In May the Council for the Defense of Belorussia and Lithuania called for the military union of the Soviet Republics. The proposal was a clever one, because it apparently did not emanate from Russia, all the while serving Lenin's purposes. Lithuanian nationalism, it seemed, could be absorbed into this binational state in which the Lithuanians were a minority. Finally this solution provisionally removed Lithuania from the protection that Great Britain afforded to the real independence of the two other Baltic States.

Were it not for the expedition so incautiously launched against Poland in 1920 to expand the territory of the revolution, Lithuania probably would have remained within the Russian orbit for some time. But the Polish defeat changed everything, and two of Lenin's ambitions collapsed simultaneously in the summer of 1918: the revolution failed in Poland, and military defeat and the Treaty of Riga reduced Belorussia to its original territory. It preserved its independence, to be sure, but without Lithuania. In addition it had to delegate its international representation to Russia, which represented it at the Riga negotiations, thereby establishing limits to its presumed "independence." The fate of Belorussia was determined by the fact that it was a very particular case. Because it was practically devoid of nationalism, Lenin had chosen it as a model of the "internationalism" presiding over the relations between Moscow and the former subjects of the empire. This independence, which was granted rather than asked for, disconcerted the rest of the world, and no state found any interest in assuming responsibility for it.

In the Ukraine, the Bolsheviks had to deal with an immeasurably more complex situation. In December 1917 Russia granted recognition to a Popular

Republic of the Ukraine that had been proclaimed by the Rada (assembly) on November 7, which appeared to anticipate the development of a model of which Belorussia would thereafter be the best illustration. But the model failed. As soon as it was installed in power, the Ukrainian government turned against the Soviet regime and supported General Alexei Kaledin, who organized resistance among the Don Cossacks. The Bolsheviks were faced with the question of whether self-determination was intended to allow a nationality to fight against the revolution. Above all they were confronted with the problem of food supplies; they would need Ukrainian grain, but how could they force an independent state to deliver it to them? Worried by the pressure it was under, the Ukrainian government called for French protection. The Bolshevik regime retorted by supporting the establishment of a Bolshevik government in Kharkov, then by sending its troops to besiege Kiev, the seat of the independent government.

On January 26, Kiev was occupied by Russian troops, and a Soviet Ukrainian government was installed there for a short time. It was compelled to abandon the city two months later under the combined blows of the German army and Petliura's forces. It was then the turn of Hetman Paulo Skoropadsky to govern the Ukraine under German protection.

The condition of the country, the prey of attacks by the Reds, the Whites, and the supporters of Nestor Makhno who led a local peasant rebellion from the spring of 1918 to November 1920, was chaotic.[7] Kiev was constantly falling from one force to another, and terror was used by all sides. In 1919 Soviet authority was finally established in Kharkov under Pyatakov's leadership. He was a resolute opponent of self-determination, which he called "counterrevolution," and was in violent conflict with Lenin on the point. Lenin viewed Pyatakov as nothing but a "Great Russian chauvinist" who was compromising the relations of Russia with other peoples.

At the Eighth Party Congress in March 1919, battle raged between Lenin and the left wing of the party (Pyatakov, Yevgenya Bosh), which was demanding the abandonment of the principle of self-determination except where it was of benefit to the workers. With a view toward limiting Pyatakov's influence in the Ukraine, Rakovsky was sent to replace him. But in the chaotic circumstances, the status of the Ukraine remained uncertain until 1921, and the nationalists alternated between French and German protection in order to avoid a Russian takeover.

With the end of the Polish war and Makhno fleeing to Rumania, Russia was finally able to organize the Ukraine as it pleased. It fell to a Ukrainian, a supporter of respect for federal principles, to help establish the Ukrainian Soviet Republic. Convinced that Communism would emancipate his country, Nikolai Alexeievich Skrypnik had been one of the founders of the Ukrainian Communist Party and throughout the years of chaos had constantly fought against the centralizing positions of Pyatakov. For his part Lenin was convinced that centralism could only foster Ukrainian nationalism and permanently alienate the Ukraine from Russia. For this reason, in 1920 he forcefully intervened in the conflict dividing Ukrainian Communists, supported Skrypnik against

Pyatakov, and installed him as commissar of internal affairs in the Rakovsky government. At that point the Ukraine became the focus of another confrontation. As a Soviet Republic, should it enjoy some degree of sovereignty, as Skrypnik argued, or should Russian centralization win out, as Stalin thought?

A final case of self-determination added to the chaos of the period, that of Georgia and, by extension, all of Transcaucasia. In October 1917 a Caucasian commissariat chaired by the Georgian Social Democrat Yevgeni Gegechkori unified the region and awaited from the Constituent Assembly the organization of its relations with the nationalities. But after the dissolution of the Constituent Assembly, the Bolsheviks acted as rulers while asserting that they were not the successors of Imperial Russia. They ceded Batumi and the vilayets of Kars and Ardahan to Turkey, without consulting the Georgians or the Armenians who were thereby divested of territory. In outrage, they decided to secede and proclaimed the independence of the Transcaucasian Federal Republic on April 22, 1918. On May 26 it fell apart over national rivalries and because of the manipulations of the "Commune of Baku," a Bolshevik stronghold controlled by Shaumyan. Three independent states took its place: Georgia, governed by the Mensheviks; Armenia, governed by the Dashnaks; and Azerbaijan, controlled by the Mussavat Party (the latter, however, lost its principal city, Baku). The advance of Turkish troops ended Armenian and Azeri independence in the summer of 1920. Only Georgia remained, and it sought first German and then British protection.

In the Caucasus, Lenin was from the outset opposed to self-determination. The commune set up in Baku in 1918 was a sign of Bolshevik determination to retain a presence in the region. As for the role played by the Mensheviks in Georgia, it could only irritate Lenin. He had been in conflict with them since 1909, but until 1920 he had had to wait. However, all indications are that the principle of self-determination that he defended against Pyatakov and Bukharin was for him only a momentary concession. At the Eighth Party Congress, although he had criticized his extremism, he had told Pyatakov that he was "a thousand times right: unity is indispensable for us."

Lenin frequently reiterated his respect for the sovereignty of states established after the revolution, but he constantly attempted to limit that sovereignty. He demanded deliveries of grain from the Ukraine, and on May 22, 1919, he telegraphed Trotsky that he should "seize" grain from the Ukrainians to ensure Russian military security, and that to carry out the task, "we should send a battalion of Chekists, a few hundred Baltic sailors, a detachment of workers from Moscow or Ivanovo-Voznesentsk, and serious propagandists."[8] He then established a single system of defense for Russia, the Ukraine and the Belorussian-Lithuanian union, which gave Russian institutions the task of centralizing the army and communications.[9] The sovereignty of the republics was thereby significantly eroded. Most important the Russian Communist Party intervened in authoritarian ways in the activities of local parties. In March 1920 the Central Committee decided that its Ukrainian counterpart was anti-Russian and should be immediately dissolved. This was a manifestation of the "self-determination of the workers," trampling without hesitation on that of nationalities.

Until the summer of 1920, Lenin continued to believe that the revolution would spread to the West. The breakup of the former empire was a secondary problem in his view. What did a reduction in the size of Russian territory matter while the hope of establishing a world Soviet state survived? He had seen self-determination at first as a revolutionary weapon. From 1918 to 1920, he conceived of it principally in terms of security and food supplies for his starving country which was threatened from all sides. Lenin and Trotsky agreed that it was impossible to survive without Ukrainian grain and the oil and minerals of the Caucasus.

But after the defeat in Poland and the collapse of hopes for a revolution in the West, the problem was posed in new terms. "We are alone," Lenin observed, and we will be alone for a long time. What was to be done? He did not for a moment consider giving up. He had always repeated that revolutionaries did not engage in revolution simply to add another page to the great book of failed revolutions. The example of the Paris Commune, always referred to by Marxists, was for him the one that should not be followed. Although one day he had proudly said: "We will have lasted as long as the Commune," he no longer accepted the precedent in 1920. He was going to set Russia on a course for the long term, and for that it needed territory, resources, and borders that would enable it to survive. He had to reconstruct what the policy of self-determination had broken apart.

THE BEGINNINGS OF FEDERALISM

By 1918, with the adoption of a Constitution that defined the forms of federal organization, the framework of communal life inside the Russian Republic was set. In the debate on the circumstances under which self-determination could be exercised, Lenin had always specified that it could not apply to all peoples and certainly not to those who were in enclaves. The choice for them was between integration and the adoption of a status of some degree of autonomy.

In 1919, when it was still under assault from various enemies, the Soviet regime began to organize federal integration. The first nationality with which Moscow dealt were the Bashkirs, who had established a republic led by Ahmed Validov, the dissolution of which had been proclaimed by Admiral Kolchak. Russia took advantage of Kolchak's imperial attitude to sign an agreement in March 1919 recognizing the independence of the Bashkir Autonomous Republic. But the recognition was only temporary; it forged bonds of dependency that led a year later, in May 1920, to the annexation of Bashkiria, along with the Tatar Republic and the Chuvash Autonomous Territory. The pretext invoked, the protection of these small states from White imperialism, made it possible for Lenin to integrate into Russia peoples whose fierce nationalism seemed destined to cause it to lose their vast territory.

This policy was applied during the same period in the steppes, where the Kazakhs had formed a national government, and in the Caspian region, where the regime offered the small Kalmuk people, who were of Mongol origin and

Buddhists, support in their fight against Denikin's troops. In the name of the "self-determination of the workers," which Lenin invoked explicitly in this case, workers were called on to vote on their national future. It hardly mattered that there weren't really any workers among the Kalmuks. The result of this "self-determination" was the formation on November 25, 1920, of a Kalmuk Autonomous Region, which was immediately integrated into Russia. Using the same method, Russia absorbed the Workers' Commune of Karelia and the Kirghiz Autonomous Republic in August 1920, followed by the Mari Autonomous Region. Over the course of the succeeding months, the Russian Republic continued to incorporate regions that had taken advantage of the revolution to organize themselves into independent ministates. The Caucasus, where countless peoples lay claim to autonomy, the Crimea, regions populated by Yakuts, and so on, fell one after the other under Russian control between 1921 and 1923.

The procedure was the same everywhere. The Russian government supported when it did not provoke "proletarian self-determination" to the detriment of the national governments that had initially been established. The step was easily made from the national republic to the Soviet Republic. Soon thereafter union with Russia was imperative in the name of the security of the small state and its political kinship with the Soviet Republic. The methods used to reach this result were simple. Sometimes the Russian Communist Party supported—on occasion with military assistance—small local Communist parties and ensured their success over national leaders. Sometimes Russia put pressure on a national state, not bothering with pretexts. At the end of the process, it was claimed that the "will of the workers" had determined incorporation into the fold of the great state of the revolution.

In 1923 Russia integrated in this way seventeen autonomous entities, some of which possessed only limited administrative freedom in the way of autonomy, while others, called Republics, enjoyed at least theoretical political autonomy. The disintegration of Russian territory had been halted and territorial continuity restored. But the problem of what had been the real empire remained: the periphery, which possessed incalculable resources and had provided to the Russia of the czars borders that were considered secure. After Russian territory the imperial lands had to be reconquered.

RECONQUEST BY TREATY

With its entire periphery separated from Russia, Lenin believed it desirable and necessary to put an end to those secessions as well. In this case the situation was different from what the Russian government had confronted in reconquering the peoples in enclaves. Real independent states had been established, and in 1920, five of them were free from any possibility of Russian expansion because they had outside protection. This was the case for Poland, protected by its military force, and for the Baltic States and Finland, protection of which had been taken over from Germany by the Allies. Clearly the Soviet State, while denying its connection to the empire of the czars, would never accept this loss of peoples and territories to the west of Russia, which had pushed its border to the east and deprived it of control over the Baltic Coast. Less than two decades later, Lenin's successor would strive, successfully except for Finland, to recover the territory lost in 1917. Although Lenin appeared to resign himself to this loss of territory, he had tried to regain control between 1917 and 1920. But a succession of failures, Russian isolation in 1920, and the need to assume a place in the community of major nations after trying to undermine them with revolutions forced him to accept the reduction of Russian territory in the west.

Elsewhere, on the other hand, where the vigilance of the Western states was not functioning, he endeavored to recover what had been lost. Various nations had established states whose total independence they intended to preserve: the Ukraine, Belorussia, Azerbaijan, Armenia, Georgia, and the republics of Bukhara and Khiva. Because they called themselves "People's" or "Soviet" Republics, and because they were in negotiations with Russia, most of them hoped to establish equal relations with that country. Lenin encouraged them, offering to establish those relations on a contractual basis which they believed would be enduring. In October 1920 an article by Stalin set out in detail the policy advocated by Lenin, the establishment of friendly bilateral relations the terms of which would be defined by formal treaties.[10] This was an attractive policy, because it seemed to be a break with the idea of revolutionary integration. The relations between states that were at the heart of the system did indeed assume equality between contracting parties and respect for each one's independence. But at the outset, the bilateral treaty between the RSFSR and Azerbaijan signed on November 30, 1920, revealed Lenin's true purposes.

In April 1920 Azerbaijan was the scene of a drama that was replayed elsewhere years later. The government of the Mussavat Party was overthrown by Communists under Russian protection. They set up a Military Revolutionary Committee inspired by the Russian October, which called on Moscow for help in order to "prevent a counterrevolution." In his draft of theses on the nationalities question for the Second Congress of the Comintern, Lenin was already asserting that Russia and Azerbaijan were linked in a federation.[11] This declaration is dated July 5, whereas the treaty was not signed until five months later. But Lenin believed that the de facto situation should immediately be given official recognition.

This treaty, which was to serve as a model for all the others, provided for a military and economic union and for joint action in various areas, notably transportation and communications. Signed by Chicherin, the Russian commissar of foreign affairs, it seemed to be accompanied with all the guarantees of a treaty between states. But one-sided clauses (particularly Azerbaijan's obligation to establish its production plans, primarily for oil, in agreement with Russia) were drafted with no concern to respect the forms. In the end the document was closer to an ultimatum than a treaty of alliance between equals. The fact is that Lenin was obsessed by the need to restore Russian access to the oil of the

Caucasus, which was located in Azerbaijan. Without it Russia would be unable to survive.

The terms of the bilateral treaty with the Ukraine signed on December 28 were distinctly more cautious, but the Ukraine carried a good deal more weight than little Azerbaijan. In particular it was supported from outside by the government in exile that had some audience in the international community. As a result the treaty, drafted in terms that respected the sovereignty of the country, seemed to leave room for the genuine existence of a state. The Ukraine preserved control over its foreign policy, which Azerbaijan had had to surrender from the outset to Russia. The Bolsheviks heading the Ukrainian government, Rakovsky and Skrypnik, were of course loyal followers of Lenin, but they had little inclination to support a puppet government. Russia could also gain advantages from giving the Ukraine the appearance of a separate state. Indeed, Rakovsky's Ukraine symbolized the two facets of Russian policy, the state and the revolutionary program. Since 1919 Rakovsky had in fact been both head of the Ukrainian government and head of the southern department of the Comintern. Angelica Balabanov was secretary of the Comintern and, she writes, was also asked to replace him "as Ukrainian commissar of foreign affairs." To be sure, when the bilateral treaty was signed, the southern bureau of the Comintern had already been sent back to Moscow (where it would be promptly dissolved), and the separation between state and Comintern functions was in the process of being erased. It was nevertheless true that the autonomy of foreign policies was not yet a crucial problem, and in addition to the acknowledged independence of the Ukraine, Rakovsky embodied the bonds of solidarity of the Communists with Russia.

A few weeks later Belorussia signed a treaty with the RSFSR that resembled the one with the Ukraine, but some clauses suggested a lesser degree of independence. Moreover an additional agreement dealing with financial problems signed in June 1921 introduced into the Belorussian government a Russian representative who had a deciding voice on financial matters, and even on more general economic questions.

Barely visible bonds were thus often forged behind the mask of alliance agreements. With the exception of the Ukraine in the early stages, Russia asserted its authority over neighboring independent states step by step, and the process provoked no crises.

Lenin could feel satisfied. His publicly stated intention was to develop friendly relations with the former Russian possessions without awakening the suspicion that Russia would want to go beyond those ties. The head of government placed that policy within the framework of normal relations between states, thereby confirming for the outside world that Russia had become a state like other states. He was eager to reassure his immediate interlocutors as well as the rest of the world, but his real intention was nothing other than the reconstruction of the land that had been broken up.

Were it not for Georgia, this political double game might have developed peacefully. But Georgia turned out to be a recalcitrant negotiator, and Lenin lost control over relations with it. In this particular case, he came up against Stalin, who had a personal policy for Georgia. Its objective, to bring Georgia back into the Russian orbit, was, to be sure, the same as that pursued by Lenin, but the means were very different. With Stalin concealment of the goal was replaced by a direct and brutal strategy of conquest.

RECONQUEST BY FORCE

From the outset Lenin found it impossible to act in Georgia as he had elsewhere. He was not dealing with complicit Bolsheviks, but with a government of Mensheviks and a nation determined to preserve the independence it had recovered. Was it possible to accuse Mensheviks, Socialists, of threatening the revolution? They were furthermore very active on the international scene, having secured de jure recognition for their country from many states, and even de facto recognition from the RSFSR by the treaty of May 7, 1920.[12] European social democrats such as Henri de Man and Emile Vandervelde traveled to Georgia to hail the coming to power of "true" Socialists and repeated over and over again that Bolshevik Russia could not possibly cross the Kura, the river on the border. For Lenin, Georgia thus posed two challenges. He considered it an outpost of the Entente on his borders. How could he Bolshevize Azerbaijan and Armenia if the third Transcaucasian state was outside his authority and the Russian model? Finally, could the unified Transcaucasia that Lenin intended to bring about put up with this Social Democratic enclave?

From Lenin attempting tactical maneuvers to the supporters of the most brutal solutions, all the Bolsheviks agreed that the case of Georgia was weakening Russia. The question was how Georgia could be weakened in return. An advocate of resolution by force, Stalin, whose special knowledge of Georgia no one dared challenge, defined what was at stake with precision: "The Caucasus is decisive for the revolution, because it is a source of raw materials and food products. But it is also decisive because of its position between Europe and Asia, Europe and Turkey, because economic and strategic routes of considerable importance go through it. We must control the region."[13]

These remarks, which were adopted by all the Bolsheviks, revealed a change in perspective. In 1917 the foundation of the Soviet state was the revolution. In 1921, on the contrary, the Soviet state organized and defined itself in terms of strategic interests and economic resources.

Lenin had three assets that he could use to reintegrate rebel Georgia into Soviet territory: the presence of the Eleventh Army that had conquered Baku in 1920 and was camped in the Caucasus; the May 7 treaty, which no doubt recognized Georgian independence, but contained a secret clause compelling Georgia to legalize the Communist Party and ensure it total freedom of action; and finally the Caucasian bureau of the Central Committee (*Kavburo*) working in liaison with the Eleventh Army and preparing the reconquest of the country.

Georgia was subjected to twofold pressure, internally from the Communists, and externally from the Kavburo. Lenin, who was hesitating over what tack to take, was also exposed to the aggressive impatience of his colleagues.

Particularly Ordzhonikidze, also a Georgian, who argued from his knowledge of Georgia, and Sergei Kirov, both of whom wanted to send in the Eleventh Army to "protect" the Georgian Communists. This would have been more or less a repetition of the Azerbaijan scenario. Even Chicherin, though more moderate, claimed the right to intervene because, he said, the Georgians were constantly violating the May 7 treaty. The model proposed was clearly the one that had prevailed in Azerbaijan: provoke an internal insurrection and intervene to respond to the appeal for help from the "true" revolutionaries, the Communists. On May 5, 1920, Lenin sent a telegram to Ordzhonikidze prohibiting him from "self-determining Georgia," but then he agreed to do it.[14] The precedent of Azerbaijan suggested that the operation was feasible and would go relatively unnoticed. But before giving his agreement, he had hesitated for a long time, and the debates in the Central Committee had been particularly stormy. Once the order was given, the operation was efficiently carried out. The Eleventh Army entered Georgia on February 15. On February 25 Tblisi fell, and the Soviet Republic was proclaimed. In appearance everything had been simple; the success of the military expedition was unquestionable. On May 21, 1921, Georgia in turn signed the bilateral agreement that Russia imposed on the Soviet Republics and thus seemed to be aligned with the others.

The Georgian case, which had been much more difficult than the others, remained difficult after the signature of the treaty. It was also revealing of the difficulties Lenin was experiencing in Russia. For these two reasons, it is worth considering in some detail.

First of all, the debate over the Sovietization of Georgia demonstrates the special concern that Lenin had at the time for the Russian "state." He feared that a premature or excessively blatant operation would provoke a British reaction that would once again threaten the international security of Russia and compromise its efforts to join the community of nations, which was a priority in early 1921. He was also concerned about the reactions of Turkey, with which Russia had begun negotiations that would lead to a treaty of friendship on March 16, 1921. In this political vision of a Russian return to the international scene, it was in Lenin's view more important to seal a pact of friendship with Mustafa Kemal's Turkey (with no prospect of a revolution, it goes without saying) than to drive the Georgian Mensheviks from power. He finally gave in to his colleagues' urgings because Chicherin had convinced him that Great Britain would agree to leave the whole of the Caucasus within the Russian sphere of influence. Lloyd George had said as much to Krasin. What London wanted was for Russia to confine itself to that sphere and to forget all its hopes for revolution elsewhere, particularly in Europe. In short, what was implicitly being negotiated around Georgia was the recognition of the territorial interests of Russia in exchange for social peace and the end of the revolutionary enterprise in Europe. The bargain made with Mustafa Kemal was of the same nature; he would close his eyes to the reconquest of the Caucasus, but Lenin would abandon Enver Pasha and the Turkish Communists as the price for the agreement. In the end Lenin gave the green light to the operation of bringing Georgia to heel because his colleagues had been able to demonstrate to him that it would not frighten the capitalist world, which consciously accepted the terms of the implicit bargain that it concealed.

The Georgian affair is no less interesting for what it reveals about the development of the Russian political system at the time. Two instruments played a decisive role, the Kavburo and the Eleventh Army. The former was established in April 1920 to coordinate the activities of Communist organizations in the Caucasus and was placed under the authority of Dzerzhinsky, who very soon secured unchallenged authority, informing Lenin about local problems that the latter was in no position to verify. The Kavburo also profited from the autonomy that the Eleventh Army had arrogated to itself. When Lenin gave the authorization to intervene on February 14, 1921, the Kavburo and the Eleventh Army had already begun operations on the spot forty-eight hours earlier. Trotsky was also a victim of this quasi-independence of the organs of power in the Caucasus. As commissar of war, he was compelled to undertake an investigation on February 21 (nine days after the beginning of operations) to find out how the decision had been made in the field and who had made it.[15] Although the Soviet state was growing stronger during this period, it is obvious that some dilution of central authority was showing up at the periphery, where those who had some institutional authority (like Ordzhonikidze with the Kavburo) acted like veritable proconsuls, as the Georgian crisis of 1923 was amply to demonstrate. Moreover, Lenin's representatives in the field had no hesitation in providing him with inaccurate information in order to secure his agreement. In February, Ordzhonikidze assured him that the Caucasus was beset by disorders due to a conflict between Georgians and Armenians and that the intervention necessary to put an end to them would be limited. After the intervention the Georgian Communists who had in fact prepared it, Budu Mdivani and Filip Makharadze, denied that the conflict used as a pretext had ever existed and attributed authorship of the scheme to the Kavburo. Lenin soon understood that this affair, even though he too thought that Georgia should return to the Russian sphere of influence, was more manipulated by his colleagues on the spot than it was controlled by him. He was in favor of caution, and again on March 3, he sent a message recommending that Ordzhonikidze find a compromise with the Menshevik president, Noi Zhordania, for the formation of an acceptable coalition instead of "imposing the Russian model." But he was not heard.[16]

Forced Sovietization was also carried out without restraint or precautions. Emissaries from the Cheka arrived from Moscow to assist in establishing the new order. The Georgian Party was placed under the authority of a loyal associate of Ordzhonikidze, Mamia Orakhelashvili, and within a few months, Georgia took on the air of an occupied country. The consequences would soon become apparent and would justify after the fact all Lenin's advice to move cautiously.

The question that arises here is that of the relative weakness of Lenin in dealing with Ordzhonikidze's encroachments on his authority. Stalin was just as guilty of this in 1921, but Lenin was as yet unaware of that and trusted his judgment.

The explanation seems to lie principally in the importance that Lenin attached at the time to problems of government. Because Russia had to become a state like other states, carrying on normalized international relations, he focused on putting that in place, which involved on his part a sharp change of direction and considerable effort. He was no longer operating in the dual register of state and revolution; he was working with reference to the long term not the provisional, and everything had to be built from the ground up. Leaders had to be specialists (in the state as well as in the Comintern and in Communist organizations), and managers had to be trained for specific tasks. In the early stages of this general transformation, it was natural that a degree of uncertainty would show up in decision making and practices. Russia's size, which had just increased in 1921, did not make this adaptation any easier.

Nevertheless the Georgian matter seemed to have been settled by the summer, and the year ended with a series of similar treaties (after the one that had begun the list, Khiva, on September 20, 1920) with Bukhara on March 4, and Armenia on September 30, 1921. The language of self-determination, which had attracted support for the revolution, seemed to have paid off. Russia had been reconciled by treaty with the imperial possessions that had at first broken away. Further, these treaties were at first sight not open to much criticism, even though the means used to secure them were in some cases violent. They established classic alliances between equal states and dealt with military and economic cooperation. They said nothing about a common foreign policy. But behind that impeccable legal facade, two elements that doomed it in advance and prefigured the final stage were already visible in 1921. First was the military aspect. The treaties spoke of cooperation in this area, but the Red Army was omnipresent and had already brought about the coming unity. As for independent diplomatic activity, only the Ukraine was in a position to maintain appearances for a time. Two Ukrainian representatives were present at the signing of the Treaty of Riga, but they were included in a combined Russian-Ukrainian delegation, which already suggested a semifederal arrangement. At the signing of the Russo-Turkish agreement of March 1921 settling the border problems of the Transcaucasian Republic, the presence of delegates from that entity was certainly anticipated, but all its clauses were negotiated by Russia alone, and the Caucasus representatives did not make their appearance until the signing of the Treaty of Kars.

The fiction of the independence of the republics was hardly convincing to European governments. This is why only Russia was invited to the Genoa conference in 1922. The Ukraine did not see things the same way and asked to be represented, but it was fighting alone, because everything had already been decided in Moscow. On January 27 Mikhail Kalinin, chairman of the All-Russian Central Executive Committee, declared that Russia would represent the interests of the eight Soviet Republics in Genoa. The decision was made by the CEC; there was nothing for the republics to do but to give way before Moscow's authority. On February 22 they gave the RSFSR the mandate to speak and sign in their name all documents at the Genoa conference.[17] The fiction of independence had fallen to pieces.

The bilateral alliances between equal states bore a strong resemblance to pacts of union. Yet Lenin was not entirely satisfied, because he was confronted with two problems. Formally independent states established a context that favored the renewal or development of tendencies toward real independence, and the consequent weakening of Russia; on the other hand, conflicts arising from nationalistic frustrations were coming to the fore at the same time, both in the Russian Republic and in the Soviet Republics.

Domestically, the opposition broke out in the Communist Party in the Tatar region. Sultan Galiev bluntly posed a question that had come up in a less explicit form at the Baku congress: Did proletarian internationalism have any meaning when it was applied to relations between nations at unequal levels of development? He answered in the negative, opening the way to dissidence that was all the more serious because it called into question the solidarity of the working class.

A nationalist rebellion began in Central Asia, whose fighters, the Basmachis, threatened the policy of union throughout the region.[18] Their movement was not fully defeated until years later, and until then, the Soviet government experienced insecurity on this border as well.

Finally Georgia continued its opposition to Russian policy. Brought into line and occupied, beginning in the summer of 1921 it resisted through the voices of the local Communists who a short time earlier had been in favor of Russian intervention. They were the very men (Makharadze and Mdivani) who in the past had sided with Rosa Luxemburg in her condemnation of Lenin's indulgence toward national movements. Confronting intense Russian pressure, they suddenly remembered that they were Georgians and claimed they were defending a policy based on the national interests of their republic. On December 13, 1921, Alexis Svanidze, Stalin's brother-in-law, complained, "Ordzhonikidze is beating us with the heavy bludgeon of central authority."[19] Georgian complaints denouncing infringements on the sovereignty of the republic proliferated in Moscow. Early in the year, Lenin had tried to impose a more gradual integration in Georgia, but by year's end he thought the time had come to organize the reconquered territory in a final way. It was necessary to provide Russia, after War Communism, with the borders, institutions, and economic resources of a consolidated state. The transitional phase of bilateral treaties was over, and the time for union had come. Georgian complaints and internal party debates were of little concern. Russia was about to become a federal state while endeavoring at the same time to demonstrate that it was no longer the empire of yesterday. Procedures for unification and definitions of ties all had to be based on a new Constitution, but before defining the legal framework of the future Russia, it was advisable to include all the still disparate states in the new structure, which would become a federation.

FORCED UNION

Union of the independent republics with Russia was imperative in 1922 principally because the economic disorganization that had led to the adoption of the

NEP had to be gradually overcome by a rational use of existing resources. Economic unity would thus help to achieve political unity.

The movement was begun in 1921. As a first step, Lenin encouraged regional associations that would be the source of another crisis in the Caucasus. The Armenians and Azeris accepted the principle of the development of regional ties, but Georgia challenged it; it intended to lead its own existence on a footing of equality with all the republics. Like the other republics of the Caucasus, in the course of the year 1921 it had been compelled to accept the uniform rules and single leadership in the region presiding over the restoration of rail transport and foreign trade. But remaining customs barriers and different currencies indicated the intent of local leaders to preserve a separate identity. Lenin therefore gave Ordzhonikidze the task of establishing unity in a Transcaucasia that he found too unsettled and complicated. Assisted by Dzerzhinsky and Molotov, Ordzhonikidze worked out with the Caucasian Bureau and the central authorities a plan for a Transcaucasian federation.[20] The local elites were hardly consulted. The Georgian Communists again appealed to Lenin, not only against a formal union that they considered bureaucratic and useless, but even more against the method used, a federal process decided on in Moscow with no consultation of the national leadership and imposed by force. This time Lenin was entirely on the side of Ordzhonikidze and the Caucasian Bureau. At the Tenth Party Congress in Moscow, factions had just been banned; opposition to the federalization of the Caucasus was factional activity, in other words opposition to the decisions of the majority of the party. Threatened with expulsion, the Georgian opposition had to capitulate and agree to the adoption of a federal status by the conference for the unity of the Caucasus in Tblisi on March 12, 1922. The Transcaucasian Soviet Federal Socialist Republic was born.

Imposed on a reluctant Georgia, the federation fostered undying resentment in the country. It did leave some autonomy to the three republics, but that was soon limited by a succession of treaties with Russia. Good Communists and Internationalists until March 1921, the Georgian leaders did not really accept what had been imposed on them and continued to submerge Lenin with protests and to attempt to mobilize their compatriots against a Caucasian federation behind which they saw in fact emerging a federal Soviet state. Lenin remained deaf to their appeals. Moreover the Georgian Communist leaders, Makharadze and Mdivani, installed in power after the Sovietization of 1921, were summoned to Moscow, dismissed, and replaced by a new Central Committee judged to be more pliable. It is customary to attribute to Stalin the violence of the methods used against the Georgians. In his excellent biography of Stalin, Robert Tucker suggests that as early as the middle of 1921, for various reasons helping to keep Lenin away from things (summer vacation in 1921, illness from December 1921 to March 1922), Stalin made many decisions on his own and that, for this reason, his later conflict with Lenin was already taking shape.[21] But the entire unfolding of the Caucasian crisis on the contrary shows that, in 1921 and 1922, until the major stroke that left him paralyzed in December 1922, Lenin considered Stalin his confidant and played a personal role in the matter of the Caucasus. In late 1921, and until the dismissal of the Georgian Communists, he very explicitly supported the actions of the Caucasian Bureau and rejected any discussion of two questions of principle: the necessity for the unity imposed on Transcaucasia with a view toward integration into the Soviet Federation in preparation and the fact that the organization of the Caucasus was being decided from above, not by the rank and file or according to national inclinations.

In the conflict between Moscow and the Georgians, the views underlying the program imposed on Tblisi were not independent from the changes taking place at the same time throughout Russia. The Soviet state was being built in order to keep the revolutionary achievement of 1917 alive. It had to have sufficient resources not only to last but also to impose itself on the external world. For that purpose reconquest and rational organization of land and resources were indispensable.

It is impossible to overestimate the depth of the transformation carried out by Lenin in 1921. As soon as he stopped believing in the possibility of exporting the revolution, he devoted all his efforts to building the Soviet state and mobilized all the resources at his disposal—party, Cheka, army—for that purpose. Although he had been full of counsels of moderation for Ordzhonikidze in early 1921, having to do essentially with the "pace" of the Sovietization of Georgia, he had disapproved of neither the intention nor especially the result. And when the dispute over the Transcaucasian Federation brought the Georgians to seek his arbitration, far from softening the position of the Caucasian Bureau, he emphasized the authority of Moscow and the party over an unruly rank and file. He therefore expressed his agreement with the dismissal of the Georgian Communists and their replacement by men obedient to decisions from the center. It was Lenin's view of the party, one he had been developing since the beginning of the century, that was implemented in this period in order to unify the Caucasus. Democratic centralism imposed authority from above even if the rank and file might be consulted (but when they disagreed, as the Georgians did in the spring of 1921, they were dismissed).

By late in the year 1921, a whole series of measures—contractual agreements, pressure from the party and the Cheka, and so on—had put an end to national resistance everywhere. The Russian Communist Party exercised complete authority over all the Communist organizations of the periphery. Economic necessity was a powerful means of (not only an argument for) centralization. For example, the Baku region, so vital for Moscow because of its oil resources, was placed under the direct economic authority of institutions of the RSFSR.

By early winter 1922, Russia was dealing only with Sovietized republics. They were few in number—the Ukraine, Belorussia, Transcaucasia—and their integration was only a matter of working out the details. They had lost the prerogatives of independence in all areas; what reasons would they have for resisting?

WHAT KIND OF FEDERATION?
THE CONSTITUTIONAL CONFLICT

The success of the enterprise of "recovery of the lost lands" was not without an echo of the "recovery of Russian lands" carried out by the monarchs after their victories over the Tatar invader, which led in less than four centuries to the formation of the powerful empire of the czars. In 1922 this success was unquestionable; there is no doubt that it resulted from the general vision of Russia that Lenin had developed after the failure in Poland in the summer of 1920. Then he had stated, "While recognizing federation as an intermediate stage on the way to complete unity, it is indispensable to make federal bonds constantly tighter."[22] When he spoke of federation, Lenin did not have a precise model in mind. In his view practice would determine what ties were sufficient, and he in fact thought of two kinds of federal organization: one, *contractual*, would link the RSFSR to republics maintaining some degree of sovereignty; the other, *organic*, was based on the autonomy of national entities integrated into the Russian Republic. In this view the first model applied to the Ukraine and Transcaucasia, the second to the Tatar region and Bashkiria. Reality, however, was more complex; it turned out that in the early 1920s there was a third category which covered Belorussia and Turkestan, states combining contractual relations and autonomy.

It was primarily the different reactions of the interested parties that were important and helped to forge Lenin's policy. In 1920 and 1921, Belorussia accepted not only the development of federal links, but also a dynamic view of those links that would one day lead to complete unity. The Georgians and Ukrainians, for their part, were recalcitrant. And Ukrainian opposition brought Lenin to think that it was necessary to speed the development of common institutions and to federalize the nation as a whole in order to break down resistance. He said this bluntly at the Eleventh Party Congress, held from March 27 to April 2, 1922. He spoke there of "breaking down" the opposition of the Ukrainians that was being expressed even within the party.

At the Tenth Party Congress in March 1921, the general line on national questions had been defined by Stalin, who presented the report on the subject. But at that time he was still the loyal if not obsequious spokesman for Lenin's views, and his report did nothing but express them.[23] The projected federation, he explained, was the framework for union; its model would be the Russian Federal Republic which would also one day serve as the model for a future world federation of socialist states. He was reiterating an idea expressed by Lenin in 1918: "The federation that we are building will be a step toward the unity of the different nationalities of Russia in a single, democratic, and centralized Soviet state." Hence there was no disagreement in early 1922 between Stalin's report and Lenin's long-term national vision.

But the program had to be put into practice, and a constitutional commission was set up on August 10, 1922, with the central leadership represented by Stalin, Molotov, V. V. Kuibyshev, Ordzhonikidze, Rakovsky, and Sokolnikov, and including representatives from the five republics directly concerned. Stalin prepared a draft, read it to the commission, and sent it to the Central Committees of the Parties of the republics in September. The draft constitution was faithful in every respect to the report presented to the Tenth Party Congress. As anticipated it extended the model of the RSFSR to the still independent republics. They were to adhere "formally" to the Soviet state and would be granted within it, like the nationalities already included, an autonomous status. The Communist parties of Azerbaijan, Armenia, and Belorussia yielded. They could hardly do otherwise, because the proposal emanated from a commission whose principal member had been general secretary of the party since April 1922, a post to which Lenin had personally appointed him. Democratic centralism required that this proposal from above be accepted.

But things were entirely different in the Ukraine and Georgia. In the Ukraine, Nikolai Skrypnik, then people's commissar of justice in the independent republic, forcefully protested against the proposed constitution. He rejected, and Rakovsky supported him, the conception of a centralized state which had nothing to do, he said, with Communism, and he demanded the abandonment of the centralizing federal plan in favor of a confederal framework. This Old Bolshevik enjoyed great authority in the party. His entry into the battle for respect of the rights of nations made as much of an impression on Lenin as the fierce resistance of the Georgian Communists. In a sense, Skrypnik had to enter into the controversy for Lenin to react, because from one crisis to the next, he had grown more or less habituated to the recriminations of the Georgian Communists. But in September 1922, their discontent turned into open opposition. The Central Committee of the Communist Party of Georgia rejected the draft proposal and insisted on its intent to preserve the marks of sovereignty. This blunt rejection and Skrypnik's emphasis on the need to maintain the status quo in relations between Moscow and the republics had the same intention, although the tone was different, diplomatic in Kiev, aggressive in Tblisi.

In September 1922 Lenin was still feeling the effects of the stroke he had suffered in May, the first of a series that would finally bring him down. He was still resting, but was not inactive, as indicated by letters to colleagues on the most varied subjects (the deportation of intellectuals or the coming elections in England).[24] Kept away from public affairs by order of his doctors, he followed them with passionate interest and commented on them. He returned to active life in late September, listened to the reactions of the Georgians and Ukrainians, and above all read Stalin's proposal. For the first time, he condemned not only Stalin's hasty behavior—"he jumps the gun"—but more important the basis of his proposals. "Autonomization" is a mistake, he said, that can only "be grist to the mill of independence supporters."[25] Indefatigable in spite of his illness, he then drafted his own outline of a proposed federation uniting equal republics to the RSFSR, but not assimilating them. "We recognize that we have equal rights with the Ukrainian SSR . . . and are ready to join with it on equal terms in a new federation." Lenin went on to say that this federation should have its own institutions of government, independent of those of Russia, standing above Russia, as well as above the other republics. In particular, he explained, there must be a government and a Central Executive Committee specific to the federation. Aware that peace among the nations was at stake, he decided to take charge of the whole matter.

Stalin was angry at the disavowal and complained to his colleagues on the Politburo: "Lenin is playing at national liberalism." He even went as far as challenging his views, saying, "The establishment of an Executive Committee for the federation alongside that of the RSFSR is, in my opinion, unacceptable." Once he had expressed his ill humor, Stalin gave in; amended his draft, taking into account Lenin's observations; and presented an irreproachable document to the Central Committee on October 6. As a skilled tactician, he carefully refrained from mentioning the recent conflict or from drawing attention to the change in the proposal, in which the word "autonomization" had disappeared to be replaced by "federation," and suggested that what was in fact a radical change in perspective was nothing but a more carefully expressed formulation.

Lenin was satisfied with the new proposal and buried the whole affair. He merely noted in a letter to Kamenev that he "declared war on Great Russian chauvinism" and that "the chairmanship of the Central Executive Committee should rotate among a Russian, a Ukrainian, a Georgian, and so on."[26]

On October 6 the proposal signed by Stalin, Ordzhonikidze, Molotov, and Myasnikov was submitted to the Central Committee and immediately approved. The conflict between center and periphery appeared to be over, along with the dispute over principles between Lenin and Stalin. However, peace on both fronts would not last long. But before getting to that, it is important to define with precision what inspired the two protagonists, Lenin and Stalin, in September 1922.

As in a number of earlier debates on the national question, the basic differences that appeared between them in 1922 should not be overestimated. Although Stalin proposed a centralizing project, it was close to the general views of Lenin, who had and would maintain until the end a centralized conception of the future of nationalities in the Soviet state. But his attitude was tempered by tactical concerns; in that respect, the Bolshevik leader, who was always a remarkable tactician, was true to himself. If he wanted to give equal status to every nation, this was not because he suddenly saw great interest or particular value in the idea and the reality of nations. They were not what counted in his view, but the consequences that the divergences that were appearing might have for the stability of the Soviet state. His concern in 1922 was in fact the same as it had been in 1913. He intended to convince national minorities of the virtues of internationalism—which in 1913 meant "common struggle," and in 1922 "common life"—and thereby to bring them one day to forget their national sentiments in favor of a conscious class solidarity. He criticized Stalin not for the content of his proposal but for his timetable. It was too soon, he thought, to promote union, because national sentiments remained strong. The best way to make them wither away was to grant them, for a while, some respect. Lenin's condemnation of Stalin's proposal was thus based on both tactical and pedagogical considerations. At the same time, he did not accept the vociferations of the Georgians (the more moderate attitude of Skrypnik, on the other hand, did not provoke his condemnation), and for the time he supported Stalin against them.

Symmetrically, the conciliatory attitude of Stalin can be explained by the fact that he had clearly understood that, at bottom, his views and Lenin's were identical. Like Lenin he believed that the future would confirm his proposal. Moreover, like Lenin he was first of all pragmatic and cynical. He remained convinced that the new law in the process of development had little importance in the face of a reality that would always win out over documents. Reality was the human and political power of Russia. It could not help but impose its preeminence in the Federation. In the face of the de facto inequality between Russia and the various other republics, legal equality would carry little weight. History was obviously to confirm that point of view.

THE GEORGIANS' FINAL BATTLE

Like the Central Committee in Moscow, all the national parties adopted the proposal amended by Stalin. But while giving their agreement, the Georgian Communists added a change that conditioned their acceptance. Setting themselves on the same level as the Ukrainians (they had fought together against the proposal), they demanded that Georgia enter the Federation on its own and not as a member of the Transcaucasian group, which would give it only indirect sovereignty.[27] The duo of Stalin and Ordzhonikidze, who because of their national origins were deemed the only experts on the Georgian question, had an entirely different view. For Stalin the Caucasus was so diverse in nationalities that it needed an intermediate body in order to prevent conflicts among nations in the region from being transposed to the federal level.[28] Moscow, he said, could not serve as the recipient of complaints and dissensions among the peoples of the Caucasus. He therefore maintained that the Transcaucasian Federation was alone authorized to enter the Union, which meant that the Georgians, and they understood this, would have merely a status of autonomy.

The entire month of October 1922 was marked by the battle of the Georgians on two fronts. In Georgia, they fought Ordzhonikidze, representative of the center in the republic. This was open warfare of extraordinary brutality among the protagonists. Armed with Moscow's support, Ordzhonikidze used classic techniques; he threatened, dismissed, and replaced the opposition with men whom he considered safe but who in the end turned against him. Lenin's old slogan, "purge," was applied wholesale by his representative on the spot. But the Georgians also fought in Moscow, appealed to Lenin, Bukharin, Kamenev, sent telegram after telegram, sent emissaries, and accused Ordzhonikidze of using force, including physical violence, against them.

Lenin, who considered the matter to be settled, greeted these complaints with outrage. He sent a stinging telegram to the petitioners, asking them to resolve the conflict "in a loyal and decent manner," and to address themselves to the secretariat of the Central Committee of the Russian Party, under the leadership of none other than Stalin, an unconditional supporter of Ordzhonikidze's policies and methods in Georgia. Being passed on to the judgment of the men who were using violence against them further mobilized the Georgians who, far from disarming, continued to resist. To make a gesture, Lenin, along with Bukharin and Kamenev, who were as indifferent as he to the Georgians' complaints, decided to send an investigating commission to the scene. The Georgians once again were faced with resolute opponents. Stalin, the general secretary of the party, had complete discretion in setting up this commission, which he placed under the authority of Dzerzhinsky whose feelings toward the Georgians (who had also complained about the Cheka) were not particularly tender. The commission had no contact with the rebels; it accepted the arguments put to it by Ordzhonikidze, and concluded that all responsibility for the crisis lay with the nationalists.[29]

Lenin had already begun to doubt what was being reported to him and asked close collaborators to inform him. His fragile health had probably not been helped by what he sensed about the behavior of Stalin and Ordzhonikidze. He was bedridden by late November, but despite suffering several strokes beginning on December 20, he wanted once again to resume control of the situation. In his view the national question was too important to be left to those whom he now started to call, referring to Gogol, *derzhimordy* ("bureaucratic brutes") or *velikoderzhavniki* ("national chauvinists").[30] He then considered nationalities policy one last time and wrote what was to be his final contribution to the discussion of this problem.[31] These were notes intended for the Twelfth Party Congress to be held the following March. He still counted on recovering, as he had so many times, and restoring order to a Central Committee in which some members were going astray. "I have been," he wrote, "very remiss with respect to the workers of Russia for not having intervened energetically and decisively enough in the notorious question of autonomization. . . . It is quite natural that in such circumstances the 'freedom to secede from the union' by which we justify ourselves will be a mere scrap of paper, unable to defend the non-Russians from the onslaught of that true Russian man, the Great Russian chauvinist, in substance a true brute and scoundrel, such as the typical Russian bureaucrat is."

Lenin's troubled reaction did nothing to slow the course of events. On November 21, despite continuing Georgian protests, the special commission of the Russian Central Committee made the timetable for national integration public, providing for publication of the definitive text of the new Constitution, followed by the signature of the act of union. On November 30, while Lenin was struggling to put his objections in writing, the Politburo adopted the resolution on the "fundamental principles of the Union." Article one provided that the Transcaucasian Federation was to join the Union. The Central Committee approved. The Georgians, whom no one had bothered to consult, held to their positions. But this time they were alone. In the Ukraine the Seventh Congress of Soviets came out in favor of the union treaty on November 13. The Federal Republic of Transcaucasia gave itself a constitution drafted and passed in haste and decided to join. Belorussia did the same on December 18. On December 30, finally, a treaty established the USSR. Its signatories were the Russian Republic and the three republics of the Ukraine, Belorussia, and Transcaucasia.

Temporarily paralyzed by the strokes that he suffered on December 13 and 22, Lenin pondered and grasped that one of the weak points in the policies adopted had been his own conviction that those involved were by definition, as

Communists, Internationalists. In considering the cases of Stalin and Ordzhon-ikidze, he noted that Communists from national minorities could conduct themselves like "Russian ultranationalists." This raised the general question of national leaders who wished to have their origins forgotten. Subsequent events would show that on this point as well Lenin's intuition was well founded.

The Constitution of the Union was drawn up in the following months by a commission chaired by Kalinin.[32] The All-Russian Central Executive Committee adopted it on July 6, 1923, at a time when the paralyzed Lenin was no longer participating in public life; the Second All-Union Congress of Soviets approved it on January 31, 1924, a few short days after his death.[33]

In literal terms this Constitution was in accordance with Lenin's wishes. The Union ratified the voluntary association of legally equal states that retained, according to article four, the right to withdraw freely. In joining the Union, the states were not giving up their sovereignty. The proposal drafted by Lenin was thus respected against Stalin's version that limited the states to the mere status of autonomy. But although he seemed to have won out in the struggle, Stalin had just as much, because the republics entering the Union turned over to it major areas of responsibility.

The interest of this document lies not only in its precise organization of the territory that had come out of the revolution. It also has to do with the fact that, unlike the 1918 Russian Constitution, the 1924 Union Constitution was intended as a permanent document covering a defined and closed territory. The 1918 Constitution anticipated dynamic developments in both time and space; it served as a transitional framework for a state that was equally transitional, and was intended to assist any nation that wanted to associate with that state. The 1924 Constitution confirmed the existence and the contours of an existing state and affirmed its rights. To be sure the first part of the document, the declaration on the founding of the Union, said that access to the Union was open not only to existing republics but also to those that would be established in the future. The territory was thus not definitively established and could be expanded. The same declaration specified that the Union, in a "world divided into two camps, the camp of capitalism and the camp of socialism," was "surrounded" by capitalism, which justified the unity that had been accomplished and implied the existence of secure borders. Was this not what Lenin had wanted in 1920 and 1921 when he signed all the treaties guaranteeing the borders of the Soviet state, with Poland, but also with Turkey, Iran, and Afghanistan?

In the end this Constitution combined the two opposing tendencies that we have seen at work in Lenin's policies since 1917: the desire for universality that gave the Soviet state its territorially open, transitory, and open character (the policy of the first three years that the failure in Poland had defeated); and the desire to preserve what existed, which led the Soviet state to assert its permanent character, to turn in on itself, and to defend itself, confirmed by the stabilized situations on the borders in 1921 and 1922. But the Constitution, and this is the interesting point, replaced the successive shifts of Lenin's policies with a synthesis of the two orientations.

It cannot be forgotten that this basic law was a monument bringing to an end both debates and a revolution. Beyond the letter of the document, those debates shed light on the intentions of the drafters. And here, too, we must recognize the duality underlying it. It accounted for a definitive fact, the triumph of the revolution and the setting in motion of a transformation of political and economic structures destined to change society and social consciousness. At the same time, it was a transitional constitution insofar as it was federal and established the state by combining different nations. The purpose of the revolution and of the Soviet state, in its 1918 or 1924 form, was, while taking into account a situation that was still in flux and the backwardness of those still attached to the nation, to help them to go beyond that stage to reach true class consciousness. The Constitution and the Federation that it established were in the end only temporary concessions to the specific situation of Russia (its national heterogeneity) and to the demands of the moment (the capitalist encirclement that helped to exacerbate and perpetuate national differences). Like the slogan of "self-determination" a few years earlier, federalism was principally a pedagogical tool, a school for internationalism. This was how he continued to interpret it in the heat of his conflict with the *derzhimordy*. Although the methods used in 1922 were certainly not to his taste, Lenin had not been betrayed. It was his long-term vision that lay behind the 1924 Constitution. That vision would shape the entire course of Soviet development in the years when he was no longer there to suggest more suitable tactics for particular concrete situations. What was really at the heart of the program imposed on the national minorities in 1924 was what he had been fiercely defending since October 1917, or at least since 1920: the intent to secure a shared future for all the peoples living in the territory of the former empire. The state framework was essential to enable that community to assert itself. In order for differences to be overcome, it implied centralization and a tightening of controls. In the final analysis, the underpinning of the entire construction was democratic centralism.

Living or dead, Lenin remained the true ruler of the federal multinational state that officially came into existence in 1924.

Chapter Fourteen

"ONE STEP FORWARD, TWO STEPS BACK"

We have achieved great successes, and we have secured a position where from an economic perspective it is clear that we will have a base, a foundation, if we take grain. . . . taking into account the difficult situation we have endured, we are saying that if once again we unite our forces and concentrate them on the winter campaign, we are certain to achieve victory.[1]

THE REPORT THAT LENIN PRESENTED ON BEHALF OF THE CENTRAL Committee to the Ninth Party Conference, held from September 22 to 25, 1920, was a glorious one. But these lines are taken from the secret portion of his report, principally devoted to explaining to the party the defeat of the Red Army in Poland and its strategic consequences. In his speech Lenin justified the Polish expedition by his conviction that in August 1920 world revolution was at hand, and that at the time the Bolsheviks had every likelihood of breaking out of their isolation. Once he acknowledged that moment of hope, Lenin moved on to a recognition of failure and explained what that implied for the future of Russia: isolation of the revolution, and the necessity of surviving in the teeth of universal opposition by mobilizing all of the nation's economic resources.

From 1918 to 1920, with the expectation of world revolution, the Bolsheviks had responded to the dangers of civil war with War Communism, that is, the direct and harsh intervention of the state in every area in order to mobilize all the human and economic resources needed for the struggle against internal and external enemies. To be sure the Bolsheviks had justified this statist policy (known as *ogossundarstvlenie*) as an emergency measure, but they had also gradually made it into a "socialist principle." In his September 1920 speech to the Party Conference, Lenin proposed its continuation, particularly in the vital area of requisitions of grain from the peasantry, presented as an enduring success that he thought the "winter campaign," was likely to consolidate.

The winter of 1920–1921 was to disappoint his hopes of domestic consolidation just as cruelly as the summer had compelled him to recognize the failure of his international hopes. That winter's major crisis therefore forced him into a total political retreat, the abandonment of War Communism and concessions to a society that was suddenly in open rebellion. The NEP (New Economic Policy) was the domestic counterpart to the international agreements reached in 1920 and 1921 with neighboring states and Great Britain and the military contacts with Germany.

THE PEASANTRY IN REVOLT

"[W]hen 260 million poods (a pood is a Russian weight equivalent to slightly over 36 pounds) of grain a year are in the hands of the state, which requisitioned it from the peasantry by quotas . . . we will resolve freely the task of correct distribution [of food]."[2] These words from the September 1920 report emphasize the vital (and satisfying, in Lenin's view) character of the policy that had been followed to feed the population.

In 1918 Trotsky had taken charge of the commissariat of food supplies (*Narkomprod*), and held that responsibility until late 1921. The concurrent holding of responsibility for war and food supplies is enlightening, suggesting that relations with the peasantry were conceived of in terms of violent conflict. The fact that this took place in the context of a civil war should not conceal the fundamental hostility of the Bolsheviks toward the peasants. They declared war on peasant society, the consciousness of which they thought irremediably dominated by the desire to own property (*sobstvennichestvo*) and by capitalist leanings. The instruments for this war were the Committees of the Rural Poor (*kombedy*), given real power in 1918[3] and the Food Army (*prodarmya*), established and given defined duties by a series of decrees from May to July 1918.[4] If we add to this the workers' requisitioning brigades, it is easy to see that by 1918 the peasantry was surrounded by a network of institutions designed to take its production by force. The *kombedy*, considered too close to the peasants and therefore not sufficiently controllable, were abolished in late 1918 and replaced by detachments of workers and especially soldiers, thus in the end, by the army.

Despite Lenin's optimistic statements about the virtues of the system, by 1920 the food supply situation in Russia was catastrophic.[5] After a trip to the Urals in February, Trotsky presented a report to the Central Committee, acknowledging the ineffectiveness of requisitioning and proposing that it be replaced by a tax in kind. He explained that if the peasants were unable to purchase industrial products, they had no interest in increasing agricultural production. What he was suggesting, in fact, was nothing other than a resurrection of the market.

These proposals met with the opposition of Lenin, who in 1920 was defending a continuation of the policies that had been followed toward both peasants and workers. With respect to food supplies, his response to the failure of requisitioning was an increase in military operations. The peasant reaction matched the government's hardening, and disorders proliferated. The army sent against the peasants often acted in its own interest, requisitioning for itself alone. Deserters from the Red Army joined by hungry workers went over to the side of the peasants and sometimes even fought by their side.[6]

Trotsky's proposal was taken up again in the second half of 1920 by a number of local leaders, who asked Moscow to stop the violence and requisitioning and for a policy of cooperation with the peasantry, the only way, according to these isolated voices, to put an end to growing rebellion in the countryside and to counteract a famine that was spreading with great speed. But the orders that came down from the commissariat of food supplies at the center were merciless. Peasant rebellion should be met with reprisals, villages should be burned, rebel peasants shot, and particularly entire families taken hostage and executed in order to dissuade the others from resisting. Violence against violence, those were Trotsky's orders; having had his proposals for a change in policy disavowed, he aligned himself unhesitatingly with Lenin's intransigence.[7]

February 1921 marked the height of the crisis. A general rebellion had broken out in Tambov Province, fertile agricultural land, and was spreading eastward toward the Volga, the Urals, and Western Siberia. Not only did the peasants no longer accept requisitioning, they no longer recognized the authority of the Bolsheviks and imposed their own law. They halted grain convoys traveling from the steppes to Moscow and plundered them. The troops sent to the scene confronted not isolated peasants, but an entire countryside in revolt, in solidarity with the rebels who hid among them. In areas not yet in revolt, the disaster was no less great; one-fourth of the land cultivated before 1913 lay fallow, harvests had decreased by 40 percent, and agricultural machinery was not maintained, much less replaced. The total break with the peasantry and the ineffectiveness of violence pointed out by Trotsky a few months earlier could be observed everywhere, and the army was neither large enough nor reliable enough to deal with the spreading revolt. The government was thus faced with the question: Could it stick to its hostile policy or was it forced to compromise? Was it possible to lose all of the Ukraine in rebellion under the leadership of Makhno and to allow the peasants of Saratov cheerfully to massacre anyone who was a loyal Communist?

Until the winter of 1920, it was customary to blame the difficulties of the rural world on the "peasant capitalist," the kulak, the "bagman." Suddenly everything changed. The peasantry was in revolt, the army was raising questions, and finally the working class in turn recognized the lack of reasons to support the men who claimed to represent it.

THE KRONSTADT INSURRECTION

By their uprising the Kronstadt sailors, whom Trotsky had called the "pride and glory of the Russian revolution," not only illustrated in a particularly tragic way the gulf between society and government, but they also gave the Russian working class the opportunity finally to demonstrate its opposition to the policies followed by Lenin up to the spring of 1921.

To understand the Kronstadt mutiny and the workers' rebellion that was grafted onto it,[8] it is worth once again considering the choices that Lenin had made. At the Ninth Party Congress in March and April 1920, he had argued that an authoritarian structure had to be imposed on the production process, eliminating the working class from management and decision making. Three measures were considered decisive in this regard: the use of non-Communist specialists (following the example of the army); the institution of a single management in the production process; and, finally, in the Communist Party and the unions, the replacement by appointment from above of election by the rank and file provided for in the rules. In the last instance, this was not a clearly expressed principle but a convenient practice justified by the need for rapid and effective action.

By 1920 these orientations promoted by Lenin had given rise to two groups that vigorously opposed them, led by Bolsheviks who frequently enjoyed prestige in the working class.

First was the Workers' Opposition led by Alexander Shlyapnikov, a member of the Central Committee since 1918, and Yuri Lutovinov, a worker who headed the metalworkers' union. It was made up of Communist militants in the unions and argued in favor of union control of the production process; it also constantly denounced the rapid bureaucratization of the party, asked that the organization be purged of all elements outside the working class, and finally demanded a return to the principle of elections for all leadership positions. This was an indictment of all the policies promoted by Lenin.

A second group was set up to defend genuine democratic centralism. Led by Nikolai Osinsky, Timofei Sapronov, and Vladimir Smirnov, it denounced galloping bureaucracy and the existing centralism, and attacked both Lenin and Trotsky.

The conflict between the party leadership and these two groups exploded in December 1919 in the Central Committee, when Trotsky argued for the need to militarize labor. It was then that Lenin collided with these opponents along with Bukharin, who gave them voice in *Pravda*. Lenin had accused them of anarcho-syndicalism, while nevertheless hesitating to support Trotsky's radical proposals. The Ninth Party Congress had not resolved these deep differences. It was thus left to the Tenth Party Congress to decide, but it had as a backdrop an event that shook the Bolsheviks, the Kronstadt insurrection, which changed everything.

The insurrection was preceded by widespread agitation among the workers sparked by the near famine conditions in the cities. Throughout the winter of 1920–1921, the working class held countless rallies and marches to protest against its status, against the "dictatorship" in factories, and against shortages. On February 23, 1921, a meeting held in one of the largest factories in Petrograd, Trubochny Zavod, showed the state of mind of the workers: It passed a resolution demanding an increase in food rations and the immediate distribution of shoes and winter clothing. On the following day, the workers in the same factory murdered the Bolshevik chairman of the Council of Petrograd Unions, named Antselovich, who had come to enjoin them to return to work, and then went to other factories to advocate solidarity with their movement. Agitation spread throughout the city. Zinoviev, head of the Petrograd Committee of Defense, tried to calm the crisis by removing the barriers that had just been set up at all the exits from the city and allowing the inhabitants to go to the country-side to get—meaning to confiscate—food.

The revolutionary flame had already spread to the Kronstadt naval base, the pride of the regime, where the sailors proclaimed their solidarity with the strikers and announced that a Provisional Military Committee had abolished the city Soviet and that a new one would soon be elected. "The Soviet without the communists" was the slogan that united the rebellious peasants in the Tambov region and the Baltic sailors. The revolutionary Commune established by the sailors, which lasted for sixteen days, took over from the striking workers and proposed a program in direct opposition to the political system in force since 1918: general dissolution of the Soviets and free elections by secret ballot to replace them; freedom of the press and assembly for socialists, anarchists, and unions; freedom for the peasants to dispose of their harvests, abolition of the requisitioning brigades in the countryside, and prohibition of property searches; and freedom of labor for artisans not employing paid labor.

Of course, as Lenin said, Kronstadt was not all of Russia, but its Commune was a troubling symbol of the rejection of the Communist government by those who had been its greatest supporters. It was also evidence of a link among all the revolts, of the Tambov peasants, the Ukrainians behind Makhno, all of the Russian countryside. The government saw the Socialist Revolutionaries rushing to join the insurgents, in the countryside but also at Kronstadt, where Viktor Chernov came to advocate calling the Constituent Assembly and a return to legality. Most important, after hesitating, the anarchists joined the sailors and would attempt to avert the final confrontation with the government.

Old reflexes were also awakened in places, notably anti-Semitism, which resurfaced in both cities and countryside. Trotsky and Zinoviev were targeted and denounced because of their origins. Banners were displayed in many places with the slogan "Russia, the first Jewish Republic!" Pogroms took place in the provinces of Minsk and Gomel, provoking a strong feeling in the Jewish section of the party (*Yevsektsya*).[9] It appealed to Lenin who asserted that "the Jewish population is gaining the impression that the Soviet government is not capable of defending the civilian population from bandits" (that is, peasants of neighboring villages), or else adopted the accusations of some Jewish farmers convinced that pogroms were made with the knowledge of the government.[10] Weren't the rulers of Russia happy to shift peasant anger against the traditional scapegoat, as the Bolsheviks' predecessors had done in the imperial past?

These fears and suspicions of Jewish Communists were strengthened by the silence with which Lenin had already greeted their first complaints, in late 1920, when they had informed him of pogroms carried out by detachments of the Red Army on their return from Poland. Thus, on at least two occasions, Lenin had been informed of the awful resurgence of violent anti-Semitism when the frustrations of the army and the peasants took Jewish communities as their target. Asked to react, to send investigating bodies to the scene, Lenin merely noted on the documents: "Into the Central Committee archive." There is no trace of an order to take action to put an end to the outrages.

Lenin's attitude toward the Jews, which was at the very least ambiguous, was confirmed by draft theses of the Central Committee intended to guide the conduct of Russian authorities in the Ukraine, when it was reoccupied after Denikin's defeat. This document, which was dated November 21, 1919, and was adopted by the Politburo on the same day with a few minor amendments in Lenin's handwriting, contains the following paragraph 7: "Treat the Jews and urban inhabitants in the Ukraine with an iron rod, transferring them to the front, not letting them into government agencies." In the margin Lenin added: "Express it politely: Jewish petty bourgeoisie." The paragraph was adopted with Lenin's changes.[11]

Perhaps it is appropriate to recall here that in a 1911 polemic against Trotsky, Lenin had called him a "little Judas."[12]

It is true that there are many documents from this period appealing to his sense of equity or the most elementary pity for individuals and groups attacked or interned in inhuman conditions that were given the same comment: "Into the archive." This makes it all the easier to understand the steady increase in popular anger that suddenly turned into an anti-Communist explosion in the countryside and in Kronstadt in February and March 1921. The fury was everywhere accompanied by the same demand, from the peasants as well as the sailors: "Give freedom to produce and exchange back to the peasants!" Russian society as a whole understood that to survive in this terrible crisis, it was first of all necessary for the peasants to be safe from terror and confiscation.

Confronted with the Kronstadt Commune, Lenin remarked, "The 'bagman' is so powerful that, armed with the slogan of freedom of exchange, he has even invaded the Kronstadt fortress." And, he might have added, to supplement this very relevant judgment, "has threatened the Bolshevik regime with death." Although Lenin did not say so bluntly, he had suddenly understood that he could no longer ignore the existing situation and that he had to give ground.

His choice was clear—because everything depended on the peasantry, he would compromise with them, but first he had to limit and then destroy the workers' rebellion.

The decision to use violence against the Kronstadt Commune was taken without hesitation and almost unanimously by all groups in the party, who were otherwise so divided. From every viewpoint it was unthinkable, impossible, to accept that the working class, the sailors, Bolsheviks until then, could oppose the regime. The only way to settle the problem was to eradicate it with force.[13] While Chekists arrested striking workers, demonstrators, and union militants in Petrograd, elite troops under the command of Tukhachevsky were sent to Kronstadt and for ten days, from March 8 to 18, 1921, supported by the air force and artillery, fought the insurgents in the name of the *Internationale*. In order to justify the repression, the Kronstadt Commune was characterized as a "petty bourgeois, anarchist, and peasant movement." Nevertheless the assault by the Soviets deeply disturbed the working class. In Tsarskoe Selo, Oranienbaum, and elsewhere, railway workers attempted to block troop transports and called on soldiers to mutiny against their officers and join the camp of the defenders of democracy. Nothing worked; the forces deployed were too great, and, more important, the decisions of the Tenth Party Congress, which restored ties with the peasantry, prevented soldiers, who were usually of peasant origin, from rushing to the assistance of the insurgents. The adoption of the NEP, of which the army was informed by March 15, ensured that it would support the government. After that the battle would come to an end.

The consequences were frightful. The dead amounted to thousands on both sides. The army, which had had to march over ice fields, suffered nearly ten thousand dead, wounded, or missing. After the victory, it massacred the defeated, executing those considered leaders without even the pretense of a trial. Then the Cheka judged and sentenced hundreds if not thousands of the survivors, put them before a firing squad or sent them to concentration camps that had been in operation in the far North since 1918, the camps that Solzhenitsyn memorialized, whose existence has been fully corroborated by the archives that have become accessible since then.[14] Following the Tenth Party Congress, Dzerzhinsky suggested that the survivors of Kronstadt be sent to the "Ukhta penal colony," and joined Lenin in deciding to enlarge the concentration camp system with the construction of a "penal colony" in Kholmogory.

Thus, at the very moment when the state and the party were in the process of making peace with society with the adoption of the NEP, the system of concentration camps was growing, indicating that social compromise was being worked out in the shadow of increasing repression. Moreover political peace did not at all coincide with social peace. Dzerzhinsky arrested all the Mensheviks, anarchists, and Socialist Revolutionaries employed by the state in government offices or factories, while Tukhachevsky, as soon as the Kronstadt insurrection was crushed, was given the mission of crushing the peasant rebellion in Tambov. He did it without mercy, killing armed peasants and their families, pursuing those who fled into the forests, using poison gas to overcome a desperate population, and finally sending the conquered prisoners to the camps that were constantly increasing in number. Concentration camps with inhuman conditions and gassing the people, those were the weapons that Lenin's government used against all who did not follow it blindly and without protest. This was the background to the NEP that the Party Congress decided to launch at that very moment.

A PEASANT BREST-LITOVSK: THE NEP

On March 15, 1921, while the Red Army was attacking the Kronstadt insurgents, the Tenth Party Congress, meeting from March 8 to 16, adopted a series of measures favoring agriculture. They constituted the New Economic Policy (NEP), which the Marxist theoretician David Ryazanov called the "peasant Brest-Litovsk." The first measure passed was a halt to requisitioning, the only way in which the government could regain the confidence of the rural world. It was followed by the establishment of a progressive tax in kind taking the place of forced levies, and recognition of the peasants' freedom to dispose of their surpluses, in other words, the restoration of the market.

There is no doubt that the decision to carry out such a radical shift was made in March 1921 because the disintegration of Russia made it necessary. Indeed,

Lenin said that the Kronstadt uprising was the final event illuminating the picture presented to the Bolsheviks, whose underlying reality was the revolt of the Russian peasants of the heartland. To persuade the still hesitant Party Congress, he went on to say: "Only an agreement with the peasantry can save the Russian revolution and allow it to survive until revolutions break out elsewhere."

But the problem of reconciliation with the peasants had been posed for months, and the debate on the issue raises two questions: What was Lenin's role in the decision? What meaning did he give to the NEP?

It must be recognized that he hesitated for a long time to accept the retreat. When Trotsky proposed to renew ties with the peasantry early in 1920, the suggestion was rejected by Lenin,[15] who decided on the contrary to speed up the militarization of production.[16] It may be that he was still counting on world revolution. At the Ninth Congress of Soviets, the Mensheviks and SRs took up Trotsky's idea. In the interim Trotsky had enthusiastically rallied to War Communism, and although in 1921 he went along with the rest of the party in the debate on adopting the NEP, by that summer he was arguing in favor of the establishment of a central economic authority. Conversely Lenin was converted to the shift in policy in early 1921, and the proposed reform was soon debated by the Politburo, on February 8, by the Central Committee on February 24, and placed on the agenda for the Tenth Party Congress, at which Lenin argued that, in the absence of concessions to the peasantry, the political crisis would definitively destroy the regime.

This was a belated conversion brought about by the society's rejection of the Bolshevik regime. But Lenin had always believed that reality imposed tactical choices. However, it was not until the summer of 1923 that he drew the theoretical conclusions from his 1921 decision. He did this in a commentary on Sukhanov's notes on the revolution, in which he acknowledged the truth of the proposition: "The development of the productive forces of Russia has not attained the level that makes socialism possible." However, he went on to ask: "If a definite level of culture is required for the building of socialism . . . why cannot we begin by first achieving the prerequisites for that definite level of culture in a revolutionary way, and *then*, with the aid of the workers' and peasants' government and the Soviet system, proceed to overtake the other nations?"[17] These are surprising remarks on the part of an orthodox Marxist who had always battled the populists on this question, and they indicate his disquiet at the consequences of Russian backwardness.

In fact he did not have to struggle against his colleagues very much at the Tenth Party Congress. The majority of them were more interested in questions concerning unions and party organization than those dealing with the rural world. The Congress transcripts show that less than 10 percent of the proceedings was devoted to the NEP. But Lenin was not unaware of the fact that he was going to come up against the Workers' Opposition, and he was therefore cautious in presenting his proposals, attempting to characterize them as limited measures.

What meaning should be given to the NEP? What meaning did Lenin give to it? Was it a concession to the reality of Russian society that he knew could not be transformed quickly? Or was it a mere breathing space intended to save the revolution? The expression "peasant Brest-Litovsk" clearly shows the breadth of the debate and the depth of the perplexities. As on Brest-Litovsk, the political class was divided on the meaning of this reconciliation with the peasantry. For Lenin—as indicated by a careful reading of his own writings and of his 1923 commentary on Sukhanov—it was merely a breathing space (like Brest-Litovsk), and he never contemplated making permanent concessions. This observation raises another and more complex question: Did he think of it as a brief pause, enabling the Bolsheviks to pacify the society, to restore their power, and to take the Russian people in hand again before resuming their forced march toward Socialism, or on the contrary as a more durable retreat, linked of course to Russian backwardness but also to the delay in the outbreak of world revolution?

Considering Lenin's attitude in 1917 as set forth in *The Immediate Tasks of the Revolution* or his first actions in October and November 1917 tends to support the hypothesis that he thought of it as a lasting pause. After all, he declared at the Tenth Party Congress: "We must deal with the peasants continuously, because transforming the small farmer, changing his entire psychology, is a task that will take decades." Similarly, referring to the effort necessary to build modern industry, the basis for social transformation, he also spoke of decades. In 1921 he therefore seemed to be agreeing with the Mensheviks against whom he had fought so much, but with one distinction. All his efforts were directed to holding power and maintaining the monopoly of the Communist Party over every area of activity.

This strategic turn aimed at adjusting policy to social reality was difficult for the party as a whole and the unions to accept. The unions recognized that, through the NEP, the peasantry would become the principal force in Russian life, and that the transformation of the country would henceforth be dependent on it. This transformation would end up by depriving the workers of their privileged position, and they found the role assigned to the peasantry intolerable. The same thing was true for many Communists. But in order to impose the change on all its challengers, the authority of the party was indispensable, and in 1921, it was divided and weak.

It was also difficult to imagine that the peasantry would not seek to broaden the role assigned to it, to strengthen and perpetuate it. In order to limit peasant independence to the economic sphere alone, to control it, and rein in its ambitions, there needed to be a strong, centralized, and authoritarian party.

This is the source of the other important reform promoted by Lenin and adopted by the Tenth Party Congress, the reform of the party itself. It is impossible to understand the meaning of the NEP in Lenin's view without linking the NEP to party reform. In combining the two, we again encounter Lenin's general perspective on the relations between party and society. For him, adaptation to reality (choosing the NEP) was acceptable only if the means of controlling society and maintaining unlimited Bolshevik power were certain. We can therefore see that his conversion to the NEP, a manifestation of his usual pragmatism, did not imply any change in his global vision of the priority of the political dimension.

A PRIORITY: PARTY UNITY

If the Tenth Party Congress deserves to be given a decisive place in Soviet history, it is not because it transformed the party, but because it put the finishing touches on the plan he had conceived early in the century, when he was merely dreaming of revolution. In 1921 Lenin established in the life and operation of the party what until then had been implicit: It was monolithic and all opposition was banned. But didn't the slogan of "purging," used as the epigraph to *What Is to Be Done?* when he invented the party, contain in embryo the monolithic form of 1921? And hadn't Lenin's practice as party head from 1903 to 1917 already confirmed the intention that was given the force of law by the resolutions of the Tenth Party Congress?

A major question was on the agenda: What was the political role of the unions? But behind that question there lay another one, that was more decisive: What was the real source of power, the leadership or the rank and file?

The first problem, the one that was formulated explicitly, had been inflamed in the months preceding the Party Congress by personal conflicts, particularly by a veritable plot fomented against Trotsky, whose leader (or tool) was none other than Zinoviev. After the muted disputes of 1920, this conflict burst out at the Tenth Party Congress on the occasion of a debate about various programs and proposals, the course of which pitted Trotsky against the Workers' Opposition. Trotsky advocated subordinating unions to the requirements of production and integrating them into administrative structures. The Workers' Opposition fought for union independence and wanted management of the economy turned over to a congress of producers. Lenin tended to agree with Trotsky, but he condemned the bluntness and intolerance with which Trotsky intended to impose his views. There were no serious divergences between the views of Trotsky and Lenin; it was the way of arguing for them that distinguished the two men and gave the false appearance of a conflict between them.

Because Trotsky and the Workers' Opposition confronted one another in a Party Congress in which their antagonism took on exceptional importance, the adversaries attempted to organize victory over one another by aligning their supporters by means of the preparation of "platforms," not a usual procedure in the party in 1921. The *History of the Communist Party of the Soviet Union (Bolsheviks): Short Course*, published in 1938, during the period of Stalin's omnipotence, relates the episode in these terms: "Despite Party discipline, Trotsky made his differences of opinion known by declaring in his own name and that of his political friends his disagreement with the Central Committee. He proclaimed that the Congress would have to choose between two principal platforms, his and Lenin's."

This account is typical of the Stalinist manipulations of history. To begin with, far from wanting to defend his position on the basis of a platform, Trotsky had on the contrary pointed out that this procedure would freeze positions and thereby make debate impossible. Moreover, although the Party Congress was certainly marked by disputes, they were much more complex than a simple duel between Lenin and Trotsky. The debate on the unions involved several platforms. Trotsky was supported chiefly by Bukharin, Preobrazhensky, and Leonid Serebriakov. Lenin on his side had put together a group of ten signatories in favor of the position advocating an independent existence for the unions. Zinoviev and Stalin were the vehement spokesmen for this Platform of Ten, both of them clashing directly with Trotsky rather than discussing the role of the unions. The Workers' Opposition was led by Shlyapnikov and supported by an illustrious recruit, Alexandra Kollontai, whose ideas on human relations and particularly on women shocked Lenin's well-known prudery. The Workers' Opposition denounced both the militarization of labor and the lack of democracy in the party and called for the adoption of an egalitarian conception of economic activity, which Preobrazhensky took apart on grounds of economic realism. Their positions were also vigorously criticized by Trotsky, who did not accept the idea of union independence. They were also criticized by Lenin, who assigned to the unions the role of "schools of communism" for a backward working class, and intended to maintain party control over them; his view of union independence was in the end very limited.

The Party Congress adopted an intermediate position based on Lenin's arguments: "In the unions, it is essential to ensure elections to all bodies and to abolish the method of appointments. The choice of the leadership of the union movement should take place, it goes without saying, under the control of the Party."

The resolution of which this is a part was in conformity with the Leninist concept of democratic centralism. It gave union organizations the duty of leading and defending the workers, and it took into account the grievance over bureaucratization reiterated by the Workers' Opposition, by reintroducing the principle of elections. Simultaneously, it unambiguously imposed on the unions permanent party control, that is, control by a superior authority.

The Workers' Opposition was defeated in the debate, but the party spared it humiliation by appointing Shlyapnikov to the Central Committee. This was another example of Lenin's singular method, consisting of eliminating not his opponents but their ideas, allowing the losers to remain in the governing bodies and thereby avoiding fixing them in their opposition. This is what had happened to Zinoviev in October 1917, when he had declared himself an implacable opponent of the insurrection. In this way Lenin succeeded both in imposing his views on his adversaries and, despite their criticisms, in maintaining party unity.

With calm thereby restored, after the election of the Central Committee, in the closing minutes of the Congress, Lenin successfully introduced two resolutions that were to have decisive influence, one on party unity, and the other on the anarcho-syndicalist deviation. This presentation, almost outside the Congress, of such important proposals by Lenin in person was a clear indication of his desire to avoid debate and amendments that would have weakened them; it also indicated the importance he attached to their adoption.

The resolution on party unity prohibited the publication of ideas condemned by the majority; they could be discussed only in appropriate forums. Making a learned distinction between "deviation," "the beginning of an orientation that must be subject to assessment by the Party," and "faction," "incompatible with membership in the Party," the resolution banned all factions. Simultaneously with the adoption of this principle, the Party Congress immediately ordered the dissolution of groups organized around particular platforms and charged all party organizations with the duty of preventing factional activity. Point 7 of the resolution, which was to remain secret, gave the Central Committee the role of enforcing party discipline and, in case of violation, applying all the sanctions provided for, including expulsion. For the members of ruling bodies, expulsion would be decided by a plenary session of the Central Committee and of the Central Control Commission, and requiring a two-thirds majority. Lenin asked for secrecy on this provision which would be invoked only in exceptional circumstances, he said, when the party was in danger of splitting. The soothing words he offered deceived no one; many of his colleagues foresaw that the banning of factions and the procedure for expulsion could one day become the rule rather than the exception and apply to them as well. Radek said it very clearly but, despite anxiety that was broadly shared, he voted for the resolution, explaining that he thought it was the only guarantee for party unity.

Lenin had once again shown himself to be a clever tactician. He had been able to persuade his colleagues of the absolute necessity of giving priority in their vote to party unity. He had been able to prevent the public expression of doubts by presenting the resolution at the conclusion of the proceedings, which explains its adoption although a number of Bolsheviks sensed its nefarious consequences, which the near future was to demonstrate.

The balance sheet of the Tenth Party Congress was in the end contradictory, because it ratified two opposed political orientations: a degree of liberalization with respect to society (the NEP; rejection, even if it was partial, of Trotsky's authoritarian views); and conversely, a more authoritarian politics than ever within the party itself.[18] What was new in 1921 was the adoption of these principles and of the mechanisms intended to ensure that they were respected. Of course, Lenin had always favored iron discipline in the ranks of the party; but in 1921, he had the Party Congress ratify what had until then been only a matter of practice, and transformed it into an immutable principle. To be sure he justified this absolutism by his ultimate concern to preserve democracy in the party, but the treatment inflicted on the Workers' Opposition at the Tenth Party Congress and the purges that followed clearly showed that "democratization" had little place in the arrangements that had been adopted.[19]

The Party Congress ratified significant changes in the ruling personnel. The three secretaries of the Central Committee who had attempted to support the most tolerant positions, particularly with reference to expulsion to which they preferred open discussion, Krestinsky, Preobrazhensky, and Serebriakov (the last two had sided with Trotsky in the union fight), were not reelected. Old Bolsheviks rose in the principal bodies: Ordzhonikidze, Mikhail Frunze, Voroshilov, Molotov, and, above all, Stalin, to whom a number of those promoted were close. Having become the dominant figure in the secretariat because of the elimination of the three preceding secretaries, Molotov would closely associate Stalin with it.

At the following Party Congress, the Eleventh, held from March 27 to April 2, 1922, Stalin was to become general secretary, a title hitherto nonexistent in the party, and he would be assisted by Molotov and Kuibyshev.[20] Formally, the nomination of Stalin was moved by Kamenev at a plenary session of the Central Committee. But, noting how attentive Lenin was at the time to Stalin's virtues (he had appointed him to the Workers' and Peasants' Inspectorate in 1919), Volkogonov points out that the choice of Stalin as general secretary could only have been the result of a decision by Lenin.[21] This was confirmed by Molotov in the conversations he had over a number of years with the writer Felix Chuev, where he said explicitly, "Opposite the name of Stalin, Lenin had personally written 'General Secretary.'"[22]

At the same time, the party was going through a substantial purge among the rank and file. One hundred thirty-six thousand eight hundred members were expelled for various reasons, ranging from passivity and lack of discipline to acts of pure delinquency. It was a harsh purge, affecting more than 20 percent of the membership.

The Tenth Party Congress had thus drawn the conclusions from the difficulties with which Russia was struggling. The difficulties were linked to the directions dictated by War Communism, and the NEP was the response. Most important, it had ratified Lenin's observation that it was impossible to wait for salvation from some hypothetical world revolution. Russia could count only on itself, and he had been reiterating this since 1920. What came to the fore in the spring of 1921 was a stabilized state, turned in on itself, and mobilizing all its resources to survive and grow. The Third Congress of the Comintern would confirm that stabilization and the beginning of the confusion between the interests of the Soviet state and those of world revolution.

The pause decided on at the Tenth Party Congress would nevertheless come up against the most cruel reality, a great famine. The absolutist orientations of the Party Congress were reinforced on the occasion of that tragedy, notably in the religious policy then adopted by Lenin. Social peace was hardly a beneficiary.

THE GREAT FAMINE: A RETURN TO RIGOR

On July 12, 1921, Sverdlov's successor as chairman of the Central Executive Committee of the Congress of Soviets, Mikhail Kalinin, declared in an "Appeal to Citizens" published in *Pravda,* that, afflicted with an extraordinary drought that had put the harvest at risk, Russia was faced with the likelihood of a serious problem of food supply.[23] These cautious remarks, accompanied by the usual explanations about "profiteers" and "saboteurs," masked a tragic reality: Famine had struck Russia. The drought was far from explaining everything. Forced requisitioning and the violence inflicted on the countryside had destroyed rural networks, starved the peasants, and destroyed their productive capacities. Famine was particularly visible in some regions of the middle and lower Volga, and the northern Caucasus, and in part of the Ukraine. Available statistics show that 40 million people living in thirty-five regions were starving and that 60 percent of the cultivated land of Russia had been damaged.[24] Five million dead, several million homeless children reduced to wandering and delinquency, those were the consequences. It was of course the result of the drought, but it was principally the price paid for the policy that had made the peasant into an enemy who could be exploited at will. Never in the past, despite numerous natural calamities, had Russia suffered a human catastrophe of such enormous dimensions. The famine was so severe that it brought some of the starving to feed on corpses or even to kill in order to eat. When the Politburo was informed, it decreed that cannibals could not be punished according to ordinary laws, but that they would be "isolated" without trial.

In order to fight this calamity, the government set up a commission chaired by Kalinin and including Kamenev and Rykov to collect and centralize all data.[25] Patriarch Tikhon and Maxim Gorky launched a joint appeal to Europe and America for aid to Russia, and the appeal was answered. In France, collections were taken up by the French Children's Fund. The Red Cross and the Nansen Committee coordinated the European effort, while in the United States the American Relief Administration headed by Herbert Hoover provided substantial aid.[26]

While appeals for help to the starving were coming in from all sides, Lenin seemed completely unaware of one of the principal causes of the disaster, the coercion exercised against the peasantry. On July 30, 1921, he sent a telegram to all the provincial and regional Party Committees ordering measures that he considered appropriate responses to the crisis. What did he propose, or rather order? An immediate restoration of the requisitioning apparatus and mobilization of a large number of militants to support it, and the reinstatement of those who had already carried out those duties. One sentence perfectly sums up Lenin's position: "The chief condition for resolving the food crisis lies in the successful collection of taxes in [the form of] food."[27]

Thus, at the moment of greatest danger, Lenin's instructions amounted to requisitions and force, a cruel indication of his determination to ignore the real reasons for the disaster and his inclination to rely on violent solutions no matter what the circumstances. The fact that he proposed this line of action a few short months after the adoption of the NEP is a revealing indication of his view of the "pause." It was indeed for him a tactical retreat which he could reverse at any moment.

Moreover, not very grateful for the foreign aid that would save Russia, Lenin was outraged at Herbert Hoover's demand that the Russian government allow the personnel of the American Relief Administration to operate freely. Unable to oppose this without risking a rupture of the agreement with the United States, he put in place an elaborate system for spying on the Americans who had come to help his compatriots and for infiltrating the American committee sent to Moscow to organize relief. In a secret note to Molotov on August 23, 1921, he ordered the Politburo to "create a commission with the task of preparing, working out, and conducting through the Cheka and other agencies the strengthening of surveillance and reporting on foreigners." He went on: "The main thing is to identify and mobilize the maximum number of Communists who know English, to introduce them into the Hoover commission and for other forms of surveillance and intelligence."[28]

The famine also provided Lenin with the opportunity to settle accounts with God, more concretely, with the church. It has already been noted that Lenin was baptized in the manner appropriate to someone of his background and that he was married in a religious ceremony. But he showed no attachment to or curiosity in a faith that he had lost at an early age, if he had ever had it in the first place. He once said that he had "thrown his cross in the trash" at the age of sixteen.[29] His philosophical position with respect to religion was simple, involving little debate, unlike Bogdanov and Lunacharsky. As early as 1905, he had set out his views in "Socialism and Religion,"[30] and he confirmed them without change in many subsequent articles. In his view, religious faith was the product of the oppression of the people, of its need for consolation, and he frequently reiterated the blunt formulation of the fathers of Marxism: "Religion is the opium of the people." He also assigned to religion a precise political role: in the service of the powerful, it had always and everywhere legitimated the enslavement of the masses, and the Orthodox Church had played this role of "ideological knout" at the service of the regime in Russia.

However, he made a distinction between party and state with reference to religion. From the point of view of the state, religion was a private matter, which implied the separation of church and state and the abolition of all religious teaching. But the party could not be satisfied with mere neutrality, because it was not an ideologically neutral organization. Its philosophy was materialist and therefore atheist and anticlerical. Hence, the duty of the party was to produce antireligious propaganda, to educate its members and society in a spirit of militant atheism. In the final analysis, antireligious propaganda was one of the elements of class struggle, not an autonomous form of thought, and it could in no case be identified with free thought. Hostile to the institutional Church, Lenin was no less hostile to philosophical movements that attempted to compromise with religion, such as the "God-builders," because a religious impulse masked by the language of progress was, in his view, just as distant from atheism.

Before the revolution Lenin had supported the idea of a separation between church and state with the aim of depriving the imperial state of its religious legitimation, but after October, he had to develop an explicit religious policy. The separation was already in progress; the church had prepared the way by restoring the patriarchate at its August 1917 Council. For Lenin, the line to follow—although he briefly seemed inclined to make some tactical concessions to believers—was that religion had no place in Socialist society. The decrees on the separation of church and state and on the church and the schools were issued on January 23, 1918. From the outset, priests and nuns were subjected to violence, arrested, or publicly humiliated. Churches and monasteries were shut down and plundered. The regime was silent when militants organized antireligious carnivals and blasphemous assemblies around places of worship and relics. In Lenin's view the clergy were nothing but "counterrevolutionaries in cassocks." The cautious Patriarch Tikhon, elected by the Council, attempted to calm the storm, avoided the involvement of the church in the civil war, and multiplied requests for an audience with Lenin to try to establish a modus vivendi. The effort was futile; Lenin refused any contact.

The famine gave the ruler of Russia the opportunity to move from an insidious struggle against religion to open warfare. After appealing for help for the starving, the patriarch had established an All-Russian Church Committee to organize famine relief. It was promptly banned; the church could not be involved in the affairs of the nation. On February 19, 1922, in order to assist the famine victims, the patriarch ordered that all objects of value in churches be donated, except for those used for the sacraments. On February 23, a decree was issued, "personally approved by Lenin," according to Volkogonov, ordering the general confiscation of consecrated valuables. Here and there, clergy and worshipers attempted resistance, and this was the signal for terrible massacres and repression. A "top secret" letter from Lenin to Molotov, dated March 19, 1922, intended for Politburo members alone, sheds sinister light on Lenin's attitude on the matter. Beginning with the conviction, which was never confirmed, that the "Black Hundred clergy" had conceived a plan taking advantage of the confiscation of church valuables to engage in a battle against the Soviet government, Lenin wrote:

[F]or us this moment is . . . the only moment when we can, with ninety-nine out of a hundred chances of total success, smash the enemy [the church] and secure for ourselves an indispensable position for many decades to come. It is precisely now and only now, when in the starving regions people are eating human flesh, and hundreds if not thousands of corpses are littering the roads, that we can (and therefore must) carry out the confiscation of church valuables with the most savage and merciless energy. . . .

We must, come what may, carry out the confiscation of church valuables in the most rapid and decisive manner, so as to secure for ourselves a fund of several hundred million gold rubles. . . . Without this fund, no government work in general, no economic construction in particular, and no defense of our position in Genoa especially is even conceivable.

In order to accomplish this, Lenin ordered brutal and implacable confiscations in the same letter, "unconditionally stopping at nothing," and the "arrest [of] as many representatives of the local clergy, petty bourgeoisie, and bourgeoisie as possible. . . . The greater the number of representatives of the reactionary clergy and the reactionary bourgeoisie we succeed in executing . . . the better."

The document itself is merciless for its author. Kept secret until the late 1960s, clandestinely taken from the archives and brought to France where it was made public in 1970, it was published and thereby definitively authenticated by the official organ of the Central Committee of the Communist Party of the USSR in 1990.[31] This letter, which was long claimed to be apocryphal, leaves no doubts about Lenin's manipulation of the whole matter in his determination to take advantage of the circumstances to destroy the church and to incite against it the hostility of a peasantry whose religious beliefs were still strong .

Lenin's instructions on executions were followed. Nearly eight thousand clergy were "liquidated" in accordance with his wishes in 1922. For that year alone, Nikita Struve has counted 2,691 priests, 1,962 monks, and 447 nuns, figures confirmed by a Soviet historian in 1990.[32] To these martyrs of the church should be added many believers who were shot down in the course of confrontations in which they tried to defend priests and monks. Most bishops were arrested and sent to camps, with the alleged "plot" used as justification for their deportation. Only the patriarch was spared. He was arrested briefly, but there was such a wave of protest in the West that Lenin had to resign himself to placing him under house arrest in exchange for a signed confession saying, "Raised in monarchist society and until my arrest under the influence of anti-Soviet people, I was hostile to the Soviet government, and that hostility sometimes moved from a passive state to actions. . . . I regret these faults."[33]

The self-criticism that Stalin later imposed on everyone he wanted to get rid of had made its entry into Soviet politics. But this was in 1923, when Lenin was at the peak of his power, so that Stalin cannot be incriminated for having invented the procedure of forcing the person who is about to be liquidated to deny himself and thereby justify those who are getting ready to crush him.

Lenin did not merely hand out general instructions, but followed the matter closely. On March 11, 1922, he sent a note to Trotsky asking him about what stage they had reached in "cleansing" the churches, that is plundering them, and he asked for precise figures.[34] He also asked for information on the number of arrests and executions of priests.[35] On May 4, 1922, a decree instituted the death penalty for priests. At the same time, Lenin published a long article entitled "On the Meaning of Militant Materialism," indicating his intent to give high priority to the struggle against religion.[36]

What can be learned from this twofold tragedy in which Lenin linked a terrible famine to open warfare against the church? In the first place, the pretext chosen by Lenin to combat the church was absolutely mendacious. The secret letter is remarkable in that it refers to the famine only to note how it has created a favorable context for unleashing the program of confiscation and antireligious terror. When he enumerates the reasons justifying the seizure of church property—economic construction, the Genoa conference, and so on—he does not breathe a word of help to the starving. The patriarch had given the order to sell church valuables to feed the hungry; Lenin did not devote a single ruble to that cause.

But he emerged the winner from the confrontation that he had sought. The church was leaderless (the patriarch, under house arrest and completely isolated, died in 1925); a schismatic body called the Living Church was set up by the Soviet government. The church was for long condemned to silence and its servants to martyrdom. Atheism, as Lenin had wished, then became a decisive component of the ideology of the state.

ECONOMIC RECOVERY

After the immense tragedy of 1921–1922, Lenin recognized the need to return to a policy that would appease the peasantry and make it possible to feed an exhausted society. It was indeed impossible to expect from a desolate country-side—fields lying fallow, herds decimated, equipment abandoned—an exceptional effort in the absence of confidence. The Agrarian Code of 1922 marked a return to the intentions proclaimed in the NEP. The Code did attempt to maintain the hope of giving pride of place to the common ownership of land, and it did give legal status to the old rural commune, renamed "land society," but the peasants were free to choose the forms of their participation in communal farming. In particular they might join together for a time during periods of intense labor but remain owners of their family holdings; this was the choice of the majority of peasants. They might also, keeping only their dwelling and a patch of land, join an artel, where everything was owned in common—land, draft animals, equipment, seeds—a solution that attracted only the poorest and the unlucky. They could, finally, join a commune, where everything was collective, but attracted very few.

In 1923 Lenin wrote an article entitled "On Cooperation," in which he expressed his preference for cooperative farming, likely, in his view, to persuade the peasants of the need for and their interest in rapidly changing the patterns of life and work in the rural world.[37] But he did not succeed in convincing the peasantry of the virtues of cooperation. Quite the contrary, the peasants found loopholes in the Code that made it possible for them to restore rural property ownership.

Warned by the preceding year's experience, the government decided to compromise. In 1922 it had already limited the tax in kind to 10 percent of production and prohibited the seizure of cattle for nonpayment. The Twelfth Party Congress held from April 17 to 25, 1923 further reduced levies in kind, which were abolished in 1924 and replaced by an agricultural tax entirely payable in currency, thereby stabilizing peasant incomes. In the same year, the Thirteenth Party Congress established the Agricultural Bank and restored credit in the countryside. In May 1922 a decree had recognized the peasants' right to dispose of their land and, most important, to hire paid labor, which was even given official status in 1924. More than one and one-half million agricultural laborers worked legally for better off peasants. These concessions revived agriculture, and harvests increased from 1922 on.

But how could peasants be stimulated to increase production if manufactured goods were absent from the market? The complement of the NEP was the rebirth of industry, which had been paralyzed by War Communism. On July 7, 1921, a decree authorized small-scale private enterprises to employ as many as twenty people. In December nationalized enterprises with ten workers were denationalized, and the measure was later extended to those employing twenty. The limited private sector was supplemented by state capitalism arising from cooperation between private business and the Socialist state, in two forms: "leasing," which permitted former owners to return "contractually" to their firms and "concessions" granted to foreign companies. Large industry remained in the hands of the state, although its management practices were made more flexible in order to meet competition from the private sector. Thus, by 1922, there was a restoration of capitalism in industry, although limited and strictly controlled.

At the time that the NEP was established and implemented, the spirit of War Communism, the pride in having destroyed commercial exchange and abolished the currency, nevertheless survived for many Bolsheviks. They believed it was possible to combine concessions made to the peasantry and the barter economy that had been established. The economist Stanislav Strumilin, a Menshevik who had belatedly rallied to Lenin, and who had been an advocate of a nonmonetary economy (and was later a proponent of Stalinist planning), had that illusion in 1921. But the Bolsheviks soon had to give it up and accept a return to money and commerce. This emerges in the August 9, 1921, decree on "the monetary form of exchange." In May 1922 a commissariat of domestic commerce (*Komvnutorg*) was established. To deal with the problem of a stable currency, the government established the State Bank, at first merely a department of the people's commissariat of finances, but soon transformed into a central bank controlling credit establishments. The aftermath of the revolution had seen a flourishing of *sovznaks* (analogous to the *assignats* of the French Revolution), the value of which had continuously depreciated. On October 24, 1922, a decree introduced a new currency, the *chernovetz* (the name of an old Russian gold coin) guaranteed by the gold and foreign currency reserves of the State Bank, which entered into competition with the soznak in 1924 (one chernovetz was worth 50 thousand soznaks). Real currency reform took place in 1924 with the abolition of competing currencies and the restoration of the ruble. Finally, foreign trade resumed; its first step was the Anglo-Russian trade agreement signed by Leonid Krasin.

The effects of these policies were rapidly felt. Freed from multiple constraints, agriculture recovered very quickly. Industry, subject to more control, recovered more slowly, not experiencing measurable progress until 1925. One of the consequences of this return to normality was the repopulation of cities. The urban population had fled cities where it could find neither work, nor food, nor heat. Gradually the major centers recovered their prewar population levels, or even increased them, giving rise, particularly in Moscow, to severe housing shortages. Life in cities was not easy. New arrivals were often uprooted and ruined peasants could not be absorbed by recovering industry. Unemployment became a constant, increasing from five hundred thousand in 1922 to seven hundred thousand two years later; by 1927 the figure had more than doubled.

The working class of the 1920s did not resemble that of the revolutionary period. It was disenchanted, obsessed with material problems, not very energetic, and politically untrained. How different it was from the working class eager to study and debate, aware of the condition of Russia, that had crowded Nadezhda Krupskaya's courses before the revolution and seized control of industry in 1918. It was not so much a social class as an amorphous mass matching the description Lenin had given of it early in the century. The party did not have or no longer had a social base; this time, Lenin was right.

THE "NEW MAN"?

The communist revolution was not carried out only with the idea of changing the political system. As a utopia, although Lenin had little to say on the subject, Communism intended to create a radically new world, for which the moral transformation of the individual was a decisive element. The rapidity of the revolutionary process in Russia and the chaotic circumstances in which the Bolsheviks took power left little place for the development of a coherent moral and social model. All changes had taken place in emergency conditions, by means of scattered and disparate, if not contradictory, measures, and they had not given the new leaders of Russia the time to provide a clear definition of their conception of the "new man." However, the policy adopted toward religion, some party decisions, and the attitude toward the press and some books and films makes it possible to discern a moral model intended to shape the man of the new world, or rather the "new man," as he was seen during the years when the personality of Lenin dominated his country.

The first aspect of a policy dedicated to the formation of the Communist consciousness, although it was not identified as such, was the prompt abolition of all freedom of the press. The newspapers of the liberal, and even the Socialist, political parties disappeared. The party press dominated the news, while de facto control was gradually established over every form of writing because of the shortage of paper. In 1919 the government established the state publishing company *Gosizdat*, which controlled all publications through its control over allocations of paper. Nevertheless, with the end of War Communism and the revival of private businesses, literary life was able to recover a relatively autonomous status.

Literary expression was only one aspect of the decisive question of culture. In the aftermath of the revolution, there was a debate over the role of culture in the postrevolutionary state, which pitted two positions against one another.

Bogdanov and Lunacharsky, who were close to Lenin early in the century, were fervent supporters of a radically new "proletarian culture" emanating from the proletariat, which was to educate the "new man." These advocates of a truly revolutionary culture believed that it should be constructed independently of any cultural contribution from the past and any external influence, including that of the state and its teachers, in order to enable the proletariat to discover and develop its own culture by itself. This was *Proletkult*, which had an organization, the All-Russian Proletkult Council, and a journal intended to spread the movement's teachings.

This approach was unacceptable to Lenin. As early as 1905, in an article on the party and literature, he had of course pointed out that any writing should respect party spirit (*partiinost*), but specifying with reference to literature: "There is no question that literature is least of all subject to mechanical leveling, to the rule of the majority over the minority."[38] As this article indicates, in Lenin's view, conformity to "Party spirit" concerned the press, not literature.

During the years of War Communism, the Bolshevik press multiplied attacks against writers accused of ignoring or criticizing communism. For the advocates of Proletkult, the answer lay precisely in the replacement of a "historically obsolete" culture by the culture of the proletariat. But, in accordance with his ideas of 1905, Lenin argued against them that there was a firm distinction between culture, which belonged to no one, and ideology, which for the proletariat was Marxism.[39] Trotsky, accustomed to dealing with cultural problems and more interested in the subject than Lenin, clarified matters in 1922 by pointing out that one of the historical advances of the revolution consisted precisely of having taken culture away from a particular class in order to make it universally available. "The culture to which the revolution of 1917 has opened the door" was, in his view, humanistic and universal, not "proletarian." He explained: "Art [understood in the broad sense of creative activity] is an area in which the Party does not have to command."[40]

Rather than engaging in polemics, Lenin acted.[41] He decided that the Proletkult Council would be subordinated to the people's commissariat for education, headed by none other than Lunacharsky. This decision caused such turmoil in the ranks of the party that *Pravda* promptly published a "Letter from the Central Committee" justifying it but also affirming that the independence of creative artists would not be affected.[42]

This debate was not only theoretical; it had practical consequences. It was a matter of not alienating the non-Communist intellectual elite that was more or less sympathetic to the Bolshevik revolution and of not driving it into opposition. By refusing to link culture and Marxism, Lenin attracted these fellow travelers to his side. What counted for him was, on the one hand, to avoid the spread of political ideas foreign to communist ideology, for which the press monopoly was sufficient; and on the other hand, to maintain cultural activity and to use the most distinguished cultural figures to shape the contours of a Soviet culture. An excellent illustration of this program is the "use" of Mayakovsky, who wrote in 1922: "Did the revolution have to be accepted? The question did not arise for me, it was 'my' revolution." The poet's enthusiasm was the sign of the rallying of all the futurists to the revolution. He put his talent at its service, devoting time to designing propaganda posters intended to spread civilized manners among an uncivilized people (such as his "comic strips" on the need for basic hygiene, washing hands, cleaning shoes, and the like). Although recognizing the usefulness of his contribution, Lenin had little esteem for him and was suspicious of him. Mayakovsky was to commit suicide in April 1930.

In the end what dominated Lenin's attitude in his view of the "new man" and the means of bringing him into existence was the idea already worked out in

What Is to Be Done? which summed up the dialectics of historical development as a conflict between spontaneity (*stikhiinost'*) and consciousness (*soznatel'nost'*). In Lenin's view human progress consisted of drawing society, or individuals, away from spontaneous consciousness in order to lead them gradually toward true consciousness. The "new man" was to be the end point of that progress, but there had to be a vanguard just as there had been one to bring about the revolution. The struggle against spontaneity was incumbent on the party and on Marxism, and it assumed the dismissal of political ideas foreign to Marxism. Religion, an essential component of the old Russian social consciousness, which had defined most of the values to which the society was attached, particularly the political order and family solidarity, therefore had to be eradicated from people's minds, not only in its institutional form. This is why the persecution of religious institutions and clergy was supplemented by 1922 with a whole apparatus of antireligious education through propaganda and ridicule. Publications addressed to different social and professional groups, along the lines of the Communist publications of 1917, sacrilegious carnivals, and the mobilization of permanent personnel to carry on this propaganda all give evidence of the magnitude of the program. Religious consciousness, which in Lenin's view was a part of the hated spontaneity that had shaped Russian thought for centuries, therefore had to disappear, he thought, in order to leave room for progress toward a consciousness shaped by communist ideology alone.

There is one final area that cannot be neglected, that touching on legal culture and the notion of law. At the time of the revolution, the disappearance of constraints, the conviction that everything was now permitted, and the belief in the native virtue of the proletariat replacing any form of legality were supposed to lead to the advent of a "proletarian law" arising from the consciousness of the proletariat, or so the utopians thought. For a short time, referring to the fable of the "cook" and his remarks on the disappearance of state institutions in *The State and Revolution,* they were able to believe that they had Lenin's support. But in the summer of 1919, in a lecture delivered at the Communist University in Moscow, turning his back on utopia, he affirmed the need to develop a legal culture in order to advance toward Communist society.[43] The bearer of an innate consciousness of legality was no longer the proletariat but legal professionals such as Pashukanis, the leader of the new school. Of course, Marxism was the backdrop for the new law in the process of development, but the essential point was the intent to provide revolutionary society with a legal "superstructure" based on strict principles worked out by lawyers, and not based on listening to the wishes of the proletariat. In a resolution on the question of legality, the Eleventh Party Conference in December 1921 gave a precise indication of Lenin's intent: "The immediate task is to provide all areas of [individual and social] life with rigorous principles of revolutionary legality." The essence of this formulation lies in the word "legality" more than in its "revolutionary" aspect. The end point of this development was the establishment of the Supreme Court of the Soviet Union by the Constitution of 1924 "in order to establish and consolidate revolutionary legality throughout the territory of the Union."

The development of the cultural and ideological program between 1917 and 1922 was swift and impressive to judge by the magnitude of the change that could be observed in 1922. In 1917 the hero of the revolution was the proletariat, even though the revolution had been the work of the party. Utopia remained powerful. The moral model to which many Bolsheviks referred, intellectuals and especially workers, was the model of the proletarian, that is, the ordinary man, the rank and file, the ideal representative of a mythicized working class. The "new man" was the man who had the native virtues and knowledge of the proletarian. The ideal society was fraternal and egalitarian, following the model of the man without particular qualities who embodied the proletariat. Whether it was Proletkult claiming to put culture to school to the proletariat and transform creative artists into mere spokesmen or scribes for the rank and file proletarian, or legality destroyed in favor of proletarian law, everything was working toward translating this vision of the man and the society of the future into reality. Although it was flattering to a working class that was paying a very heavy material price for political change, the utopia offered to it had only a very brief existence. It very early came up against the culture of the party and the state advocated by Lenin, the work of professionals. In the army, the law, institutions, professionals evicted proletarians, "little men," and surreptitiously introduced into the budding political culture of the Soviet state a hierarchy that official ideology would take pains to ignore for a few more years.

The development of the ideological and moral model defended by Lenin expressed the conflict in *The State and Revolution* between the "cook" capable of running the state, symbol of the "new man" cherished by the utopians, and the organizers of "the single office and the single factory." Lenin's practice between 1917 and 1922 and his own view of the "new man" are a response to the question raised by a reading of *The State and Revolution*. Between the spontaneity embodied by the "cook" and conscious organization, Lenin clearly chose the latter. By doing so he remained true to himself. From the critique of spontaneity in 1902 to the organizational choices made between 1917 and 1922, the continuity of his thought was strengthened by his action. The "new man" was the man whose spontaneity the party and the state attempted to destroy and whom they attempted to lead toward a certain degree of real consciousness. In short Lenin did not really believe in the new man. His slogan, repeated in 1922 and 1923, was "study," or, "learn first; then learn, and learn again."

Chapter Fifteen

THE DECLINE OF A MIND

LENIN'S PERSONALITY WAS MARKED BY TWO CHARACTERISTICS that often had contradictory effects: a will of iron that nothing could ever sway; and a nervous system that he himself knew to be fragile—he referred in a letter to his sister Maria to his "irremediably bad nerves." As Volkogonov notes, many addresses for specialists in nervous diseases were found in his papers. Even before the revolution, he was often compelled to drop everything and rest because of his nervous troubles. With the revolution, his activity of greater intensity than any he had hitherto known and the pressure of events together weighed on his nervous stability, though the situation made it impossible for him to follow the remedy that had periodically been prescribed by Krupskaya of a long vacation and calming nature walks. This constant tension was probably the cause of the final cerebral collapse the first symptoms of which appeared late in 1921. From then on Lenin periodically suffered crises that reduced his activity and finally removed him from the government almost a year before his death.

The first signs of the illness appeared in the summer of 1921 in the form of extreme irritability and fatigue that might certainly be explained by the tragic period of the famine following the nearly total collapse of the system. At the time, it was impossible for Lenin to limit his activities; he had never been compelled to make as many urgent decisions as in those months in which all Russia was rejecting his revolution. He paid the price in May 1922; he was felled by an attack on May 25 and temporarily removed from the government. This time he was not suffering from fatigue or depression but from a cerebral attack characterized by Doctor Kramer, one of his physicians, as a "severe disorder of the blood vessels in the brain."[1]

Lenin was ill, and Russian and foreign doctors crowded around his bedside. He returned to work in October, but only for a short time. When he appeared at the Fourth Congress of the Comintern, held from November 4 to December 5, the participants took note of the change in his demeanor. The Lenin they saw in front of them was frailer, spoke with less vigor, was less incisive, and especially kept his distance from the debates.[2] Of course he had already developed the habit of behaving like a head of government and hence attending meetings of the world party of revolution only in the background. Even so fatigue did not prevent him from delivering a one-hour speech in German with no hesitations or mistakes. But he confessed his worry to the doctors watching in the corridors; he had the impression that he had had a "gap" and, more troubling, he had felt cramps in his legs that made him afraid that he would not be able to finish his speech. In any event contemporaries noted that, in December 1922, he was a man who was very different, both physically and in his manner of speech. It was not that his intelligence appeared to be impaired, but the slowness of speech had replaced his former vigor. Indeed, he was on the point of collapse; beginning on December 13, a series of alerts presaged a new attack on December 16 that paralyzed him and forced him to give up all political activity, but not yet to stop thinking and making decisions. He wanted to keep up with everything and argued with the doctors who intended to force him to rest, as he did with the Politburo, which had decided in July that it had the authority to decide whether Lenin would participate in any meetings. Although ill, Lenin could not stand being infantilized in this way. He demanded the dismissal of the German doctors, and complained that his right to receive visits on political questions was being limited.[3] The fact that he expressed his grievances to Stalin in a friendly tone in the summer of 1922 is a clear sign that he still had confidence in the man he had promoted to the position of general secretary of the party.

In spite of his exhaustion, during the period from December 1922 to March 1923, Lenin worked on a number of problems, and then, starting on March 6, a series of strokes affected his speech, and then on March 10, the damage became irremediable. He completely lost the ability to speak, could no longer draft the notes that he had so passionately written throughout his life, and was almost totally paralyzed. His wife's desperate efforts to teach him an elementary vocabulary again and treatment by an impressive number of doctors nevertheless brought about some minor improvement. Living in the countryside near Moscow, he was taken to the Kremlin in October 1923 for a last look at the place where he had exercised his immense power. This was his condition until the end, which came on January 21, 1924, removed from political life and lacking in consciousness, despite sometimes optimistic reports on the improvement of his condition, or even his possible return to work.

The autopsy and his doctors' reports, along with the testimony of many witnesses, suggest that the reality of his condition after March 10, 1923 corresponded in no respect to the official accounts. "Lenin's brain was dying," was the conclusion confirmed by the account of a visit to Lenin in December 1923 by the painter Yuri Annenkov, who found him "reclining on a chaise longue, wrapped in a blanket and looking past us with the helpless, twisted, babyish smile of a man in his second infancy. . . ."[4] In any event, the judgment is plausible; looking at the last photographs taken of Lenin in a wheelchair in the park at Gorki, one cannot fail to be impressed by his wild look, the appearance of a man who has nothing but a vague resemblance to the father of the revolution.

Illness is no doubt a private matter, particularly when it affects the mind. But in this case the cerebral deterioration that began in May 1922 cannot go without mention, because Lenin made serious decisions at least up to the winter of 1922-23, and then left a kind of testament. Those decisions and that "testament" should also be considered in the light of his intellectual capacities at the time. It is therefore important to investigate the changes in character and judgment that may have resulted from the increasingly impaired cerebral condition of this sick man who occupied a special position because of the authority that he still held up to late March 1923.

THE DEPORTATION OF INTELLECTUALS

On May 19, 1922, shortly before his first stroke, Lenin sent a letter to Dzerzhinsky asking that the GPU (as the Cheka had been renamed in 1922) that he headed establish a list of intellectuals–writers and teachers–suspected of counterrevolutionary sympathies to be deported from Russia.[5] When Dzerzhinsky displayed little enthusiasm to condemn his staff to examine documents allowing them to choose the victims of this plan of deportation, Lenin returned to the attack in July 1922, after illness had removed him from the government. He then wrote to Stalin to ask what reason lay behind the delay in carrying out the operation he had initiated before his illness. He listed names of Socialist Revolutionaries, Mensheviks, and writers, and specified: "Arrest several hundred and without stating the reasons–out with you, gentlemen!"[6] He was extremely impatient, because on September 17, 1922, still on sick leave, he demanded explanations from Unshlikht, Dzerzhinsky's deputy: "Be so good as to see to it that all the attached papers are returned to me with notations of who is exiled, who is in prison, who has been spared from deportation (and why)."[7] He returned to the question again on December 13, the day on which a series of cerebral attacks began, in a letter to Stalin for the Central Committee, in which he expressed outrage that the Menshevik historian Nikolai Rozhkov, a not very eminent figure, had not yet been deported and demanded that it be done immediately. The irritation Lenin showed over the Rozhkov case in the month of December 1922, at a time when he was concerned with more important matters, points to an obsession rather than a coherent political program. At the same time, this fury against an elite who he suspected were not fully submissive to the Bolsheviks was in accordance with his general conception of freedom of thought.

The deportation of intellectuals provoked a sharp reaction from Gorky, who was in Germany and wrote to Lenin to express his feelings. Lenin's reply to a man whom he had until then tried to accommodate is characteristic of his authoritarianism in this area as in so many others. On September 15, 1922, he answered in these terms: "The intellectual forces of the workers and peasants are growing and getting stronger in the struggle to overthrow the bourgeoisie and their accomplices, the intellectuals, the lackeys of capital, who think they're the brains of the nation. In fact, they're not its brains, they're its shit."[8]

Of course Lenin was sick when he insisted on trampling in this way on the Russian intellectual elite. But his orders were promptly transmitted by Stalin to Dzerzhinsky and finally carried out, because his authority, of which he had no doubt, still existed. The deportation of intellectuals that he called for is evidence of his inability to accept anything that he considered an opposition, even in moments when doubt and sometimes despair afflicted him. Indeed, he asked to be provided with poison to be in a position to commit suicide, because by 1922, he was alternating between phases when he felt a strong desire to recover and to act and phases of pessimism in which he thought he would never get well.[9]

HOW TO LAST *(PRODERZHATSIA)*

Removed from the government for periods of months, Lenin was nevertheless kept informed of the life of the country by his wife and his secretaries. Because his authority was necessary to his colleagues, even though it could no longer really be exercised, they kept up the myth of his prompt return and in exchange had to keep him abreast of public affairs and answer his questions and instructions, as, for example, in the matter of exiling intellectuals. In 1922 and 1923, Lenin was thus in an unusual situation for a government figure; removed from affairs, but psychologically present and armed with the uncertainty weighing on his ability to return, he could think about the course of events and about his work, and still try, because he had not lost power, to modify the system, to correct the mistakes he saw, and even to speed up certain developments. Lenin had already carried out this meditation from a distance in which statesmen indulge after they have left power while he was still *in* power, and it is for this reason that this final period of his life is so important. It was precisely the nature of the power that he had established that mobilized him in his last months of conscious reflection, which he was still able to share because he was writing or rather dictating. For example, after reading Sukhanov's notes on the revolution, he wrote a furious commentary on them.[10] Had revolution been premature, given the condition of Russia? No, he answered, once the circumstances lent themselves to it. Although he was so sensitive to Sukhanov's criticism and opposed to it his voluntaristic vision, he was nevertheless going through a period of doubt. Observing the country on which he now had little capacity to act, he saw that Russian Socialism had come up against two significant obstacles: the world revolution that had been hoped for but had slipped away and the internal problems of Russia. In "Better Fewer, but Better," the last article he was able to dictate, on March 2, 1923, one week before the stroke that would permanently deprive him of any means of expression, he set out a desperate assessment of the situation:

> [W]e have destroyed capitalist industry and have done our best to raze to the ground the medieval institutions and landed proprietorship, and thus created a small and very small peasantry, which is following the lead of the proletariat because it believes in the results of its revolutionary work. It is not easy for us, however, to keep going until the socialist revolution is victorious in more developed countries merely with the aid of this confidence."[11]

After having treated the peasants as enemies, having watched them die of hunger without a single word of pity, confronted with the future of his work, Lenin suddenly grew worried about a possible break between the proletariat and the peasantry: "That would be a disaster for the Soviet Republic."

In the end his analysis was close to that of Sukhanov and led him to question the nature of Socialism in these precarious circumstances. His answer was the one that he always gave, the exercise of political will and the decision to hold on at any cost. Faithful to his old convictions, in 1923 he reasserted the primacy of politics. The task of his companions in government was to make Russia advance, to bring its economic infrastructure into line with the system of government established in 1917. In this last article by Lenin, achieved Socialism is seen, as it was in 1917, as a matter of power, not as the outcome of the social will and collective effort of the people. His successors had the duty of organizing and governing; those were his final recommendations.

The instructions he gave them in this final meditation started from the backwardness of the country, the very complex national question, and the conflicts between government and society. If the masses were unable to adapt to the new political order, this was because of the intellectual backwardness of Russia. And this backwardness had to be overcome through a cultural revolution to which Lenin constantly returned. He saw this revolution of mind and consciousness, as he had amply demonstrated by his condemnation of Proletkult, in an entirely traditional light: "Eliminate illiteracy by any means necessary"; "Learn how to read and write, and understand what you read"; "[W]e hear people dilating at too great length . . . on 'proletarian' culture. For a start we should be satisfied with real bourgeois culture." And he pointed out that Russia in 1923 was in a state of "semi-Asiatic backwardness." To move from there to a minimal cultural level, it was necessary, he wrote, to "go through a period of cultural development."

In the countryside the cultural revolution had to be accompanied by the establishment of institutions acceptable to a peasantry that, Lenin pointed out, understood nothing about Communism. In his final reflections, these institutions were summed up for him by "cooperation," about which he had written in January 1923.[12] He condemned the idea of bringing Communist ideas to the countryside: "That would be harmful to communism," he wrote. He presents cooperation as the foundation for long-term progress in rural society. Of course he forgets neither industrialization, nor electrification, nor state power. But the essential lies in the NEP, which has made it possible "to organize the population of Russia in cooperative societies on a sufficiently large scale." Thus, in the end, Lenin finds in cooperation the dimension of the Socialism that is to be built: "[G]iven social ownership of the means of production, given the class victory of the proletariat over the bourgeoisie, the system of civilized cooperators is the system of socialism."

By establishing this equivalence between cooperation and socialism, Lenin granted real status to the NEP. Although it was possible to wonder about what meaning he gave it in 1921–breathing space or long-term solution–the article on cooperation suggests that he saw it as a long-term solution, allowing the system to "last" (*proderzhatsia*), a word that recurs frequently in his final writings.

Who would be able to give force to this system of cooperation, to invigorate and orient it? Lenin's answer was clear; the state was to prepare the way for economic growth, establish directions, and mobilize resources. But, although he clearly indicated in 1923, in contrast to the illusions of 1920 and 1921, that he saw the policy of the continuation of cooperative Socialism as a long development and a long process, he also raised the question of the risks that would be run: how to avoid the dissolution of authority, the development of opposing interests between workers and peasants, and the weakening of the government through popular demands.

The only guarantee making it possible to preserve Socialism and the revolution from these dangers lay in Lenin's view, in 1923 as in 1902, in the party; a Party that had been transformed, enlarged, and adapted to the exercise of state power, but one that remained the real instrument of social progress. Lenin knew only one way to strengthen the Party and avoid internal conflicts and splits, to increase the size and the powers of the ruling organs. On December 23, 1922, he proposed a reform of the top of the party, an enlargement of the Central Committee from less than 30 to about 100, and joining to it a Central Control Commission with at least 75 members, the two bodies thus forming a new Central Committee of nearly 200 that would meet six times a year.

The source of these proposals was what he had observed when he briefly returned to the government in the fall of 1922. He had been shocked by the personal rivalries, more openly expressed than in the past. He had also discovered the proliferation of useless administrative organs, and growing rivalry between government and party. By proposing a reorganization of the Central Committee, he hoped both to swallow personal rivalries in a larger body and to give this body new responsibilities, covering both governmental and Party work. In the end his plan aimed at restoring the party, which he had helped to weaken in favor of the government he headed since 1917, to the center of the political system, thereby settling the question of the respective scope of state and party activities.

The party, he thought in 1923, had the mission of building a new state apparatus appropriate for the new stage of development on which the country had embarked, and the Central Control Commission was particularly capable of carrying out that mission. Didn't the state apparatus that he intended to renew have to be subject to constant control? How was that control to be established? In 1923 Lenin saw the urgent necessity for this, but, perhaps because he was ill, and probably also because that was his natural inclination, he was unable to come up with solutions different from those already familiar to him. In 1920 he had established the Workers' and Peasants' Inspection (*Rabkrin*) headed by Stalin to supervise the administration as a whole. When Stalin left the Rabkrin in 1922, it had become an administration with twelve thousand employees, ponderous, nit-picking, and totally ineffective, according to Lenin. During the period of the NEP, bureaucracy grew and prospered in an organ designed precisely to combat it. In 1923, Lenin raised the question: "How We Should Reorganize the Workers' and Peasants' Inspection."[13] Between January 9 and 14, he dictated notes in the form of "materials," and then on January 23 the proposal for reorganization intended for the Twelfth Party Congress, scheduled to meet from

April 17 to 25, a time when illness had irrevocably excluded him from political life.

No doubt the most effective means of reducing the bureaucratic cancer would have been to impose some popular control. But Lenin did not consider this for a moment. The solution that he adopted and proposed to the party was as bureaucratic as the evil he denounced. The Rabkrin would be limited to a small number of bureaucrats with the duty of supervising both the party and the state. For supervision of the state administration, it would meet jointly with the Central Control Commission. This was a paradoxical proposal: in order to overcome bureaucracy, Lenin suggested the creation of a new bureaucratic organ, a "superbureaucracy." What he wanted to create was an "administrative vanguard" parallel to the revolutionary vanguard that had come out of *What Is to Be Done?* In both cases the principle governing these vanguards was the same: because social consciousness was backward in relation to political plans and possibilities, Lenin decided that it would be driven by a conscious elite to the assigned goal. The presumed virtues of that administrative elite were the same as those of the party elite: discipline, organization, loyalty, and consciousness of their historic mission.

There was another area that was just as important, to which Lenin devoted some final efforts, the national question. The Georgian crisis of 1922 had opened his eyes to the persistence of national oppositions and national feelings among Communists. He had, of course, imposed his views on Stalin concerning the federation and the concessions to be made to the demands of the nationalists of the Caucasus, who were, it must be remembered, Communists (the 1922 conflict, which was subsequent to the annexation of Georgia, had indeed eliminated everyone who was not a party member). Because it was between Communists and because the brutality of the language used shocked him, the conflict had deeply shaken Lenin. The notes dated December 30 and 31 are also of interest because in them he acknowledges, uncharacteristically, his own mistakes. The confession is full of pathos, but in fact it masks the continuity of his underlying vision. To be sure Lenin accuses himself of not having recognized the persistence of Great Russian chauvinism and the degree to which the imperious mentality of the Russian bureaucrat had interfered with a real solution to the national problem. He clearly saw that the guilty parties were not only survivors from the past, archaic figures, but also the highest level of party officials who had adopted as their own the legacy of imperialist thinking. To correct this terrible deviation, he advocated an inegalitarian policy that would favor the small nations so recently oppressed. It was a sort of affirmative action before the fact.

The relevant analysis of national oppositions and the proposals put forth to correct them could not hide the essential point. In fact Lenin did not believe in the autonomy of the national problem. Although he proposed a bold strategy in this area, the goal he was pursuing was the disappearance of the national minorities, and the instrument for this disappearance remained the party. Of course he recognized that the party had made enormous mistakes in its relations with the minorities. However, it was on the party, with which Lenin shared a sense of guilt, that he relied to correct the mistakes that had been made and to see to the development of genuine internationalism. Lenin's thinking here followed the same course as in the Rabkrin affair; although he was clearheaded about the revolution's stagnation and the failings of the party and its leaders, it was nevertheless that small and compromised core that carried his hopes for the future. His directives were all aimed at strengthening the party by developing institutions and supervision.

All things considered, what was new in Lenin's thinking in 1922 and 1923 was the assessment of failure or semifailure that he despairingly drew up. What was not new were the remedies he proposed. His thinking, so capable of recognizing the difficulty, was unable to stray from the paths he himself had set out in order to find the remedy. Was this the effect of the illness that was daily making him weaker, or his own system of thought that led him from clear analysis to dead ends. History will retain the fundamentally mistaken character of the solutions he proposed, that were so tragic for his country and his people.

Before history projects its harsh light on the work he accomplished, it remains to examine a final episode related to the doubts and the final wishes of Lenin, the episode of his succession, which is closely linked to his break with Stalin.

AN AMBIGUOUS LOOK AT THE FUTURE

Lenin had frequently worried about the future of the political system after his death. By the summer of 1922, in moments of discouragement, he had sometimes thought of withdrawing, sometimes of interim solutions. In a letter to Stalin of September 11, he suggested that new responsibilities be given to Trotsky and Kamenev to assist Alexander Tsyurupa, his deputy at the head of the government, who was overburdened with work.[14] It is true that at the time the doctors were assuring Lenin that he would be able to resume his activities (gradually, of course) beginning in early October. When the Politburo voted on the question, Trotsky opposed a categorical refusal. Lenin was all the more irritated by this because, unlike other leaders such as Stalin, Trotsky was not among the most assiduous of visitors during his illness. He was also angry because he had the justified impression that his unavailability was diminishing his authority over his colleagues and that his instructions were being followed with reluctance. His repeated notes on the deportation of intellectuals indicate the unease that he felt in the face of what he considered their lack of discipline.

Despite the Georgian crisis, until late in 1922 it was to Stalin that he sent complaints, requests, and instructions; Stalin was his most frequent visitor, because of his official position, of course, but also because of the bonds of confidence that had been established between the two men between 1917 and 1922. However, in the final months of his conscious life, Lenin was to break with Stalin, try to restore ties with Trotsky, and think deeply about his political associates.

At bottom, the disagreement with Stalin was linked to the Georgian affair. Lenin had gradually become aware of his protégé's brutality and, more important, of the excessive authority he arrogated to himself, ignoring the instructions sent to him by the man who remained the ruler of Russia. But an incident precipitated the break, one that was linked to the hidden conflict that had always existed between Stalin and Trotsky.

Troubled by Stalin's habitual manipulations, Lenin gradually turned toward Trotsky and asked him to present his concerns to the Twelfth Party Congress. They had to do with the party's abuses of national minorities, which he set out in notes drafted on December 30 and 31, 1922, that he sent to Trotsky with all the information he had been able to gather on the problem, despite the obstacles set up by Stalin.[15] Bukharin said that Lenin had "given a bomb" to Trotsky to destroy the general secretary of the party who had been appointed less than a year earlier. Lenin's sudden confidence in Trotsky was also shown on December 21, when he dictated a note asking him to preserve the monopoly of foreign trade and to mobilize the Party Congress for this struggle, which he considered decisive in view of Russia's economic weakness.[16] On this point as well, Stalin had in the spring of 1922 thought that he could take a position contrary to Lenin's,[17] which explains why Lenin turned to Trotsky, while informing Stalin: "I have made an agreement with Trotsky on the defense of my opinions with respect to the monopoly of foreign trade."[18] By late 1922, angry and distressed by the shift in Lenin's feelings about him, Stalin nevertheless thought he had an effective means of preventing Lenin from weakening his political position—making it impossible for him to communicate with the outside world.

In fact, on December 18, the Central Committee entrusted him with the care of Lenin to make sure that his doctors' advice for rest and caution was strictly followed.[19] Stalin thus became responsible for the patient's health and, using doctors' orders, did not hesitate to prohibit any activity, especially to prohibit his associates from sending him information and documents or taking down dictation from him. Indeed, Lenin soon developed the suspicion that the doctors were not the source of the instructions that Stalin was enforcing, but that it was Stalin who had compelled the doctors to give such strict instructions.[20]

The role of nurse that Stalin had assumed was the immediate cause of the final break between the two men. Learning that Lenin had dictated a short letter for Trotsky to Krupskaya on December 21, Stalin called her the following day to criticize her for ignoring the doctors' instructions. The telephone call was characteristically Stalinist, that is, so harsh and insolent that the next day Krupskaya complained to Kamenev, to whom she wrote: "Stalin subjected me to a storm of the coarsest abuse yesterday. . . . he takes it upon himself to threaten me."[21]

When did Lenin learn of this incident? There are several possible hypotheses. We know that his condition suddenly worsened between December 22 and 23 and that he became very agitated. Because Krupskaya had told him about Stalin's outburst, or because he had noticed his wife's distress? It is very plausible that in the immediate Krupskaya kept silent, contenting herself with appealing to Kamenev in order to avoid increasing the distress of a Lenin who was all too aware of the limitations on his activity. In any event Lenin's public reaction to the incident came on March 5, 1923, when he sent Stalin a threatening letter demanding that he apologize to Krupskaya, "or we will break off all relations."[22]

This belated formal break was preceded by a real one, contained in what is usually called "Lenin's Testament," which is in reality a "Letter to the Congress" dictated by Lenin on December 23 and 24, 1922.[23] The document is very representative of the feelings troubling Lenin at the time—he felt that the future no longer belonged to him and that he therefore had to orient the party so that it would entrust the highest responsibilities to the best men. But it is also extremely ambiguous—the intentions and even the judgments that it contains are very difficult to interpret.

His notes, transcribed under the very difficult circumstances described in his secretaries' Journal, started from the recognition that the situation of Russia was going to become even more difficult because the international climate was not favorable, and in Russia itself, personal and group rivalries threatened party unity. In order to ward off this danger, Lenin proposed reforms, including the enlargement of the party's ruling bodies, in an additional note dictated on December 29.[24] In his detailed analysis of the Russian situation, he insists on the indispensable solidarity between peasants and workers, but even more on the problems posed by the individual rivalries in the ruling circles. Here he examines the six personalities which the document suggests are in a position to succeed him. Lenin makes precise judgments on all of them, marked by an obvious concern for fairness, the avoidance of judgments that are too personal, and an overriding concern to take a position. He did not wish that after his death one of these men could rely on his judgment to lay claim to any particular legitimacy. The way in which the six figures are presented, in pairs and with a subtle mixture of praise and criticism, indicates his intent to leave the Central Committee free to make its own choices.

The first to come on stage (Lenin is indeed organizing a dramatic presentation) are Bukharin and Pyatakov. The first, he writes, is a brilliant theoretician, "the entire Party's favorite," but he has "never fully understood dialectics." For his part Pyatakov is a competent administrator, but precisely too focused on administration. The youth of both men made it possible to hope that they would correct these inadequacies.

After them come Zinoviev and Kamenev, who, Lenin recalls, were unable to correctly appreciate the historical situation and hence opposed his decision to initiate the insurrection in October 1917. Lenin asks that this momentary lapse not be used by the party against them in the future.

Finally, in the foreground, Lenin compares the two men whose rivalry he feared the most: Stalin and Trotsky. He acknowledges that both have eminent qualities that have brought them to occupy a central place in Russia since the revolution. Stalin is, however, characterized by the fact that he "has concentrated boundless power in his hands, and I am not convinced that he will always manage to use this power with sufficient care." As for Trotsky, Lenin points to his "outstanding ability," and notes that he "is personally the most capable man in the present Central Committee." The reservations following this praise are nevertheless many: Trotsky had come to the Party by a devious route, "he has an excess of self-confidence," and "an excessive preoccupation for the purely administrative side of affairs." To be sure Lenin expresses the wish that his belated joining of the Bolsheviks not be held against him: "It should not be used personally against him," he specifies. But in recalling it, making numerous critical remarks, and placing Trotsky on the same level as Stalin, Lenin weakened the position of the man whom he had at the same time made his spokesman at the Party Congress in order to defend his positions on burning questions.

On the basis of this catalog, it is hardly possible to decide on Lenin's preferences in late December 1922. In the days and weeks before dictating these notes, he had attempted to establish ties with Trotsky. Yet he did not designate Trotsky as his heir. However, very shortly thereafter, on January 4, 1923, he added to his Letter to the Congress a note that removed all ambiguity about his feelings toward Stalin:

> Stalin is too crude, and this inadequacy, which is wholly acceptable in our milieu and in exchanges among us communists, becomes intolerable in the post of General Secretary. I therefore urge comrades to think of a method for transferring Stalin from this position and to appoint another person to this position who in all other respects differs from comrade Stalin through the one advantage of being more tolerant, more loyal, more polite and more attentive to comrades, less capricious, and so on.[25]

This note, which is significant in many ways, shows that by the end of 1922, Lenin had formed a negative judgment of Stalin which he did not subsequently change. This was not a personal break, but the recognition that the position of general secretary gave a man like Stalin "unlimited resources to exercise dreadful power." In a few months, Lenin had understood that the man he had promoted to the position of general secretary had used it to assume increasing power that he abused. The qualities Lenin sought in a possible successor to Stalin provide an inverse and hardly flattering portrait of him. According to Lenin, he was in reality neither patient, nor polite, nor balanced, nor, especially, "loyal." This word, set down among the others, is unquestionably one of the principal grievances that Lenin addressed to the man that he was suddenly treating as an enemy. Indeed, he had himself experienced Stalin's characteristic disloyalty, concealed as long as Lenin was in power, but allowed to show forth once Stalin thought Lenin was dying.

As for the epithets used in this document, they indicate how precise Lenin could be in his judgments. The Russian word *grub* ("*Stalin slishkom grub*") or *grubost'* means both rudeness and brutality. Lenin used the same word in the note announcing his break with Stalin, in which he reproached him for the rudeness (*grubost'*) of his behavior toward Krupskaya. Although he was a cultivated man, Lenin had never hesitated to heap the most frightful insults on his opponents. His disputes with the Mensheviks and with factions of every variety provide documents containing an astonishing anthology of vulgarities and invectives. Lenin's sudden reaction to a man whose natural rudeness could not have escaped his notice earlier is revealing of the emotionalism that illness and the isolation to which Stalin had condemned him had exacerbated. The anxiety over his work, which he believed to be threatened, was also a contributing factor to the writing of this note.

He also knew that his comrades were not very clearheaded about Stalin's serious shortcomings. Such major figures in the party as Bukharin and Trotsky had nothing but contempt for administrative tasks and saw the position of general secretary as that of a mere manager. None of them understood the importance of the position given to Stalin in April 1922 or the power that was bound up with it. On the contrary they were grateful to a man for whom they had little consideration or whom they did not know for taking on tasks for which they had the deepest contempt. From his sickroom Lenin could clearly see the weakness of his potential heirs, their failure to recognize the real center of power. That explains the precise and reasoned suggestion for Stalin's removal. In the short time between December 23 and January 4, Lenin had radically changed his attitude. From the desire not to influence the decisions of the Central Committee that characterized his Letter to the Congress, he suddenly shifted to command. Above all his January 4 note expresses a condemnation of Stalin with no extenuating circumstances.

This pattern—a letter followed by an additional note—is fully in accordance with his behavior throughout his life. In December 1922 he recognized that enormous dangers were threatening the party; that its leaders had serious failings or that they were dangerous for the apparatus. But as always he knew only one remedy for so many dangers, for the party to take on the matter and settle everything. However shaky it might be, the party remained in his eyes the last resort.

THE DYING MAN BETRAYED BY HIS COMRADES

In the last two months of his life, Lenin struggled fiercely, against the doctors, against Stalin who held him in check, against his own failing powers, to speak out on every question, and he counted on the party to give his thoughts and warnings the necessary follow-up. He was not writing for history but for the upcoming Party Congress. His colleagues, notably Trotsky in whom he confided, were not very attentive to the wishes of a sick man whom they thought was already close to his end; they betrayed his intentions with no hesitation and no shame.

This was first of all the case for "Better Fewer, But Better," which Lenin wanted to have printed in *Pravda*. Bukharin, then editor in chief of the party newspaper, was reluctant to publish an article largely aimed against Stalin's authoritarian practices. He asked for the Politburo's opinion, which was against publication, one member even suggesting that they simply lie to Lenin.

Kuibyshev proposed that the article be printed in a single copy of *Pravda* prepared for Lenin alone. The scheme failed in the face of the combined opposition of Trotsky and Kamenev, but it gives a measure of the offhand way in which his colleagues were beginning to treat Lenin.[26]

Trotsky paid just as little attention to his requests. On March 6 Lenin sent him the notes he had dictated on December 30 and 31, along with the file on Georgia accompanied by a very insistent message: "I urgently request you to take upon yourself the defense of the Georgian affair at the Central Committee of the Party. The thing is at present under 'prosecution' at the hands of Stalin and Dzerzhinsky, and I cannot rely upon their impartiality."[27] At the same time, he informed the Georgians that he had taken steps in their favor, and his message rang out like a threat against the men he held responsible for the entire matter: "I am horrified at Ordzhonikidze's arrogance and Stalin's criminal alliance with him. I am preparing memoranda and a speech in your defense."[28] This vindictive letter fortified the Georgians and indicated to them, and to Trotsky, that the break with Stalin and the men that Lenin considered his accomplices was complete. It supplemented the note sent to Stalin denouncing him for his rudeness to Krupskaya. As he had done so often in the past, Lenin rejected, purged, and relied (this was new) on an ally to whom he offered great prospects for the future. But Trotsky made no use of the situation, and Stalin, who in the early part of March seemed politically condemned and, from all accounts, suffered great anxiety, was to come out of the ordeal triumphantly; the great loser was Lenin himself.

It is true that at the moment when the Party Congress that would have been decisive in the duel that now opposed Lenin to Stalin was about to open, a more severe stroke than the earlier ones transformed Lenin into a living shadow. The stroke occurred on March 10, 1923. A few days later, Trotsky assured Kamenev of his hostility to any change within the party. On March 20 he published an article in *Pravda* on the national question, but he adopted a very neutral tone and made no mention of the notes that Lenin had sent to him. When the Party Congress met, Trotsky finally referred to the notes, but the cautious silence he had adopted in *Pravda* now cost him very dear. Lenin, paralyzed and speechless, was unable to intervene, and Stalin recovered all his arrogance and accused his rival of having concealed from the party and kept notes from Lenin for himself. This fierce counterattack, inconceivable if Stalin had not known the real condition of the illustrious patient, destroyed Lenin's desperate effort to be present at the Congress through Trotsky and to redress the situation in the party. Bukharin took up the torch, defended the Georgians, and fought at their side, while Trotsky remained silent. All the hopes that Lenin had placed in this Congress were futile. Stalin was reelected as general secretary. Discouraged by Trotsky's passive behavior, Bukharin then decided to support Stalin—wasn't he the real victor in the confrontation with Lenin, the manipulator who had been able to turn to his own advantage a situation that was at first sight desperate?

At the conclusion of the Party Congress, Stalin was able to proclaim, with some impudence: "Comrades, it has been a long time since I have seen a Congress so united, so inspired by a single conviction."

When Lenin died on the evening of January 21, 1924, it was the head of the party and the founder of the USSR who disappeared. His absence from the political stage, his conflict with Stalin, and his repeated warnings about the dangers threatening the party all faded before the myth that was almost immediately forged. Already at the Thirteenth Party Conference, held from January 16 to 18, the dying man had been elected as a member of the presidium as though he had been kept from the meetings by a mere cold. It was Stalin who informed all party bodies, at every level and in every region, of Lenin's death. Was that not one of his duties as general secretary? It was in any event a final insult to Lenin's wishes.

Л Л Л

What if Lenin had lived? Some historians, including Moshe Lewin in his detailed and stimulating study of the final months of his life, have concluded that everything would have turned out differently in the USSR.[29] They assert that Lenin's last days, his final battle against Stalin, provided him with the opportunity to discover the human dimension in history. In short the final Lenin is said to be a man concerned with concrete human beings, not with the abstractions of proletariat and bourgeoisie whose shadows were hovering at his bedside.

A reading of his various writings of the final months of his life makes it difficult to support this position. It is true that during his illness Lenin paid more attention than before to the failings of the men around him. For many years he had tended to consider the events and the obstacles that he encountered through the prism of necessity and historical conditions. During his illness he added to the causes of the party's failings the brutality and cynicism of Stalin and a few others. He had previously given social or purely political explanations for the erring ways of his opponents. The "renegade Kautsky" and the "little Judas" Trotsky never enjoyed an analysis or even a description of their character. Lenin was satisfied with describing their misdeeds. The explanation for them was simple: they had not followed his principles nor obeyed the apparatus he had established. The national question had been a revelation for him, enabling him to understand that the apparatus also depended on the quality of the men it was composed of. In 1922 he had declared to the Eleventh Party Congress: "What counts are men, the choice of men." It was for this reason, in "Better Fewer, but Better," that he counted on the elite of the party to eliminate bad Communists. Of this abstract elite that he evoked, he said: "They are the best elements we have." But along the way he had forgotten that the men he attacked in 1923 had seemed to him the best in 1920 or 1922. The human failings that troubled Lenin were those that harmed the party. At no point did he raise questions about the relations of the men whose brutality toward Communists he denounced—notably Dzerzhinsky, inventor and head of the Cheka, who imprisoned, tortured, and executed without restraint—with the rest of society, with ordinary men. At the very moment when Lenin was insisting on the necessity of promoting "the best," he was calling for the deportation of writers who asked to stay in the country. And he had no words of regret for the suffering peasantry or the martyred clergy. His horizon remained the unity of the party he had established and shaped according to his principles—purging and excluding—and whose failings were unbearable to him. In this he was loyal to the convictions that had animated him for a quarter century and that had enabled him to transform his country. But to infer from this desperate effort to restore to his party its necessary virtues that the dying Lenin looked on his work with horror and deplored the absence of the ordinary man behind the organization cannot withstand scrutiny. Of course, like all utopians, Lenin still wished for the happiness of humanity, but like all founders of utopias, he neglected human beings in favor of abstract entities.

On the threshold of death, Lenin had hardly changed.

CONCLUSION

"[Revolutions] begin as anarchistic movements against the bureaucratic state organization which they inevitably destroy; they continue by setting in its place another, in most cases a stronger, bureaucratic organization, which suppresses all free mass movements."[1] In asserting what he considered a veritable law of revolutions, the author of these lines, Franz Borkenau, an eminent historian of the International, was particularly interested in the case of Russia. But by integrating it into a series and claiming that it followed a law, he suggested that the Russian revolution, the work of Lenin, was far from being, as a number of historians have asserted, the specific product of Russian culture and Russian conditions in the early twentieth century. He thereby subscribed to the position of Lenin, who had always denied that he represented a particular variant of Marxism and had constantly based his thinking and his actions on the affirmation of his adherence to orthodox Marxism.

In doing so, Borkenau neglected three particular aspects of Lenin's work that gave it an exceptional character.

In the first place, it must be acknowledged that before 1917, Lenin carried little weight in the international workers' movement. At a time when Social Democracy was at its peak, seemed able to mobilize the European working class around its programs, and was dominated by prestigious figures, Lenin enjoyed little renown in its ranks. His writings could not replace the works of Kautsky or Rosa Luxemburg. He was considered an unscrupulous agitator, while the major Social Democratic figures held his rivals, such as Plekhanov, in the highest regard. Moreover his party was considered nothing but a sect that would one day be compelled to dissolve in the main current of Russian Socialism. Neither the man, nor his positions, nor his party seemed to have any future at all. But it was this sect that was to become the embodiment of authentic Marxism and to give birth to a powerful party and to the Third International, for both of which it served as a model. An explanation for the victory of a sect that everyone believed condemned to a swift disappearance is indispensable.

A second, no less unexpected, characteristic of Lenin's career was the success of his seizure of power. In 1917 Russia in turmoil was more or less well reflected by the major socialist parties, the Socialist Revolutionaries and the Mensheviks. Their leaders were on the scene, in the countryside and in the Soviets, and they seemed destined for power. But it was Lenin who seized it, at the head of a handful of men whose life, like his own, had largely taken place in the reading rooms of the Bibliothèque Nationale and the British Museum, if not in prison. At the outset of the revolution, the party had only twenty four thousand members, not very many for enormous Russia. However, it was this small group, guided by a leader who had just returned from exile, that won out. Of all the hypotheses that might have been proposed before April 1917, the success of the Bolsheviks was the least plausible.

Finally, this professional revolutionary, who always thought only in terms of destruction of the existing government and its replacement, but who had no experience of the exercise of power, instantly transformed himself into the manager of a state in which everything had to be created from scratch. He exercised power for only four years, a very short period consumed by events that hindered the consolidation of that power. However, those four years sufficed to build a state of incomparable power and to establish a system that survived its founder for sixty-seven years. Everything was accomplished in four years, and thereafter there were only "Lenin's successors." The work had been his.

These particularities of Lenin's success deserve an explanation. The German Marxist Karl Korsch provided a personal response by insisting on the surprising combination of "the orthodox theory and the totally orthodox practice of the revolutionary Lenin."[2] It is not possible to accept fully the first proposition. Lenin drove Marxism in a direction that suited him, of an essentially "political" order. But he decreed that the Marxism he was developing was orthodox Marxism, and accused anyone who disagreed with him of reformism or heresy. This was the case for Bernstein, who shared his pessimistic analysis of working-class consciousness, but drew different conclusions from that analysis. In the name of the orthodox Marxism with which he identified himself, Lenin was always opposed to Bernstein, whom he accused of reformism. It is worth noting in this context his great capacity to impose on his opponents his conception of what constituted genuine Marxism. He acted similarly with the Mensheviks. He succeeded in imposing his judgment, his truth, in part because his opponents– Plekhanov and Kautsky–did not consider him significant enough to take the insulting epithets he heaped on them seriously. Because they long underestimated Lenin, these brilliant minds, who were certain they were the best, allowed him to occupy wrongly the field of orthodox Marxism.

We must always come back to the fact that everything turned on the ideas set out in *What Is to Be Done?*–an occasional pamphlet that nevertheless had an extraordinary historical fate. The "spontaneity" (*stikhia*) of the proletariat, so prominent in the analyses of many Russian revolutionaries, was the enemy that Lenin flushed out and against which he forged his fighting tool, the party, the true bearer, in his view, of the class consciousness of the workers. It may be thought that in developing this negative conception of the proletariat, Lenin was taking into account the specific situation of Russia, characterized by weak industrialization and a nascent working class. His reasoning would be legitimate if the intent were to help the new working class to become aware of its situation and its goals. But that was not his procedure. Far from being confined to Russia, whose backward stage of development explained the weak class consciousness of its proletariat, Lenin's analysis was general, and even more severe for the workers of the capitalist world. He made his views on the subject explicit in the succeeding years. For Marxism, the development of capitalism, industry, and the working class had always been an essential condition for the progress of the revolutionary movement. Lenin also thought that the development of capitalism was desirable for Russia. He did not conclude from that, however, that the class consciousness of the workers would progress, but saw on the contrary the increasing danger that the working class would surrender to its trade union inclinations. Hence, it was not the economic and social condition of Russia that justified to Lenin his view of the party, but a pessimistic vision of the proletariat, whatever the level of the development of the country in which it was located. The party was the weapon that Lenin brandished against spontaneity, the weapon that was to enable him to compel the working class to act in the name of a class consciousness that the party embodied, not by following a spontaneous view of its interests.

At the same time, Lenin condemned a specifically Russian variant of spontaneity, linked to the dominant position of the peasantry in society. He was not, by far, the only one who thought of the Russian future in terms of revolution. Indeed, he came up against rival movements attempting to reach the same goal by taking as a starting point the social conditions of Russia in the early twentieth century, that is, a peasant society with communitarian reflexes, marked by latent anarchism and violence leading to terror or collective uprisings. The populists, followed by the Socialist Revolutionaries, made those spontaneous tendencies the basis of their revolutionary program. On occasion they claimed to follow Marx and his ambiguous reflections on the possibility of avoiding the capitalist stage. Lenin constantly crossed swords with them; he argued against them, simultaneously and in complementary fashion, the necessity for capitalist development and the necessity for preparing society for that by establishing the party. In dealing with all the revolutionary hypotheses, *What Is to Be Done?* is thus an answer based on two elements: a condemnation of spontaneity and the invention of its antidote, the party.

Through this harsh vision that condemned the proletariat to follow a vanguard for an indefinite time, Lenin had accomplished a strange masterstroke. *What Is to Be Done?* is in fact a short book outstanding for neither style nor depth of thought. Yet Marxism is rich in work with real literary quality, dominated by philosophical debate and discussion on the meaning of history and man's place in it. Compared with the brilliant works of Kautsky, Rosa Luxemburg, and many others, Lenin's pamphlet seems colorless. The same holds true in comparison to Russian revolutionary literature. However, this pamphlet survived and became a Bible for all the Communist parties in the world. The virtue of *What Is to Be Done?* was to focus primarily on revolutionary tactics. Moreover, Lenin supplemented it in 1905 with *Two Tactics of Social Democracy in the Democratic Revolution*, a veritable manual of revolutionary methodology.[3] It therefore hardly matters that his writings are ponderous and colorless, because they had real practical consequences. Lenin liked to quote Goethe, for whom "dogma is gray, but life is green."[4] And life was to lead him to move from the gray to the green, to use the spontaneity that he had always condemned.

Speaking to young Swiss workers in January 1917, he told them: "We must not be deceived by the present grave-like stillness in Europe. Europe is pregnant with revolution. . . . in Europe, the coming years . . . will lead to popular uprisings under the leadership of the proletariat against the power of finance capital, against the big banks, against the capitalists; and these upheavals cannot end otherwise than . . . with the victory of socialism. We of the older generation may not live to see the decisive battles of this coming revolution."[5] Lenin spoke of the reasons for his optimism—the possibility that the "older generation" would not see the revolution is a rhetorical flourish—before this young audience electrified by his remarks. He returned to the question in more detail in an article written in September 1917, in feverish expectation of the event. These reasons had to do with the spontaneous mass movements he saw developing in the country, about which he noted: "There can be no doubt that the spontaneity of a movement is a sign of its depth and invincibility."[6] The confidence he expressed in the popular spontaneity developing in Russia provides one of the keys making it possible to understand his success in 1917. Until then, he had relied on his party, whose influence in the population remained very weak. In the name of unity, Lenin had moreover often weakened it by anathemas, exclusions, and above all his rejection of any compromise with the Mensheviks. But when he returned to Russia in 1917, what immediately met his eyes was a revolution whose wellspring was spontaneity. Indifferent to any definition and any program, the society was agitating neither for liberalism nor for socialism. It was simply defending interests: bread and peace for everyone, land for the peasants, control over factories for workers, emancipation for the national minorities. The revolution that Lenin saw developing was the result of the combination of those spontaneous demands. What he recognized was thus contrary to all his convictions. But this was where his political genius, previously held in check by the lack of opportunities, was to shine forth. With no hesitation he followed along behind all the spontaneous movements and made his party their spokesman. Bread, peace, land, national self-determination, these were so many dispersed and contradictory demands in which social consciousness was diluted and society fragmented. But it immediately became the program of Lenin and his party. "All Power to the Soviets!" was a slogan which, from the point of view of theoretical Leninism, was unacceptable; from the viewpoint of revolutionary tactics, it was a masterstroke. This was also the case for *The State and Revolution*, written at the same time, which was an undisguised call for spontaneity.

Beginning in April 1917, Lenin's practice was thus in complete contradiction to the theory that he had developed in book after book since 1902. But this was not a total surprise, except if his readers had failed to take note of two essential aspects of his thinking. "Marxism," in his view, had always been identified with "revolution" and "power." Tactical concerns trumped everything else, or rather were inseparable from the theory which could not be imposed in the absence of appropriate tactics. Always and above all, Lenin had concentrated on the political side of Marxism. This explains why, before the revolution, and even before the war, he had constantly thought about the conditions and the resources that would make it possible to transform theory into political action, that is, into revolution. For this reason, almost alone in the Marxist movement, he broadened his thought to a genuinely international, not merely European, scale. In the strategy that he developed for national minorities and colonies, he had already integrated the spontaneous consciousness of the national and colonial masses. Sensing very early on that the chances for the revolution were there, he turned his back on orthodoxy and on his own contribution to Marxism, keeping in mind only the tactical interests of the revolution.

In considering Lenin's development in the prewar years, we are forced to recognize that even his thinking, which seemed so rigid and that he imposed mercilessly on his followers and his opponents, went through extraordinary shifts whenever the interests of the revolution seemed to require it. It was the same compromise that he chose to make with the reality of the popular movements beginning in April 1917 that this time brought him to power.

Once power had been taken, after a very brief period of adjustment, Lenin once again demonstrated exceptional political instincts. A professional revolutionary completely ignorant of the art of exercising power, he instantaneously transformed himself into a man of power in order to hold on to it. And no less swiftly, he returned to the authoritarian view of relations with the proletariat that he had expounded in 1902. To hold on to and consolidate power, he could no longer stand for the spontaneous impulses of a society that was hostile to him. It was therefore the party alone that was to determine the path to be followed. The principal motto of the revolution had been "freedom," and its major social hope the Constituent Assembly. From the outset, Lenin suppressed both, on the grounds that, in order to be expressed, social consciousness had to be in accord with the party (with its newspapers alone, for example), and that, by electing a Constituent Assembly in which the Bolsheviks were in the minority, the proletariat had shown attachment to a past world and a judgment foreign to class consciousness. Against the spontaneity and anarchism that had been encouraged a short time earlier, Lenin favored centralism and party unity, and immediately transferred them to a reconstituted state power, because he thought that real power depended on statist institutions. In doing so he once again condemned spontaneity. The state had always been the hated enemy. Bakunin had said as much, and Tolstoy had preached it to his compatriots. For Lenin, on the contrary, the reconstitution of the state was the indispensable counterweight to the anarchistic tendencies of society. The party then changed roles, becoming the ideological guardian of the new state. The party would legitimate the government, the reconstituted state, and its violence as well. It would attest that all the state's actions were in accordance with the laws of historical development long defined by Marxism.

To reduce Lenin simply to his strategic genius would not be equitable. His thinking contained two other aspects that establish some degree of originality for him within the Marxist family. First of all he was inspired throughout his life by a fierce desire for Westernization. Like all his compatriots, Lenin inherited the old debate on the nature of Russia and the paths that should be followed in order to achieve progress. Was Russia European or Asian? Was it a country that, in order to make progress, had to find inspiration in its own political and social culture, as the Slavophiles, Bakunin, and the populists had all thought? Or was it a country like other countries that had to follow the common path? Lenin's answer was unambiguous; he felt European in every fiber of his being. Moreover, he spent most of his adult life in Western Europe. He was fascinated by the German intellectual model (German philosophy was particularly attractive to the Russian elites at the turn of the century), by German science and technology, and by the German talent for state and military organization. Compared with Germany, Russia represented for him "Asiatic barbarism." He further thought that it was no accident that Marxism had been invented and developed by Germans. When he thought about Russia, he considered revolution the only certain way of lifting it out of its backwardness, its "Asiatic barbarism," and one day, after great effort, making it into a copy of Germany.

He had always identified Marxism with the revolution and the party, but also with the means of finally resolving the problem of the Westernization of Russia; he hated not only its backwardness but also its cultural particularities. One of the most tragic and paradoxical consequences of Leninism was precisely the fact that the revolution he desired took place in a country that had barely begun to overcome its backwardness. The reforms of the last three reigns had, of course, not been enough to anchor Russia in modernity, but the country had already started down that path. And the February Revolution, despite the difficulties and the failings of the successive holders of power, had outlined the course of political modernization. In his fierce determination to Westernize through revolution, by applying his view of the relations between government and society, Lenin stopped the modernization in progress, replaced advancing democracy with a totalitarian system, and separated Russia from the Western world for a long time. Perhaps history does not like to be hurried. Didn't Marx say that it was necessary to respect its natural course?

A second characteristic aspect of Lenin's thinking was his worldwide vision. To be sure, Marxism had a global aim of emancipation of the proletariat, but the vision was limited to Western Europe. As for the European workers' movement, it had always given priority to the national framework in both thought and action, although it had endeavored more or less to conceal that fact behind internationalist language. The 1914 war was a cruel demonstration of the reality. In Lenin's case, on the contrary, both thought and programs had always been rooted in a real international framework. In his view the Russian revolution was merely the "spark" that was to set the world on fire. He leapt into the adventure of the Russian revolution because it was within his reach. But beforehand he had dreamt of setting it off in Switzerland or in any other country. As an internationalist he was ready to call any country home where there was a possibility of carrying out a revolution. But he was forced to choose Russia. Had the spark fulfilled the role that Lenin assigned to it, his action would have taken place in a framework going well beyond the borders of his country. With the revolution accomplished in Russia and delayed elsewhere, he could not imagine that in spite of everything it would not finally spread. In a first period lasting until 1920, the hope for the spread of the "revolutionary flame" did not have as a basis the desire to save Russia; he was simply incapable of thinking that the revolution could be contained within the limits of a single country.

After 1920, with all revolutionary hope gone, his pragmatic temperament, which drove him to reject theory when he felt that necessary, resurfaced. He adapted to the isolation, until then inconceivable, of the Russian revolution and endeavored to save the "country of the revolution," hence "revolution in one country." Although no one acknowledged that definition, after 1920, it underlay all Lenin's actions. He agreed to subordinate his ideas to the necessities of a strong state by consolidating its borders, and even restoring control over former imperial territories. Not only did he accept the survival of capitalism, but he compromised with it, inventing the "peaceful coexistence" of Socialism and capitalism before the fact, a phenomenon that the founding fathers of Marxism had probably never imagined. But Lenin was convinced that this compromise with reality required the support of Marxist theory and its guardian, the Russian Communist Party, that the revolution and the will of Lenin had made into the exclusive embodiment of Marxism. Even in his worst nightmares, Marx had never imagined such a seizure of his legacy. Beginning in 1920, the date of the Second Congress of the Comintern, Marxism became identified with Lenin's Marxist theory, hence with his theoretical justifications for shifting practices, and the Second International and the Fourth International of the Trotskyites were both consigned to the hell where heretics were condemned to burn for eternity.

Lenin was in the end a man of many contradictions. As an individual to begin with, it is difficult to reconcile the image of this short, good-natured man of ordinary appearance, so concerned with his health and comfort, so happy with his family and concerned for their well-being, used to long walks in nature, bicycling calmly through the streets of Paris, shut up in libraries, with the charismatic leader who mobilized crowds with repetitive and emphatic speeches that stirred men's souls. It is difficult to reconcile the ordinary man with the myth whose image reigned for a long time alongside those of the founding fathers, Marx and Engels, forming a trinity that was revered as icons and relics had been in the past, by both Communists and even by many who were not. It is difficult to reconcile language whose dominant theme was the good of humanity with a practice based on the misfortune of men for which Lenin never spoke a word of pity, much less of remorse.

No doubt all utopias have led to this kind of contradiction. But in the history of utopias the case of Lenin is unusual in two ways. First, no utopia, Plato's no more than Thomas More's, ever gave rise to a lasting state. At the very most, precarious "communes" have appeared in a few places, soon swept away by the currents of history that have little patience for social experiments. Moreover, the contradiction between humanistic speech and dehumanizing practice should have been enough to condemn Lenin's work, but he long succeeded in avoiding the condemnation that weighed on his creation. It was Stalin, accused of being "power-crazed" or a monster, who was held responsible for the perversion of Lenin's work. Lenin is exempt from judgment, or he was for a long time, because the view of Karl Korsch was adopted, according to which he was the embodiment of orthodox theory and hence of Marx's program.

Lenin the man is just as enigmatic if we consider the reasons for his success. How can he be defined? Cynical, pragmatic, opportunistic, obsessed with the plan for revolution, persuaded that he had the innate knowledge of how to achieve it? Lenin always claimed that the party was the "bearer" of class consciousness and historical "knowledge," but at the same time, he always imposed his own will and his own thinking on the party, thereby inwardly identifying his thinking with the class consciousness embodied by the party, even before his successors made that identification official.

Lenin was thus simultaneously an extraordinary tactician and a political genius, a man who invented the means of transforming a utopia into a state that claimed universal status. If his attempt had failed and he had ended his days in exile, wandering from one European capital to another, he would probably appear in the history books as a secondary Marxist figure, more or less a visionary. But he transformed his dream into reality, and this success, which justifies nothing of the tragedies inherent in the Leninist enterprise, has granted him an exceptional position in the history of this century, probably the most important of all because of the influence that he exercised. It is tempting to conclude that, although he was a rather mediocre theoretician, he was nonetheless an extraordinary political "inventor"–the only one in this century in which dictators have followed the paths laid out by others leaving no trace of their passage but in the shifting soil of the killing fields.

SELECT BIBLIOGRAPHY

This book is not a work of scholarship, but one of reinterpretation and rethinking. It is, in short a "revisited" *Lenin*, because the end of Communism encourages a new look at the man and at the meaning of his experience.

This bibliography makes no claim to being exhaustive. It is not a state of the art, but a record of the readings that have over the years nourished the author. The same is true of the archives. What has been helpful to me is already in the work of the late General Volkogonov, who generously shared his discoveries with me, and in that of R. Pipes. This is why their work is cited here.

This book is based primarily on Lenin's writings. Five editions were published in the USSR, four of them after his death. The most complete, and the one used here is the fifth. This book is also based on Party Congresses and various official documents of the time.

I. LENIN

Polnoe sobranie sochinenii. 55 vols. and 2 vols. of index. Moscow, 1958–65.
Sochineniia (third ed.) (edited among others by Bukharin and with annotations).
Leninskii sbornik. 39 vols. Moscow-Leningrad, 1924–80, containing miscellaneous works.

Some documents (particularly letters and notes) were not included in the complete works. Some were published in *Istoricheskii Arkhiv* in 1992. Many documents remain buried in theoretically open archives (Russian Center for the Preservation and Study of Documents of Recent History), but their availability is problematic.

II. CONGRESSES OF THE BOLSHEVIK PARTY

Pervyi s'ezd RSDRP: dokumenty i materialy mart 1898 (First Congress of the RSDLP). Moscow, 1958.
Piatyi (Londonskii) s'ezd RSDRP (b), aprel-mai 1907 goda., Protokoly (Fifth Congress of the RSDLP). Moscow, 1963.
Chestoi s'ezd RSDRP (bolshevikov) august 1917 g., Protokoly (Sixth Congress of the RSDLP (b). Moscow, 1958.

329

Sed'moi s'ezd RKP (b) Mart 1918, Protokoly (Seventh Congress of the Russian Communist Party). Moscow, 1959.

Desiatyi s'ezd RKP (b) Mart 1920, Protokoly (Ninth Congress of the Russian Communist Party). Moscow, 1960.

Desiatyi s'ezd RKP (b) Mart 1921, Stenograficheskii ochet (Tenth Congress of the Russian Communist Party). Moscow, 1963.

Odinadsatyi s'ezd RKP (b) mart-aprel 1922 goda, Stenograficheskii ochet (Eleventh Congress of the Russian Communist Party). Moscow, 1961.

Dvenadsatyi s'ezd rossiiskoi Kommunisticheskoi Partii bol'shevikov, Stenograficheskii ochet (Twelfth Congress of the Russian Communist Party). Moscow, 1923.

Sed'maia (aprel'skaia) Vserossiskaia Petrogradskaia Konferentsiia RSDRP (b) aprel 1917 g. (ed. Orakhelashvili) (Seventh All Russian Conference of Petrograd). Moscow, 1934.

Collections of Documents

Protokoly tsentral'nogo komiteta RSDRP (b) August 1917. Feval 1918 (Protocols of the Central Committee of the RSDLP (b), August 1917–February 1918). Moscow, 1958.

Anikeev, U. V., ed. *Perepiska sekretariata TSK RSDRP (b) s mestnymi partiinymi organizatsiami: Sbornik dokumentov i. mart. okt. 1917* (Correspondence of the Secretariat of the Central Committee of the RSDLP (b) with Local Party Organizations. Collection of Documents, March–October 1917). Moscow, 1957.

Belov, G. A. *Iz istorii Vserossiiskoi Chrezvychainoi Komissii 1917–1921. Sbornik dokumentov* (History of the All Russian Special Commission. Collection of Documents). Moscow, 1958.

III. STATE POWER

Dekrety Sovetskoi vlasti (Soviet Government Decrees). 15 vols. published. Moscow, 1957.

IV. THE SOVIETS

Pervyi Vserossiiskii s'ezd Sovetov rabochikh i soldatskikh deputatov. 1917 Protokoly (First Congress of Soviets of Workers' and Soldiers' Deputies) (ed. V. N. Rakhmetov and N. P. Miamlin). 2 vols. Moscow-Leningrad, 1930–31.

Vtoroi Vserossiiskii s'ezd Sovetov rabochikh i soldatskikh deputatov. Protokoly (Second Congress of Soviets of Workers' and Soldiers' Deputies) (ed. K. G. Kotel'nikov). Moscow-Leningrad, 1928.

V. COLLECTIONS OF DOCUMENTS

Browder, R. P. and A. Kerensky. *The Russian Provisional Government 1917. Documents.* Stanford, 1961.

Bunyan, J. and H. Fisher. *The Bolshevik Revolution 1917–1918. Documents and Materials.* Stanford, 1965.

Lenin i Vcheka. Sbornik dokumentov (Lenin and the Cheka: Collection of Documents). Moscow, 1976.

VI. ACCOUNTS BY CONTEMPORARIES

Antonov-Ovseenko, V. A. *Zapiski o grzhdanskoi voine* (Notes on the Civil War). Moscow-Leningrad, 1924.

Balabanoff, A. *Impressions of Lenin.* London, 1964.

_____. *My Life As a Rebel.* New York, 1968 [1938].

Bonch-Bruevich, V. D. *Na boevykh postakh fevral'skoi i oktiabr'skoi revoliutsii* (At Battle Stations in the February and October Revolutions). Moscow, 1931.

_____. *Izbrannye sochineniia,* vol. 3: *Vospominania o Lenine 1917–1924* (Selected Works: Memoirs on Lenin). Moscow, 1963.

Bukharin, N. *Politishskoie zaveshchanie Lenina* (Lenin's Political Testament). Moscow, 1929.

Dan, T. *The Origins of Bolshevism.* New York, 1964.

Fotieva, L. A. *Iz vospominanii o V. I. Lenine Dekabr' 1922 g. Mart 1923* (Memoirs on Lenin). Moscow, 1964.

Gorky, M. *Vladimir Ilich Lenin.* Moscow, 1924.

Kautsky, K. *Le Bolchevisme dans l'impasse.* Paris 1982 [1930].

Kerensky, A. *The Catastrophe: Kerensky's Own Story of the Russian Revolution.* London, 1928.

_____. *Istoriia Rossii.* Irkutsk, 1996.

Kremer, A. and Y. Martov. *Ob agitatsii* (On Agitation). Geneva, 1896.

Krupskaya, N. *Vospominaniia o Lenine* (Memoirs on Lenin). 2 vols. Moscow, 1957 and 1972.

Latsis, M. *Chrezvychainye komissii po bor'be s kontrrevoliutsiei* (The Special Commissions in the Struggle Against the Counterrevolution). Moscow, 1921.

Lunacharsky, A. V. *Revolutionary Silhouettes.* London, 1967.

_____. *Lenin, Tovarishch, Chelovek* (Lenin: The Comrade, the Man). Moscow, 1987.

Martov, Y. *Zapiski sotsialdemokrata* (Notes of a Social Democrat). Berlin, 1922.

Mikoyan, A. *Mysli i vospominaniia o Lenine* (Thoughts and Memoirs on Lenin). Moscow, 1970.

Miliukov, P. *Istoriia vtoroi russkoi revoliutsii* (History of the Second Russian Revolution). 3 vols. Sofia, 1921–23.

_____. Vospominaniia *1917–1959* (Memoirs). New York, 1959.

Nikitine, B. *The Fatal Years.* London, 1938.

Pascal, P. *En communisme.* Paris, 1918–21.

Radek, K. *Les Voies de la révolution russe.* Paris, 1971 [1922].

_____. *Vneshnaia politika sovetskoi Rossii* (Foreign Policy of Soviet Russia). Moscow-Leningrad, 1923.

_____. *Piat' let Kominterna* (Five Years of the Comintern). 2 vols. Moscow, 1924.

Raskolnikov, F. F. *Kronstadt and Petrograd in 1917.* London, 1982.

Roy, M. N. *Roy's Memoirs.* Bombay, 1964.

Shlyapnikov, A. *Semnadsatyi god.* 4 vols. Petrograd 1923.

Stassova, E. *Vospominaniia.* Moscow, 1969.

Struve, P. B. *Razmyshleniia o russkoi revoliutsii* (Reflections on the Russian Revolution). Moscow, 1991.

Sukhanov, N. N. *Zapitski o revoliutsii* (Notes on the Revolution). 7 vols. Berlin-Petrograd-Moscow, 1922–23. Quoted here from *The Russian Revolution : A Personal Record.* ed. J. Carmichael. London, 1955.

Trotsky, L. *Sochineniia.* 12 vols. Moscow, 1925–27 (esp. vols. 3 and 11).

_____. *O Lenine.* Moscow, 1924.

_____. *History of the Russian Revolution.* 3 vols. London, 1932–33.

_____. *La Jeunesse de Lénine.* Paris, 1970.

Tsereteli, I. *Vospominaniia o fevral'skoi revoliutsii* (Memoirs on the February Revolution). 2 vols. Paris-The Hague, 1963.

Ulyanova, M. I. *O V. I. Lenine i sem'e Ulinaovykh* (On Lenin and the Ulyanov Family). Moscow, 1988.

Valentinov, N. *Encounters with Lenin.* London, 1968.

_____. *Maloznakomyi Lenin* (The Ill Known Lenin). Paris, 1972.

Vishniak, M. *Vserossiiskoe uchreditel'noe sobranie* (The All Russian Constituent Assembly). Paris, 1932.

Zetkin, C. *Souvenirs sur Lénine.* Paris, 1968.

VII. BIOGRAPHIES AND STUDIES OF LENIN

Besançon, A. *Les Origines intellectuelles du léninisme.* Paris, 1980.

Colas, D. *Le Léninisme, philosophie et sociologie politique du léninisme.* Paris, 1982.

Crisenoy, C. de. *Lénine face aux moujiks.* Paris, 1978.

Ganetski, I. *O Lenine. Otryvki vospomaninanii* (On Lenin: Excerpts from the Memoirs). Moscow, 1933. (In this book Ganetski is designated as Hanetsky.)

Gorky, M. *Vladimir Ilich Lenin.* Leningrad, 1924.

Krzyzhanovsky, G. M. *Velikii Lenin* (The Great Lenin). Moscow, 1982.

Laloy, J. *Le Socialisme de Lénine.* Paris, 1967.

Lazitch, B. *Lénine et la IIIe Internationale.* Paris, 1951.

Leggett, G. *The Cheka: Lenin's Political Police.* Oxford, 1981.

Lewin, M. *Le Dernier Combat de Lénine.* Paris, 1967.

Luxemburg, R. *The Russian Revolution.* Ann Arbor, 1961.

McNeal, R. *Bride of the Revolution: Krupskaya and Lenin.* Ann Arbor, 1972.

Meyer, A. *Leninism.* New York, 1962.

Page, S. *Lenin and World Revolution.* New York, 1959.

Payne, R. *The Life and Death of Lenin.* London, 1964.

Pipes, R., ed. *The Unknown Lenin.* New Haven, 1996.

Polan, A. *Lenin and the End of Politics.* Berkeley, 1984.

Reddaway. P. and L. Schapiro, eds. *Lenin: The Man, the Theorist, the Leader.* London, 1967.

Rigby, T. H. *Lenin's Government: Sovnarkom, 1917–1922.* Cambridge, 1979.

Service, R. *Lenin: A Political Life.* 3 vols. Bloomington, 1985–95.

Shaparov, I. P. *Lenin kak chitatel'* (Lenin as a Reader). Moscow, 1990.

Shub, D. *Lenin: A Biography.* Harmondsworth, 1966 [1948].

Solzhenitsyn, A. *Lenin v Tsurihe.* Paris, 1975.

Treadgold, D. *Lenin and His Rivals: The Struggle for Russia's Future, 1898–1904.* New York, 1955.

Ulam, A. *The Bolsheviks.* New York, 1965.
Vladimir Ilich Lenin. Biografia. ed. P. N. Pospelov. Moscow, 1963.
Volkogonov, D. *Lenin: A New Life.* New York, 1994.
Wolfe, B. *Three Who Made a Revolution.* New York, 1948.
Zbarski, B. O. *Mavzolei Lenina* (Lenin's Mausoleum). Moscow, 1949.

VIII. GENERAL WORKS

Anweiler, O. *Les Soviets en Russie, 1905–1921.* Paris, 1972.
Baturin, N. *Ocherki istorii sotsial demokratii* (Outlines of a History of Social Democracy). Saint Petersburg, 1906.
Broué, P. *Rakovski, le socialisme dans tous les pays.* Paris, 1996.
_____. *Histoire de l'Internationale communiste, 1917–1943.* Paris, 1997.
Brovkin, V. N. *The Mensheviks after October: Socialist Opposition and the Rise of Bolshevik Dictatorship.* Ithaca, 1987.
Carr, E. H. *The Bolshevik Revolution 1917–1923.* 3 vols. London, 1950.
Chamberlain, W. H. *The Russian Revolution, 1917–1921.* 2 vols. New York, 1965 [1935].
Cohen, S. *Bukharin and the Bolshevik Revolution.* Oxford, 1980 [1974].
Daniels, R. V. *The Conscience of the Revolution.* Cambridge, Mass., 1960.
_____. *Red October.* New York, 1967.
Deutscher, I. *The Prophet Armed: Trotsky, 1898–1921.* New York, 1965 [1954].
Dubnow, S. M. *History of the Jews in Russia and Poland.* 3 vols. Philadelphia, 1917–20.
Elwood, R. C. *Roman Malinowski: A Life Without a Cause.* Newtonville, Mass., 1977.
_____. *Inessa Armand: Revolutionary and Feminist.* Cambridge, 1992.
Ferro, M. *La Révolution de 1917.* 2 vols. Paris, 1967–76.
Figes, O. *Peasant Russia, Civil War: The Volga Countryside in Revolution (1917–1921).* Oxford, 1989.
Footman, D. *The Civil War in Russia.* London, 1961.
Fremkin, M. *Tragediia krest' aniskikh vostanii v rossii 1917–1921* (The Tragedy of Peasant Insurrections in Russia). Jerusalem, 1987.
Haimson, L. *The Russian Marxists and the Origins of Bolshevism.* Cambridge, Mass., 1955.
Hasegawa, T. *The February Revolution: Petrograd 1917.* Seattle, 1981.
Haupt, G. and J. J. Marie, eds. *Les Bolcheviks par eux-mêmes.* Paris, 1968.
Heller, M. and A. Nekrich, *Utopia in Power: The History of the Soviet Union from 1917 to the Present.* New York, 1986.
Keep, J. L. H. *The Rise of Social Democracy in Russia.* Oxford, 1963.
_____. *The Russian Revolution: A Study in Mass Mobilization.* London, 1975.
Kennan, G. *Russia and the West under Lenin and Stalin.* Boston, 1961.
Kindersley, R. *The First Russian Revisionists.* Oxford, 1962.
Kolakowski, L. *Main Currents of Marxism.* 3 vols. New York, 1982.
Latours, S. de. *Toukhatchevski.* Paris, 1996.
Maiski, I. *Foreign Policy of the Russian Soviet Federated Republic.* Moscow, 1923.
Malia, M. *The Soviet Tragedy: A History of Socialism in Russia, 1917–1991.* New York, 1994.
Nettl, J. P. *Rosa Luxemburg.* 2 vols. London. 1966.
Pipes, R. *The Formation of the Soviet Union: Communism and Nationalism, 1917–1923.* Cambridge, Mass., 1954.

_____. *Social Democracy and the Saint Petersburg Labor Movement*. Cambridge, Mass., 1963.

_____. *Struve: Liberal on the Left, 1870–1905*. Cambridge, Mass, 1970.

_____. *The Russian Revolution, 1899–1919*. New York, 1990.

Rigby, T. H. *Communist Party Membership in the USSR, 1917–1967*. Princeton, 1968.

Schapiro, L. *The Origin of the Communist Autocracy: Political Opposition in the Soviet State, First Phase, 1917–1922*. London, 1977 [1955].

_____. *The Communist Party of the Soviet Union*. New York, 1960.

Werth, N. *La Vie quotidienne des paysans russes de la révolution à la collectivisation, 1917–1922*. Paris, 1984.

_____. "Un État contre son peuple," in *Le Livre noir du communisme*. Paris, 1997.

Wheeler-Bennett, J. *Brest-Litovsk: The Forgotten Peace*. New York, 1938.

Zeman, Z. A. B., ed. *Germany and the Revolution in Russia, 1915–1918*. London, 1958.

_____. and W. B. Scharlau. *The Merchant of Revolution: The Life of Alexander Israel Helphand (Parvus), 1867–1924*. London, 1965.

CHRONOLOGY

1870	*April 10*	Birth of Lenin (V. Ulyanov) in Simbirsk
1871	*March 8*	Paris Commune
1872		Russian publication of the first volume of Marx's *Capital*
1881	*March 1*	Assassination of Alexander II
1883		Plekhanov establishes the Emancipation of Labor group in Geneva
1887	*May 8*	Execution of Lenin's brother Alexander Ulyanov; Vladimir Ulyanov completes secondary school with a gold medal
1893–95		Vladimir Ulyanov lives in St. Petersburg and meets Nadezhda Krupskaya
1895	*December 9*	V. Ulyanov is arrested and imprisoned until 1897
1897		Ulyanov leaves for Siberian exile where Krupskaya joins him
1898	*March 1*	The Russian Social Democratic Labor Party is founded in Minsk and immediately broken up
1899–1900		Student agitation in Russia
1900	*February*	Ulyanov leaves Siberia for Switzerland and becomes Lenin
1900	*December 11*	Publication of the first issue of *Iskra*
1901–2		The Socialist Revolutionary Party is founded
1902		Lenin writes *What Is to Be Done?*

335

1903	*July 17–August 10*	Second Congress of the Russian Social Democratic Labor Party (RSDLP) in Brussels and then London; Bolsheviks and Mensheviks split
1904	*January 27*	Beginning of the Russo-Japanese War
	February–May	Lenin writes *One Step Forward, Two Steps Back*
1905	*January 9*	Bloody Sunday and the beginning of revolution in Russia
	April 4–27	Third Congress of the RSDLP in London
	August 25	Treaty of Portsmouth ends the Russo-Japanese War
	September 7–9	Conference of Social Democratic organizations in Riga; Lenin returns to Russia
	October 17	Imperial Manifesto promising a constitution
	October	General strike in Russia
	December 6–17	Insurrection in Moscow
	December 12–17	First Conference of the RSDLP in Tampere
1906	*April 27*	Elections to the First Duma, dissolved on July 8
	April 10–25	Fourth Congress of the RSDLP, known as the "Unification" Congress, in Stockholm
	November 7–11	Second Conference of the RSDLP in Tampere
	November 9	Stolypin's agrarian reform
1907	*February 2–June*	Second Duma
	April–May	Fifth Congress of the RSDLP in London
	August 3–5	Kotka Party Conference
	November 1	Election of the Third Duma; Lenin leaves Russia for Switzerland
	November 5–12	Fourth Party Conference in Helsinki
1908	*December*	Fifth Party Conference in Paris
1910	*January*	Plenum of the Central Committee of the RSDLP; last attempt at reconciliation between Bolsheviks and Mensheviks

1911		School for party leaders established in Longjumeau
	September 1	Stolypin assassinated in Kiev
1912	*January*	Sixth Party Conference in Prague; it becomes the RSDLP (Bolshevik)
	April	Striking miners in Siberia fired on
	April 23	Publication of first issue of *Pravda*
	Summer	Lenin moves to Cracow
	August	Trotsky organizes a conference in Vienna: the "August Bloc"; definitive break between Bolsheviks and Mensheviks
	November	Opening of the Fourth Duma
	November 24	Basel Congress of the Second International against war
1914	*June 28*	Archduke Franz-Ferdinand assassinated in Sarajevo
	July 23–30	President Poincaré of France visits Russia
	July 28–30	The International meets in Brussels
	August 1	Germany declares war on Russia; St. Petersburg is renamed Petrograd
	Late August	Russian defeat at the Battle of the Masurian Lakes; Lenin returns to Switzerland
1915	*September 5–8*	Zimmerwald conference
1915–16		Lenin writes *Imperialism, the Highest Stage of Capitalism*
1916	*February*	Kienthal conference
	March	Russian offensive on the Northern Front to relieve the French army engaged in the Battle of Verdun
	December 17	Rasputin assassinated
1917	*February 23–25*	Revolution in Petrograd
	February 27	Taking of the Winter Palace; Soviet established in the Tauride Palace
	March 2	Provisional Government formed; Nicholas II abdicates

March 9	The United States recognizes the Provisional Government
April 3	Lenin arrives in Petrograd
April 4	The *April Theses*
April 24–29	Seventh Conference of the RSDLP (b)
May 5	Coalition government formed
June	First All Russian Congress of Soviets
July 3–5	"July Days"; Bolsheviks arrested; Lenin flees
July 26–August 3	Sixth Party Congress, known as the Unification Congress; Trotsky joins the Bolsheviks
August 27	Kornilov attempts a coup d'état
September 25	Released from prison, Trotsky elected president of Soviet
October 10	The Central Committee decides on insurrection
October 25	Insurrection and seizure of power; Second All Russian Congress of Soviets
November 12–27	Elections to the Constituent Assembly
December 2	Armistice between Germany and Russia; Brest-Litovsk negotiations
December 7	Cheka established
1918 *January 5–6*	Meeting and dispersal of the Constituent Assembly
January 10–18	Third All Russian Congress of Soviets
January 21	The Sovnarkom repudiates all debts contracted by the old regime
February 1	Russia adopts the Gregorian calendar
March 3	Treaty of Brest-Litovsk signed
March 6–8	Seventh Party Congress
March 10–14	Moscow becomes the capital of Russia
May	Civil War begins
June 28	Beginnings of War Communism

	July 6	The Left Socialist Revolutionaries oppose the Bolsheviks
	July 17	Imperial family assassinated
	August 30	Fanny Kaplan attempts to assassinate Lenin
1919	*January*	Paris Peace Conference begins
	January 15	Rosa Luxemburg and Karl Liebknecht assassinated
	March 2–7	First Congress of the Communist International in Moscow
	April–October	Kolchak and Denikin offensives against the Red Army
	December 2–4	Eighth Party Conference
	December 27	Beginnings of the militarization of labor
1920	*January*	Whites routed in Siberia
	March 29–April 5	Ninth Party Congress
	April 24	Polish War begins
	July 21–August 6	Second Congress of the Communist International
	August	Red Army before Warsaw; Polish counterattack and Russian defeat
	September 1	Baku Congress
	October 12	Peace treaty with Poland
	October 25– November 16	Offensive against Wrangel's army leads to his defeat
1921	*January–March*	Uprising of Tambov peasants
	March 2–17	Commune of Kronstadt
	March 8–16	Tenth Party Congress; beginnings of the NEP
	June 22–July 12	Third Congress of the Communist International
	August	Purge of the party
	October 12	State Bank established
1922		Famine in Russia
	February 6	The Cheka renamed the GPU

	February 26	Confiscation of church property; antireligious campaign
	April 3	Stalin appointed general secretary of the party
	April 10–May 19	Genoa Conference
	April 16	Russia and Germany sign a non-aggression treaty in Rapallo
	May 26	Lenin's first cerebral stroke; he goes on leave until October
	August–September	Conflict between Stalin and the Georgians
	November 4–December 5	Fourth Congress of the Communist International
	December 16	Lenin's second stroke
	December 23	"Letter to the Congress," known as "Lenin's Testament"
	December 30–31	Lenin dictates notes on the national question
1923	*January 4*	Lenin dictates a note asking that Stalin be removed from power
	January–March	Lenin dictates his last articles
	March 6	Lenin breaks with Stalin
	April 17–25	Twelfth Party Congress, in Lenin's absence
1924	*January*	Thirteenth Party Conference; Trotsky's views condemned
	April 21	Lenin dies; Rykov succeeds him as head of government

GLOSSARY

Apparatchik	Party functionary
Bund	Jewish Socialist Party
CC	Party Central Committee
CCC	Party Central Control Commission
CEC	All Russian Central Executive Committee of the Congress of Soviets of Workers' and Soldiers' Deputies (also VTsIK)
Cheka	Political police
Comintern	Third International
Duma	Lower house of the Russian Parliament
Gulag	Administration of the camps, more broadly the system of concentration camps
GPU	Name given to the Cheka in 1922; see Cheka
Ispolkom	Executive Committee
Kadets	Constitutional Democratic Party
Kavburo	Caucasian Bureau of the Party
Kolkhoz	Collective farm
Kombedy	Committee of the Rural Poor
Kulak	Rich Peasant
MRC	Military Revolutionary Committee or REVCOM
Narkomindel	People's commissariat for foreign affairs
Narkomnats	People's commissariat for nationality affairs
Rabkrin	Workers' and Peasants' Inspection

RSDLP	Russian Social Democratic Labor Party
RSDLP (b)	Lenin's Bolshevik faction
RSFSR	Russian Socialist Federated Soviet Republic
Soviet	Council
Sovkhoz	State farm
Sovnarkom	Council of people's commissariats (government)
SR	Socialist Revolutionary Party
Ukase	Decree
USSR	Union of Soviet Socialist Republics
Zemstvo	Autonomous provincial assembly

NOTES

(References to Lenin's works are generally to the fifth edition of *Polnoe Sobranie Sochinenii*, cited as *PSS.*)

FOREWORD

1. "Chto govoriat rabochii" (What do the workers say?), *Rabochaia Moskva*, January 25, 1924.
2. *Za Leninizm. Sbornik statei* (For Leninism, collection of articles) (Moscow. 1925). G. Zinoviev, *Leninizm. Vvdenie v izuchenie Leninizma* (Leninism. Introduction to its Study) (Leningrad and Moscow, 1925). J. Stalin, *Problems of Leninism* (Moscow, 1953).
3. "Partiia lenina s vami. Put' vam ukazhet Khristos" (Lenin's Party is with you. Christ will show you the way), *Komsomol'skaia Pravda*, February 4, 1998.

CHAPTER ONE

1. *Deiateli okt'iabroski revoliutsii*, Entsiklopedicheskii slovar' ruskogo instituta Granat (The Participants in the October Revolution), Encyclopedic Dictionary (Seventh edition) (Moscow, 1927–29).
2. K. Pobedonostsev, *Pisma Pobedonostseva k Alexandru III* (Pobedonostsev's Letters to Alexander III) (Moscow, 1925-26), vol. 1, p. 3.
3. A. S. Poliakov, "Vtoroe 1go Marta 1887" (Another March 1, 1887), *Golos Minuvshego* (Moscow, 1918), pp. 10ff.
4. G. Haupt and J. J. Marie, *Les Bolcheviks par eux-mêmes* (Paris, 1969), p. 151.

CHAPTER TWO

1. H. Norman, *All the Russias* (London, 1902), p. 2: "Russia! . . . it would be easier to say what is *not* Russia."
2. J.-B. Duroselle, *Les Français 1900–1914* (Paris, 1972), pp. 60–61. J.-L. Bodiguel, *La Durée du temps de travail enjeu de la lutte sociale* (Paris, 1970), pp. 77–78.
3. R. Pipes, *Russia under the Old Regime* (London, 1974) devotes an entire chapter to "The Missing Bourgeoisie," pp. 191–221.

4. F. Starr, *Decentralization and Self-Government in Russia 1830–1870* (Princeton, 1972), pp. 48ff.

5. *Russia Under the Old Regime*, pp. 313–15.

6. Ibid., p. 311. P. A. Zaionchkovski, *Rossiskoe samoderzhavie v kontse XIX^{go} stoletiia* (Russian Autocracy in the Late Nineteenth Century) (Moscow, 1970), pp. 168ff.

7. In 1890 and 1891, ten thousand Jewish artisans were banished from Moscow on the grounds that they lacked residence permits. H. D. Löwe, *The Tsars and the Jews: Reform, Reaction, and Antisemitism in Imperial Russia, 1772–1917* (New York, 1977), p. 111.

8. *Svod zakonov rossiiskoi imperii* (Collection of Laws of the Russian Empire) (Saint Petersburg, 1892), vol. II.

9. "In order to insure that workers have true freedom of conscience, the Church is separated from the State." Basic law of the Russian Soviet Federated Socialist Republic, 1918, ch. V § 13. But the restoration of the patriarchate by the council of 1917 was a de facto separation.

10. Pyotr Chaadayev was placed under house arrest. He later qualified his views on Russian history in *Apology of a Madman* and the continuation of his *Philosophical Letters*.

11. A. S. Khomiakov, *Polnoe Sobranie Sochinenii* (Complete Works) (Moscow, 1904), vol. 1, p. 636, wrote that the Slavophiles had revived the idea of the traditional commune and founded a new spiritual movement.

12. M. Confino published letters from Bakunin to Nechaev in *Daughter of a Revolutionary* (London, 1974), pp. 238–70, indicating their very close relations. See also Confino, "Bakunin et Netchaev," *Cahiers du monde russe et soviétique* VII, 4 (1966), pp. 666ff.

13. Quoted by Franco Venturi, *Les Intellectuals, la revolution et le pouvoir,* (Paris, 1972), vol. 1, p. 635.

14. In 1834, Pushkin published a history of Pugachev's rebellion in Saint Petersburg. See Pierre Pascal, *La Révolte de Pougatchev* (Paris, 1971).

CHAPTER THREE

1. Letter from Engels to Sorge, June 26, 1883. Engels says that he found two cubic meters of material on Russia in Marx's papers.

2. Flerovsky was the author of *Situation of the Working Class in Russia* (St. Petersburg, 1869) and *Alphabet of the Social Sciences* which inspired praise from Marx: "Works like those of Chernyshevsky and Flerovsky do honor to Russia." Quoted by M. Molnar, *Marx, Engels et la politique internationale* (Paris, 1975), p. 177.

3. Letter to Engels, December 12, 1870, preface to the Russian edition of the *Communist Manifesto*.

4. M. Rubel, "K. Marx, F. Engels, écrits sur le tsarisme et le communisme russe," *Économie et sociétés* III, 67 (July 1969), p. 1360.

5. On Petr Bernardovich Struve (1870–1946), see R. Pipes, *Struve, Liberal on the Left, 1870–1905* (Cambridge, Mass., 1970), which deals with this period.

6. M. A. Silvin, "Kbiografi V. I. Lenina" (For a Biography of Lenin), *Proletarskaia Revoliutsiia* no. 7 (1924), p. 66.

7. *Chto Takoe Druzia naroda i kak oni Voiuiut protiv sotsial demokratos* (Who Are "The Friends of the People" and How Do They Fight Against the Social Democrats?) *PSS*, vol. 1, pp. 125–346.

8. *Kriticheskie zametki k voprosu ob ekonomicheskom razvitiie rossii* was published by Potresov in St. Petersburg in the fall of 1894.

9. Quoted by R. Pipes, *Social Democracy and the Saint Petersburg Labor Movement* (Cambridge, Mass., 1963), p. 72.

10. I. Getzler, *Martov: A Political Biography of a Russian Social Democrat* (Cambridge, Mass., 1967), pp. 28–29.

11. Z. Gittelman, *Jewish Nationality and Soviet Politics* (Princeton, 1972), p. 24.

CHAPTER FOUR

1. *Zadachi russkikh sotsial demokratov*, *PSS*, vol. 2, pp. 433–70.

2. N. Valentinov, *Maloznakomyi Lenin* (Paris, 1972), p. 55

3. *Chto delat'*, fall 1901, February 1902, *PSS*, vol. 6, pp. 1–192.

4. Letter to Joseph Weydemeyer, March 5, 1852, in M. Rubel, *Pages de Karl Marx* (Paris, 1970), vol. 2, p. 80.

5. In two letters to Radchenko in July 1902, Lenin had explained how he could manipulate the agenda and the voting. "Pismo I. I. Radchenko," July 3 (16) and July 9 (22), 1902, *PSS*, vol. 46, pp. 201–3 and 204–7.

6. "Proekt Ustava partii" (Proposed Party Statutes) (First version, May–June 1903), *PSS*, vol. 54, pp. 448–53; "Proekt Ustava RSDRP, vol. 7, pp. 256–58.

7. "Shag vpered, dva shaga nazad, otvet Rose Liuksemburg" (One Step Forward, Two Steps Back, Reply to Rosa Luxemburg), September 2 (15), 1904, *PSS*, vol. 9, pp. 38–65.

8. Lenin replied with a polemic to *The Crisis of German Social Democracy*, published under the pseudonym of Junius, *PSS*, vol. 30, pp. 1–9.

9. *Shag vpered, dva shaga nazad. Krizis v nashei partii*, February–May 1904, *PSS*, vol. 8, pp. 185–414.

10. Lenin noted his version of events as early as September 1903, "Raskaz o II[m] s'ezde RSDRP" (Account of the Second Congress of the RSDLP), *PSS*, vol. 8, pp. 1–20.

CHAPTER FIVE

1. On 1905, see P. Miliukov, *La Crise russe* (Paris, 1907); Martov *et al.*, eds. *Obshchestvennoe dvizhenie v rossii v nachale XX[go] veka* (The Social Movement in Russia in the Early Twentieth Century) (Moscow, 1906), 2 vols.

2. A. Mazlemoff, *Russian Far Eastern Policy 1881–1904* (Berkeley, 1958).

3. J. Schneiderman, *Sergei Zubatov and Revolutionary Marxism* (New York, 1976).

4. Father G. Gapon, *The Story of My Life* (New York, 1906).

5. O. Anweiler, *The Soviets* (New York, 1974).

6. Note from the Granat encyclopedia; see *Les Bolcheviks par eux-mêmes*, p. 52.

7. N. Valentinov, *Maloznakomyi Lenin*, p. 82.

8. On Marya Andreeva and Lenin, see A. Vaksberg, *Le Mystère Gorki* (Paris, 1997), p. 36.

9. *PSS,* vol. 12, pp. 99–105; *The Lenin Anthology,* ed. Robert C. Tucker (New York, 1975), pp. 149–50.
10. *Maloznakomyi Lenin,* p. 32.
11. "Krovavye dni v Moskve" (Bloody Days in Moscow), September 27 (October 10), 1905, *PSS,* vol. 11, pp. 313–18; "Politicheskaia stachka i ulichanaia bor'ba v Moskve" (Street Battles in Moscow), vol. 11, pp. 418–21.
12. "Sotsial demokratiia i izbiratelniye soglasheniia" (Social Democracy and Electoral Agreements), second half of October 1906, *PSS,* vol. 14, pp. 73–96.
13. "Sotsial demokratiia i vybory v Dumu" (Social Democracy and the Elections to the Duma), January 13–14 (26–27), 1907, *PSS,* vol. 14, pp. 249–73.
14. "Melkoburzhuaznaia taktika" (A Petit-Bourgeois Tactic), February 22 (March 7), 1907, *PSS,* vol. 15, pp. 49–53.
15. Quoted in Isaac Deutscher, *Stalin: A Political Biography* (New York, 1949), p. 78.
16. "O Boikote" (On the Boycott), August 12–25, 1906, *PSS,* vol. 13, pp. 339–47.
17. "O Sovremennom momente demokraticheskoi revoliutsii" (On the Present Moment of the Democratic Revolution), February 15–18, 1907, *PSS,* vol. 15, pp. 3–4.
18. "O Stat'e Plekhanova" (On Plekhanov's Article) October 29, 1907, *PSS,* vol. 16, pp. 150–51 and vol. 15, pp. 6–8; "O Taktike oportunizma" (On the Tactics of Opportunism), February 23, 1907, *PSS,* vol. 15, pp. 57–62.
19. *Les Bolcheviks par eux-mêmes,* p. 93.
20. See the introduction by B. Nikolaevsky to the memoirs of Tsereteli on his role and his prestige in the Duma, I. G. Tsereteli, *Vospominaniia o fevral'skoi revoliutsii* (Paris, 1963), vol. 1, p. xiii.
21. Criticisms by Lenin in the materials prepared for the Third Conference of the RSDLP (July 21–23, 1907), "Plan-konspekt rechi po voprosu o professional' nom s'ezde" (Plan for a speech on the question of a professional congress), *PSS,* vol. 16, p. 478.
22. *Dve taktiki sotsial demokratii v demokraticheskoi revoliutsii,* June–July 1905, *PSS,* vol. 11, pp. 3–7 and afterword, pp. 105–31.
23. *Agrarnaia programma sotsial demokratii v pervoi russkoi revoliutsii: 1905–1907 godov* (The Social Democratic Agrarian Program in the First Russian Revolution), November–December 1907, *PSS,* vol. 16, pp. 193–413 and after–word, pp. 412–13.
24. Ibid.
25. "Revoliutsionnaia demokraticheskaia diktatura proletariata i khrestianstvo" (The Revolutionary Democratic Dictatorship of the Proletariat and the Peasantry," March 30 (April 12), 1905, *PSS,* vol. 10, pp. 20–31 and preparatory materials, vol. 10, pp. 366–69.
26. *Trotsky, 1905,* fourth edition (Moscow, 1925), pp. 225–26.
27. At the time, he wrote "Revoliutsionnaia armiia i revoliutsionnoe pravitel'stvo" (The Revolutionary Army and the Revolutionary Government), June 27 (July 10), 1905, *PSS,* vol. 10, pp. 335–44.

CHAPTER SIX

1. Tsereteli, pp. xi–xii.
2. *Agrarnaia programma sotsial demokratii . . .,* *PSS,* vol. 16, pp. 193–413; "Agrarnyi vopros i sily revoliutsii" (The Agrarian Question and the Forces of Revo-

lution), April 1, 1907, vol. 15, pp. 204–7; "Novaia agrarnaia politika" (The New Agrarian Policy), February–March 1908, vol. 16, pp. 422–26.

3. Valentinov, p. 127.
4. Kropotkin, *Paroles d'un révolté* (Paris, 1978), "L'expropriation," pp. 235–66.
5. Ibid., p. 250.
6. R. Arsenidze, "Iz vospominanii o Staline" (Memories of Stalin) *Novyi Zhurnal*, no. 72 (June 1963), p. 232; Trotsky, *Stalin* (New York, 1941), pp. 104–5.
7. Ibid., pp. 102–3 (on the boyeviki).
8. Valentinov, p. 104. He claims that Shmit committed suicide in prison and was neither tortured nor murdered.
9. See the Protocols of the Transfer of the Shmit Funds to the Bolshevik Center, signed by six people, including Lenin, Zinoviev, and Kamenev, in R. Pipes, ed., *The Unknown Lenin: From the Secret Archive* (New Haven, 1996), pp. 20–21.
10. Ibid. The whole story is delightfully told by Valentinov, pp. 101ff.
11. Ibid., p. 116.
12. Dmitri Volkogonov, *Lenin: A New Biography* (New York, 1994), p. 59.
13. Lenin's deposition in the Malinovsky affair, May 26 (June 8), 1917, *The Unknown Lenin*, pp. 35–40.
14. See § 7 of the draft resolution of the Executive Committee of the Party, November 1909: "Regarding Trotsky, the faction acknowledges the maximum concession to *Pravda* to be an agreement to leave *Pravda* in Vienna." Pipes, *The Unknown Lenin*, p. 23.
15. "Vybory i oppozitsiia" (The Elections and the Opposition), June 24 (July 7), 1912, *PSS*, vol. 21, pp. 369–72.
16. Answer sent to Camille Huysmans, October 3, 1912. *Correspondance entre Lénine et Huysmans*. ed. G. Haupt (Paris, 1963), p. 118.
17. Answer to Huysmans, ibid., p. 117.
18. *The Unknown Lenin*, p.25 (May 10 or 11, 1914); I. S. Rozental, *Provokator, kariera Romana Malinovskogo* (A Provocateur: The Career of Roman Malinovsky) (Moscow, 1994).
19. Liquidator was an insult coined by Lenin against the Mensheviks, whom he accused of "liquidating" the revolution by subordinating themselves to the demands of the working class. "O likvidatorstve i o gruppe likvidatorov" (On Liquidationism and the Liquidators' Group), January 1912, *PSS*, vol. 21, pp. 150–52; "Protiv ob'edineniia-s likvidatorymi" (Against Union with the Liquidators), February–March 1912, pp. 161–66.
20. See Lenin's 1903 speech on the Bund at the Second Congress of the RSDLP, "Plan rechi po voprosu o mesti Bunda v RSDRP" (Outline of a speech on the place of the Bund in the RSDLP), July 19–20, 1903, *PSS*, vol. 7, p. 425; "Polozhenie Bunda v Partii" (The Position of the Bund in the Party), October 22, 1903, vol. 8, pp. 65–76.
21. "Pismo A. M. Gor'komu" (Letter to Gorky), *PSS*, vol. 48. pp. 160–63.
22. The second representative was B. I. Krichevsky, replaced in 1904 by the SR Rubanovich, Haupt, ed. *Correspondance*, p. 19.
23. Ibid., p.42.
24. *VIIᵉ Congrès socialiste tenu à Stuttgart du 16 au 24 avril 1907* (Brussels, 1908); commentary by Lenin, *PSS*, vol. 16, pp. 67–71.
25. *Le Peuple* (Brussels newspaper), August 18, 1907.
26. See his commentary, "Khoroshaia rezoliutsiia i plokhaia rech" (A Good Resolution and a Bad Speech), December 1913, *PSS*, vol. 24, pp. 211–13.

27. *The Unknown Lenin* contains letters not found in the complete works; see also Volkogonov, pp. 41ff.; Solzhenitsyn, *Lenin v Tsiurikhe* (Lenin in Zurich) (Paris, 1975), pp. 70–74.
28. Editions of the complete works of Lenin include many letters to Inessa for the month of December 1913, but they are expurgated, *PSS*, vol. 48, pp. 238, 242–43, 248–49. Quotations here are from *The Unknown Lenin*, pp. 26–30.
29. Volkogonov, p. 40.
30. Letter to Inessa Armand, June 23, 1914, *The Unknown Lenin*, p. 27; incomplete text, "Pismo I. F. Armand," *PSS*, vol. 48, pp. 299–300.
31. Gorky, *V. I. Lenin*, p. 10.

CHAPTER SEVEN

1. "Pismo A. M. Gor'komu, *PSS*, vol. 48, p. 155 (written after January 12, 1913).
2. *VIIe Congrès socialiste international*, p. 99.
3. "O lozunge prevarashcheniia imperialisticheskoi voiny v voinu grazhdanskuiu" (On the Slogan of the Transformation of the Imperialist War into a Civil War), *PSS*, September 1914, vol. 26, p. 36.
4. J.-B. Duroselle, *La Grande Guerre des Français* (Paris, 1994), p. 17.
5. *The Unknown Lenin*, p. 27.
6. "Novaia Demokratiia" (The New Democracy), January 19, 1913, *PSS*, vol. 22, pp. 302–3.
7. "Zadachi revoliutsionnoi sotsial demokratii v evropeiskoi voine" (The Tasks of Revolutionary Social Democracy in the European War), *PSS*, vol. 26, pp. 1–7.
8. Valentinov, p. 147.
9. "Pismo A. G. Shliapnikovu," October 1914, *PSS*, pp. 12–16, 20–28.
10. "Plan stat'i o tsimerval'dovskoi Konferentsii" (Outline for an Article on the Zimmerwald Conference), after August 26, 1915, *PSS*, vol. 54, pp. 462–63; Angelica Balabanoff, *My Life As a Rebel* (New York, 1968 [1938]), pp. 133–42.
11. K. Kautsky, *Sozialismus und Kolonial Politik* (Berlin, 1907); R. Luxemburg, *Die Akkumulation des Kapitals* (Berlin, 1912); R. Hilferding, *Das Finanzkapital* (Berlin, 1910).
12. *PSS*, vol. 16, pp. 67–71.
13. *Imperializm kak vyshaia stadiia kapitalizma*, *PSS*, vol. 27, pp. 299–426; "Imperializm i raskol sotsializma" (Imperialism and the Socialist Split), October 1916, vol. 30, pp. 163–79; outline for this article, vol. 30, pp. 370–72.
14. *Tetradi po imperializmu*, 1915–16, *PSS*, vol. 28, pp. 1–740 (22 notebooks).
15. "O brochiure Iuniusa," *PSS*, vol. 30, pp. 1–16.
16. "Plan referata po natsionalnomu Voprosu" (Outline for a Report on the National Question), before June 26, 1913, *PSS*, vol. 23, pp. 444–48; "O kulturno-natsionalnoi avtonomii" (On Cultural-National Autonomy), November 28, 1913, *PSS*, vol. 24, pp. 174–78.
17. *O prave natsii na samo opredelenie*, February–May 1914, *PSS*, vol. 25, pp. 255–320; outline of the work, vol. 25, pp. 435–40.
18. Otto Bauer, *Die Nationalitätenfrage und Sozialdemokratie* (Vienna, 1907).
19. *PSS*, vol. 25, p. 275.

20. See the account of criticism addressed to Lenin by the Bundist A. Litvak, to which Lenin paid no attention, Litvak, *In Zurich and in Geneva during the First World War: Reminiscences* (New York, 1954), p. 246.

21. "O natsional'noi gordosti velikorossov" (On the National Pride of Great Russians), *PSS*, vol. 26, pp. 106–10.

22. See Radek's arguments of April 1916, O. Gankin and H. Fisher, eds. *The Bolsheviks and the World War: The Origins of the Third international* (Stanford, 1940), pp. 223–29 and 507–11.

23. "Sotsialisticheskaia revoliutsiia i pravo natsii no samoopredelenie–tezisy," January–February 1916, *PSS,* vol. 27, pp. 252–66; "Zametki k tezisam," p. 457.

24. "O natsional'noi programme RSDRP" (On the National Program of the RSDLP), *PSS*, vol. 24, pp. 223–29.

CHAPTER EIGHT

1. N. N. Sukhanov, *The Russian Revolution 1917*, ed. and trans. Joel Carmichael (London, 1955), p. 5.

2. A. Senn, *The Russian Revolution in Switzerland,* pp. 60–74.

3. Vakhabov, *Tashkent v period trekh revoliutsii* (Tashkent in the Period of the Three Revolutions) (Tashkent, 1957), p. 168.

4. *Vospominaniia o Fevral'skoi revoliutsii* , p. 150.

5. Angelica Balabanoff, *My Life As a Rebel* (New York, 1968 [1938]), p. 144.

6. Ibid.

7. Z. A. B. Zeman and W. B. Scharlau, *The Merchant of Revolution: The Life of Alexander Israel Helphand (Parvus), 1867–1924* (London, 1965) pp. 204ff.

8. Bernstein made this estimate in *Vorwärts,* January 14, 1921.

9. Balabanoff, p. 144.

10. Tsereteli, p. 239, quoting remarks by the minister of foreign affairs Tereshchenko concerning the suspicions under which Grimm labored.

11. Ibid., pp. 240–41.

12. Sukhanov, p. 270.

13. Ibid., pp. 272–73; *Izvestia,* April 5, 1917.

14. *Leninskii Sbornik,* vol. 21, p. 33.

15. A. S. Alliluyeva, *Vospominaniia* (Memoirs [Moscow, 1946], pp. 165ff., on Stalin's return to *Pravda;* Stalin's editorial, "O voine" (On the War), *Pravda,* March 17, 1917.

16. Shlyapnikov notes this disagreement and the circumstances under which Kamenev, Stalin, and Muranov took control of *Pravda,* A. Shlyapnikov, *Semnadsatyi god, kniga vtoraia* (The Year 1917, Book Two) (Moscow and Petrograd, 1923), p. 180.

17. "Pisma iz daleka," *PSS,* vol. 31, pp. 9–57. Five letters dated March 7, 9, 11, 12, and 26, 1917; draft of the fifth letter, pp. 58–59.

18. E. N. Burdzhalov, "O taktike bol'chevikov v marte-aprele 1917 goda" (On Bolshevik Tactics in March and April 1917), *Voprosy istorii* 4 (1956), pp. 48–50; Lenin's comments, *PSS,* vol. 31, pp. 501–4.

19. Sukhanov, pp. 286–87.

20. Contradicted by Sukhanov, p. 287, who points to Miliukov's lucidity.

21. "O zadachakh proletaria v dannoi revoliutsii," April 4–5, 1917, *PSS*, vol. 31, pp. 113–18.

22. E. N. Burdzhalov, "Esche o taktike bol'chevikov v marte-aprele 1917 g." (Again on Bolshevik Tactics in March and April 1917), *Voprosy istorii* 8 (1956), pp. 109–14.

23. *Sed'maia (aprel'skaia konferentsiia, vserossii skaia i Petrogradskaia obshchegorodskaia konferentisii RSDRP (b) aprel' 1917 g.)* (Documents of the Seventh Party Conference), ed. M. Orakhelashvili; details on votes, pp. 190ff.

24. "Pismo 1-pervyi etap, pervoi revoliutsii" (First Letter, First Stage of the First Revolution), *PSS*, vol. 31, pp. 11–22.

25. On this delay, see Tsereteli's explanations, pp. 474–90.

26. "Tezisy po povodu deklaratsii vremennogo pravitel'stva" (Theses on the Proclamation of the Provisional Government), not before May 4, 1917, *PSS*, vol. 32, pp. 437–38.

27. Tsereteli, pp. 271–85.

28. Balabanoff, p. 156.

29. Sukhanov, p. 352.

30. Volkogonov, *Lenin*, p. 118; Pipes, *The Russian Revolution* (New York, 1990), p. 411.

31. Sukhanov, p. 380.

32. Tsereteli, vol. 2, pp. 53ff.

33. B. V. Nikitine, *The Fatal Years* (London, 1938), pp. 110–16.

34. Sukhanov, pp. 386–88; F. F. Raskolnikov, *Kronstadt and Petrograd in 1917*, trans. Brian Pearce (London, 1982).

35. D. Shugayev, *Revoliutsionnoe dvizhenie v iule 1917* (The Revolutionary Movement in July 1917) (Moscow, 1959), pp. 290ff.

36. Nikitine, pp. 149–50.

37. Sukhanov, pp. 471–72.

38. Alliluyeva, pp. 176–82.

39. Ibid., p. 190.

40. There is an excellent account of the entire July crisis in Alexander Rabinowitch, *Prelude to Revolution: The Petrograd Bolsheviks and the July 1917 Uprising* (Bloomington, 1968), pp. 233ff.

41. *Shestoi s'ezd RSDRP (bol'shevikov) August 1917 goda–Protokoly* (Protocols of the Sixth Congress of the RSDLP (b)) (Moscow, 1958).

42. Ibid., p. 118.

43. Ibid., pp. 27–28 and 35–36.

44. E. Martynov, *Kornilov* (Leningrad, 1927); Shugayev, ed. *Revoliutsionnoe dvizhenie v Rossii v auguste 1917. razgrom Kornilovskogo miatezha* (The Revolutionary Movement in Russia in August 1917. The Crushing of the Kornilov Putsch) (Moscow, 1959).

45. Sukhanov, p. 523.

46. "Bol'sheviki dolzhny vziat' vlast," Letter to the Central Committee and to the Petrograd and Moscow Committees of the RSDLP, March 12–14, 1917, *PSS*, vol. 34, pp. 239–41.

47. "Marxizm i vosstanie," Letter to the Central Committee of the RSDLP, September 13–14, 1917, *PSS*, vol. 34, pp. 242, 247.

48. "Pismo v tsk mk PK i chlenam sovieta Pitera i Moskvy bol'shevikam, *PSS*, vol. 34, pp. 340–41 and 347–50.
49. "Krizis nazrel," September 9, 1917, *PSS*, vol. 34, pp. 272–83.

CHAPTER NINE

1. Sukhanov, p. 535.
2. See the July 1917 article, "O konstitutsionnykh illiuziakh" (On Constitutional Illusions), *PSS*, vol. 34, pp. 33–47 and 403.
3. Sukhanov, p. 556.
4. "Pismo k tovarishcham" (Letter to the Comrades), October 17, 1917, *PSS*, vol. 34, pp. 398–418.
5. Two conversations of the author with Kerensky, in Stanford in May 1967, and in Paris on September 10, 1967.
6. Pipes, *The Russian Revolution*, p. 489.
7. "Pismo predesedateliu oblastnogo komiteta armii flota i rabochikh Finlandii i. t. Smilge" (Letter to the Chairman of the Committee of Workers, Soldiers, and Sailors of Finland, I. T. Smilga), September 27, 1917, *PSS*, vol. 34, pp. 264–68.
8. Trotsky, *History of the Russian Revolution* (New York, 1937), vol. 3, p. 355.
9. *Les Bolcheviks par eux-mêmes*, pp. 262 and 264.
10. *Dekrety sovetskoi vlasti*, I.
11. Sukhanov, p. 627.
12. L. de Robien, *Journal d'un diplomate en Russie* (Paris, 1967), p. 144.
13. S. P. Melgunov, *The Bolshevik Seizure of Power* (Oxford, 1972), provides a detailed account.
14. *Vtoroi vserossiiskii s'ezd sovetov* (Second All Russian Congress of Soviets), ed. Kotel'nikov (Moscow and Leningrad, 1928).
15. Sukhanov, p. 653.
16. Ibid., p. 655.
17. E. N. Gorodetsky, *Rozhdenie Sovetskogo gosudarstva 1917–1918* (The Birth of the Soviet State 1917–1918) (Moscow, 1964), pp. 156ff.
18. Sukhanov, p. 656.
19. *L'Illustration* presented portraits of the members of the Russian government, emphasizing the fact that almost all of them were Jewish. "Petrograd sous la Commune," *L'Illustration*, no. 3491 (September 11, 1918), pp. 259–60.

CHAPTER TEN

1. J. Sadoul, *Notes sur la révolution bolchevique*, p. 73.
2. *Gosudarstvo i revoliutsiia*, August–September 1917, *PSS*, vol. 33, pp. 1–120; afterword to the first edition, November 30, 1917, p. 120.
3. "Marksizm o gosudarstve," January–February 1917, *PSS*, vol. 33, pp. 123–307.
4. "Plany, konspekty i zametki k knigi gosudarstvo i revoliutsiia," January–September 1917, *PSS*, vol. 33, pp. 308–28.
5. Lenin takes this passage from *The Civil War in France: Address of the General Council*, Karl Marx, *The First International and After*, ed. David Fernbach (Harmondsworth, 1974), p. 212.

6. J.-B. Duroselle, *La Grande Guerre des Français*, p. 290.

7. Sadoul, p. 81.

8. A. Popov, ed. *Oktabr'skii perevorot: fakty i dokumenty* (The October Coup: Facts and Documents) (Petrograd, 1918), pp. 402ff.

9. P. Vompe, *Dni okt'iabr'skoi revoliutsii i zheleznodorozhniki—materialy* (The Days of the October Revolution and the Railway Workers) (Moscow, 1924), pp. 21–26.

10. Leon Trotsky, *Stalin* (New York, 1941), p. 240.

11. "Kak obespeechit' uspekh uchreditel'nogo sobraniia—(o svobode pechati)" (How is the Success of the Elections to the Constituent Assembly to Be Assured—On the Freedom of the Press), September 15, 1917, *PSS*, vol. 34 pp. 208–13.

12. David Shub, *Lenin* (Baltimore, 1966 [1948]), p. 314.

13. *Les Bolcheviks par eux-mêmes*, p. 75.

14. "Tezisy ob uchreditel'nom sobranii," *PSS*, vol. 35, pp. 162–66.

15. "O konstitutsionnyh illiusiah," July 26, 1917, *PSS*, vol. 34, pp. 34–47.

16. Balabanoff describes Zinoviev's opportunism, *My Life as a Rebel*, p. 221.

17. "Deklaratsiia prav trudiashchtegosiia i ekspluatiruemogo naroda," drafted at the latest on January 3 (16), 1918, *PSS*, vol. 35, pp. 221–23.

18. "Tezisy (proekt dekreta o rospuske uchreditel'nogo sobraniia) (Theses [Proposed Decree on the Dissolution of the Constituent Assembly]), January 6, 1918, *PSS*, vol. 35, pp. 232–35.

19. Shub, *Lenin*, p. 328.

20. See especially "Mir ili voina" (War or Peace), February 23, 1918, *PSS*, vol. 35, pp. 366–68.

21. "The Germans are both nervous and threatening." Sadoul, p. 192.

22. Ibid., p. 237.

23. *KPSS v rezoliutsiiah i resheniiah, s'ezdov konferentsii i plenumov TSK 1898–1903* (Moscow, 1953), vol. 1, p. 405.

24. Sadoul, p. 260.

25. On the change of capital, see A. F. Fraiman, *Revoliutsionnaia zashchita Petrograda v Fevrale-Marte 1918* (The Revolutionary Defense of Petrograd in February and March 1918) (Moscow and Leningrad, 1964); letter from Lunacharsky to the Sovnarkom of March 1918 in *Lenin i Lunacharski—Pisma, doklady, dokumenty* (Moscow, 1971), p. 59.

CHAPTER ELEVEN

1. Quoted by Shub, p. 344.

2. M. Latsis, "Tov. Dzerzhinsky i Vchk" (Comrade Dzerzhinski and the Cheka), *Proletarskaia revoliutsiia* no. 56 (1926), p. 81.

3. Trotsky, *Kak vooruzhalas' revoliutsiia* (How the Revolution Armed), vol. 1, pp. 186–95.

4. Ibid., vol. 1, pp. 127–31.

5. Sadoul, p. 370.

6. Ibid., p. 302.

7. "Groziashchaia katastrofa i kak s nei borotsia," September 10–14, 1917, *PSS*, vol. 34, pp. 151–59.

8. "Deklaratsiia prav trudiashchtegosiia i ekspluatiruemogo naroda," January 3, 1918, *PSS*, vol. 35, pp. 221–23.

9. Volkogonov, *Lenin*, p. 227.
10. Balabanoff, *My Life as a Rebel*, p. 188.
11. Krupskaia, *Vospominaniia o Lenine* (Memoirs on Lenin) (Moscow, 1957), p. 316.
12. This article, entitled "Shest' tezisov ob ocherenykh zadachakh sovetskoi vlasti" (Six Theses on the Tasks of the Soviet Government) was published in *Izvestia*, April 28, 1918, and reprinted in *PSS*, vol. 36, pp. 277–80.
13. "O levom rebiachestve i o melko burzhuaznosti" (On Leftism and the Petit-Bourgeois Spirit), May 15, 1918, *PSS*, vol. 36, pp. 283–314.
14. This document from the secret archives addressed to "Comrades Kuraev, Bosh, Minkin, and other Penza Communists" has been published in full in Richard Pipes, *The Unknown Lenin*, p. 50.
15. Memorandum of 3 or 4 September 1918, ibid., p. 56. Lenin explains, "initially this can be done secretly."
16. S. P. Melgunov published *The Red Terror in Russia* in London in 1925.
17. Decree published in *Izvestia*, September 10, 1918, on the Red Terror. George Leggett, *The Cheka: Lenin's Political Police* (Oxford, 1981), pp. 100ff. and 215–16.
18. P. Holquist, "Conduct Merciless Mass Terror: Decossackization of the Don, 1919," *Cahiers du monde russe et soviétique*, 38 (January–June 1997), pp. 127–62.
19. Balabanoff, p. 180.

CHAPTER TWELVE

1. *Sed'moi s'ezd Rossiiskoi Kommunisticheskoi partii* (Moscow, 1923), p. 195.
2. Sadoul, p. 313.
3. *Leninskii sbornik* (1933), vol. 21, pp. 252–53.
4. "Pismo chlenam gruppi spartak" (Letter to Members of the Spartakus Group), October 18, 1918, *PSS*, vol. 50, pp. 195–96.
5. *Proletarskaia revoliutsiia i renegat Kautsky*, written between late October and November 10, 1918, *PSS*, vol. 37, pp. 235–338.
6. Letter to Stalin, July 17, 1922, *The Unknown Lenin*, p. 168.
7. Letter to N. A. Rozhkov, January 29, 1919, ibid., pp. 62–63.
8. "Pismo k rabochim evropy i ameriki," *PSS*, vol. 37, pp. 454–62.
9. "The Cossacks in their majority would have remained hostile to us . . . we supplied Denikin with a significant number of soldiers." Secret memorandum from Trotsky to the Central Committee, October 1, 1919, Pipes, *The Unknown Lenin*, pp. 70–71.
10. "Denikin is an incomparably more serious enemy than Kolchak." Ibid., p. 71.
11. Balabanoff, p. 209.
12. For the foreign Communist Parties, Karski (Poland), Rudnianszki (Hungary), Duda (Austria), Rozin (Latvia), Sirola (Finland), Rakovsky (Balkans), and Reinstein (USA).
13. P. Broué, *Histoire de l'Internationale communiste, 1919–1943* (Paris, 1997), pp. 76–78.
14. "Tezisy i doklad o burzhuaznoi demokratii i diktature proletariata," March 4, 1919, *PSS*, vol. 37, pp. 491–509.
15. On these beginnings, see Broué, pp. 86–90; documents in J. Degras, ed., *The Communist International, 1919–1943: Documents I, 1919–1922* (New York, 1956), pp. 43ff.
16. Balabanoff, "Lénine et la création du Komintern," in J. Freymond, ed. *Contributions à l'histoire du Komintern* (Geneva, 1965), pp. 33ff.

17. Balabanoff, *My Life as a Rebel*, pp. 216–18.
18. P. Broué provides an excellent picture of this revolutionary outburst, pp. 99–109.
19. *Destskaia bolezn' 'Levizny' v kommunizme*, April–May 1920, *PSS*, vol. 41, pp. 1–104.
20. On this notion, see *Documents on the Foreign Policy of the USSR* (Moscow, 1957), vol. 2, pp. 370–71.
21. "Tezisy po II kongressu kommunisticheskogo internatsionala," June–July 1920, *PSS*, vol. 41, pp. 159–212.
22. On the conditions for joining, see "Usloviia priema v kommunisticheskii internatsional", *PSS*, vol. 204–11, and "Dvatsatyi punkt uslovii priema v kommunisticheskii internatsional," p. 212.
23. "Tezisy"; "Pervonachal'nyi nabrosok tezisov po natsional'nomu i kolonial'nomu voprosam. Dlia vtorogo s'ezda kommunisticheskogo internatsionala" (Preliminary Version of Theses on the National and Colonial Questions for the Second Congress of the Comintern), *PSS*, vol. 41, pp. 161–68; "Pervonachal'nyi nabrosok tezisov po agrarnomu voprosu" (Preliminary Theses on the Agrarian Question), pp. 169–82.
24. "Doklad o mezhdunarodnom polozhenii i osnovnykh zadachakh internatsionala" (Report on the International Situation and the Basic Tasks of the Comintern), July 19, 1920, *PSS*, vol. 41, pp. 215–35.
25. Proceedings of the Second Congress were published in four languages: German, English, French, and Russian. Quotations are taken from the Russian edition, *Vtoroi kongress Kominterna* (Moscow, 1921).
26. C. Zetkin, *Reminiscences of Lenin* (London, 1929), pp. 19–22.
27. "Doklad na II$^\mathrm{m}$ vserossiiskom s'ezde kommunisticheskikh organizatsii Vostoka" (Report for the Second All-Russian Congress of Communist Organizations of the East), *PSS*, vol. 39, pp. 318–31.
28. G. Safarov, *Kolonial'naia revoliutsiia opyt Turkestana* (Moscow, 1921).
29. Ibid., p. 97.
30. S. Galiev, "Sotsial'naia revoliutsiia na Vostoke" (The Social Revolution in the East), *Zhizn' Natsional'nostei*, nos. 38 [46] (October 5, 1919); 39 [47] (October 12, 1919); 42 [50] (November 2, 1919).
31. Archaruni and Gabidullin, *Ocherki panislamizma i pantiurkizma v rossii* (Moscow, 1931), pp. 76–91, esp. p. 78.

CHAPTER THIRTEEN

1. E. Pesikina, *Narodnyi komissariat po delam natsional'nostei* (Moscow, 1950); *Spravochnik narodnogo komissariata po delam natsional'nostei* (Moscow, 1921), p. 5.
2. *PSS*, vol. 34, pp. 304–5.
3. *PSS*, vol. 36, p. 76.
4. *Dekrety sovetskoi vlasti* (Moscow, 1968), vol. 4, pp. 15–18.
5. *PSS*, vol. 35, pp. 286–90.
6. O. V. Kuusinen, *Revoliutsiia v Finlandii* (Petrograd, 1919), pp. 12ff.
7. N. Makhno, *Pod udarami Kontrrevoliutsii* (Under the Blows of the Counter-revolution) (Paris, 1936); P. Archinoff, *Le Mouvement makhnoviste* (Paris, 1924); Y. Ternon, *Makhno, la révolte anarchiste* (Brussels, 1981).
8. Telegramma L. d. Trotskomu, May 22, 1919, *PSS*, vol. 50, pp. 320–21.
9. *Dekrety sovetskoi vlasti* (Moscow, 1971), vol. 5, pp. 259–61.

10. *Pravda* October 10, 1920; *Zhizn' natsional'nostei,* December 15, 1920.

11. *PSS,* vol. 41, pp. 161–68.

12. H. C. Luke, *Cities and Men* (London, 1953), pp. 137–60.

13. Stalin, "Commentary on the Caucasus," *Pravda,* November 30, 1920.

14. G. K. Zhvania, *V. I. Lenin, Tsk Partii i bol'sheviki zakavkaziia* (Lenin, the Party Central Committee, and the Transcaucasian Bolsheviks) (Tblisi, 1969) pp. 238–39.

15. N. Zhordania, *Moia zhizn'* (My Life) (Stanford, 1968), pp. 110ff.; *The Trotsky Papers, 1917–1922* (The Hague, 1971), vol. 2, p. 385.

16. *PSS,* vol. 51, p. 152.

17. *Dokumenty vneshnei politiki SSSR* (Moscow, 1961), vol. 5, pp. 110–11.

18. J. Castagné, "Les Basmatchis," *Revue du monde musulman,* 11 (1922), pp. 174–78, and manuscript notes.

19. S. V. Kharmandarian, *Lenin i stanovlenie zakavkazhskoi federatsii, 1921–1925* (Lenin and the Establishment of the Transcaucasian Federation) (Yerevan, 1969), p. 218.

20. Ibid., p. 361.

21. R. C. Tucker, *Stalin as Revolutionary* (Princeton, 1973), p. 240.

22. *PSS,* vol. 41, p. 164.

23. *Desiatyi s'ezd RKP (b) Mart 1921 goda* (Moscow, 1960), pp. 192–93.

24. Letters of September 17, 1922 to Unshlikht and September 28, 1922 to Radek, *The Unknown Lenin,* pp. 174–75.

25. "Pismo L. B. Kamenevu–ob obrazovanii SSSR" (Letter to Kamenev–on the formation of the USSR), September 26, 1922, *PSS,* vol. 45, pp. 211–13.

26. "Pismo L. B. Kamenevu," October 6, 1922, *PSS,* vol. 54, p. 292.

27. Kharmandarian, p. 344.

28. Miasnikov, *Izbrannye proizvideniia* (Selected Works) (Yerevan, 1965), pp. 423–24.

29. Kharmandarian, pp. 369–70.

30. *PSS,* vol. 45, pp. 356–62; L. Fotieva, *Iz vospominanii o V. I. Lenine–Dekabr' 1922–Mart 1923 g.* (Memoirs of Lenin, December 1922–March 1923) (Moscow, 1964), pp. 54 and 63.

31. "Pismo k s'ezdu" (Letter to the Congress), *PSS,* vol. 45, pp. 343–48, 354–55.

32. *Vtoraia sessiia Tsik sovetskikh sotsialisticheskikh respublik* (Second Session of the CEC of the Soviet Socialist Republics) (Moscow, 1923), pp. 11ff.

33. *Vtoroi s'ezd sovetov soiuza Sovetskikh sotsialisticheskikh respublik* (Second Congress of the Soviets of the USSR) (Moscow, 1924), pp. 129–36.

CHAPTER FOURTEEN

1. "Politicheskii ochet tsk RKP (b)" (Political Report of the Central Committee of the RCP (b), September 9, 1920, *PSS,* 41, pp. 281–85; complete text in *The Unknown Lenin,* pp. 95–114.

2. Ibid., p. 112.

3. *Kombedy bednoty–Sbornik dokumentov* (Committees of the Rural Poor–Collection of Documents) (Moscow, 1937).

4. A. Stanziani, "La gestion des approvisionnements et la restauration de la gosudarstvennost'," *Cahiers du monde russe et soviétique,* 38, 1–2 (January–June 1997), pp. 82–112.

5. G. Sokoloff, *La Puissance pauvre* (Paris, 1993), p. 293.
6. M. M. Fremkin, *Tragediia krestianisikh vosstanii v rossii 1917–1921 g.* (The Tragedy of Peasant Insurrections in Russia) (Jerusalem, 1987), pp. 55ff.; V. Danilov and T. Shanin, *Krestianskoe vostanie v Tambovskoi gubernii v 1919–1921* (The Peasant Uprising in Tambov) (Tambov, 1994).
7. S. Courtois, et al., *Le Livre noir du communisme* (Paris, 1997), pp. 131–32.
8. *Kronstadt–1921. Dokumenty* (Moscow, 1997); A. Ciliga, *The Kronstadt Revolt* (London, 1942); P. Avrich, *Kronstadt 1921* (Princeton, 1970).
9. Z. Gitelman, *Jewish Nationality and Soviet Politics* (Princeton, 1972), p. 106; Dimanshtein, *Revoliutsiia i natsional'noi vopros*, vol. 3, pp. 34 ff.
10. *The Unknown Lenin*, pp. 10, 116, 128–29.
11. Ibid., p. 77.
12. "O kraske styda u Iudushki Trotskogo" (The Little Judas Trotsky's Blush of Shame), January w (15), 1911, *PSS*, vol. 20, p. 96.
13. Trotsky, "Shumikha vokrug Kronstadta" (The Fuss about Kronstadt), *Biuleten oppozitsii*, May–June 1938, pp. 22–26; "Eshche ob usmerenie Kronstadta" (More on the Pacification of Kronstadt), ibid., October 1938, p. 10.
14. A. Solzhenitsyn, *The Gulag Archipelago* (New York, 1974–78).
15. *Le Livre noir du communisme*, pp. 153–54.
16. "Zamechanie k proektu tezisov Trotskogo: ocherednye zadachi khoziaistvennogo stroitel'stva" (Remark on Proposed Theses of Trotsky; the Immediate Tasks of Economic Construction), March 3, 1920, *PSS*, vol. 40, pp. 90–91.
17. "O nashei revoliutsii (po povodu zapisok N. Sukhanova)" (Our Revolution [Apropos of N. Sukhanov's Notes]), January 16 and 17, 1923, *PSS*, vol. 45, pp. 378–82.
18. *Desiatyi s'ezd RKP (b) mart 1921 goda stenograficheskii ochet* (Moscow, 1963).
19. Ibid., pp. 564–71.
20. *Pravda*, April 4, 1922.
21. Volkogonov, pp. 306–7.
22. F. Tchouev, *Conversations avec Molotov* (Paris, 1995), p. 173.
23. *Pravda*, July 12, 1921; *Pravda* had already mentioned the famine on June 27, 1921.
24. M. Wehner, "Golod 1921–1922 gg" (The Famine of 1921–1922), *Cahiers du monde russe et soviétique*, 38, 1–2 (January–June 1997), pp. 233–42.
25. They were published in *Rapport sur les conditions économiques de la Russie* (Geneva, 1922).
26. B. Weissman, *Herbert Hoover and Famine Relief to Soviet Russia, 1921–1923* (Stanford, 1974).
27. Telegram of July 30, 1921, *The Unknown Lenin*, pp. 130–31.
28. Ibid., p. 133.
29. G. M. Krzyzhanovsky, *Lenin Tovarishch Chelovek* (Moscow, 1987), p. 212.
30. "Sotsializm i religiia" (Socialism and Religion), December 3 (16), 1905, *PSS*, vol. 12, pp. 142–47.
31. *Vestnik khristianskogo dvizheniia*, no. 52 (1970), pp. 62–65; *Izvestia TSK*, April 1990, pp. 190–93; *The Unknown Lenin*, pp. 152–55.
32. N. Struve, *Deux mille ans de christianisme* (Paris), p. 39.
33. *Pravda*, June 27, 1923.
34. *The Unknown Lenin*, p. 150.
35. Volkogonov, p. 377.

36. "Oznachenie voinstvuieshtego materializma," March 12, 1922, *PSS*, vol. 45, pp. 23–33.
37. "O kooperatsii," January 4 and 6, 1923, *PSS*, vol. 45, pp. 369–77.
38. "Partiinaia organizatsiia i partiniia litteratura" (The Party Organization and Party Literature), November 13 (26), 1905, *PSS*, vol. 12, pp. 99–105.
39. "O proletarskoi kulture" (On Proletarian Culture), October 8, 1920, *PSS*, vol. 41, pp. 336–37; Y. Yakovlev, "O proletarskoi kulture i proletkulte," *Pravda*, October 24 and 25, 1922.
40. "Litteratura i revoliutsiia." *Pravda*, September 15 and 16, 1922.
41. *V. I. Lenin o litterature i Iskustve* (Moscow, 1967).
42. "O proletkulte. Pismo TSK RKP," *Pravda*, December 1, 1920.
43. "Ogosudarstve. Lektsia v Sverdlovskom universitete" (On the State. Lecture at Sverdlov University), July 11, 1919, *PSS*, vol. 39, pp. 64–84.

CHAPTER FIFTEEN

1. Volkogonov, p. 411.
2. A. Rosmer, *Moscou sous Lénine* (Paris, 1953), p. 231.
3. Letter to Stalin for the Politburo, 15 June 1922 and Note to Stalin, 7 July 1922, *The Unknown Lenin*, pp. 165–66.
4. Yuri Annenkov, "Vospominanie o Lenine," *Novyi zhurnal* 65 (1961) 141–42; quoted, Volkogonov, p. 429.
5. "Pismo F. E. Dzerzhinskomu," May 19, 1922, *PSS*, vol. 54, pp. 265–66.
6. Letter to Stalin, 17 July 1922, *The Unknown Lenin*, pp. 168–69.
7. Ibid., p. 174.
8. Quoted by Volkogonov, p. 361.
9. Trotsky, *Stalin*, pp. 376–77. Molotov confirmed this in his conversations with Tchouev, p. 167.
10. "O nashei revoliutsii," *PSS*, vol. 45, pp. 378–82.
11. "Luche men'she da Luche," March 2, 1923, *PSS*, vol. 45, pp. 389–406.
12. "O kooperatsii," January 4 and 6, 1923, *PSS*, vol. 45, pp. 369–77.
13. "Kak nam reorganizovat' rabkrin" (How to Reorganize the Rabkrin), January 23, 1923, *PSS*, vol. 45, pp. 383–88; background material for the article, vol. 45, pp. 442–50.
14. *The Unknown Lenin*, p. 171.
15. Fotieva notes in her diary that Stalin asked her: "How does Lenin know about what is going on?"
16. "O monopoli vneshnei torgovli" (On the Monopoly of Foreign Trade), December 13, 1922, *PSS*, vol. 45, pp. 333–37.
17. "Pismo I. V. Stalinu i. M. Frumkinu i poruchenie sekretariu" (Letter to Stalin, Frumkin, and the Secretary), May 15, 1922, *PSS*, vol. 54, p. 260.
18. "Pismo I. V. Stalinu o monopolii vneshnei torgovli," October 13, 1922, *PSS*, vol. 45, p. 338.
19. *PSS*, vol. 45, p. 608; *The Unknown Lenin*, p. 188.
20. (Fotieva's Diary) "Dnevnik dezhurnykh sekretarei v. I. Lenina" (Diary of Lenin's Permanent Secretaries), November 21, 1922 and March 6, 1923, *PSS*, vol. 45. pp. 455–88, esp. p. 485.

21. The complete text was made public in the secret speech to the Twentieth Congress; excerpts in *PSS*, vol. 45, pp. 674–75.

22. According to Volodicheva, "Dnevnik dezhurnykh sekretarei," *PSS*, vol. 45, p. 486.

23. "Pismo k s'ezdu" December 23 and 24, 1922, *PSS*, vol. 45, pp. 343–48 and 354–55.

24. Addition to the preceding, "K otdelu ob uvelechenii chisla chlenov TSK" (On the Increase in Membership of the Central Committee), December 29, 1922, *PSS*, vol. 45, pp. 354–55.

25. "Dobavlenie k pismu ot 24 dekabria 1922 g" (Addition to the letter of December 24), January 4, 1923, *PSS*, vol. 45, p. 346.

26. The article was published in *Pravda* on March 4, 1923. See also, M. Lewin, *Le Dernier Combat de Lénine* (Paris, 1967), p. 124.

27. "Pismo L. d. Trotskomu," March 5, 1923, *PSS*, vol. 43, p. 329.

28. "Pismo tovarishcham Mdivani, Makharadze i drugim," March 6, 1923, *PSS*, vol. 54, p. 330.

29. Lewin, pp. 131–42; F. Fejtö, *L'Héritage de Lénine* (Paris, 1973) takes a more nuanced position on the issue.

CONCLUSION

1. "State and Revolution in the Paris Commune, the Russian Revolution, and the Civil War," *Sociological Review* 29 (1937), p. 67, quoted by J. L. H. Keep, *The Russian Revolution: A Study in Mass Mobilization* (New York, 1976), p. x.

2. By 1926, Korsch was saying that "Lenin's Marxism is no better than Kautsky's," quoted by D. Lindenberg in Châtelet, Pisier, and Duhamel, eds. *Dictionnaire des œuvres politiques* (Paris, 1995), p. 601.

3. "Dve taktiki," February 1 (14), 1905, *PSS*, vol. 9, pp. 254–63.

4. Quoted by A. Ulam, *The Unfinished Revolution* (London, 1979).

5. "Doklad o revoliutsii 1905 goda" (Lecture on the 1905 Revolution), written before January 9 (22), 1917, *PSS*, vol. 30, pp. 306–28.

6. "Russkaia revoliutsiia i grazhdanskaia voina" (The Russian Revolution and the Civil War), first half of September 1917, *PSS*, vol. 34, pp. 214–28.

INDEX